REFORM AND REGRET

REFORM AND REGRET

The Story of Federal Judicial Involvement in the Alabama Prison System

Larry W. Yackle

New York   Oxford
OXFORD UNIVERSITY PRESS
1989

Oxford University Press

Oxford New York Toronto
Delhi Bombay Calcutta Madras Karachi
Petaling Jaya Singapore Hong Kong Tokyo
Nairobi Dar es Salaam Cape Town
Melbourne Auckland
and associated companies in
Berlin Ibadan

Copyright © 1989 by Oxford University Press, Inc.

Published by Oxford University Press, Inc.,
200 Madison Avenue, New York, New York 10016

Oxford is a registered trademark of Oxford University Press

Library of Congress Cataloging-in-Publication Data
Yackle, Larry W.
    Reform and regret : the story of federal judicial involvement in
the Alabama prison system / by Larry W. Yackle.
        p.   cm.
    Bibliography: p.
    Includes index.
    ISBN 0-19-505737-6
    1. Prisons—Law and legislation—Alabama.   2. Prisoners—Legal
status, laws, etc.—Alabama.   3. Criminal justice, Administration
of—Alabama.   4. Prison administration—Alabama.   I. Title.
KFA588.Y33 1989
344.761′035—dc19
[347.610435]   88-18793
                                                        CIP

9 8 7 6 5 4 3 2 1

Printed in the United States of America

Preface

I collected materials for this bittersweet story during the ten years I spent in the South, where I taught at the University of Alabama and where I observed, at close hand, a struggle for social reform worth recounting. As I unpacked my books in the summer of 1974, I realized that the men and women around me were freshly launched on a grand adventure. Their purpose was to achieve dramatic change in Alabama's penal system; their instrument was constitutional litigation before Frank M. Johnson, Jr., one of the South's great federal judges. School desegregation cases in the previous decade had demonstrated that the federal courts could be recruited to the cause of social betterment. Judge Johnson in particular had condemned racial discrimination in the public schools and had issued injunctive decrees pointing the way to integrated public education. More recently, Johnson had issued similar injunctions in lawsuits involving inmates of Alabama's mental institutions and prison hospitals. Those cases, *Wyatt v. Stickney* and *Newman v. Alabama,* encouraged reformers to employ still more lawsuits in an attempt to end the horror in the state's penitentiaries.

These were ordinary, middle-class people, all southerners, moved to act by their state's deplorable policy of warehousing criminal offenders in maximum security penal facilities located in rural areas, where inmates languished in shocking, debilitating living conditions. There were two lawsuits, *Pugh v. Sullivan* and *James v. Wallace.* I monitored their progress for a decade—in conversations over dinner, strategy sessions in lawyers' offices and, occasionally, formal proceedings in court. At times, I was more active. I advised the prisoners' lawyers regarding legal issues surfacing in their work. When Judge Johnson invited a team of psychologists from the campus into the prison system to classify inmates, I went along as legal counselor. And when the Alabama Civil Liberties Union contested the state attorney general's decision to revoke a liberal interpretation of state sentencing laws, I wrote the brief and made the oral argument in the Alabama Supreme Court. With respect to the primary reform efforts in federal court, however, my role was peripheral. Others lived the story that follows.

The core of that story is a thorough description of the *Pugh* and *James* cases. There is value in a full record for its own sake, and I will treat events in as much detail as the enterprise will bear. The information I have collected can contribute to an understanding of the society in which each of us lives. For a quarter century, this society has relied on lawsuits in federal court to ignite efforts, however meager, to contend with crowded and dilapidated prisons. I will review the circumstances that gave rise to litigation over prison conditions, and I will describe the institutions in Alabama that were the focus of *Pugh* and *James*. Those prisons were monstrous in the extreme; they were so bad that state authorities conceded that the prisoners forced to endure them were subject to cruel and unusual punishment in violation of the Eighth Amendment. To appreciate both the way in which the effort to achieve penal reform came to such a pass and the course of the movement thereafter, however, it is necessary to do some backing and filling. I will discuss the prisoners themselves, the lawyers, the state officials. I will treat the legal theories, the tactical maneuvers, the preparations for trial, the trial itself, the appeals and, most important, the arduous implementation stages. And I will trace the appellate courts' attitude toward the *Pugh* and *James* cases over the years—from apparent encouragement when the prison cases were initiated in the mid-1970s to grudging tolerance as they staggered into the 1980s. Behind the appellate courts' change of heart lies the related story of shifts in the national political climate and the concomitant diminution of support for the penal reform campaign from the U.S. Department of Justice.

The Alabama prison cases were hardly isolated from their social and political environment. They were part of their own milieu and served within it as a catalyst for reform efforts touching numerous political power centers. No participant in the events depicted here seriously believed that change could be achieved by the mere issuance of a judicial decree commanding state authorities to abandon fundamental policies. Quite the contrary, the reform campaign used the *Pugh* and *James* cases only to approach an intricate web of political arrangements that had to be altered, and altered significantly, if public resources were to be channeled away from more popular uses and toward a prison system housing the most despised and least politically influential of all citizens.

Judicially inspired reform necessarily was adjusted to public fears, demands, and aspirations. Indeed, the most formidable task faced by the reform movement was the recurrent necessity of gauging the realistic role of judicial action in making Alabama politics responsive to prison inmates. Reformers had to determine what state officials could be ordered to do, when they could be expected to produce results, what means should be employed to spur them into action and whether, in the nature of things, they should be permitted to escape with reluctant compliance, both partial and tardy. Irresolution regarding such questions as these repeatedly undercut progress. Accordingly, I will treat developments across the range of the state's public life in an effort to capture the richness of the relations between and among the players who had some impact on the course of the reform effort. The story of the Alabama prison cases is in a real sense the story of Alabama politics at a time when those cases focused public attention on penal institutions.

The reform movement to which the *Pugh* and *James* cases contributed form and direction had only limited success within Alabama itself, albeit Judge Johnson's dramatic orders became important precedents for similar cases elsewhere. The world is a frustrating place; social progress typically comes slowly, or in fits and starts—if, indeed, progress comes at all. In this instance, the dazzling number, variety, and complexity of the barriers in the path of reform thwarted all but modest improvements in the penal system. The lawsuits came to an inconclusive pause in November 1984. The formal dismissal order was provisional, holding open the possibility of further proceedings if conditions in the prisons should deteriorate in the near term. Yet the truth of the matter was plain: the litigation had finally been dragged to a halt by the relentless, grinding power of settled arrangements to defy change of any kind, at every turn, and to the last hour. The court monitored developments in the prison system after 1984, and conditions in the prisons were the better for it. Any genuine influence on state officials, however, was minimal. The *Pugh* and *James* cases worked no profound transmutation in the policies governing the disposition of criminal offenders in Alabama or in the nature of the institutions in which prisoners were confined. In the main, state authorities responded to demands for reform by refurbishing existing facilities to eliminate the worst of their deficiencies and by expanding the prison system's capacity to house convicts in institutions of the kind Alabama had employed since the nineteenth century. The fundamental policy at work, the punishment of offenders by caging them for extraordinary lengths of time under primitive conditions, remained what it had always been.

There were reasons for shortfall. As the narrative progresses, I will ascribe significance to personal animosities, bureaucratic inertia, administrative incompetence, and political demagoguery. I will also note points at which different strategies open to the prisoners' lawyers or to Judge Johnson might have advanced the reform cause a bit further. Paradoxically, Johnson's attempts to cooperate with state authorities, his deference to state concerns, his flexibility and boundless patience, often failed to generate the synergy he intended and, indeed, exacerbated resistance to judicial interference in penal affairs. Occasionally, at least, a more resolute posture might have produced better results sooner—and greater acceptance into the bargain. I hasten to make clear, however, that my criticisms do not reflect reservations regarding the very enterprise in which Judge Johnson was engaged: the judicial development and enforcement of constitutional standards for prison conditions. There are those who doubt that the federal courts should attempt such a task and who regard failure of any substantial sort as evidence that penal reform should be pursued by other means, namely legislative or executive action at the local level. I do not share those misgivings. In my view, even marginal social progress is a thing to be accepted warmly. Our champions are those who enter the lists and take the most tentative initial steps.

This is a book about reform. And reform there was as the direct result of the *Pugh* and *James* cases. Alabama's penal institutions became cleaner, less crowded, safer; the agony of prisoners' daily life was mitigated. This is also a book about regret. Yet if I confess a full measure of disappointment that more ground was not gained, I do so against the backdrop of unflagging appreciation for the valiant efforts I watched for so long and with such wonder. Under circumstances that would have baffled less committed men and women, a small band of advocates and an extraordinary jurist did what could be done to improve the conditions under which thousands were forced to suffer. The players in this drama did something of value with a decade of their lives. This is the bright side of the story I have to tell.

Boston   L.W.Y.
June 1988

Acknowledgments
and Sources

My work on this project was supported by a Travel and Study Award from The Ford Foundation. I am indebted to Karl Menninger for recommending the project originally, to Marjorie Fine Knowles and Sanford Jaffe at Ford for approving it, and to William P. Gormbley for permitting me two extensions so that I might complete it with all deliberate speed. I am also indebted to the libraries at the University of Alabama, the University of Texas, and Boston University, where I studied the relevant secondary literature, and to the dozens of men and women familiar with the Alabama prison cases who opened their files and memories to me. I had access to the official files maintained by Jane P. Gordon, Ruth Ann Hodges, and Ann Rittenour at the U. S. District Court in Montgomery, and also to unofficial files kept by attorneys and other participants. In particular, I wish to acknowledge the cooperation I received from Alvin J. Bronstein of the National Prison Project, who gave me a free hand to sift his files for noteworthy documents, memoranda, and correspondence. Sharon Goretsky and Janice Lothers guided me through the cartons and cabinets, and Melvin Gibbons made copies of anything I wanted. Assistant U.S. Attorney Kenneth Vines permitted Antrena B. Gardner to show me pertinent files in the U.S. attorney's office in Montgomery. Phillip A. Butler, John L. Carroll, Ira DeMent, Ralph I. Knowles, Jr., and George P. Taylor were equally free with their materials. I received no timely response to my formal request to examine Justice Department files, but Stephen Whinston arranged access to materials covering the years prior to the Reagan administration. On the defendants' side, I was allowed to review files kept by W. Scears Barnes, Jr., who represented the penal authorities, and the lawyers who represented the Alabama attorney general. With Judge Johnson's permission, M. Roland Nachman, Jr., and George Beto allowed me to see previously confidential Human Rights Committee files. Raymond D.

Fowler and Stanley Brodsky gave me access to their voluminous notes on the Prison Classification Project.

Many others helped me more than they know. Janice S. Dawson, Denise Flowers, Gina W. Rudder, and especially Rebecca Jean Cook spent weeks transcribing interviews. Charlotte Gliksman, Cindy Malone, Leslie Muth, Cindy Ross, Camilla Roper, Karen Sacratini, and Karen Zarkades typed multiple versions of the manuscript. Roy R. Wade assisted me with countless administrative problems. James D. Thomas and Forrest McDonald helped me locate materials on Alabama history, E. Culpepper Clark gave me valuable lessons on oral history techniques, and Carl B. Clements introduced me to the relevant psychological literature. Others contributed insights in hundreds of conversations and telephone calls. An incomplete list includes Kathryn Abrams, William D. Barnard, Michael J. Churgin, Hugh G. Collins, Colin S. Diver, Russell J. Drake, Tony A. Freyer, Jerome A. Hoffman, Iredell Jenkins, Jennifer Johnston, Virginia L. Looney, Ira C. Lupu, Howard Mandell, Martha I. Morgan, Judith Resnik, Lawrence G. Sager, Allen E. Smith, Aviam Soifer, Mary Weidler, Carol Weisbrod, Jeanette F. Yackle, and especially Ralph Knowles and Steve Suitts.

To fill out the skeletal account of the prison cases established by the documentary record, I conducted formal interviews with key participants. Their names, together with the places and dates of the interviews, follow.

Interviews

Bennett, Larry D., Commissioner of Corrections, Montgomery, Ala., July 28, 1982; March 9, 1983.

Beto, George, Consultant, Human Rights Committee, Huntsville, Tex., June 28, 1982.

Britton, Robert G., Commissioner of Corrections, Birmingham, Ala., July 13, 1982.

Brodsky, Stanley, Associate Director, Prison Classification Project, Tuscaloosa, Ala., May 18–19, 27, 31, 1982.

Bronstein, Alvin J., Director, National Prison Project, Washington, D.C., August 17–18, 1981; April 21–22, 1982; March 28, 1983.

Carroll, John L., Director, Southern Poverty Law Center, Montgomery, Ala., May 31, 1983.

Coleman, James P., U.S. Circuit Judge, Ackerman, Miss., April 25, 1983.

DeMent, Ira, U.S. Attorney, Montgomery, Ala., July 20, 1982.

Fowler, Raymond D., Director, Prison Classification Project, Tuscaloosa, Ala., June 23, 1982.

Gordon, Jane P., Clerk, U.S. District Court, Montgomery, Ala., August 4, 1982.

Gwaltney, M. Lewis, U.S. Magistrate, Montgomery, Ala., August 19, 1982.

Hale, John H., Director of Public Information, Board of Corrections, Montgomery, Ala., July 28, 1982.

James, Worley, Named plaintiff in *James v. Wallace,* Mt. Meigs, Ala., November 20, 1980.

Johnson, Frank M., Jr., U.S. District Judge, Montgomery, Ala., April 19, 1983.

Knowles, Ralph I., Jr., Attorney, National Prison Project, Tuscaloosa, Ala., April 20–21, June 21, 30, 1983.

Lamar, Robert S., Jr., Counsel, Board of Corrections, Brimingham, Ala., August 2, 1982.

Littlefield, Patricia G., Attorney, U.S. Department of Justice, Washington, D.C., March 29, 1983.

McMillan, George D. H., State Senator, Birmingham, Ala., March 21, 1983.

Myers, Matthew L., Attorney, National Prison Project, Washington, D.C., August 19, 1981; April 23, 1982.

Nachman, M. Roland, Jr., Chairman, Human Rights Committee, Montgomery, Ala., May 11, 24, 28, 1982; March 15, 23, 1983.

Robinson, Richard, Member, Board of Corrections, Alexander City, Ala., July 23, 1982.

Samford, William J., Jr., Counsel, Governor James, Montgomery, Ala., May 31, 1983.

Segall, Robert D., Counsel, *Pugh* plaintiffs, Montgomery, Ala., April 11, May 29, 1982.

Smith, Fred V., Commissioner of Corrections, Montgomery, Ala., July 30, 1986.

Suitts, Steve, Executive Director, Civil Liberties Union of Alabama, Clifton Forge, Va., May 17, 1985.

Taylor, George P., Counsel, *James* plaintiffs, Tuscaloosa, Ala., March 8, 1982.

Varner, Robert E., U.S. District Judge, Montgomery, Ala., August 21, 1982.

Vickers, John E., Chairman, Board of Corrections, Demopolis, Ala., July 26, 1982.

Warren, Kenneth, Director of Professional Services, Board of Corrections, Montgomery, Ala., July 21, 1982.

Whinston, Stephen, Attorney, U.S. Department of Justice, Washington, D.C., March 29, 1983.

Wright, Cathy, Law Clerk to Judge Johnson, Birmingham, Ala., August 17, 1982.

Contents

REFORM AND REGRET

1

Conditions Precedent

The common starting point for anyone familiar with the evidence is that the American criminal justice system is in scandalous condition. Nothing seems to work. At least, that is, nothing seems to work well enough to summon consensus support. To begin, we are divided regarding the kind of human behavior we should discourage by imposing a criminal penalty. When we agree that specified forms of aberrant behavior may properly be labeled criminal, giving rise to a societal authority to impose punishment, we are at odds regarding the appropriate sanction. When and if we are able to agree on a suitable penalty—a term of incarceration, for example—we are divided once again over the length of an appropriate sentence and the character of the penal institution in which the offender should be housed. Only here do penal authorities play a role. Coming near the end of the process, prison officials must contend not only with their own shortcomings, but with the failures of others at anterior stages. Indeed, wardens typically explain their difficulties on precisely this ground. They control neither the front nor the back doors of their institutions. Their only authority, and thus their responsibility, is to deal with inmates while they are in custody.

Conflicting policies, grounded in ignorance and uncertainty, only feed more bodies into already crowded and quickly deteriorating facilities. From 1930 to 1939, in the desperate years of the Depression and for a time thereafter, the prisoner population grew by 39 percent. There was a 29 percent decline during the war years, 1940 to 1944, but, when young men returned home, the prison population began to rise yet again—by 72 percent between 1945 and 1961. The Vietnam War accounted for another decline from 1962 to 1968, but, as American involvement in Southeast Asia tapered off, the inmate population back home grew at a disproportionate rate. Initial increases were dramatic, but then the figures became startling. In the five-year period from 1973 to 1978, the prison population grew by 54 percent. The result was cat-astrophic. Large numbers of disturbed people were simply herded together in dilapidated structures for extended periods of time. Prison-ers arrived at the gate undifferentiated, the killer in the same bus with the sneak thief. Undertrained, overworked penal authorities could only accept them, hold them, and hope that the inevitable trauma could be held to a minimum. Shocking conditions developed in short order. Vio-lence was close behind. The Attica uprising occurred in 1971; the Okla-homa state penitentiary at McCalister burned to the ground in 1973; similar episodes of violence broke out in many other states. Instead of coming to grips with problems now of astonishing proportions, public officials across the country roundly ignored the agony of life in penal institutions. State legislative and executive authorities alike abdicated their responsibilities entirely, leaving state penitentiaries to degenerate into bedlams of brutality, disease, and death.[1]

It was in this context that help was sought from the federal courts, which in the previous decade had grappled with another vexing social issue—racial segregation in the public schools. In 1954, the Supreme Court had held in *Brown v. Board of Education*[2] that "separate but equal" schools denied black children the equal protection of the laws guaranteed by the Fourteenth Amendment. Thereafter, trial-level judges in federal district courts across the South had assumed primary responsibility for desegregating schools "with all deliberate speed." In lawsuit after lawsuit, those judges developed an array of techniques for gradually forcing state officials to restructure the administration of pub-lic schools in order to conform to constitutional requirements. The fed-eral courts' success in the desegregation endeavor was mixed. Yet they demonstrated extraordinary capacity to manage elaborate lawsuits whose design was not merely to vindicate constitutional rights but, in a real sense, to reform the operations of complex public institutions. That record, in turn, encouraged reformers committed to change in penal institutions to seek the federal courts out for new service.

In many instances, prisoners sued on their own behalf. They leafed through law books in the prison library, identified plausible constitu-tional claims against their keepers, and filed formal complaints in court. In time, however, sympathetic organizations outside the walls, partic-ularly the American Civil Liberties Union (ACLU) and the NAACP Legal Defense Fund (LDF), took up the cause. In the 1960s, the ACLU sponsored two small teams of lawyers and law students, one in New York and the other in Virginia, whose purpose was to sue state penal officials to achieve prison reform. In 1972, those programs were merged to form the National Prison Project with offices in Washington, D.C. In some cases, the Prison Project and the LDF assumed responsibility for the representation of inmates in need of legal assistance; in others, they participated in litigation as amici curiae—friends of the court. The latter status permitted trained lawyers to appear in court, question witnesses, and file briefs on legal points much as though they were retained by the prisoners concerned. During the same period, the U.S. Department of Justice occasionally played a similar role in prison cases. It was unclear at the time whether the Justice Department could formally represent prison inmates in lawsuits against state penal authorities; accordingly, government lawyers purported to act only for the United States, which scarcely could be denied the status of a friend of the federal courts.[3]

Lawyers specializing in prison work employed the same processes used in the school desegregation cases. The most common procedural vehicle was the Ku Klux Klan Act of 1871 which, in its modern form, authorized aggrieved citizens to sue state officials who had interfered with "rights . . . secured by the Constitution." For a century after its enactment in the aftermath of the Civil War, that statute had been used only rarely. In the 1960s, however, it was revived for new duty as a general enforcement mechanism for Fourteenth Amendment rights. In some instances, litigants sought money damages in compensation for their injuries at the hands of state authorities. In others, including prison reform cases, the preferred remedy was an injunction—an explicit order from the court instructing state officials in what they must do to eliminate constitutional violations. To ensure that such orders were as effective as possible, lawyers often sued not on behalf of a single inmate, complaining of an isolated episode of mistreatment, but on behalf of an entire class of prisoners joined in one lawsuit on the basis of a common claim or set of claims against state officials. These classes of prisoner-plaintiffs were drawn as broadly as possible, often including every inmate in a state's penal system and anyone who might be confined there in the future. If, then, the class claims were sustained, the court's injunctive order could alter penal practices well into the future, in order to protect both prisoners now incarcerated and class members who would later enter the prison system as inmates. In this manner, penal reforms wrung from federal litigation could enjoy genuine staying power.[4]

Class action lawsuits were expensive. Many lawyers were typically involved, collecting documents, interviewing witnesses, and writing memoranda and briefs on legal issues. Experts in penology and allied fields were needed to tour prisons and report their findings in court. Organizations such as the National Prison Project and the LDF were thus necessary to ensure adequate support for the reform effort. Moreover, in some instances the federal courts appointed private lawyers to represent prisoners unable to hire their own attorneys. Those lawyers often cooperated with the Prison Project and LDF, glad to benefit from the experience gained in other cases around the country. Early on, appointed lawyers were compensated from the federal treasury but, in the 1970s, some courts required the states whose penal insitutions were successfully attacked to pay reasonable attorneys' fees and costs to the prisoners' attorneys. The Supreme Court put a stop to that practice in 1975 but, in the following year, Congress enacted legislation allowing the award of attorneys' fees whenever plaintiffs suing pursuant to the Ku Klux Klan Act were successful. The prospect of winning not only an injunction reforming a penal facility but reimbursement for the costs of the lawsuit plainly encouraged the growth of prison litigation for the remainder of the decade.[5]

The claims raised in prison reform lawsuits varied. The National Prison Project initially contended that the fact of incarceration did not foreclose prisoners' exercise of many constitutional rights they would have enjoyed in the community. Inmates were entitled, for example, to worship freely, to express themselves in private correspondence, to read controversial literature and, when charged with violating prison rules, to be given a fair hearing. Lawsuits pressing claims of that kind were often successful; in two years, the Prison Project won a deserved reputation for legal actions that made a tangible difference in prisoners' lives. At the same time, two other legal theories promised even more dramatic possibilities. First, it was argued that the due process clause of the Fourteenth Amendment required all state policies to bear some rational relation to legitimate governmental purposes. In the Alabama mental hospital case, *Wyatt v. Stickney*,[6] for example, Judge Johnson held that if the purpose for which mental patients were confined was to subject them to treatment, then they must actually be treated. Similar arguments on behalf of prison inmates were available and, indeed, were explored in the initial stages of *Pugh* and *James.* Yet the due process theory in *Wyatt* was worrisome, suggesting few firm guidelines for judicial judgment and, in some minds, leaving courts too much discretion to determine what policies must be instituted to achieve state objectives "rationally."[7]

The second theory proved to be more popular. Harsh living conditions within American prisons were condemned as "cruel and unusual punishment" in violation of the Eighth Amendment. Inasmuch as punishment schemes of the past had been extremely brutal, some observers initially doubted whether conditions in contemporary prisons could be considered unconstitutional, however objectionable they might seem to federal judges. When, however, diligent lawyers established that prison conditions were far worse then outsiders had imagined, and when experts explained that such conditions were wholly unnecessary, the courts brought the Eighth Amendment into play. Occasionally, particular practices in a prison system were found to be so intolerable that they constituted cruel and unusual punishment in themselves. Typically, however, the federal courts examined all aspects of prison life and then rested judgment on the "totality of conditions" to which the class of prisoner-plaintiffs was exposed. In *Holt v. Sarver,*[8] the notorious Arkansas prison system was declared to be unconstitutional on this Eighth Amendment ground. Judge Johnson also relied on the Eighth Amendment in the medical care case, *Newman v. Alabama.* Similar litigation was soon under way in many jurisdictions. By 1978, the penal systems in thirteen states were operating under court order. By 1982, the number had increased to thirty-one. Broad-ranging judicial decrees regarding the treatment of prison inmates thus became a fixture of American penal administration.[9]

The Supreme Court was ambivalent with respect to these developments. Partaking of the so-called hands-off doctrine, the justices insisted on the one hand that the lower federal courts lacked both the expertise and the resources to meet the problems facing state penitentiaries, however urgent those difficulties might be. Judicial restraint in this field reflected "no more than a healthy sense of realism." Generally, then, state prison administration should be left to the officials concerned. On the other hand, the Court proclaimed that the federal courts should remain watchful lest "valid constitutional claims" arising in the penal context be neglected for insubstantial, not to say practical, reasons. The Supreme Court thus explicitly confirmed that district judges presented with prison cases must "discharge their duty to protect constitutional rights."[10]

An understanding of the way in which the penal reform movement in Alabama invoked the constitutional rights of prison inmates to effect change demands some appreciation of the history of penology in that state, Judge Johnson's career on the bench, and earlier reform litigation that laid the groundwork for *Pugh* and *James.* For it was the long and troubled history of penal institutions in Alabama that presented the judge with such a daunting challenge, it was Judge Johnson's managerial style that made litigation in his court an effective instrument of reform, and it was Johnson's experience with other cases, particularly *Wyatt,* that suggested the means for making genuine progress.

Penal measures in the American colonies mirrored those in contemporary England. Punishments were as primitive as the times. The death penalty was routinely available even for minor offenses, and mutilation augmented capital punishment. In time, however, the colonies seized the opportunity in the New World to begin afresh, to invest intellectual effort in the development of new and different penal systems. There were early starts, notably at the Walnut Street Jail in Philadelphia. Then, the same nineteenth-century trend toward institutionalization took hold in both psychiatry and penology. In this, the Quakers of Pennsylvania played the leading role. They brought an end to public spectacles and, in the alternative, established workhouses in which prisoners labored in private. Precisely why institutions were thought to hold promise is anything but clear. The incarceration of the poor, the sick, and the wayward may simply have been part of the "reforms" ushered in under a blind faith in change for its own sake. Then, too, institutions may have served the interest of a growing industrial society to keep the lower classes at work, even if that could be accomplished only through forced labor at detention centers.

The ideology of the times also played a critical role. Asylums were designed, first, to reform the persons assigned to them, and, second, to provide an example of explicit social organization to the society at large, to preserve some order and structure in the face of chaos. Almshouses, homes of refuge for juveniles, and mental hospitals thus sprang up everywhere to provide the structured, stable environment that human beings sought and needed but were denied in open society. In Alabama, in particular, the commitment to the asylum was ostensibly complete. By the early decades of the twentieth century, there was an Alabama Boys' Industrial School, an Alabama Reform School for Juvenile Negro Lawbreakers, a State Training School for Girls, a Vocational School for Girls, a Girls' Rescue Home, two Alabama Hospitals for the Insane, and an Alabama Home for the Feebleminded. Every form of human grief seemed destined to have its own institution, always further divided to maintain the Jim Crow rule. Hastings H. Hart, who served as a Russell Sage Foundation consultant to Governors Henderson and Kilby, declared in 1922 that "[i]n the past four years, Alabama [had] advanced from the rear rank to the front rank of the states of the Union in her social progress." Indeed, Hart recommended the establishment of yet another segregated institution for retarded blacks. "There is the same reason," he wrote, "for providing for the Negro feeble-minded that has led to State provision for insane Negroes, Negro criminals, and Negro delinquent children."[11]

Penal institutions emerged from the same intellectual history. First, the Quaker "separate" system, under which inmates worked alone in solitary cells, was established at the Eastern Pennsylvania Penitentiary in Philadelphia, known as Cherry Hill. Then, the "silent" system, under which prisoners slept in single cells but worked together during the day, was developed in New York at Auburn in Cayuga County. Of the two schemes, the Auburn plan proved to be more viable, for the unremarkable reason that convicts laboring in groups could be more efficient, produce more output, and help pay for their own upkeep. Cellular penitentiaries following the Auburn model soon were in place throughout the Midwest. From there, they spread south—first to Georgia and Louisiana and then to Alabama, which located such a prison, called the "Walls," at Wetumpka in 1846. Yet the southern states typically took little more than architectural guidance from Auburn. While there were attempts, early rather than late, to house prisoners in single cells at night and to engage them in congregate labor through the day, the new southern institutions were operated in the main without hint of isolation. Crowding was the immediate problem, subordinating any thought of isolation to the necessity of finding places for prisoners to sleep and frustrating attempts to involve inmates in productive employment.

The prisons established in Alabama over the next century suffered these shortcomings in the extreme. Occasionally, to be sure, public officials articulated objectives that were enlightened even by modern standards. Governor Bagby said in 1840 that the "great objective" of the "Walls" was to "reform" criminal offenders. An 1888 report on the prisons similarly insisted that imprisonment itself was the punishment for crime and that any "other or different punishment" within a penal institution was "unjust." Another report by W. H. Oakes in 1914 argued that it was "futile" to subject criminal offenders to "indignities" that would cause them to "hate" the very law it was hoped they should respect and to turn out men who were as much the enemies of society as the "law could make [them]." In fact, however, Alabama was never true to any such ideas. The conditions of confinement in state institutions were never such as to avoid the deterioration of inmates' capacity for living as ordinary citizens; certainly, those prisons never promised seriously to change criminal offenders for the better. From the earliest days, and increasingly after the Civil War, the Alabama penal system was charged at once to pay for itself and to accommodate large numbers of inmates, most of them ex-soldiers and manumitted blacks. These two themes, the requirement of self-support and crowding, were ever in conflict; the attempt to reconcile them condemned the Alabama prison system to failure.[12]

Within a year after the "Walls" was opened, state authorities discovered that prisoners crowded into the building were unable to support themselves. Accordingly, Alabama joined other southern states in adopting a convict lease system, which moved prisoners out of the prison to coal mines, where they served private masters under notoriously oppressive conditions. The press scored penal officials and lessees for flagrant abuses at the mines. Prisoners who refused to work were subjected to a curious and brutal "water torture." More refractory prisoners were routinely flogged or segregated in a disgusting disciplinary structure known as the "doghouse." After visiting some of the mines, a member of a legislative committee declared: "The present convict system is a blot upon the civilization of this century and a shame upon the State of Alabama." In 1888, Robert Dawson, representing the state in its first appearance at the annual conferences of the National Prison Association, spoke directly to the question that troubled his audience: "The lease system must go, as slavery went, and as the dramshop is bound to go." Even so, Alabama was not prepared to surrender so lucrative a business summarily. In 1890, W. D. Lee took the floor at another meeting of the Prison Association to defend his state against attacks on the lease system. While Lee conceded that the leases were "wrong in principle and bad in practice" and that they should in due course be abolished, he insisted that Alabama had adopted the lease system out of necessity, after imprisonment in an institution had failed both to generate revenues and to accommodate the great crush of inmate bodies.[13]

When the legislature finally discarded the leases, the state launched an aggressive construction campaign in order to house prisoners returning from the mines. In 1923, a new 900-place prison, named for Governor Kilby, was erected near Montgomery. Kilby Prison was to be the centerpiece of a new regime in which, once again, it was proposed to reform criminal offenders. Incoming inmates were to be interviewed and tested to determine what Hart called their "remedial defects." Then they were to be assigned to other institutions for a "systematic course of reformatory treatment." In 1939, Draper Correctional Center was established at Speigner; in 1942, the old prison at Wetumpka was refurbished and opened as the Julia Tutwiler Prison for Women. Atmore Prison, later renamed the G. K. Fountain Correctional Center, was opened in 1949 to house the thousands of prisoners working the system's agricultural lands in rural Escambia County. Hundreds more, most of them black, were sent to the State Highway Department's road camps scattered over the state. Still more were sprinkled over other agricultural lands at the Red Eagle Honor Farm north of Montgomery and at the State Cattle Ranch near Greensboro. In the late 1960s, Kilby deteriorated dramatically and had to be razed. In its place, the Mt. Meigs Medical and Diagnostic Center was established near Montgomery in Elmore County, and Holman Prison was constructed near Fountain to the south. Holman was opened in 1969, Mt. Meigs a year later. The state's best institution, the Frank Lee Youth Center in Deatsville, a few miles north of Draper, was opened in 1964 to house approximately 100 first offenders.[14]

Still, however, the same two factors that had previously frustrated enlightened objectives surfaced again. The persistent drive to make prisoners pay for their own upkeep augured against changes in penal policy that threatened to reduce the income the state could derive from inmate labor. Thus the farms were now filled with unskilled inmate crews, not in any serious attempt to reform prisoners' behavior, but simply and frankly to meet the costs of their maintenance. And the system's overpopulation rendered meaningful examination and classification of new prisoners impractical. New inmates arriving at Mt. Meigs were sent wherever there was space for them and were employed in whatever labor program promised to bring the most economic benefit to the state. These difficulties were exacerbated when the rate at which Alabama incarcerated citizens skyrocketed along with the national trend. During the early 1970s, the population of Alabama's prisons increased at an accelerating rate—20 percent during the ten months immediately preceding trial in the *Pugh* and *James* cases. Now there were far more prisoners than could be employed in *any* manner. Alabama's prisons, like those in other states, were troubled by violence. Indeed, the level of assaults throughout the period demonstrated a consistent pattern of physical abuse in the daily lives of inmates.

These were the circumstances in which Alabama prison inmates raised constitutional claims in Judge Johnson's court, claims that Johnson was duty-bound to examine pursuant to the Supreme Court's then recent admonitions. Prisoners' allegations revealed a penal system permitted to degenerate into unrelieved squalor. Most inmates were housed in large, unsupervised dormitories, where the strong had their

way with the weak. Instead of making architectural changes or supply-
ing sufficient numbers of guards to prevent violence, the authorities
instituted a disciplinary regime of mindless brutality. None of the
state's institutions met ordinary public health standards or the state fire
safety code. Medical care was inadequate by any professional measure.
Prisoners were poorly fed throughout the system. They were denied
adequate exercise and reasonable opportunities to visit with family and
friends. Relatively few educational and vocational programs interrupted the oppressive monotony of prison life. Alabama prisons were
nothing more than human warehouses that contained but hardly contended with an overwhelming population of idle criminal offenders.
The state's penal system, in short, was in administrative bankruptcy.

The plaintiff in the *Newman* case filed his own complaint. He
described the prison system's medical care system in shocking detail.
Since his arrival, six men had died in the prison hospital, most of them
on weekends when no physician or nurse was available. Newman
alleged that one inmate had died without attendance of any kind and
that maggots had been found in another's wounds. In still other cases,
he charged deliberate abuse. In one particularly egregious illustration,
an inmate had arrived at the hospital unable to control his bowels. The
staff quickly tired of changing the prisoner's bedding and, in Newman's
telling, attempted to discourage bed-wetting by forcing the inmate to sit
upright on a wooden bench next to his bunk. There the prisoner sat for
"days and weeks and months," until "both feet and legs became solid
sores." The prisoner's "[f]lesh turned black." In the end, one leg was
amputated to save the inmate from gangrene. "[H]e lived one day after
the amputation."

Similar instances of abuse could be found in other facilities, and
nowhere more plainly than in the disciplinary unit at Draper Prison. To
visit that facility was to descend to the depths of human depravity in
our time. Situated in what still was called the doghouse, the punishment
cells measured only thirty-two square feet in area—the size of an ordinary door. The doghouse was accessible to visitors only with great difficulty. As much as a half hour might pass before a guard could locate
the keys and open the main door, described by one witness as a "tomb-
stone." Inside, there were twelve cells housing men whose offenses were
often insignificant; these were prisoners who had cursed an officer or
missed morning roll call. Inmates in the doghouse had no beds, no
lights, no toilets, no running water, no reading matter. They were fed
once a day and allowed to shower once in eleven days. They were never

released for exercise. They were crushed together, as many as six men to a cell, for weeks at a time.

Even routine conditions in the prison system were virtually as bad. The complaint in another lawsuit, filed by David W. Tanner, revealed that forty-five prisoners at the Mt. Meigs facility were forced to sleep "crossways" on the floor in a hallway six feet wide. Tanner complained that there was only one toilet bowl for all the men in the hallway. There was no place to wash himself or to brush his teeth. He had been unable to change clothes in six weeks. Rapes and beatings were common, there being no guards on duty to keep order at night.

The twin themes of crowding and violence appeared as well in the complaint filed by Jerry Lee Pugh. He was one of comparatively few white prisoners assigned to live with a large number of black inmates in a 200-bed dormitory at Fountain. Racial tensions ran high, and Pugh became convinced that violence was imminent. Inmates brandished nightmarish weapons—"sharp blades" up to sixteen inches long, "[s]teel bars" as long as thirty-six inches, as well as "hatches" [*sic*] and "pick handles." Pugh's repeated requests to be transferred to safer quarters were turned back by guards who, for their own safety, stayed well away from the dormitory after dark. Prisoners locked inside were left to fend for themselves. When violence finally erupted in the summer of 1973, Pugh was badly beaten and, by his account, left for dead under a bunk. Other inmates rescued him after order was restored and probably saved his life by bringing him forward for emergency treatment at nearby hospitals. Medical records showed that Pugh suffered multiple lacerations and fractures; a part of his skull was crushed. There were allegations of a different order, notably the claim developed in the *James* case that prisoners were entitled not only to protection from abuse at the hands of penal authorities and other inmates, but to educational and vocational programs for their benefit. The immediate catalyst for judicial action, however, was the utter depravity of the prison system as it was described by prisoners who faced each hour with dread.

The prisoners' right to relief in the *Pugh* and *James* cases was established after a grueling trial in the summer of 1975. The testimony regarding the conditions in the Alabama prison system was devastating and, on the evening of the sixth day, the defendants and their lawyers decided they had seen enough. Next morning, Robert S. Lamar, Jr., the defendants' chief trial attorney, carried the message to opposing counsel and ultimately to Judge Johnson. Shortly before the luncheon recess, the lawyers joined in a request for a conference in chambers. When they emerged a short time later, Lamar proclaimed in public what he had already conceded in private.

> Your Honor, the Defendants in this case, the Alabama Board of Corrections and several of its officers, rest their case at this time. They rest their case based upon the amended complaints filed and upon the overwhelming majority of the evidence, which shows that an Eighth Amendment violation has and is now occurring [*sic*] to inmates in the Alabama Prison System. On that theory the Defendants have nothing further to offer to the Court and at this time rest.

Lamar's statement was ambiguous on several key points. The precise meaning to be taken from it would prove debatable in due course. Yet for the moment the speech was widely understood to represent a complete capitulation—a matter-of-fact recognition that the Alabama prison system was itself a violation of the Constitution. Perhaps more important, Lamar not only conceded that the plaintiffs had demonstrated that cruel and unusual punishment was being visited on prisoners. He acknowledged a judicial authority to act, to commit the power and prestige of a federal court order to redress prisoners' grievances against the Alabama penal system. There could be no doubt that sweeping relief would be forthcoming. By the end of the day, Judge Johnson had ordered the defendants to close the notorious doghouse at Draper. Next day, he instructed them to cease accepting more prisoners into state facilities until attrition diminished the population to "design capacity." Five months later, he issued a comprehensive order touching numerous aspects of penal administration relating to the physical treatment of inmates.

Frank Johnson was no ordinary judge. If he had been, the Alabama prison cases would never have been litigated with such vigor, and with such monumental hopes, in his courtroom. Born and reared in Winston County in the hills of north Alabama, he attended the University of Alabama in Tuscaloosa and later the university's law school. Like his father before him, Johnson was a conservative Republican—in contrast to his friend and law school classmate, George C. Wallace, who at the time was considered a liberal Democrat. Political labels earned early in life did not follow either man far. Johnson enlisted immediately after graduation and served a tour of duty with the Third Army in France. Wounded on two occasions, he was later assigned to a depot in Lichfield, England, where, ironically, he once defended several stockade guards against charges that they had mistreated prisoners in their care. After the war, Johnson returned to Alabama to practice law and enter

GOP politics. He was a delegate to the party's national conventions in 1948 and 1952 and campaigned in Alabama for both Dewey and Eisenhower. His early support for Eisenhower over Taft won him an appointment as U.S. attorney in the Northern District. Two years later, Eisenhower gave him the district judgeship in Montgomery. Johnson was then 37 years of age, the youngest federal judge in the country. He took the oath in the fall of 1955, just over a year after the Supreme Court's decision in *Brown*.[15]

Immediately on assuming his new position, Johnson joined other southern judges who not only accepted the Supreme Court's announcement that public schools must be desegregated, but extended the principle of racial equality to other circumstances. He struck down racial discrimination in municipal buses, parks, libraries, and museums in Montgomery and fashioned desegregation plans for state agencies and public schools. He invalidated the poll tax and enjoined interference with the Freedom Riders. On other fronts, he reapportioned the Alabama legislature to enforce the principle of "one person, one vote" and restructured state property tax levies to ensure that wealthy landowners were not given invalid advantages over the poor. It seemed that every public issue of significance found its way to his chambers, there to be treated in a sensitive, methodical manner. More than one observer asked rhetorically whether Johnson was not the "real governor" of Alabama. Justice Douglas counted him among his "champions." He was that and more. And he suffered for it.

In the 1960s, Johnson was condemned in his native state for the very actions that elicited praise elsewhere in the country and had put his picture on the cover of *Time* magazine. He received threatening phone calls and hate mail. In some quarters, he was socially ostracized. Crosses were burnt on his lawn, and his mother's house was bombed. His own home was placed under armed guard. Yet times changed. By the 1970s, it was no longer socially acceptable to use overtly racist rhetoric in public discourse. As racial slurs vanished from campaign speeches, harsh attacks on Judge Johnson also receded. Locally, he was no longer a pariah, but was widely admired for decisions that only recently had been bitterly decried. Political reality may account for such a remarkable change in so short a time. Granted access to the polls by Johnson's orders of the previous decade, Alabama blacks developed significant political strength—particularly in Birmingham to the north and in the agricultural region near Montgomery. Soon it was politically inexpedient to neglect the new black electorate and, perhaps, to abuse the man who had made that electorate possible. Not only Yale and Boston University, but his alma mater, the University of Alabama, awarded him an honorary degree.

Johnson disclaimed any general authority to develop social policies and to order that they be enforced. He protested that he was "just a judge" who could not "reach out and get cases" but must be content to "evaluate the facts" in lawsuits brought by interested litigants, to determine "what the law is" with respect to those facts, and to "decide the case accordingly." To put even more distance between himself and the making of public policy, he essentially blurred any distinction between the substantive force of the Constitution and his own judicial pronouncements. His rhetorical device for this purpose was an oft-stated commitment to the "supremacy of law." His famous address to the all-white jury in the *Luizzo* case, in which Klansmen were charged with violating Mrs. Luizzo's civil rights by murdering her, put the idea in the extreme. Neither he nor the jurors, Johnson insisted, could be concerned with the "wisdom or the policy of the law." Instead, it was a matter of duty to "accept the law" and "make a proper and an unbiased application of it in any given instance." Judicial decisions and orders, by this account, were the concrete embodiment of the Constitution itself.[16]

In most circumstances, Judge Johnson found the law easy enough to ascertain. "In retrospect," he said, "I didn't find any tough factual or legal question in any of the civil rights and human rights cases." In Johnson's mind, for example, the Supreme Court's decision in *Brown* outlawed racial discrimination in all manner of public facilities. His own opinions simply applied that equality principle—for the straightforward and sufficient reason that it was the law and due to be obeyed. Once the law was identified, moreover, it must apply to everyone. Johnson rejected civil disobedience on the part of civil rights activists and the Ku Klux Klan alike. He refused to credit the proposition that anyone might claim a moral authority to violate the law, regardless of the ultimate justice of a cause. His conduct of lawsuits in court underscored the point. A 1976 survey of lawyers in Alabama turned up no one who claimed unfairness in Johnson's rulings from the bench. Said Governor Wallace's long-time counsel, John Kohn: "Johnson is the finest judge I've ever seen. I always felt he was totally fair."[17]

If Judge Johnson acknowledged responsibility for substantive law-making at all, he claimed to act only when state officials abdicated their own duties and thrust them on the court. Taking a favorite line from the growing literature on his work, he ascribed the demand for judicial action to the "Alabama Punting Syndrome." The history of federal civil rights litigation in Alabama was, in Johnson's telling, "replete" with instances in which state officials might have avoided judicial decrees if they had only taken responsibility to meet constitutional objections to their behavior. "[T]ime after time," he insisted, the courts had found it necessary to "step into the vacuum left by the state's inaction." In effect, state officials in Alabama consistently "punted" the state's problems to the federal bench. By common account, the most egregious offender was George Wallace, Johnson's law school classmate, who became governor of Alabama in 1962.[18]

Judge Johnson understood that state officials in civil rights cases required highly detailed instructions and that, to ensure that his orders were carried out, he was typically forced to retain judicial supervision over such cases for considerable time. Yet recognizing the "delicate" nature of the "balance of power" in the federal system, he designed his orders to "keep to a minimum the disruption of state institutions and the intrusion into state functions." He punctuated his opinions with careful language conceding the primary responsibility of state administrative officers—even as he acknowledged that his accompanying orders promised to reduce the "autonomy and flexibility" those officials would otherwise have enjoyed. He explained his continued involvement at the implementation stages as the by-product of his general deference to state prerogatives. Instead of insisting on immediate compliance with specified standards, he routinely permitted state officers to formulate and present their own plans for change. When those plans were inadequate, however, he instituted his own—to drive home the point that the matter at hand was serious and that genuine change was necessary. An old Alabama story provided an illustration.

> Everyone in Winston County knows that mules are the most stubborn characters in the world. This fellow had a mule he couldn't train. When he told it to giddy-up, why, the mule would stop. But when he'd tell it to whoa, the mule would get up. You'd tell it to gee, it would haw. You'd tell it to haw, it would gee. He finally decided he had to take it to a mule trainer, and he did. He took it across the county, left it, and told the man what he wanted. . . . [T]he mule trainer picked up a singletree, a piece of wood about three feet long. . . . So, he knocked the mule in the head with it. . . . [T]he owner of the mule says, the man says, I wanted you to train my mule. I didn't want you to beat him to death. And the man says, Well, I haven't even started training your mule. He says, I'm just trying to get his attention.[19]

Even when Johnson established his own prescriptive standards (to get the defendants' attention), he remained patient in the face of intransigence. If he continually prodded state authorities to act, it was only because he declined, out of deference, to mandate immediate and complete satisfaction of his orders. The Supreme Court had been content to order desegregation of the public schools "with all deliberate speed," and Judge Johnson was no less willing to wait.

Johnson rarely unsheathed the court's ultimate weapon—the power to hold recalcitrant parties in contempt and to fine or jail them until they met judicial orders. In one of his many celebrated confrontations with George Wallace, this one when Wallace was still a local judge in Barbour County, Johnson stated publicly that he would issue a contempt citation if Wallace did not comply with an order to release local voting records to the U.S. Commission on Civil Rights. The stratagem was successful; Wallace gave the records to a grand jury, which made them available to the commission. In Johnson's view, the episode demonstrated not that state officials could fruitfully be held in contempt to force them to respect his orders, but that the *threat* of a contempt citation could accomplish what a genuine order might not. Patience, reinforced by the menace of contempt, held out the only real promise of success. The serious question for Johnson was not whether the state's policies must be brought into compliance with constitutional standards he himself identified, but "[h]ow fast are we going to do it?"[20]

Johnson's handling of school desegregation cases tracked his public explanations. In an early case, *Shuttlesworth v. Birmingham Board of Education,*[21] he joined with Judge Richard Rives to uphold a state statute giving school officials authority to decide which schools students would attend. It was clear that the statute could be used to enforce racial segregation, but Johnson and Rives refused to hold in the abstract that it could not be employed in a nondiscriminatory fashion. "We must presume," they insisted, "that [the statute] will be so administered." At the same time, they admonished the defendants to proceed with care. If in application the statute produced segregation, the judges promised to award black plaintiffs appropriate relief.

Johnson behaved in much the same way in his next case, a straightforward challenge to segregation in the public schools in Macon County. In his initial opinion in *Lee v. Macon County Board of Education,*[22] the judge concluded that the board had unconstitutionally assigned both students and faculty on the basis of race. Yet he withheld an immediate desegregation decree, thus allowing state authorities time in which to meet constitutional standards without further judicial coercion. Events in the next few months demonstrated no such cooperation. Governor Wallace ordered the board to delay the opening of classes for one week, apparently in hopes of discouraging black students from attending, and dispatched state troopers to the school to prevent any student from entering. In succeeding days, most white students left Tuskegee High to enroll at other, all-white public schools in the county and at Macon Academy, a new private school in Tuskegee. The governor provided state patrol cars to transport white students to all-white schools, and later, acting in his capacity as ex-officio president of the state board of education, he obtained a resolution closing Tuskegee High entirely. The effect was to solidify the assignment of white students to other segregated schools and to channel blacks to Tuskegee Institute High, an all-black school.

It was apparent that Johnson had not yet caught the attention of state education authorities. Accordingly, he issued a series of orders enjoining Wallace and the state board from interfering with integration at Tuskegee High, preventing the use of state funds for the purpose of maintaining race discrimination in the public schools, and demanding that the Macon County board prepare a "realistic" plan for desegregation. Most important, he took advantage of the very stratagem used by Wallace to inject himself and the state board into the Macon County case. Inasmuch as the governor and the state board had assumed control of all the state's public schools, albeit to frustrate desegregation, the judge was able to extend the reach of his injunction, originally limited to Macon County, to every public school in Alabama. Johnson's patience had been rewarded with recalcitrance. He, in turn, rewarded resistance with more sweeping decrees—and yet more patience.[23]

Notwithstanding his public statements to the contrary, there was novelty in much of Judge Johnson's work. He took innovative measures to ensure that civil rights litigation was properly handled. Impressed by the federal government's representative in the field, John Doar, Johnson occasionally drafted the Justice Department to provide assistance to private litigants. In the Macon County case, he flatly ordered the department to "appear and participate as a party." His authority to issue such an order was questionable at best. Yet in the heady atmosphere of the times, federal authorities made no complaint. Drawing on the experience of Judge Ronald N. Davies in the Little Rock, Arkansas, case, Johnson also took advantage of the Federal Bureau of Investigation (FBI). Employing the same skills they used in criminal investigations, FBI agents produced volumes of sensitive information that might not otherwise have been available to litigants attacking segregation. Johnson's use of the Justice Department and the FBI tended to undercut his insistence that he had little control over the matters to come before him for decision. In some instances, at least, he did not simply respond to disputes brought to his door, but took the affirmative step of bringing a particularly resourceful and powerful litigant, the United States, into civil rights actions. He went further in the institution cases of the 1970s; he enhanced the ability of mental patients and prisoners to make their arguments by appointing excellent lawyers to represent them and by designating professional organizations and the National Prison Project to participate as amici curiae.[24]

Judge Johnson not only channeled litigation by influencing the identity and capacity of litigants, but also pioneered the give-and-take methods employed by district judges to enforce unpopular federal standards. All district judges understood that conventional remedies, such as the payment of damages, were inadequate in cases in which litigants challenged the operations of state institutions. Only injunctions could redress the grievances about which civil rights litigants complained. Indeed, even traditional, "preventative" injunctions were ineffectual. It was hopeless merely to order defendants to cease violating the Constitution; they required affirmative guidance—"reparative" orders telling them not what they could no longer do, but what they must do in the future. Johnson took matters a step further. He developed the "structural" injunction—a judicial order designed to reorganize a dysfunctional social institution.[25]

In the end, and notwithstanding his public protests, Johnson treated the business at hand for what it realistically was—a challenge to respond to generalized grievances regarding public policy put forward by a class of similarly situated citizens. His cases reached well beyond the parties immediately involved, affected a range of competing interests and goals and, accordingly, demanded a high degree of judicial management in order that all the social conditions at stake were thoroughly explored. Johnson took evidence in court not merely to determine the relevant facts, but to establish a basis for a remedial decree that promised to correct abuses of power in the future. And, certainly, he recognized that his own role was not finished when the judgment and order were entered. The issuance of an injunction only initiated a long-term relationship in which Johnson intervened again and again with supplemental orders, relaxing deadlines and establishing new ones, in the course of shaping an institution's operations into satisfactory order. The initial decree, indeed, served only as a triggering device, invoking a pattern of judicially inspired management.

Judge Johnson's critics insisted that his work trespassed into the realm of policy-making. To the extent he superintended social arrangements over time, he seemed to broker political power in the manner of the executive and legislative branches of government and thus undermined the authority of his orders as *law* instead of as political claims for dominance. Within the critics' case, Johnson's unwillingness, or inability, to hold state authorities in contempt played a curious, even paradoxical, role. If, it was charged, Johnson genuinely had the great power he asserted to order state officials to rework existing arrangements, then he should be willing, and able, to coerce their immediate compliance—on pain of fines or imprisonment if they refused. Thus Johnson's preference for giving state authorities ample time in which to change their ways and only threatening to exercise his contempt power was put forward as evidence that his orders were questionable in the first instance.

Proponents of the work that Judge Johnson and other federal judges did in civil rights cases responded that the courts had undertaken a similar management role in other fields, namely in cases in which railroad corporations were reorganized and in which disputes over child custody were resolved, often through highly detailed injunctive decrees contemplating close judicial supervision over time. The rub in civil rights cases, they charged, was that judicial techniques previously employed in less controversial contexts were now being used to the advantage of the poor, racial minorities, and institutional inmates whose claims Johnson's critics did not fully respect.

On the question whether Johnson should or must enforce orders by holding state officials in contempt, the Supreme Court's signals were quite clear, at least at first. Johnson was not instructed to use harsh means to bring state officials to heel, but he was openly commended for his own, more accommodating methods. Indeed, the Supreme Court's warm reception for his handling of school desegregation cases encouraged the judge to apply the same techniques in the mental health and prison cases. Another school case, *Carr v. Montgomery County Board of Education*,[26] provides an illustration. The evidence in *Carr* was overwhelming, and Johnson had no difficulty finding a constitutional violation. Yet he was content to order state authorities to "take the necessary steps to desegregate" some grades by the beginning of fall classes. Once again state officials defaulted, and once again the judge engaged his strategy for obtaining compliance with federal standards. He cajoled the defendants. He nudged them. He threatened them with contempt when they made no progress and complimented them when they reported even modest success. He demanded annual reports from them and held periodic hearings whenever more specific guidance proved necessary. He took serious account of the defendants' views regarding the wisdom and efficacy of specific actions. When he finally established yet another plan for the elimination of segregated schools in Montgomery, his specific requirements prompted both sides to appeal. The Fifth Circuit Court of Appeals, which encompassed Alabama, affirmed in most respects but made occasional modifications. In the Supreme Court, however, Johnson was totally vindicated. Justice Hugo Black's opinion for a unanimous bench extolled Johnson's flexibility as a virtue. In Black's words, Johnson's "patience and wisdom" were "written for all to see and read on the pages of the five-year record" before the Court. Accordingly, the circuit's modifications were vacated, and Johnson's order was embraced "as he wrote it."[27]

Judge Johnson's experience with segregation in the public schools emboldened him to invoke similar techniques in litigation regarding other state institutions. He had seen resistance in the school cases and had learned to contend with it. In *Wyatt,* in which he addressed the problems besetting Alabama's mental patients, he felt the weight of bureaucratic inertia as well. Now the judge dealt with unfortunate men and women forced to live in dilapidated hospitals that, like the prisons, had been left over from the Jacksonian period. Johnson's experience with the mental hospitals took law reform litigation in Alabama well beyond the requirements of school desegregation and laid the predicate for the prison cases to come.

The treatment of institutionalized people in Alabama was initially challenged in 1969 when a private attorney, Ira DeMent, discovered a young black woman who had been placed in a detention cell on the third floor of the Montgomery courthouse. When DeMent learned that the lights had failed on Friday afternoon and his client had spent the weekend in the dark, he filed a petition insisting on her release. Resting on the common law doctrine of *parens patriae,* under which the state stood in place of the girl's parents, DeMent demonstrated that the conditions in the detention cell were intolerable. The case captured considerable notoriety in the local press and, in the end, DeMent was successful not only in winning his client's freedom, but in drawing attention to the general question of the conditions under which the state's captives were forced to live.[28]

Like Judge Johnson, DeMent was from Winston County. When he opened a small law practice in 1958, the celebrated cases that would build Johnson's reputation were only beginning. DeMent was drawn into them in various capacities—primarily as Assistant City Attorney in Montgomery. In the troubled 1960s, when Montgomery was the scene of friction between civil rights demonstrators and the police, DeMent served as legal advisor to Police Commissioner L. B. Sullivan, who later became a key defendant in the prison conditions suits. Back in private practice, DeMent again turned his attention to state institutions housing poor blacks. He became convinced that the Alabama Industrial School for Negro Children was little better than a "slave camp" where unwanted black children were sent for safekeeping. Accordingly, he filed a class action lawsuit in Judge Johnson's court, relying once again on the theory that state authorities must improve deteriorated facilities to fulfill their role as surrogate parents. While the *Stockton*[29] case was pending, President Nixon appointed DeMent to the post of U.S. attorney for the Middle District. Instead of giving up the case, DeMent persuaded the Department of Justice to intervene. Here again, the department's authority for becoming involved in constitutional litigation initiated by private litigants was questionable. Yet the matter was serious, and in the wake of the department's role in the Alabama school cases, the authorities in Washington acquiesced. *Stockton* was settled out of court and, accordingly, drew little public attention.

Race discrimination supplied the initial occasion for litigation touching the major asylums, Bryce Hospital and Partlow State School for the Retarded in Tuscaloosa and Searcy Hospital at Mt. Vernon. Bryce and Partlow were predominantly white, with black patients and residents assigned to separate quarters to the rear. Searcy was all-black. As early as 1965, the Department of Health, Education, and Welfare (HEW) warned state authorities that the continuation of segregation would mean the termination of federal financial support for the hospitals. The Alabama Mental Health Board gave assurances that something would be done, but the board's limited efforts were frustrated when Governor Wallace opposed desegregation in the mental health system just as in the public schools. Three years later, after repeated attempts to persuade Alabama to abandon that stance, officials at HEW withheld further federal monies. The Alabama attorney general filed a federal lawsuit, *Alabama v. Finch*,[30] asking Judge Johnson to declare the federal action invalid. HEW responded with a counterclaim to enforce its decision to cut off funds, and the Justice Department intervened to help. In the meantime, attorneys working with the LDF filed a separate suit, *Marable v. Alabama Mental Health Board*,[31] on behalf of patients and residents demanding an end to Jim Crow. Johnson made short work of the claims in both cases. Racial segregation violated the equality principle established in the school cases. Nothing further need be said regarding the substance of the parties' contentions. Coming to the appropriate relief, however, Johnson was characteristically restrained. He found it "unnecessary" to issue a "formal injunction" immediately and preferred, instead, to defer to the "sober judgment of experienced personnel" in Alabama—who, he insisted, were better situated to devise "ways and means" for desegregating the mental health system. And, of course, he deemed it "desirable" to give state authorities time to end segregation "in a manner that works a minimum of disruption on the ongoing programs of the institutions."

Stockton, Finch, and *Marable* focused federal attention on Alabama's mental institutions. The more far-reaching litigation in *Wyatt* came close behind. Decades of neglect had left Bryce, Searcy, and Partlow in wretched shape. Overextended and underfinanced, those facilities served only as crowded detention centers for thousands of people who were unwelcome in the community at large. The situation was ripe for yet another lawsuit in Judge Johnson's court, this one challenging the constitutionality of holding mentally ill and handicapped people against their will under conditions making it impossible to care for them properly. That lawsuit came, but in an unlikely package.

In the summer of 1970, the Alabama commissioner of mental health, Dr. Stonewall B. Stickney, announced that the Mental Health Board was running out of money and that scores of professionals at Bryce would have to be discharged. Some of the psychologists scheduled for dismissal retained a Florida attorney, George Dean, to represent them. Dean was a veteran civil rights lawyer with personal ties to Alabamians, among them Alberta Murphy in Tuscaloosa and Ira DeMent in Montgomery. Murphy and her husband, Jay, introduced Dean to Dr. Raymond Fowler, chairman of the Department of Psychology at the University of Alabama and an outspoken opponent of Stickney's plans. Together, the four pondered the theory Dean would put to Judge Johnson. It would be essential to protect the psychologists' jobs indirectly, by insisting on the interests of their patients. If the purpose of committing mentally ill people to Bryce was treatment, Dean would contend, it followed that the Mental Health Board was obligated to provide professional care to anyone confined there. Stickney's plan to dismiss large numbers of professionals threatened the board's ability to meet that obligation. Dean obtained the cooperation of guardians for several patients and, when his secretary listed one of those patients, Ricky Wyatt, as the first named plaintiff in the class action suit, the *Wyatt v. Stickney* case was born.

Judge Johnson's experience in the earlier cases had made him painfully aware of the plight of Bryce patients. He anticipated, moreover, that sooner or later the deeper problems of patient care would come his way, in the same manner that other public issues had come to him when state authorities proved unable or unwilling to address them. The pattern at Bryce was a familiar one, and this might well be the case in which to face issues left untouched in the race discrimination cases of the previous year. In an early hearing, Johnson said that if Dean was prepared to argue that involuntarily committed mental patients had a constitutionally protected "right to treatment," the judge would take such an argument seriously. The primary focus of the *Wyatt* litigation shifted then and there. In due course, Dean withdrew the staff members' claims altogether, leaving only the patients' contentions in the case. Thereafter, staff levels were considered only as evidence that the deplorable conditions at Bryce frustrated adequate care. Johnson held a hearing in the case in January 1971, and in March he issued an opinion collecting his preliminary findings and announcing his legal judgment.[32]

The judge quickly concluded that the administration of Bryce was in chaos. The very mission of the institution was in doubt. While Bryce was apparently intended to serve the needs of mentally ill patients in need of psychiatric care, thousands of mentally handicapped and geriatric patients were held there for a variety of other reasons. The "programs of treatment" until recently, he said, "failed to conform to any known minimums established for providing treatment for the mentally ill." Turning to legal theory, Johnson was on uncomfortable ground. The Supreme Court had never held that state mental health authorities must actually give patients the treatment for which they were ostensibly confined, but the judge found some help in a series of opinions written by Judge David Bazelon, holding that certain federal statutes entitled patients at federal hospitals to adequate care. Those statutes were inapplicable to state institutions like Bryce, but Johnson could build on Bazelon's aside that the Constitution might establish a right to treatment where federal statute law did not reach. The constitutional basis for the right to treatment was the Fourteenth Amendment's due process clause. In this, Johnson did not mean that the procedures by which patients had been committed were inadequate; he dealt with the necessary procedural safeguards for civil commitments in another case. He held in *Wyatt* that, regardless of the process employed, state authorities were bound in a substantive sense to keep their implicit promise to provide the treatment for which patients were committed in the first instance.[33]

The choice of the due process clause as the basis for the right to treatment recognized in *Wyatt* was theoretically explosive and practically troublesome. To be meaningful, the right to treatment must be a right to adequate treatment. And there was no immediately apparent standard for determining whether even the feeble efforts currently being made at Bryce were sufficient to satisfy the Constitution. Judge Johnson understood as much and chose to meet the problem in a familiar way. He waited to see what Stickney could and would do on his own. Johnson recognized that the matter would require "thorough study" and "professional judgment and evaluation." Stickney, he said, was up to the task—if he was given sufficient financial support. Accordingly, Johnson allowed the commissioner six months to "promulgate and implement" standards for adequate care at Bryce. If he failed, the judge made it clear that professionals of the court's choosing would be appointed to appraise the situation and propose standards that Johnson himself would impose on the system.

Johnson was cautious. Even as he gave Stickney and the Mental Health Board an opportunity to set their own house in order, he called on old allies to help. He explicitly invited various agencies of the federal government, including the Justice Department, HEW, and the U.S. Public Health Service, to enter the case as amici curiae to assist the court in evaluating the plan that Stickney was ordered to produce. That action brought the new U.S. attorney, Ira DeMent, into the case. He quickly renewed his friendship with Dean and Fowler and worked closely with them on the *Wyatt* case. A Tuscaloosa attorney, Russell Jackson Drake, entered the case with Dean, and David L. Norman, an assistant attorney general in the Civil Rights Division, participated on behalf of the Department of Justice. Other amici, including the American Psychological Association, the American Orthopsychiatric Association, and the ACLU, were soon involved. And the case was expanded to include not only Bryce Hospital, but Searcy and Partlow as well.

Local and national newspapers carried numerous stories about the *Wyatt* case—reports on DeMent's surprise inspections of the three hospitals and exacting studies of the conditions those inspections uncovered. At the end of the six-month period, Johnson concluded that the defendants had performed well enough to warrant yet another trial period and again deferred "turning over the operation of these institutions to a panel of masters." He was not so impressed, however, that he could leave matters there. Noting the defendants' failure to complete the task set for them, he scheduled an evidentiary hearing at which the parties and amici would propose and defend standards for the operation of the three facilities.[34]

The hearing, held in early 1972, proved to be an impressive show of strength for the forces of reform. In Johnson's own words, some of the "foremost authorities on mental health in the United States" appeared to testify. Specialists on both sides tended to agree on both ultimate objectives and immediate strategies. When Judge Johnson came round to new opinions and orders in the case, he found that the defendants had stipulated to 90 percent of the proposed standards offered by the plaintiffs and amici. In that sense, the resulting decrees were not so coercive as at first they seemed. Still, they were by far the most detailed injunctive orders yet issued in cases of this kind.

Within Alabama, *Wyatt* was the catalyst for the University of Alabama's Center for Correctional Psychology, built around Dr. Fowler's work on the psychological effects of involuntary confinement. Established at the urging of Dean and DeMent and financed at DeMent's insistence by the Law Enforcement Assistance Administration, the center played an important role in the prison cases three years later. Outside the state, *Wyatt* received widespread press coverage and generated a rich and vigorous academic literature, touching both the validity of the standards Johnson embraced and the legitimacy of their establishment by judicial decision. Johnson held the *Wyatt* case on his docket for nearly fifteen years and, even then, he did not close the file but passed it on to another district judge, Myron Thompson. Over the course of the litigation, Johnson employed techniques never attempted before but due to be used again in the prison cases.[35]

While Judge Johnson deferred in many respects to the good faith and assumed expertise of the state authorities charged with operating Bryce, Searcy, and Partlow, he nonetheless established mechanisms for the enforcement of his decree. His options in that vein were several. For example, he might have taken the implementation of his order into his own hands—bringing state authorities into court for periodic hearings and maintaining constant, personal surveillance of their behavior. Johnson, however, wished to restrict his own day-to-day involvement in the operation of the hospitals, both to reserve time for other matters on his docket and to avoid the appearance of undue judicial meddling. The judge also rejected two other possibilities: the appointment of a "master," a federal magistrate or private lawyer who might have served as his surrogate in further hearings and other proceedings, and the appointment of a "receiver," a professional administrator who might have assumed responsibility for the hospitals directly. Both those ideas appeared extreme, at least so long as state mental health authorities promised genuine efforts to meet the court's demands.

Judge Johnson chose a fourth option. He appointed panels of citizens, called "human rights committees," to superintend compliance with his orders at each institution. The committees, in turn, appointed their own professional staff to monitor the treatment of patients. Johnson's tactic was to involve respected Alabamians in the *Wyatt* case, make them understand the reasons for his actions, and have the benefit of their experience in meeting public criticism of his orders. As always, the judge relied on the Justice Department, and on Ira DeMent, to carry the weight of the litigation by providing expert witnesses and other, critical support. He also relied on DeMent to represent the human rights committees in their disputes with state authorities. Finally, Johnson insisted again and again that it was insufficient to respond to his instructions with complaints of inadequate funding. He rejected Dean's suggestion that he direct the Alabama legislature to provide the funds necessary to operate the hospitals properly, yet he admonished state officials to recognize the "grave emergency" and authorize the wherewithal to end it.[36]

Certain events in the long history of *Wyatt* are of special importance here. Inasmuch as Stickney and others consented to most of the provisions of the *Wyatt* orders, Alabama Attorney General William J. Baxley initially announced that there would be no appeal. In short order, however, Governor Wallace declared that he had conceded nothing and would appeal on his own through personal counsel. Baxley soon acquiesced and pursued an appeal on behalf of Stickney and other mental health officials named as defendants in *Wyatt*. While the case was before the Fifth Circuit, Judge Johnson rejected proposals from the human rights committees that might have drawn the court deeper into the internal affairs of the state institutions. But when the appellate court affirmed his orders in all respects, he once again turned to the time-consuming and painful task of guiding the state toward compliance. Finally, it must be said, the genuine accomplishments of the *Wyatt* litigation were at least questionable. Instead of providing expensive services to thousands of hospitalized people, state authorities discharged as many as possible into the community. The release of many patients was hardly disturbing standing alone. Observers were convinced that many people held in Alabama's hospitals did not need close supervision and should have been released into less restrictive environments much sooner. Still, the state did little to establish alternative homes for the patients and residents who were discharged, and many found their way into nursing homes and similar facilities where conditions were extremely bad, even by the standards set by Bryce itself. The people for whose benefit the litigation was pursued suffered in a different way, perhaps, but they suffered nonetheless.[37]

Public schools and institutions for the mentally ill were one thing. The beneficiaries of Judge Johnsons' desegregation orders and the litigation in *Wyatt* were morally blameless and, in the popular mind, perhaps entitled to the essentials of decency that Johnson's orders established. Prisons, housing men and women who had committed serious crimes, were quite another. When Johnson took up cases involving prison inmates in Alabama, he found it difficult to persuade a doubtful public that convicts, too, were worthy of sympathy and redress. Years later, he insisted that the people of his state accepted his decisions in the prison cases, just as they had accepted his work in the 1960s. He observed that judicial orders could be enforced against the popular will only in the short run. Ultimately, they must enjoy wide support. "If [judicial decisions] violate the conscience of the people," he said, "they won't stand." Nevertheless, the long and ugly history of penal institutions in Alabama gave ample testimony that public education regarding prisons would not come easily. There came a time when Judge Johnson turned to the state prisons. When he did, he committed himself to litigation that continued until he left the district court bench in Montgomery.[38]

2

Genesis

Three early decisions foreshadowed the more significant prison conditions suits in Alabama. In *Washington v. Lee*,[1] Judge Johnson joined
with Judge Rives and Seybourn H. Lynne, another district judge from
Birmingham, to invalidate racial segregation in the prisons, and in
Beard v. Lee[2] and *Lake v. Lee*,[3] Judge Virgil Pittman in Mobile held
that confinement in punitive isolation at Holman and Fountain constituted cruel and unusual punishment. Judge Johnson's major work
began with the medical care case, born of a 1971 letter to the judge from
an inmate at Mt. Meigs, complaining about conditions at the prison
hospital there. The prisoner, who gave the name N. H. Newman,[4] provided details—names, dates, and numbers accumulated over weeks of
study. Prisoners, he said, were "openly and flagrantly being denied . . .
medication and proper care which are essential to life." This was not
the ordinary, handwritten scribble from a desperate man seeking assistance wherever he could find it. Newman had typed his message to the
court and styled it, however crudely, as a "[p]etition for relief from
existing conditions imposed on petitioner and other state prisoners."
Newman intended to initiate a lawsuit and not only a lawsuit but a class
action against the state of Alabama, the state attorney general, the warden at Mt. Meigs, and various members of the hospital staff. On the day
he received Newman's letter, Judge Johnson sent a memorandum to Ira
DeMent.

> I am enclosing a copy of a civil action that I have authorized to be
> filed . . . this date. As you will note, a petitioner raises extremely serious
> . . . 8th Amendment questions. You may want to give consideration to
> intervening in this matter; if not, I will want to give consideration to
> appointing you as amicus.[5]

The message was clear. Johnson meant to take Newman's petition
seriously, and he expected help. His experience in the *Wyatt* case had

taught Judge Johnson that institutional litigation could be time consuming and expensive. DeMent had provided necessary firepower in that instance. Now, Johnson again called on him to commit the resources of the United States on behalf of indigent litigants in Alabama. This was to be the first thorough examination of conditions in the state's prisons, albeit limited to the medical care program. Patterns set in the *Newman* case were repeated in the later litigation in *Pugh* and *James*. Thus an understanding of Judge Johnson's experience in *Newman* is essential to an appreciation of further, even more expansive investigations of the prison system that came later.

Ira DeMent responded to Judge Johnson's memo with a letter of his own, addressed to David Norman, the Justice Department lawyer with whom DeMent had worked in *Wyatt*. DeMent "strongly" recommended that "we intervene in this case immediately." Norman was sympathetic but doubtful. The Justice Department still had no statutory authority to sue local authorities over the administration of state institutions. Norman therefore thought it inadvisable for DeMent to attempt to join the *Newman* case as a formal plaintiff. Amicus participation had now become familiar in Alabama, however, and Norman was prepared to recommend that course. Accepting Norman's advice, James P. Turner, then acting assistant attorney general, instructed Jesse Queen, head of the Justice Department's fledgling Office of Institutions and Facilities, to convey directions to DeMent: "[I]f the judge enters an order making us amicus, we'll be glad to participate." DeMent, for his part, requested an FBI investigation of Newman's allegations. He also asked the FBI to follow up similar claims included in a letter received earlier in the summer by Harold Martin, publisher of the *Montgomery Advertiser*. In that letter, the plaintiff in one of Judge Pittman's cases, Joe Donald Beard, had described a dozen or more instances of alleged maltreatment at Mt. Meigs and Holman, including three deaths in the preceding six months. Federal agents interviewed Newman himself and, one by one, all the living inmates mentioned in his complaint.[6]

The FBI learned that Newman had spent nearly ten years in the old prison hospital at Kilby Prison before transfer to the new institution at Mt. Meigs. There he had been assigned to the hospital unit, where he was employed as an orderly. He administered "sick call," dispensed medication, checked vital signs, and performed other standard tasks. Always, in his telling, Newman had kept notes on the treatment of other inmates. Those notes formed the basis of his petition in Judge Johnson's court. Questioning Newman and the hospital director, the FBI discovered that Newman had presented his complaints to prison officials before writing to Judge Johnson and had sought judicial help only when his allegations had been rejected and he had been challenged to sue. After that confrontation, Newman had been scheduled for transfer to another institution—ostensibly because he was rumored to be dealing in drugs at Mt. Meigs. When Newman learned what was afoot, he persuaded a guard to mail his complaint to Judge Johnson.

The investigation verified that the men Newman had mentioned in his complaint actually existed, that there was corroborating evidence for at least some of his allegations regarding their treatment, and that many other prisoners had received inadequate care both at Mt. Meigs and at Holman. There was more talk of maggots in a prisoner's wounds, gangrene, and other indications of gross neglect. As the agents moved from inmates to staff members, their results were mixed. Superiors tended to disclaim knowledge or to issue broad denials of deliberate mistreatment. Yet other staff members volunteered their own criticisms of hospital practices and management. They complained of inadequate staff, antiquated equipment, improper medication, sloppy record keeping, and other deficiencies. In the end, the FBI report painted a grizzly picture of routine maladministration. DeMent had what he wanted. Newman's assertions might be exaggerated and imprecise in some respects, but the core of his complaint was accurate. Real, flesh-and-blood people were suffering without adequate medical care throughout the Alabama prison system. There was substance to this lawsuit.[7]

In the meantime, Attorney General Baxley was busy preparing a formal answer to Newman's allegations. Baxley insisted that the charges were grossly overstated and in all critical respects untrue. Judge Johnson was unimpressed. Two days later, now with DeMent's acquiescence, the judge ordered the federal government to enter the *Newman* litigation as amicus curiae, "to assist the Court in the speedy and just determination of the issues involved." The "public interest," Johnson said, should be represented in the case. Shortly after Christmas, DeMent filed a response to Baxley's answer. He acknowledged that Newman's petition was poorly drafted and that it failed clearly to identify the theory on which the prisoners sought relief. DeMent argued, however, that Newman's assertions of fact, if true, would establish a violation of the "right to adequate medical treatment and care," derived from the Eighth Amendment ban on cruel and unusual punishment. The issues were joined; Judge Johnson scheduled a hearing in the case for early spring.

At the same time, and curiously late in the proceedings, Johnson appointed a private attorney as the prisoner-plaintiffs' formal representative. His choice was surprising. Johnson selected Joseph Phelps, the Montgomery attorney who had served as counsel for the *defendants* in *Wyatt* and in Montgomery's fiercely fought school desegregation case of the previous decade. It was Johnson's way to seek out professional ability instead of personal zeal and to call on a good lawyer to use his talents in the service of a worthy cause. The judge recalled the way in which Phelps had conducted himself in the equally volatile school desegregation case and concluded he needed such a lawyer again in the *Newman* litigation. The appointment of Phelps underscored the view Johnson, and he hoped others, would take of *Newman*. If there were problems in the prison system, then right-thinking Alabamians would want to know about them; having identified deficiencies, they would want to act decisively to eliminate injustice. Moreover, in anticipating the difficulties he might face in enforcing an unpopular injunctive order, Johnson wanted the benefit of an early association with a local lawyer whose credentials were unimpeachable and whose professionalism would ensure a vigorous presentation of the evidence. The judge was not disappointed. Phelps set to work immediately. Cooperating with Patricia G. Littlefield, the Justice Department lawyer assigned to the case, he amassed overwhelming evidence that the medical care system was scandalously substandard. By February, the parties had agreed on a pretrial statement collecting their differences and identifying the issues to be tried.[8]

The first two questions were vexing enough: whether Alabama prisoners were constitutionally entitled to adequate medical care and, if so, whether they had been (and were being) denied adequate care at the hands of state authorities. The third would prove intractable. If the court should decide that the prisoners were entitled to judicial relief, what form should that relief take? Looking forward to the day when Judge Johnson might enter a decree ordering state officials to make changes in the operation of the prison hospital at Mt. Meigs and other medical facilities, Phelps asked to add Commissioner of Corrections L. B. Sullivan and the members of the Board of Corrections, among them John E. Vickers and Thomas F. Staton, as defendants. Judge Johnson granted that request, and Baxley immediately embraced Sullivan and the board members as appropriate parties in the litigation. The introduction of Sullivan and the others into the *Newman* case was only a formality. They were immediately responsible for the institutions under attack and thus were proper defendants; if the original complaint had been drafted by a lawyer, they would have been named routinely, instead of Baxley and the state of Alabama as an entity. Still, neither

Phelps nor Baxley asked to substitute the new defendants for those identified by Newman or to delete improper defendants from the pleadings. In the end, Baxley himself and the state of Alabama continued as unchallenged defendants in the *Newman* case even as their identification as parties to the litigation receded into the background—a matter that later proved significant in *Pugh* and *James.*

Trial was held in March 1972. Phelps initially offered into evidence fifty-three written statements made by state officials and twenty-four other exhibits developed from prison hospital records. Then Louis N. Thrasher, a Justice Department attorney, called John P. Braddy, the Board of Corrections' own personnel officer, to the stand. Braddy had access to the board's employment records and could authenticate what Phelps and Littlefield had learned in their investigations. Medical services in the prison system were critically understaffed. Thrasher set up charts on a tripod and took Braddy step by step through the positions the board had established, the salaries that had been authorized and, most important, the vacancies in vital "slots." Asked why the board had not hired physicians and nurses to fill over seventeen vacant positions, Braddy responded in a refrain that would be repeated over and over again: "We just have not been funded at a rate that we could fill them." Johnson interrupted, demanding to know who had decided that the system needed medical staff in the numbers suggested by Braddy's records and whether the defendants had tried to employ more trained professionals. Braddy acknowledged that the positions shown in the charts represented minimal staff for decent medical care—not an ideal program but merely an adequate one. He also conceded that the commissioner and the board were able on occasion to employ new staff members when they chose to do so. Indeed, a new pharmacist assistant and an additional registered nurse had been retained at Mt. Meigs in the last few weeks before trial. That admission was not lost on Judge Johnson. It seemed that penal authorities could find funds for the medical system on the threshold of what promised to be an embarrassing public hearing.

The next witness,[9] Dr. Joseph F. Alderete, was director of the U.S. Penitentiary Hospital in Atlanta. The Justice Department had flown Alderete to Alabama for a tour of the medical facilities in each of the state's institutions, and Littlefield now led him through his copious notes on what he had seen. Alderete was the first genuine expert to testify in Alabama prison litigation. He knew what to look for on tours of prison medical care units and could explain to the court the deficiencies he found. In addition, he could introduce professional standards in the field, promulgated by respected national organizations for the very purpose of measuring the adequacy of medical facilities. He pointed to guidelines prepared by the American Correctional Association, the Joint Commission on Accreditation of Hospitals, and even the Alabama State Board of Health. In particular, he relied on a set of standards prepared by the U.S. Department of Health, Education, and Welfare (HEW) for use in evaluating hospitals participating in the Medicare program. State authorities resisted the simplistic notion that standards published by professional organizations translated directly into constitutional guarantees. Yet Judge Johnson made use of professionally accepted guidelines at another level, just as he had in *Wyatt*. Once he identified conditions of confinement so terrible as to constitute cruel and unusual punishment, he relied on national standards, coupled with the testimony of experts who had actually toured the Alabama prison system, when he fashioned an injunctive order to remedy the constitutional violations that established his authority to act. The judge wanted to know what was wrong with the medical care program in place and, equally important, he wanted to know what to say in his order when the trial was over and the time came to shape relief.

Littlefield and Alderete gave him what he wanted—hours of it. The testimony went well beyond the fragmented allegations in Newman's complaint, providing instead an exhaustive review of the many respects in which the medical care units in the penal system failed to meet recognized standards. At the Mt. Meigs hospital, Alderete found only one physician where at least two were needed. Registered nurses were available only on weekdays. A psychologist visited only one afternoon a week, and there was no dietitian at all. The administration of the hospital was in shambles. Technicians were thinly spread and inadequately supervised, drugs were improperly stored and administered, medical records were inaccurate and incomplete. Inmates were given responsibility for critical functions that only professionals could properly perform. The list of complaints stretched on and on. If anything, the infirmary at Draper was in worse condition. The physical plant there was "terrible." A single medical assistant had charge of the entire program and was forced, in consequence, to rely on prisoners for everything from keeping records to dispensing drugs and suturing wounds.

The women's institution at Tutwiler harbored still more tragic stories. Convicts routinely gave birth in a dilapidated delivery room in which Alderete discovered equipment and techniques he had not seen elsewhere for thirty years. At G.K. Fountain to the south, the hospital equipment was "extremely old," the X-ray machine had not been

checked for leakage in three years and, in the operating room, "[h]alf
... the tile on the floor was gone." Across the highway at Holman, not
a single medical staff member was on duty. An inmate "steward" held
the keys to other prisoners' records and the drug cabinet. The steward
had run out of bandages and was tearing up bed sheets to bind inmates'
wounds.

Critical as Alderete was of what he had seen, he stopped short of
condemning the individuals working in the prison medical facilities
under attack. Indeed, he acknowledged that the hospital staff was doing
the best that could be expected under the circumstances. Phelps and
Littlefield saw little to be gained by attacking the few professionals the
penal system had managed to attract. The lawyers were convinced that
individual staff members were personally to blame in many instances.
Yet they doubted that Judge Johnson had missed that point, and they
hardly wished to provoke an already inadequate staff into mass resig-
nations. Their strategy changed, however, when the board's part-time
medical director, Dr. James F. Mracek, took the stand to answer Alderete's charges. While Mracek acknowledged various deficiencies in the
system, he insisted that conditions were "at the lower limit of adequacy" and that, in any case, improvements were already under way.
On the morning of his testimony, he had issued an order forbidding
inmates to administer "shots" in any of the facilities under his authority. He had established a new laboratory monitoring system only three
weeks earlier and was working on a plan for a new blood bank. Mracek
thus presented himself as a dedicated man making do with inadequate
resources. Under cross-examination, however, he professed ignorance
of individual inmates' care and blamed instances of apparent mistreatment on faulty record-keeping. He conceded that he lacked the staff to
enforce his new order regarding the administration of "shots" and
expressed surprise to learn that, as medical director, he had responsibility not only for the state prisons, but for medical services at the
state's 200 local jails as well. Mracek admitted that he had never visited
any of those facilities and had no idea whether the medical care available in them was adequate. In the end, he was demolished on the stand.
Immediately following the trial, Mracek and several other professionals
resigned their positions.

Ira DeMent's only witness was his old friend, Raymond Fowler,
whose testimony focused on the need for mental as well as physical
health care in the Alabama prison system and his own ability to assist
state officials in determining specific requirements and staffing programs with graduates of the Center for Correctional Psychology.

Indeed, Fowler had already spoken with Commissioner Sullivan about a proposed survey of mental health problems in the prison system, and DeMent wanted to ensure the success of that project by building it into the *Newman* case. The testimony he elicited was powerful. Relying on national statistical studies, Fowler estimated that fully one-third of the inmates in the system were mentally retarded. One in ten prisoners was psychotic. Most others were depressed, emotionally disturbed, and very likely in need of professional counseling. Fowler professed himself ready to help and, in an exchange with Mr. Lamar, who represented state penal authorities, it became clear that Sullivan would cooperate.

One key participant in the case did not take the stand. Convinced that Commissioner Sullivan was pliable, Phelps and the others permitted his stipulated statement to be read into the record. The commissioner, according to the statement, was "generally receptive" to improvements in the prison system's medical care program, but "lack of funds from the Legislature" had kept him from making needed changes. This was self-serving, of course, but the statement included a backhanded concession that the medical program was inadequate and poorly funded. Mracek's testimony behind them, counsel wanted to return once again to the strategy with which they had begun. They hoped to leave the commissioner room in which to maneuver. Sullivan had taken his new position as commissioner of corrections only a year before the trial in *Newman.* His predecessor had resigned after only six months in office, charging that he had not been allowed sufficient funds to operate the prison system properly. If Sullivan were permitted now to withdraw with dignity, he might do what would be required of him in the future instead of risking disgrace in later encounters. Moreover, DeMent had genuine sympathy for Sullivan, with whom he had worked years earlier, and wanted to spare his feelings.[10]

Immediately following the reading of Sullivan's statement, the U.S. attorney agreed that the commissioner was a "dedicated, competent administrator" with the "capacity" to administer the prison system "well" and that it was "a lack of funds" that had delayed improvements to date. DeMent's words took Judge Johnson by surprise. A brief exchange clarified the government's position and, it should be noted, protected the record the lawyers had built so carefully over three days of trial.

JUDGE JOHNSON: Do you concur—do I understand that you are saying that lack of funds is the only deficiency in the operation of the medical system?

DEMENT:	No, sir; no, sir; but I think lack of funds is the basis of what you see.
JUDGE JOHNSON:	Insofar as the Commissioner is concerned, it is lack of funds.
DEMENT:	Yes, sir.
JUDGE JOHNSON:	Insofar as the administration of the medical program is concerned, do you—do you stipulate it is lack of funds, also?
DEMENT:	No, sir.
JUDGE JOHNSON:	All right.

While Johnson's questions prevented DeMent's comments from undercutting the plaintiffs' attack on the prison medical care program, it was plain that the distinction DeMent was trying to draw could not be defended. On the one hand, he declared that the system was rife with deficiencies; on the other, he had it that the man primarily responsible for the institutions under examination was willing to make needed changes. Moreover, DeMent's virtual endorsement of Sullivan's statement lent credence to two defense theories that would plague prison litigation in Alabama for a decade. First, Sullivan was permitted to shift the blame for poor prison conditions away from himself and toward other state authorities, in this instance the Alabama legislature. Second, the commissioner was allowed to focus attention on the state's failure to commit funds to the penal system. Money was a matter of critical importance. The budget for Dr. Alderete's field hospital in Atlanta more than doubled that of the medical program for the entire Alabama system. Yet Sullivan's implicit premise was not merely that more money would resolve the problems faced by the prison system, but that the underlying penal policies that he and the other defendants were pursuing were sound and had failed, or were failing, only for want of financial support.

Back in his chambers, Judge Johnson seemed at first to be faced with a familiar dilemma. He had ample evidence from which to make findings of fact, but he lacked judicial precedents on which to rest his legal conclusion that the facts established a constitutional violation. Other courts had held that inadequate medical care might warrant judicial intervention into the administration of prison medical programs— at least in extreme circumstances. Yet the traditional hands-off doctrine posed a serious barrier. The Fifth Circuit had long recognized that prison authorities enjoyed "broad discretion" with respect to medical treatment and had routinely insisted that prisoner complaints regarding medical care should be dismissed summarily in the absence of specific allegations of an abuse of that discretion. At most, the circuit opinions down to 1970 had acknowledged medical care claims only in an ambiguous way—when the court had affirmed summary dismissals in cases in which prisoners' allegations were insufficient. Closer examination revealed, however, that the legal landscape was changing even as Judge Johnson pondered the case at hand in Montgomery.[11]

The key new decision was *Haines v. Kerner,* [12] handed down by the Supreme Court of the United States just before the *Newman* trial opened in Montgomery. In *Haines,* the Court held that federal courts should be patient with prison inmates proceeding on their own behalf and should not hold their pleadings to the ordinary standards that lawyers must meet. Prisoner complaints could be dismissed, according to the Court, only when it was clear that the petitioner could prove no set of facts warranting judicial relief. *Haines* was not primarily an action about poor medical care. Coincidently, however, the first cases to reach the Fifth Circuit in the wake of the new decision *were.* In several decisions in the summer following the trial in *Newman,* the circuit court reversed summary dismissals of prisoner complaints regarding medical treatment—remanding for more thorough consideration at the district court level. These new cases offered Judge Johnson additional authority, however tentative, on which to rest his own judgment in the *Newman* case. He relied heavily on them when he announced his decision on October 4, 1972. He ticked off a list of factual findings regarding the medical program in Alabama, declared that the defendants' "broad discretion" had been abused, and concluded that the plaintiffs were entitled to judicial relief. In nine short months, the seemingly innocuous decision in *Haines* had been transformed into a judicial precedent for one of the most dramatic orders to date in the field of prison litigation.[13]

Johnson's opinion set forth factual findings on two levels. First, relying primarily on Dr. Alderete's expert testimony, Johnson condemned the generally poor quality of the medical care program in Alabama's prisons. He found the hospital at Mt. Meigs "totally inadequate" but "remarkably good" when compared with the smaller infirmaries elsewhere in the system. He found that the staff was "overworked," that drugs and other medications were in short supply, and that necessary equipment was unavailable or in poor repair. The "cumulative effect" of those deficiencies was "profound." In the case of the mentally impaired, Johnson found "no treatment whatsoever." On a second level, he turned to illustrative instances in which individual inmates had been mistreated. These proved to be more than "isolated instances of mere negligence or malpractice." Instead, they illustrated "what can and does occur when too few reasonable men, functioning with too little supportive facilities, undertake what is, in effect, an impossible task." In this, the judge seemed to embrace the strategy DeMent had pursued at trial. In essence, he intimated, even good faith attempts to meet acceptable standards could not be successful in a system so fraught with difficulties. In the end, however, Johnson held that both the defendants' failure to "provide sufficient medical facilities and staff to afford inmates [the] basic elements of adequate medical care" and their "refusal" to "allow inmates access to medical personnel" and "prescribed medicines" constituted "wilful and intentional" infliction of cruel and unusual punishment—in violation of the Eighth Amendment.

His legal conclusion in place, Judge Johnson turned to the appropriate relief to be awarded the plaintiff class. The record in *Newman* carried no promise that state authorities would make necessary changes if the court merely condemned present conditions and called for the development of alternative plans. Accordingly, Johnson took it on himself immediately to order specific actions to bring the medical care program into compliance with relevant standards—among them HEW's Medicare regulations. In addition, he instructed the defendants to develop plans for increasing the medical staff and upgrading equipment. In yet another round of instructions, Johnson covered discrete problems from ambulance service through the use of inmates to administer drugs. Finally, he gave penal officials six months in which to file a report detailing the implementation of many of his directives. That report, he insisted, must include a current financial statement and an explanation of the defendants' plans for securing any additional funding his order might require.[14]

Johnson had done what had been anticipated but what no other judge had attempted before. The meager authorities on which he relied had dealt with individual prison inmates' complaints about their own treatment. Johnson's action in *Newman* moved from the mere recognition that poor medical treatment might violate the constitutional rights of an individual prisoner to the more dramatic proposition that a systemwide medical program could constitute cruel and unusual punishment of an entire class of prisoner-plaintiffs. He had not only declared the existence of such a constitutional violation, but he had imposed an injunctive remedy touching most aspects of medical treatment in Alabama's prison system.

The *Newman* case attracted the attention of Alabama professionals concerned about the conditions in the state's penal institutions. In September 1972, the Alabama Advisory Committee of the U.S. Commission on Civil Rights agreed to participate in a national study of correctional institutions. *Newman* was featured prominently in the Alabama group's report, published in 1975. Following up his trial testimony, Dr. Fowler entered into a formal contract with the Alabama Law Enforcement Planning Agency. Under grants from the federal government, university and state personnel cooperated in the development of a report on the prison system's mental health programs, published in 1972, and a Master Plan for Corrections in Alabama, published in 1974. Only a few months after the order in *Newman,* a newly elected president of the Alabama Bar Association, M. Roland Nachman, appointed a special Committee on Correctional Institutions and Procedures—charged to make a "complete study" of the Alabama penal system "to the end that those who offend against Alabama's criminal laws will be punished in a civilized fashion."

The *Newman* order also generated a number of personal letters to Judge Johnson. He treated well-intended expressions of concern with the appreciation they deserved but was careful to maintain some judicial distance. When, for example, Sister Caraher of the Links Society in Mobile offered to share her organization's information about prison conditions with the court, Johnson forwarded her letter to DeMent. The judge "in a case like this," he explained, "does not investigate and present the evidence. . . ." DeMent, in turn, wrote Caraher to encourage her to send along any information she and her group might have. In another instance, Judge Johnson responded enthusiastically to an offer of assistance. Two months after the order, he received a message from Maston Mims, chairman of a recently appointed Joint Legislative Study Committee, requesting an audience to discuss the prisons. Mims dropped a heavy hint that his committee had been formed to address the *Newman* order. The committee, he said, would determine the needs of the prison system and "take appropriate legislative action" to make changes wherever they were needed, "including the medical program." Within days, Johnson invited both Mims and DeMent to meet with him in chambers. That meeting, while inconsequential in itself, can be counted as the first in a series of instances in which Judge Johnson proved receptive to any indication of legislative interest in improving the prison system. Mims' committee was able to establish a new work release program; future committees also contributed useful innovations.[15]

In the meantime, the defendants reacted to the new order on two tracks at once. They refused to acknowledge the unconstitutionality of the system for which they had responsibility and thus filed motions for a new trial and for an appeal. Yet they recognized that the system had many obvious flaws and that the actions demanded by the October 4 order made sense. Accordingly, they requested no stay of that order and, indeed, purported to work toward its implementation. Sullivan and the Board of Corrections thus provided Judge Johnson with periodic progress reports, describing their efforts to satisfy his demands.

One early report drew on surveys made by the state medical and hospital associations. Preferring to see the primary documents themselves, Johnson phoned Baxley's office and requested copies. What he found was sobering. The Alabama Medical Association survey was particularly critical, making the defendants' own report seem vague by comparison and, perhaps, revealing an effort to soften the study on which it purported to rest. Johnson immediately summoned Kenneth Vines, DeMent's chief assistant, for a meeting in chambers. As it happened, Gail Littlefield was in town for other purposes related to the litigation. Johnson suggested that Vines bring Littlefield along, and the three met in his office in January. In that private setting, the judge told the government lawyers that "he wanted the United States to emphasize in its brief on appeal" that the defendants had admitted that staffing levels in the medical program failed to meet minimum professional standards. Going on, he said he tended to be "protective" of his orders on appeal. Inasmuch as the survey "substantiated" his order in *Newman,* he "wanted it to go to the press and be a part of the record." To avoid losing time, he picked up the phone while Vines and Littlefield were still in the office and called Baxley to ask whether he objected to including the survey in the record. Baxley had not yet read it and, accordingly, declined comment for the moment. He called back to voice no objection, however, and the survey was placed in the file that afternoon.[16]

The episode illustrates three matters of some significance. First, Johnson demonstrated once again his propensity to make use of DeMent's office and the Justice Department. His willingness to call Vines and Littlefield in for consultation in the absence of other lawyers in the litigation and to give them instructions for the appeal underscored his view that these lawyers did not represent adversaries in the *Newman* case at all; they appeared for the United States which, in Johnson's mind, meant they represented the public interest. Second, Johnson revealed personal concerns about appellate review. He was under no illusion that the *Newman* case had come to an end with his order. He was acutely aware that Baxley was pursuing an appeal, and he wanted to protect his judgment. Finally, Johnson demonstrated his recognition that the press, and through the press the public, must be taken into account in law reform litigation of this kind. He was not one to speak to the press himself, yet he was quite willing to make use of the media when publicity was desirable.

The publication of the survey put Commissioner Sullivan on the spot. He chose the course of self-defense. In his own press statement the commissioner insisted that he and the board had asked the Alabama Medical Association for help in the past and been refused, that the new survey was long on criticism but short on positive recommendations, and that the doctors had delivered themselves of a highly critical report calculated to create "favorable publicity for themselves" instead of genuine improvements in the prison system's medical care program. In the end, a stratagem Judge Johnson apparently had hoped would fortify his own actions in the public mind prompted an uninformative exchange between Sullivan and faceless physicians.[17]

Appellate review in *Newman* scarcely justified Judge Johnson's caution. Even as the Supreme Court insisted that the federal courts "sit not to supervise prisons," the justices who served on the Court in the early 1970s denied that any "iron curtain" could be drawn "between the Constitution and the prisons of this country." Moreover, the Court's deeds tended to undercut its rhetoric admonishing the lower courts to defer in most instances to the judgment of prison administrators. In two key decisions in 1974, the Court held that the free speech rights of prisoners had been violated. In the same period, the circuit courts moved beyond their earlier decisions condemning particularly brutal treatment of individual prisoners and addressed themselves to systemic challenges to practices throughout a penal system. While the *Newman* case was pending before Judge Johnson, another district judge in Arkansas, J. Smith Henley, launched one of the longest-running prison cases in history when he declared that the conditions in that state's prisons constituted cruel and unusual punishment. The Eighth Circuit Court of Appeals affirmed Henley's judgment in *Holt v. Sarver* in 1971, just before Johnson's order in *Newman*. Other circuits soon rendered similar decisions.[18]

Most important for Johnson's purposes, the Fifth Circuit proved particularly receptive to broad-gauged attacks on prison practices affecting large numbers of inmates. In September 1972, two weeks before Johnson's order in *Newman*, lawyers in Mississippi initiated a class action challenge to the conditions in that state's notorious prison at Parchman. In *Gates v. Collier*,[19] Judge William C. Keady appraised a wide range of conditions and concluded that Mississippi, too, was violating the Eighth Amendment rights of its inmate population. The litigation in *Gates* was primarily the responsibility of Roy S. Haber, a young attorney in the Jackson office of the Lawyers' Committee for Civil Rights Under Law. Both Haber and his supervisor in Jackson, George Peach Taylor, later made appearances in Alabama. In the circumstances, one might have expected *Gates* to follow *Newman* to the appellate court. As it happened, however, the *Newman* appeal was delayed while the parties litigated the adjacent question whether Judge Johnson had properly ordered Alabama authorities to pay attorney fees. That postponement permitted *Gates* to reach the Fifth Circuit first and, in September 1974, the appellate court affirmed Judge Keady in all respects. Once *Gates* was in place the participants in *Newman* could only anticipate that Judge Johnson, too, would be sustained.[20]

The Fifth Circuit decision, handed down in November 1974, surprised no one. Another Alabamian, Judge Walter Gewin, wrote the brief opinion for a unanimous panel. Gewin acknowledged that *Newman* was not the ordinary case in which it was alleged that state penal authorities had failed to meet their obligations with respect to a single inmate. But he made the same jump to class-based litigation that Johnson himself had made two years earlier. The egregious conditions in the Alabama prison medical system went well beyond anything that might be addressed on a case-by-case basis. The defendants' behavior amounted, in Gewin's words, to "callous indifference to the welfare of inmate-patients." Having followed Johnson this far, Gewin followed him still further to the theory of the *Newman* case. Johnson had rested on the Eighth Amendment; Gewin acquiesced. Finally, Gewin dismissed the defendants' objections to the scope and detail of the remedial order. In light of Johnson's meticulous factual findings, Gewin could not say that something less rigorous would have addressed the serious deficiencies that vexed the system. Indeed, Johnson's order tracked some of the recommendations that the state's own witness, Dr. Mracek, had offered from the witness stand. The order promised only "moderate judicial monitoring" of the defendants' efforts at implementation. In any event, Judge Gewin wrote, it was "axiomatic" that a federal district court's "remedial power" was "coterminous with the scope of the constitutional violation found to exist."[21]

Baxley's request for further review in the Supreme Court was denied summarily, and attention turned to attempts by Sullivan and the Board of Corrections to comply with the October 4 order. The board approved a new budget that, if fully funded, would have placed the medical program on a firmer financial footing. Yet the resignation of

Dr. Mracek and other professionals left most positions open and cast doubt on the commissioner's ability to fill vacancies even if a suspicious legislature authorized the necessary funds. In an effort to marshal support for his budget requests, Sullivan invited the news media to visit the state's prisons and to explain to the public what life in those institutions had become. Walter Massey, an editorial writer for the *Birmingham News,* had published an eight-part series of articles while the *Newman* case was pending before Judge Johnson. After the order was entered, Stan Bailey, also of the *Birmingham News,* covered the commissioner's attempts to obtain more money for the system, and Ed Watkins of the *Tuscaloosa News* filed his own series surveying each of the state's prisons. Still, public education was slow and painful. As 1973 dragged on, little ground was gained.

Moreover, in the same period, the attention of prison authorities was diverted to even more serious difficulties within the system. The prison population had been growing for years, but now the influx of new inmates was staggering. Frustration and anger grew in geometric proportion. The result in Alabama was what it had been at Attica in New York only two years earlier. Through the long summer and fall of 1973, local newspapers carried scattered stories of inmate violence. Reports that inmates had been stabbed, raped, or murdered became common. By official count, a total of twenty-seven prisoners lost their lives in the Alabama penal system in the 1972–1973 period. Guards were also occasionally injured or killed. The rate of incidents promised to be higher still if the legislature enacted pending bills, sponsored by Attorney General Baxley, to increase prison sentences, and thus the number of prison inmates, dramatically. Circumstances became so strained and rumors of further violence so prevalent that in early 1974 the Alabama Highway Patrol was routinely on alert should troopers be needed to put down riots at Fountain and Holman.[22]

The occasion arrived on January 18, when a dozen prisoners housed in the segregation unit at Fountain, the same cells that Judge Pittman had declared to be unconstitutional in the *Beard* case, took matters into their own hands. They overpowered two guards, took them hostage, and demanded that the warden, Marion Harding, summon several "free world" people to hear inmate grievances. Negotiations continued for only an hour. When Harding realized that the rebels had already stabbed two prisoners thought to be "snitches," he led a phalanx of officers into the cell block. Harold Martin's account was vivid.

> The guards rushed down the hall, staying flat over against the wall and shooting into some of the cells as they went.

"I thought the world was coming to an end when all that shooting started," one inmate said.

The inmates were told to come out of the cells with their hands on their heads. They were herded into the outer lobby, made to strip off their clothes, get down on their knees and crawl across the room. As they did, they were hit with what was described as "pick ax handles."

Less than a dozen inmates had participated in the uprising, but more than forty were sent to the Greenlawn Hospital in Atmore for x-rays after being beaten by the guards.[23]

Two men died. Luell Barrow, a guard, was stabbed twenty-seven times shortly before or during the officers' assault on the cell block. George Dobbins, the leader of the black activist group responsible for the uprising, was at first reported to have been shot. A "fact-finding board" hastily organized by the Board of Corrections released a statement that he had been killed by gunfire. That account was soon refuted, however, by Nelson Grubbs, the Alabama state toxicologist who examined Dobbins' body at the hospital. Grubbs reported that Dobbins had died, in Martin's words, "from nine stab wounds in his head caused by a heavy, sharp instrument wielded with enough force to penetrate the frontal bone in two places." Explanations for Dobbins' death in that manner are in conflict.[24]

The violence in January prompted renewed talk of reform in February. The *Montgomery Advertiser* introduced a series of articles by Martin with an editorial warning that the "fester" in the prisons would worsen unless the people of Alabama tore down the "mental barricades" that had prevented "thoughtful discussion of . . . penal reform" in the past. In April, a grand jury in Escambia County, where Fountain and Holman were located, issued a special report on those institutions that mixed rhetoric condemning "revolutionaries" at Fountain with calls for a return of the death penalty for homicides committed within a penal institution. In a revealing passage, however, the grand jurors expressed their impatience with a "do-nothing" legislature that had failed over the years to attend to the needs of the penal system. A cover letter by Judge Douglas S. Webb, addressed to Governor Wallace, complained that residents in the area lived "on the perimeter of a boiling, seething cauldron" that could "explode" into "tragedy" at any moment.[25]

Calls for serious attention to penal practices had been heard before in Alabama. Always they had been ignored. Now, once more, the apparent necessity for action receded from the public mind as the events at

Fountain slipped the short distance from news to memory. In Montgomery, the Alabama legislature stood silent. One legislator explained that public monies would not be appropriated for prisons for the obvious reason that "prisoners cannot vote." Maston Mims proposed no dramatic policies to address the prison system's faults. His committee called on the governor to allow the Board of Corrections an additional $2 million to build more catwalks, gun towers, and punitive cells at Fountain and to purchase more guns and riot equipment for guards. The official reaction to inmate violence was not an investigation of its causes, but a campaign to arm penal authorities to respond in kind.[26]

Prisoners in the Alabama penal system refused to suffer quietly. In the wake of the *Newman* order of October 1972, and the Fountain uprising in January 1974, they increased their letters to Judge Johnson. Two grievances in particular became routine. Prisoners complained that they continued to suffer inadequate medical care notwithstanding the *Newman* order and that they were subjected to physical abuse—usually from other inmates. The two issues, poor medical care and violence, were inextricable, often for the self-evident reason that the prisoners concerned needed medical attention for injuries received at the hands of their fellows. Johnson read all his mail from prisoners and, having identified a letter with a complaint of a particular nature, he channeled it to one of several offices, accompanied on occasion by his own suggestions for action. In most instances, DeMent was the proper recipient. In Johnson's view, DeMent had responsibility for investigating complaints touching medical care within the *Newman* framework and for appraising complaints regarding physical abuse for possible prosecution under federal civil rights statutes. In time, DeMent and his assistants also established a routine. In situations in which the complaint was administrative only, the appropriate state official, usually the commissioner of corrections, was contacted and asked to respond. In more serious instances, the FBI was summoned to make a preliminary investigation. In this way, and without the surface appearance of federal involvement, the Alabama penal system was monitored by federal officials in a routine, if limited, way.[27]

Time wore on, but the letters did not cease. In the spring of 1975, Judge Johnson grew anxious. In a letter to DeMent, he proposed a new means of assuring compliance with his *Newman* order.

> In my judgment, it is time that an in-depth investigation be conducted of the several prisons involved in the Newman case to determine if the arbitrary denial of basic medical and surgical needs continues. I am

receiving too many written complaints from prisoners regarding such denials to ignore them and to fail to have such an investigation conducted. . . .

> I request that the United States Department of Justice and your office as amicus curiae in this case at the earliest convenient time cause an appropriate investigation to be conducted and a copy of the findings of that investigation together with any motions that may be appropriate to be filed with the court.[28]

The *Newman* case was to be reopened, the defendants' success in bringing the system's medical program up to standards was to be examined and, if necessary, DeMent and the Justice Department were to ask for further relief. Plainly, the judge had concluded that in this instance not even the lawyers he had ushered into a case had ensured progress toward reform. In *Newman,* Judge Johnson himself was ever the moving force.

Yet the scheme did not work. The task of preparing a report was assigned to Littlefield, who faced various delays in interviewing prisoners, checking their complaints against official records, and scheduling tours by Dr. Alderete and other health officers. Littlefield was able to file only a preliminary report in August 1975, a bare two weeks before trial opened in the *Pugh* and *James* cases. Her final report was received in the spring of 1976, when the circumstances had changed so radically that any motions for supplemental relief in *Newman,* as distinguished from *Pugh* and *James,* would have been inappropriate. Well before that, indeed, well before the circuit's decision in November 1974, Judge Johnson had turned his attention to new cases. Both *Pugh* and *James* involved complaints touching medical care. Looking back now, it is consistent with the evidence that Johnson looked on the new cases as, in large measure, enforcement devices for the order he had already entered in *Newman.* If that explanation is accurate, the point was lost on the lawyers concerned. They were vaguely acquainted with the *Newman* litigation, but they had no notion that their own work was so closely linked with what had gone before. Continuity in an examination of the Alabama prison system rested with Judge Johnson.[29]

The experience in *Newman* taught Judge Johnson many lessons that served him well in the more important cases to come. He learned that he could entertain a class action lawsuit challenging prison conditions, that DeMent and the Justice Department could provide the necessary resources to marshal the evidence (if not to monitor compliance with injunctive decrees later), that the developing case law would permit him to identify constitutional violations, and that, if he was able to make detailed findings of fact regarding serious deficiencies in a prison system, the court of appeals would sustain even a sweeping remedial order—deferring to his authority to prescribe relief sufficient to redress the constitutional violations he might find. Prison litigation, that is, could be accommodated within the framework previously developed for the school desegregation and mental health cases. There was no doubting the difficulties presented by cases of this kind. Yet *Newman* established that it was possible to manage them, at least through trial. *Newman* opened a window to the Alabama prison system, permitting Judge Johnson and responsible citizens to look inside and to appreciate the gravity of the wrongs committed behind the walls. The evidence in that case, together with prisoner mail in the wake of the court's order, offered glimpses of a sordid story that demanded elaboration. The *Pugh* and *James* cases served as vehicles for a further investigation that required years to complete.

3

Progeny

If the original documents in *Pugh* and *James* had been merely letters, Judge Johnson would have referred them elsewhere—as was his custom in the wake of *Newman*. Crudely drawn though they were, however, these documents tracked the language and form of complaints drafted by lawyers to initiate lawsuits. Judge Johnson accepted them in that way and promptly set in motion a series of events that would see two protests from individual inmates merged in a powerful attack on current conditions and practices throughout the Alabama prison system.

Early developments can be grouped in four parts. First, Johnson appointed aggressive lawyers to represent the prisoners concerned. Those attorneys, in turn, orchestrated the lawsuits into major class actions for the purpose of achieving sweeping and permanent penal reform. In this, the involvement of the National Prison Project and, later, the federal government, proved to be critical. Second, Judge Johnson provided the prisoners' lawyers with an early evaluation of the constitutional claims they developed and, indeed, guided them to the theory on which he himself preferred the cases to proceed. The judge focused the litigation on physical conditions in large penitentiaries and, in so doing, dampened hopes that he would order fundamental changes in state penal policy—even as the lawyers generated evidence exposing the flaws in that policy. Third, state officials disclosed their initial reactions to the threat that the prisons for which they were responsible were to be examined in a federal courtroom. Those reactions, evident both in the state's own lawyers' preparation of a defense to prisoners' claims and in more public statements and activities on the part of the commissioner of corrections and other principals, provided an advance glimpse of arguments and themes to be repeated in succeeding years. Finally, the lawyers on both sides of the new lawsuits began the long and tedious task of preparing for trial.

The complaint in *Pugh,* hammered out on an old prison typewriter, described an assault at the hands of other prisoners, not state authorities. Yet it nonetheless laid the blame for Pugh's injuries on the officials in charge—Commissioner Sullivan and Warden Harding. Pugh demanded not only an injunction establishing new standards for inmate treatment, but $2 million in money damages. Hard upon the uprising in which George Dobbins had been killed, such a claim commanded serious attention. In February 1974, Judge Johnson appointed a young Montgomery practitioner to represent Pugh in the lawsuit.

Robert D. Segall was of a new generation of Alabamians. A 1971 graduate of the University of Alabama Law School, he had served as Johnson's law clerk the year the *Wyatt* case was tried and the *Newman* complaint was filed. After the clerkship, he had taken a graduate degree in law at Harvard and then joined a prestigious law firm in his hometown. Knowing of Segall's interest in civil rights cases, the judge naturally thought of him when he needed an energetic lawyer to handle unpopular litigation. Johnson had appointed Segall in *Lynch v. Baxley,*[1] a challenge to the procedures used in Alabama for the commitment of persons believed to be mentally ill, and now, in *Pugh,* he turned to him in a case destined to be even more significant. Segall read the complaint to present an explosive allegation—that state prison authorities were constitutionally obligated to protect inmates from each other. He took the assignment as a clear signal that Judge Johnson was concerned generally about assaults on inmates in the Alabama prison system and would permit the expansion of *Pugh* beyond the confines of the episode described by this single prisoner.[2]

In his earliest meetings with Jerry Pugh, Segall proposed two related strategies. First, he suggested that the prayer for damages be severed from the request for injunctive relief. That action would not only dispense with trial by jury, to which the defendants would be entitled if sued for damages, but would also redirect attention away from Pugh's personal injuries and focus it on the larger picture of violence throughout the prison system. Second, Segall proposed to convert Pugh's individual lawsuit into a class action on behalf of all Alabama prisoners subject to the kind of violence that Pugh himself had experienced. The prisoner agreed to both maneuvers, and Segall promptly filed an amended complaint. A few weeks later, Pugh had second thoughts. He apparently hoped that a lawsuit geared to his own, personal interests might create the leverage required for early parole and worried that a broader lawsuit might dilute the usefulness of the litigation for his own purposes. Acting on that possibility, Pugh wrote to Judge Johnson in late April, denying that he had authorized Segall's changes and asking for a different attorney. Johnson summoned Segall and, after a few meetings, the confusion sorted itself out. Pugh reaffirmed his satisfaction with both Segall and his tactics, and Johnson scheduled a pretrial conference for late summer.[3]

Having settled the nature and scope of the litigation, Segall next arranged logistics. His law firm gave him permission to devote his own time to the project. For funding, Segall turned to the Southern Poverty Law Center, a civil rights organization established a half dozen years earlier by Morris Dees, a wealthy young Alabama lawyer. Dees represented Joanne Little charged with homicide in North Carolina, Vietnamese refugees threatened by Klan violence in Texas, and dozens of prison inmates sentenced to capital punishment. Joseph Levin, the center's director, agreed to provide financial assistance and to work with Segall in the *Pugh* case. Moreover, through Levin, Segall met Roy Haber, counsel for the Mississippi prisoners in *Gates v. Collier,*[4] the case that had served as a precedent in *Newman.* Over the succeeding weeks, both Levin and Haber offered useful advice on the way in which the new case, *Pugh,* might be prepared for trial.[5]

Segall was creative in fashioning a theory on which to proceed. In his view, the episode described in Pugh's original complaint was not an isolated event, but part of a pattern of violence at Fountain and throughout the Alabama prison system. In particular, the practice of housing large numbers of prisoners in crowded dormitories, without regard to the violent propensities of individuals, had made brutality the common currency of prison life. The fault, according to Segall, lay not solely with the inmates who fought with each other in the dormitories, but with Sullivan, Harding, and other penal authorities who knew, or should have known, that the consequences of their policies would be violence, injury and, in some instances, death. The conditions in Alabama's prisons, conditions plainly ascribable to deliberate decisions by state penal officials, thus ensured that prisoners would be subjected to assault on a routine basis. That cold insight must be captured in legal argument. The obvious vehicle was the Eighth Amendment's prohibition on cruel and unusual punishment. Segall proposed to argue that Alabama penal authorities punished prisoners in violation of the Eighth Amendment by placing them in threatening circumstances without safeguarding them from attack. In due course, he ranged afield from that "right to protection" contention but, in the end, returned full circle to it.

The immediate problem was to identify some standard against which conditions in Alabama could be measured. As he reflected on that question, Segall came to the view that he could best explain what was wrong with the Alabama prison system by explaining what must be done to set things right. He could best provide Judge Johnson with a standard for judgment by describing a state of affairs in which prison violence would be unlikely to occur and then contrasting such a regime with the status quo. The effect would be to merge two matters that lawyers typically hold apart: what must be shown to win a lawsuit and what the winner obtains in victory. Anticipating the kind of decree that he would ask Judge Johnson to issue after judgment, Segall laid in place, at least temporarily, the linchpin connecting what may be called the negative version of his case (the claim that conditions in the prison system produced unconstitutional violence) and a more affirmative version of the case (a claim that, in order to be free from unconstitutional violence, prisoners were entitled to something positive—something that, if granted, would prevent violence).

The literature had already given that something a name. Segall borrowed that name in his own deliberations and in his conversations with advisors. He formulated the contention that prison inmates had a constitutional right to "rehabilitation." If, Segall reasoned, the elimination of prison violence could be attained only by reducing prisoners' frustration in confinement, and if prisoners' frustration could be reduced only through educational and vocational programs, then "rehabilitation [became] a prerequisite to the elimination of violence and, thus, a constitutional right." Plausible as such an idea was, Segall could not persuade the penal specialist he consulted, Dr. Stanley Brodsky, the associate director of Dr. Fowler's Center for Correctional Psychology. Despairing that he would be able to convince the judge of his "rehabilitation" theory without expert witnesses who would testify in support, Segall reoriented his thinking around the simpler "right to protection" thesis with which he had begun.[6]

Not to say that the "right to protection" theory to which Segall retreated was unambitious. It was not. Segall rather boldly proposed that "[w]hen a state denies people their liberty and forces them to live in confined quarters and without self-defense, . . . that state assumes a corresponding duty to protect these people from physical and mental harm. . . . " Although he was unaware of the nineteenth-century history on which he might have relied, in the end he put forward the familiar, commonsense proposition that "[i]ncarceration is the punishment established by law. . . . Correction officials are not entitled to add to that punishment more than what . . . are necessary concomitants of incarceration." Routine violence in the dormitories and cell blocks, by Segall's account, constituted such additional cruel and unusual punishment. On this, much would rest. Segall insisted that prisoners' right to protection existed apart from the defendants' personal knowledge or intentions regarding institution violence and, perhaps as important, apart from their financial capacity to make necessary changes.[7]

Moreover, the even more far-reaching "right to rehabilitation" theory found its way into the attack on Alabama's prisons by a different route. In retrospect, it is hardly surprising that a proposition that could attract Segall, even temporarily, would enjoy an even warmer reception among prisoners themselves. At the very time that Segall was considering the "right to rehabilitation" idea, but apparently without connection to his work, the same argument was actively being discussed within the inmate population. Only a month after Segall's consultations with Brodsky and just as Segall was reconciling himself to abandoning the rehabilitation claim, it was squarely presented to Judge Johnson in a new complaint filed by a different prisoner. Worley James had little in common with Segall's client. Jerry Pugh was a young Caucasian, first convicted in 1969 and sent to prison in 1973 only after violating the terms of probation. He was 27 years old when he filed his complaint. James was born in 1894, the son of a black sharecropper in a rural area of south Alabama. His string of felonies began in 1925. In 1944, he was sentenced to death for the murder and rape of a 12-year-old child. That sentence was commuted to a life term. He was released on parole in 1969, but was returned to prison three years later after yet another conviction for assault with intent to ravish. In June 1974, with the help of another inmate whose name was never publicly disclosed, James filed a handwritten complaint in Judge Johnson's court—faulting the state's failure to meet his medical needs and to "rehabilitate" him in prison. In addition to George Wallace, the complaint named Sullivan and William Long, James' warden at Mt. Meigs, as defendants. On the day the complaint was filed, Judge Johnson appointed a local law professor, George Taylor, to represent James in future proceedings.

Taylor was no stranger to Judge Johnson, to the great cases in which the judge had been involved, or to the institutional reform litigation those cases had encouraged. He was not a radical. Judged by contemporary standards, his political outlook was moderate. Yet he had been there when it meant something to be there. As a young lawyer in Birmingham in the 1960s, Taylor joined with David Vann and Charles Morgan to form the Young Men's Business Club, which challenged Bull Connor for political control of the city. He and Vann negotiated a peaceful settlement between Dr. Martin Luther King and city authorities in 1963; he and Morgan filed the first great reapportionment case,

Reynolds v. Sims,[8] in the same year. After a brief career in the Peace Corps, Taylor went to Mississippi to head the field office of the Lawyers' Committee for Civil Rights Under Law. During his tenure, that office handled Roy Haber's litigation in *Gates* and the Mississippi version of *Reynolds,* inherited from another lawyer, Alvin J. Bronstein. Drawn back to Alabama in 1973 to become assistant dean at the University of Alabama Law School, Taylor paid a courtesy call on Judge Johnson, mentioning in passing that he would be available periodically to accept court appointments in cases in which litigants could not afford to hire a lawyer. A year later, Johnson asked him to represent Worley James.[9]

The judge mentioned the rehabilitation claim to Taylor, and it seemed to him that it was that issue that had caught Johnson's attention. Indeed, Taylor thought he had been appointed not because of his experience in massive class action suits, but because of his academic post. He had access to an intellectual community that might guide the court toward an answer to an exciting new issue in legal theory— whether prisoners had a "right to rehabilitation." Accordingly, Taylor anticipated that the bulk of his work in the *James* case would be done in the law library. He, like Segall, immediately amended his client's complaint to state a class action challenge on behalf of all Alabama prisoners. Yet Taylor's action, unlike Segall's, was motivated by concerns tied tightly to the client's individual claim instead of by a grander plan to challenge the Alabama prison system on a wide scale. His initial interview with James generated serious doubts that a lawsuit on James' behalf alone could survive to judgment. Charged by the court to explore an innovative legal theory, Taylor found himself representing a sickly, elderly man—hardly a candidate for the rehabilitative opportunities the complaint apparently demanded. Even if Taylor could contend seriously for James' right to rehabilitation, moreover, the poor man might die before the litigation could be completed. The only course was to broaden the suit. To submerge James in the case as much as possible, Taylor asked for and obtained his permission to eliminate allegations regarding his personal medical care and to locate other, more suitable representatives of the class to be named in an amended complaint. Notwithstanding its motivation, this shift to the class action form promised to transform the case from an isolated dispute between a man and his keepers, albeit a dispute over a novel claim of right, into a powerful engine for social change not unlike forerunner cases such as *Wyatt* and *Newman.* Working with James, the younger prisoner who had actually drafted the original complaint, and Steve Suitts, director of the Civil

Liberties Union in Alabama, Taylor identified several inmates to represent the class along with James himself.[10]

Taylor was not alone in his work. Students at the law school helped him maintain contact with his inmate-clients and to research the legal issues. Taylor's approach, more academic than Segall's, began with the rich literature on the general matter of rehabilitation in prisons. The object to "reform" criminal offenders was, of course, as old as the colonies. Firmly rooted in the Pennsylvania and New York systems, reformation had been the vital element in the Jacksonian asylum that had gained such complete acceptance in nineteenth century Alabama. Penal authorities in Alabama were not turnkeys or guards; they were "correctional officers." Prisons were not gaols; they were penitentiaries or reformatories. Misbehaving citizens were detained, in hospitals and prisons alike, ostensibly because they were ill and required treatment for their cure. Like most other states, Alabama had long since written rehabilitation into the state criminal code, identifying the "treatment" of criminal offenders in a "correctional institution" as the normal sanction for violations of the law. Alabama court decisions also recognized that the punishment of offenders was understood to be in aid of their "reformation" and "rehabilitation." The federal courts, too, acknowledged the role that rehabilitation had come to play. In 1949, the Supreme Court had identified rehabilitation as one of the "important goals of criminal jurisprudence," and only three months before the complaint in *James* was filed, the Court had reiterated that penal officials were responsible for "rehabilitating" prisoners "to the extent that human nature and inadequate resources allow."[11]

Inasmuch as the language of penology linked prisons with other institutions in which people were held against their will, Taylor thought it unremarkable to propose that the "right to treatment" theory in Johnson's own decision in *Wyatt* could and should be extended to the prison context. Indeed, he was tempted to place primary reliance on the due process clause rather than the Eighth Amendment—this to underscore the intellectual relationship between *Wyatt* and *James*. At bottom, the argument in *James* could be precisely what it had been in the mental health case. Government must act rationally, employing means substantially related to the purposes sought to be achieved. Hence, if the objective of incarceration was the rehabilitation of criminal offenders, then inmates must have an affirmative right to various beneficial progams now denied to them. Indeed, Taylor speculated that Judge Johnson wanted him to test the power of the idea in *Wyatt* to win acceptance outside the circumstances that had given rise to it. Said yet another way and on a more dramatic scale, the *James* case might present an opportunity to collect the various strands of midcentury thinking about institutionalization generally and to weave them together behind a single legal theory—the proposition that citizens involuntarily detained for the purpose of treatment were constitutionally entitled to be treated.[12]

As Taylor and his students probed more deeply into the literature, however, and when they approached Fowler and Brodsky for advice (tracking in this respect the path that Segall had followed only weeks earlier), they became discouraged. However well accepted the treatment idea had been until recently, the country was now growing cold to it. To begin, respected studies had lately concluded that rehabilitative programs had been unsuccessful in changing offender behavior. Conservatives now insisted that raw punishment, unadorned by liberal attempts to "help" criminal offenders, constituted the better weapon against crime. At the same time, those who had held out hope for rehabilitation now submerged their disappointment in critical reexamination. Rehabilitation was not condemned merely because it had failed to work, but because it posed a threat to the libertarian concerns of the very progressives who had been its primary proponents. Criminal offenders were not necessarily ill or in need of any cure in the medical sense; to propose that they were was to deny their integrity as individuals responsible for their own thoughts and actions. The notion that offenders were incarcerated for treatment, moreover, comtemplated not merely that prisoners should benefit from programs provided for them, but that the state, too, had a legitimate interest in forcing inmates to endure programs to which they might object. The spectre of "drug aversion therapy" and other "behavior modification" schemes caused many supporters of rehabilitation to reevaluate their postitions. Finally, Taylor's research turned up no solid judicial precedents in support of a "right to rehabilitation" claim. While many judges had mentioned rehabilitation, none had translated what might be a marginally good idea into an affirmative constitutional right. Johnson himself had explicitly distinguished prisons from mental hospitals in *Wyatt,* and Taylor could locate no case authority that might persuade the judge to reconsider that part of his opinion and extend to prison inmates the benefits of the *Wyatt* theory.[13]

The alternative that suggested itself was to redirect the litigation in *James* away from the due process claim that prisoners were entitled to the rehabilitation for which they were ostensibly confined and toward the Eighth Amendment theory that had been so successful in previous suits over prison conditions. In that framework, educational, vocational, and other beneficial programs for prisoners could be sought as remedies for prison conditions that currently constituted cruel and unusual punishment. Taylor now felt his case growing beneath him. If *James* were to become an Alabama edition of *Gates,* it would demand heavy expenditures of time and funds—resources that, for Taylor, were in short supply. The answer to that dilemma lay in cooperation with Segall, whose work in *Pugh* plainly overlapped with the litigation in *James.* Judge Johnson had mentioned the *Pugh* case to Taylor, who had telephoned Segall only five days after his appointment. Now, however, the two men explored a much closer relationship. For if Segall and Levin were already committed to a sweeping attack on conditions in the prisons, it only made sense that Taylor should join forces with them. Segall, for his part, was pleased. The inauguration of *James* mitigated any regrets he harbored about having abandoned the rehabilitation issue in *Pugh.*[14]

If the resulting joint project promised to blossom into major litigation, Taylor and Segall could take comfort in knowing that they would have help from a mutual friend in Tuscaloosa, Ralph I. Knowles, Jr. Another graduate of the University of Alabama School of Law, Knowles had gone into practice with a classmate, Jack Drake, and together they had been involved in various civil rights cases, among them *Wyatt.* Knowles was a principal figure in the ACLU's Alabama affiliate and, with Steve Suitts, was committed to the maintenance of an ACLU voice on matters touching individual rights. He brought to the litigation not only a personal, ideological perspective, but keen intelligence, sound judgment, and an heroic capacity for hard work. Knowles was meticulous in preparing cases for trial, organizing the relevant information in exquisite detail, and orchestrating the participation of others into an efficient, single-minded enterprise. Sensing that the men and ideas swirling around the *Pugh* and *James* cases demanded coordination, Knowles set about arranging a meeting of interested parties. The conference was scheduled for early August in the Montgomery law office of another ACLU activist, Howard Mandell.

By now, Taylor faced a motion to dismiss, filed in response to Worley James' original complaint. Instead of meeting that motion forthrightly, he carried through with the plan to convert the case into a class action and to omit James' claims concerning his personal medical disabilities. Anticipating all the difficulties his research had unearthed, he articulated the rehabilitation claim in alternative forms. Initially, he alleged that the defendants had violated the Eighth Amendment in that they had "failed . . . to provide facilities, programs, and personnel for the treatment and rehabilitation of [prisoners]." He thus posited an affirmative right to rehabilitation, albeit a right based on the Eighth Amendment rather than the due process clause. He was pessimistic that any such right could be established, but he felt compelled to assert it nonetheless. He hoped that his references to inmates who needed help would diffuse concerns that prisoners might be subjected to manipulative programs against their will.

Next, Taylor set forth a more complex, second-level argument constituting yet another, indirect approach to the rehabilitation claim, but one that diverged sharply from what Segall had considered. Taylor argued that state penal authorities had violated the Eighth Amendment in that they had "failed . . . to eliminate those conditions which make impossible the . . . rehabilitation . . . of [prisoners]." If he could persuade Judge Johnson that penal authorities were constitutionally obligated to rehabilitate prisoners, Taylor would be glad to take that victory. If, however, the judge should decide against such an affirmative duty, Taylor still hoped to persuade him that the authorities could not validly place barriers in the way of prisoners attempting to rehabilitate themselves. If that point were accepted, then he hoped to convince the judge to order improved conditions and programs not on the theory that prisoners were entitled constitutionally to *be* rehabilitated but on the alternative ground that existing circumstances frustrated voluntary, individual efforts at self-improvement. This second-level argument still sounded the theme in *Wyatt*. Yet Taylor's avoidance of the due process theory employed in the mental health context and his substitution of the Eighth Amendment theory cited in other prison cases evidenced his doubt that the precedent in *Wyatt* would be helpful, or even significant, in *James*. Judge Johnson promptly overruled the motion to dismiss on the ground that Taylor's amendments superseded the original complaint to which the motion had been addressed. That was the posture of the case on August 9, when Taylor met with the group that Knowles had brought together.[15]

Discussion at the meeting in Mandell's office centered on the conceptual underpinnings of the two cases and, to a lesser extent, on the way in which the litigation could be funded.[16] Everyone agreed that the cases should be taken beyond the confines of most prison litigation to date. This was an opportunity to demonstrate the inherent flaws in the current system, in which large numbers of idle criminal offenders were incarcerated for lengthy sentences served in massive, rural penitentiaries, and to force state authorities to adopt penal policies that might actually succeed—decently and fairly. Knowles and Suitts in particular suggested that the cases could have national significance and, to that end, they urged the group to spare no expense in developing them for trial. Levin was already committed to support his own and Segall's work in *Pugh,* but he hesitated to do the same for Taylor in *James.* That turned attention to Alvin J. Bronstein, Taylor's old friend from their days in Mississippi and now director of the National Prison Project. Bronstein had been approached on prior occasions, by Taylor, Knowles, and especially Suitts, who was insistent that the ACLU's special project for prison litigation should play a major role in the Alabama cases. Bronstein had consented to journey south for the meeting and used it to determine the likelihood that a sizable investment of effort in Alabama would be worthwhile.

Al Bronstein had been involved in civil rights litigation throughout his adult life. The son of Russian immigrants, he was reared in New York City, where he worked with the War Resisters' League, the Congress of Racial Equality, and the Student Non-Violent Coordinating Committee. After graduation from the New York Law School, he went to Mississippi with the Lawyers' Constitutional Defense Committee. During the next four years, he worked in various southern states, including Alabama, and appeared before numerous southern judges, among them Judge Johnson. He continued his involvement with civil rights groups during a few more years at the Kennedy School of Government at Harvard. In 1972, he was selected to be the first director of the Prison Project. After two years, Bronstein had grown weary of pursuing the discrete claims of individual inmates and frankly wished to challenge the overarching policy of long-term imprisonment in the United States. He was not averse to considering Alabama as the site for a new and ambitious campaign against the status quo—provided lawyers in that state were willing and able to do the necessary field work.[17]

Then there was the little ACLU affiliate in Tuscaloosa, which also boasted a long, exciting history of success that suggested an organization many times its size. Most of the credit for that record was owed to Suitts, the group's first executive director and a match for Knowles in his capacity for sustained labor. Under Suitts' leadership, the local affiliate had attacked racial discrimination, election law violations, and various forms of censorship. More recently, the organization had taken an interest in prisons. Volunteers corresponded with inmates, collecting reports of mistreatment. In the year before *Pugh* and *James* were instituted, Suitts published a study of the racial makeup of the state's inmate population—demonstrating that blacks accounted for a disproportionate number of the men and women held in state custody. Yet the local affiliate lacked the resources needed to put its concerns about the prisons in the form of a lawsuit. Bronstein's program offered the where-withal for legal action, and Suitts did what he could to entice the Prison Project to Alabama. He courted the older man with periodic reports and phone calls. When concrete cases arose, he urged Bronstein to seize the opportunity they presented.[18]

Bronstein listened intently during the meeting in Mandell's office, then agreed to participate, primarily because the Alabama cases would come before Judge Johnson. There were no illusions about this judge. Whatever else he was, Johnson was a reserved southerner suspicious of litigation with an explicit policy orientation. Yet if he could be per-suaded that the circumstances warranted action, he might issue the kind of injunctive decree he had entered in *Wyatt* and *Newman*. In turn, that might advance the cause of prison reform immeasurably. Bronstein thus made the decision to go forward as soon as he could hire an addi-tional staff member to carry the weight of the new cases. He had already interviewed Matthew Myers, a graduate of the University of Michigan Law School who had worked part-time on the *Wyatt* case. When Myers joined the Prison Project in September, the commitment to the Ala-bama cases was sealed. Myers assumed responsibility for the brunt of the preparation in *James;* Knowles served as the Prison Project's local counsel.[19]

As the lawyers for the prisoners were organizing, the defense crept along seemingly without appreciation for what plaintiffs' counsel were planning. The defendants in *Pugh* were represented by Larry R. New-man, an assistant attorney general in Alabama, and Robert Lamar, a local practitioner appointed as a special assistant attorney general only for purposes of this single case. Neither man initially grasped the threat posed by Segall's argument; indeed, the matter was handled in the same manner in which states' attorneys might have responded to a lawsuit pursued by an inmate without professional representation. If anything, the defense in the *James* case was handled more casually. The case was assigned to William M. Bowen, a junior member of Baxley's permanent staff with no background in prison litigation, who then found himself opposite George Taylor, an older litigator of considerable experience. The two met for the first time in September when Judge Johnson heard argument in Montgomery on Bowen's motion to dismiss Taylor's amended complaint. Taylor took the floor first; Bowen followed with rebuttal. Probing, Judge Johnson asked the young lawyer whether there might be merit in Taylor's second-level argument which, in Johnson's understanding, amounted to the contention that prisoners had a right "not to be deprived" of an opportunity to rehabilitate themselves.

Bowen confessed he could not understand that theory, and Taylor left the courtroom thinking he had survived this early test.[20]

He was right. On September 30, Johnson issued an order overruling the motion to dismiss, accompanied by an opinion explaining his understanding of the lawsuit Taylor would now pursue. This opinion, Johnson's first in either *Pugh* or *James,* was essentially a blueprint. Myers put it succinctly: "As we all agreed, Johnson has provided us with a basic outline which we would be wise to follow." That is precisely what the judge intended. He had always expected that the lawyers would refine the issues in these cases and set before him whatever support they could locate. When Taylor arrived in court having dressed his client's original claim in a sophisticated theoretical framework but still lacking hard support in the precedents, Johnson found it appropriate and timely to register his preliminary reaction. The judge was not prepared to launch a critical examination of Alabama penology and to substitute his own judgment, or Taylor's, for that of the state officials concerned. By contrast, he was predisposed to tolerate whatever penal policies Alabama authorities wished to pursue, so long as the resulting conditions in the state's institutions did not slip beneath minimal decency. This, then, was the legal rule on which Johnson would rest. State officials were entitled to make choices in this field, but they were not free to institute a mindlessly brutal and oppressive regime that denied the essential humanity of the inmates in their charge.[21]

Taylor had now had his chance to demonstrate a link between an affirmative, constitutional "right to rehabilitation" and the "decent" conditions to which prisoners were entitled. He had produced very little. Such a claim, therefore, presented the very attempt to second-guess penal decision-making that Johnson wished to avoid. At the same time, Taylor's artful indirection did show promise. Johnson now used his blueprint opinion to "put the parties on what [he] thought was the right track." That track led to Taylor's second-level argument—the version of the claim for rehabilitative programs that the judge himself had put to Bowen two weeks earlier.

> [T]his Court is compelled to reject plaintiffs' claim of absolute entitlement to the provision of rehabilitative services on the ground that persons convicted of felonies do not acquire by virtue of their conviction a constitutional right to services and benefits unavailable as of right to persons never convicted of criminal offenses. So long as treatment, rehabilitation, and reformation services and facilities may not be demanded of the state as of right by her free citizens, this Court is unpersuaded that such services may be demanded by convicted felons.

Plaintiffs' amended complaint, however, advances other theories and allegations which do state cognizable claims and which, if proved, would entitle them to relief. . . .

On the basis of the allegations set forth, plaintiffs would be permitted to introduce evidence tending to show that the defendants, or some of them, have prohibited members of the plaintiff class from, or refused to allow them, the opportunity to rehabilitate themselves by means not inconsistent with the orderly operation of the correctional system.

Again, while Taylor's second-level contention resonated with the due process analysis in *Wyatt,* the linkage Judge Johnson found to the requirement of decent living conditions thrust the "right to treatment" trappings of the claim in *James* into the background. A claim that prisoners had a right "not to be deprived" of the opportunity to rehabilitate themselves could rest, in Johnson's view, on Eighth Amendment precedents already on the books—precedents purporting to find constitutional fault not with state penal policies, but with primitive living conditions standing alone. In particular, Johnson relied upon *Holt,* in which Judge Henley had said that the absence of training and similar programs may "militate against reform and rehabilitation." That insight, according to Judge Johnson, suggested a further, related proposition of fundamental importance.

Where conditions within a prison are such that the inmates incarcerated therein will inevitably and necessarily become more sociopathic and less able to adapt to conventional society as the result of their incarceration than they were prior thereto, cruel and unusual punishment is inflicted.

Johnson admonished Taylor that the burden of proof would be heavy. Yet if the prisoners' lawyers could make the required showing, he would compel the state to provide "basic rehabilitative services and facilities." Finally, the blueprint opinion took account of Taylor's list of the prison system's flaws. Johnson said that he would consider evidence that the few rehabilitative services available to Alabama prisoners were being administered in an arbitrary manner, that prisoners with "mental or emotional difficulties" or with "geriatric problems" were being denied appropriate care and, in an obvious overlap with *Pugh,* that prisoners with a propensity for violence were being housed indiscriminately with others, leading to assaults on weaker inmates. The road ahead now seemed clear. Taylor told his clients that "Judge Johnson pretty well told us that if we can prove certain things, we are going to win." Now, he explained, "the problem [was] to produce the evidence to support the statements we . . . made."[22]

Not even Johnson's blueprint opinion yet impressed the lawyers for the defense, who still failed to comprehend the importance of the *Pugh* and *James* cases. Two events illustrate the point. Apparently disturbed that state authorities should be called to account in *Pugh* for physical assaults carried out by prisoners themselves, Larry Newman filed a counterclaim, contending that prisoners actually engaged in violence should be enjoined from assaulting others. The tactic sorely mistook the gravity of the "right to protection" claim that Segall was making. The judge was furious. His quick order dismissing the counterclaim was laced with harsh language, denouncing what he took to be "bad faith" and an "unprofessional approach" to the litigation. Newman's stratagem thus backfired. It only prejudiced Judge Johnson's courtroom for any future moves the defense might wish to make. The second event took place in Johnson's chambers, when the judge appointed Bronstein's Prison Project to serve as amicus curiae "with authority to participate . . . to the extent that any party is authorized to participate in all future matters." Bowen's performance in that setting was so inept that Johnson candidly asked him whether he expected to "have help" from other defense lawyers. Bowen had been outclassed by Taylor from the outset. With the introduction of Bronstein, Myers, and Knowles, he was hopelessly overmatched. His solitary position in *James* thus underscored some state officials' failure to recognize the lawsuit's true scope.[23]

Commissioner Sullivan, by contrast, was fully aware that these cases had the potential to expose his system's many weaknesses. Yet the commissioner did not react negatively. He might have preferred to avoid interference from civil rights lawyers and Judge Johnson, but he understood that litigation could provide a catalyst for needed change. At all events, he refused to wait for plaintiffs' counsel to identify the prison system's flaws. He took the offensive, just as he had two years earlier in the wake of Johnson's order in *Newman*. First, Sullivan focused on the good things in the prisons. Staff members gave interviews to draw attention to praiseworthy developments and, at the least, to cast the prison system in a favorable light. Newspapers published stories applauding Governor Wallace for assigning federal revenue-sharing funds to the Board of Corrections and describing the system's better institutions to the public. The *Birmingham News* reported on new educational programs at Holman, and the *Tuscaloosa News* presented the Frank Lee Youth Center as "more like a camp" than a penal institution. Next, the commissioner revealed the system's darker side,

in hopes of obtaining financial support from the legislature to implement corrective measures. In this, he had support from board members.
The outgoing chairman, Dr. Max V. McLaughlin, said publicly that he,
too, believed it was time to "let people know what [was] happening to
get their support," and the new chairman, Dr. Staton, declared that current conditions in the prisons made a new federal court order "a definite
threat." Now, it became routine to insist that if something were not
done quickly, the prison system would face an Attica-class uprising or
a federal court order—and probably both.[24]

Particular emphasis was placed on the intractable problem of
crowding. The prison system, Sullivan said, was "like a bag. . . . [W]hen
you keep stuffing things into it, sooner or later it's going to burst. . . ."
Warden Harding was even more graphic: "Anytime it's overcrowded,
you've got an explosive situation . . . and I don't care whether you're
talking about prisoners or preachers." Harding asked visitors to imagine "living like this day in and day out; so close you can't move, so close
you can't help but bump into somebody with every step. . . . [S]ooner
or later it's going to get to you and you're going to explode." John Hale,
Sullivan's public information director, said that penal authorities were
"sitting on a powder keg that could explode at any time."[25]

The primary "bottleneck," in Hale's words, was the Medical and
Diagnostic Center at Mt. Meigs. The purpose of that institution was to
receive new prisoners, hold them for a short time for testing and classification, and then channel them to appropriate assignments elsewhere.
It was reported in February that as many as sixty-eight inmates at Mt.
Meigs were sleeping on the floor. Three days later, there were ninety-
nine, with twenty more expected the next day. The assistant warden
confessed that "prisoners [were] sleeping in the hall, in the showers and
between beds. Anywhere you can put a mattress, we put it." Five days
after that, the population swelled yet again with the arrival of more than
100 new prisoners, sent south by Sheriff Mel Bailey in Birmingham.
Bailey said that he hesitated to add to Sullivan's difficulties. But the
buildup of prisoners in the Jefferson County Jail promised to spawn
litigation *there* if nothing were done to reduce the population. A pattern
was developing. Jails across Alabama were funneling sentenced prisoners to Mt. Meigs far faster than that institution could absorb them.[26]

In early spring, Hale announced that prisoners had been on the
floor "for about four months." As yet, he said, there was "not much of
a discipline problem. . . . " But that was "probably because the men . . .
[were] new in prison" and the weather had been "pleasant." During the
approaching summer, he warned, "things [would] probably get pretty

bad." In June, Warden Long reported that more than 200 prisoners had slept on the floor the night before and that a riot might be triggered "at any time." In July, a press release warned that Mt. Meigs had "long passed the danger stage and that the likelihood of serious trouble at the prison [was increasing] with each additional inmate forced into the vastly overcrowded institution." Four days later, nineteen inmates were injured in an outbreak of violence.[27]

Newspaper reporters invited into the prisons elaborated on the conditions there. Ted Bryant of the *Birmingham Post Herald* reported that prisoners were served "thin slices of a tasteless, compacted corn-bread, turnip greens so tough they threatened injury to the gums, peas that seemed to be cooked in a sweet, greasy jelly and dried lima beans." The authorities explained that the system's farmlands could produce better provisions for prisoners, but that cash crops were grown instead to be sold for needed revenues. The *Herald* reacted with an editorial warning that if Sullivan's message were ignored there would certainly be riots and that, in the end, "the federal courts [would] step in with additional orders to clean up the present conditions." The *Eastern Shore Courier* expressed the hope that it would not be "violence and bloodshed" that would finally awaken the state to "the problems of our prisons." The *Advertiser* compared Alabama's prisons to Devil's Island.[28]

The media were not hesitant to name the officials with the duty and responsibilty to take action. The *Birmingham News* declared that George Wallace should finally "take an interest" in the prison system and see that it was properly funded. The *Mobile Register* reported that one of the visitors at Mt. Meigs had said in an aside that "[i]t wouldn't help Gov. Wallace's presidential aspirations if another Attica were to take place in Alabama." Primary attention, however, centered on the legislature. Few legislators attended the tours, and those who did were unwilling to commit themselves publicly to expensive reform measures.[29]

Sullivan offered specific proposals for change—addressed primarily to the crowding issue. On one level, he tried to reduce the sentences of some inmates and to obtain more space for all. Thus he asked that pris-oners be credited on their sentences for time spent in jail awaiting trial and that a new facility for the "criminally insane" be established to house mentally disturbed inmates. He also suggested that abandoned school buildings, an old ordnance plant near Childersburg, and an air base at Courtland should be refurbished for use by the penal system. Politics always controlled, however, and the suitability of any particular structure for use as a prison was routinely subordinated to the predilections of citizens living nearby. Courtland residents, for example, insisted that they would rather have a nuclear power plant in their neighborhood. One other possibility for absorbing the system's burgeoning population was taken more seriously. For years prior to the 1970s, the Alabama Highway Department had operated road camps at which prisoners were employed. Road gangs had been abandoned so recently that some of the facilities were still in existence and might accommodate prisoners, whether or not inmates maintained the public roads. In fact, Sullivan argued that at least a part of his current population problem stemmed from the closing of the road camps without alternative housing for the prisoners concerned. The possibility of reopening some of the camps was discussed in various quarters, but the Alabama Highway Department refused to agree to any such plan. In the end, Sullivan was forced to ask Wallace and the legislature for funds to build at least one new prison.[30]

On another level, the commissioner attempted to persuade state officials and the public to abandon Alabama's heavy reliance on large, rural prisons and to explore alternative penal policies. He said he hoped local judges would make greater use of probation, that restitution would be substituted for incarceration in property crime cases, and that more "half-way house-type programs" would be established for nondangerous offenders. He said he favored a thorough review of state sentencing policies at all levels, to the end that the prison system might receive fewer prisoners to hold for shorter terms. In the same vein, Dr. Staton declared that "work release" centers such as those established under the authority of the legislation sponsored by Maston Mims constituted the "only hope" for reducing the population in the state's major prisons.

Sullivan was gambling. He meant to establish in a public way that conditions in the prisons were bad and getting worse and thus to characterize the claim in *James* as unrealistic. He insisted that rehabilitative opportunities for prisoners were impossible in the present circumstances. With "neither the space nor the personnel," he could not hope to provide any such programs. In this, the commissioner was modestly successful. Most editorials accepted the argument that serious discussion of rehabilitation was premature. At the same time, Sullivan understood well enough that the bad publicity he deliberately generated essentially conceded the key factual points that Segall was making in *Pugh*. He acknowledged that he had little defense against claims of that kind. Indeed, the only defense he offered publicly was that he was doing his "best" with what he had. To underscore the point, Larry Newman proposed that if something were not done soon, the state would have to turn "murderers, bank robbers and rapers [*sic*] . . . out on the streets." Finally, at least, Sullivan's own concern had captured his lawyers' attention. In February, Lamar assumed responsibility for the *James* case and, in short order, the defense in both *Pugh* and *James* took on a serious cast not previously in evidence.[31]

As spring wore on and the lawsuits churned toward trial, some movement was discernible in Montgomery. Dr. Staton reported that Wallace had promised to address the board's many needs. And, in due course, the governor recommended that the legislature set aside $2 million in each of the next two years to be used for capital construction. He allotted the board another $6 million in a new state bond issue. In the legislature, a new Joint Interim Committee was formed to take up Sullivan's proposals. Chaired by Senator George D. H. McMillan, Jr., of Birmingham, and including Representative Brooks Hines, the new committee demonstrated surprising enthusiasm, prompting one reporter to ask whether there was "a new awareness" in Montgomery regarding the prisons. Not everyone was so optimistic. The *Birmingham News* recalled that similar groups in the past had made little progress against the inertia elsewhere in the government. McMillan's committee managed to push a few bills through a special session, notwithstanding Wallace's failure to support them. One permitted state prisoners to serve sentences in federal prisons; another, following Sullivan's suggestion, granted prisoners credit for time spent in jail pending trial; still another authorized the release of prisoners having ninety days or less remaining to serve.[32]

Even as Sullivan's efforts enjoyed moderate success in the Alabama legislature, reversals on three other fronts undercut his campaign to use the special focus on Alabama's prisons in 1975 to advance his proposals. To begin, the Alabama Advisory Committee to the U.S. Commission on Civil Rights published its highly critical report in April. The charges and recommendations struck heavy blows against a prison system housing a large proportion of black prisoners. This notwithstanding that Governor Wallace had recently appointed Dr. Marion Carroll, a black dentist, to be the Board of Corrections' next chairman. At a meeting with the board, one of the advisory committee's members, Father Albert S. Foley, exchanged rhetoric with Dr. Staton, and the result was hard feelings all around—undercutting Sullivan's purpose to obtain public support.[33]

Then there was the proposal by Cutter Laboratories in California, which asked to purchase blood from Alabama prisoners. Suitts and

Myers urged the board to reject the idea, primarily because the peculiar circumstances of prison inmates would render their participation inherently involuntary. Attorney General Baxley also expressed doubts, and the board ultimately rejected the plan without lengthy discussion. Coincidently, however, the plan was in the news just as George Taylor was urging Ira DeMent to become involved in *James*. Taylor was increasingly concerned that his own and Bronstein's efforts would be inadequate and pressed DeMent to participate in order to have the benefit of the federal government's enormous resources. DeMent requested authorization to "get involved immediately." His chief reason, curiously enough, was not that conditions in the prisons justified federal participation, but that the Cutter Labs "blood sucking" proposal required forceful federal opposition. Officials at the Justice Department acquiesced, and, paradoxically, the short-lived and otherwise inconsequential blood plasma plan was in large measure responsible for the introduction of the local U.S. attorney into the *James* litigation.[34]

DeMent's involvement was not without controversy in the plaintiffs' camp. There were advantages. Resources *were* in short supply, and DeMent could recruit the FBI to service. Segall pointed out in addition that DeMent could summon the Environmental Protection Agency (EPA) to support the charge that the Alabama prisons posed health and safety hazards. Desperate as he was for assistance, however, Taylor looked on the FBI with suspicion. In the ordinary course of business, agents were allied with state law enforcement authorities. In this instance, then, they would be asked to make inquiries about officials they knew personally. Taylor worried, accordingly, that they might not bring to the task a full measure of enthusiasm. Bronstein and Myers shared Taylor's concern about the FBI and extended it to other federal agencies. They balked, for example, at DeMent's suggestion that the U.S. Bureau of Prisons be asked to evaluate the Alabama prison system. While the bureau had no direct stake in the state institutions under attack, federal penal authorities might see their own facilities and, indeed, themselves as the Prison Project's next targets. The threat of one day being in Sullivan's place might motivate federal officers to defend even poor conditions in Alabama. The proposal to ask the EPA to survey the prison system raised similar concerns. In the end, neither federal agency was asked for assistance.[35]

DeMent's personality also generated conflict. In the eyes of some, he lacked discipline. He tended to go his own way without consulting the other lawyers and addressing their concerns. Myers found him frankly "unpredictable" and, for that reason, threatening to what otherwise was a thoughtful and efficient enterprise. At some point, DeMent might break ranks and lead Judge Johnson in the wrong direction. Bronstein did not share those concerns. If DeMent became difficult, Bronstein anticipated that he could prevail on friends in Washington to rein him in. At any rate, any risks associated with DeMent's impetuous ways were outweighed by the suspicion, shared by all the other lawyers, that he enjoyed a special relationship with Judge Johnson. If DeMent did not actually discuss the cases with the judge, the others believed he was at least in a better position than they to appraise Johnson's reaction to developments. Accordingly, his participation was invaluable. This last may have rested more on hope than on evidence. DeMent does not recall discussing the prison cases with Johnson; those who thought he was a conduit to the judge may have been mistaken.[36]

A third setback in mid-March was not so unambiguously frustrating to Sullivan as the civil rights commission report and the Cutter Labs episode. In a new decision, *McCray v. Sullivan*,[37] the Fifth Circuit Court of Appeals reversed a judgment by a district judge in Mobile, Judge Brevard Hand, in which Hand had rebuffed prisoners' complaints regarding crowding, violence, and poor medical care at Holman and Fountain. On the one hand, the circuit's action lent support to the plaintiffs in *Pugh* and *James*. Many of their allegations had now been acknowledged by the appeals court to warrant serious attention. On the other, the circuit court sent the *McCray* case back to Judge Hand—who probably would not be sympathetic. After all, Hand had previously disposed of these very issues in summary fashion; that is why the circuit court had reversed him. Even if he now held hearings under order, the results might well be dissatisfying. Judge Hand scheduled hearings to begin in June, and it seemed that he might well rush ahead of Johnson, decide overlapping questions, and issue an order favorable to the defense before *Pugh* and *James* came to trial. Such a judgment and order might bar further proceedings on the same questions in Montgomery.

Ultimately, this incident, too, proved to hold no value for state authorities. For when Judge Hand began to hear evidence, his reaction stirred events in an unexpected direction. Holman and Fountain were housing twice the number of prisoners for which they were designed, and violence, particularly homosexual rape, could not be controlled. At the conclusion of a single day's trial, Hand informed the state's attorneys that if they could not rebut the testimony he had heard, he was prepared to enter an order forbidding the authorities to admit more inmates to either facility until the population in each was reduced to "design capacity." That statement "shocked" state officials but, in further proceedings a short time later, Sullivan confessed that his four major institutions were now holding 1500 more inmates than they were intended to accommodate and that his staff was far too thin to keep order.[38]

At that, Judge Hand concluded that something must be done. He blamed neither Sullivan nor the board--nor Governor Wallace, whom he did not mention. In Hand's view, the fault lay with the legislature, and to drive that point home he threatened a stringent decree if the legislature did not provide needed funds in its current session. He scheduled yet another hearing for August 29 and ordered Sullivan, the members of the Board of Pardons and Paroles, the Superintendent of Education, and the commanding general of the Alabama National Guard to appear. The parole board might, of course, release prisoners earlier and in that way alleviate crowding; the superintendent might make abandoned schools available to house prisoners; the National Guard might supply other facilities, including military tents, to be used on a "temporary basis." Paradoxically, Judge Hand's delay was fatal to his participation in later events. By August 29, Judge Johnson's work in *Pugh* and *James* had overtaken Hand's treatment of *McCray*. An order entered jointly on that day collapsed the *McCray* case into the others, terminating Hand's involvement for any significant further purpose.[39]

The task of preparing the *Pugh* and *James* cases for trial was painstaking. On the plaintiffs' side, Myers prepared formal written questions, called *interrogatories,* and requests for concessions, called *stipulations,* to be put to Lamar and Newman, as well as questionnaires to be sent to prison inmates. Taylor visited the institutions frequently and collected letters, notebooks, and similar documents suggesting the testimony that individual inmates might provide. His appearance in the halls was a constant reminder that the lawsuits, in which all prisoners had some stake, were still alive and moving toward trial—when, prisoners hoped, the truth about their plight would finally be uncovered. All the Alabamians, and occasionally Myers, conducted formal interviews, called *depositions,* with prison authorities and other potential defense witnesses, in order to learn what their testimony would be at trial. Lamar was accommodating. He made arrangements for the plaintiffs' lawyers and expert witnesses to tour the prisons and provided information of various kinds on an informal basis. He answered most interrogatories in the time requested and agreed to hundreds of factual stipulations describing prison conditions. Some of those stipulations, such as Lamar's acknowledgment of the number of inmates the major institutions were designed to house, did serious damage to the defense. But Lamar saw nothing to be gained by forcing the plaintiffs to present formal proof of matters that no one could reasonably contest, and he anticipated that, if he insisted that the plaintiffs do unnecessary work, he would only anger Judge Johnson—a man who would not suffer gladly the antics of querulous advocates. The development of evidence thus proceeded efficiently through the spring and summer.[40]

Some of the information provided by state officials was defensive, but a fair share of the materials obtained prior to trial actually aided the prisoners' cause. Individual officials, including Sullivan and Staton, were unwilling to defend the most egregious conditions. Sullivan conceded that the system was grossly overpopulated and was operating "in the red." He could not afford to provide more space or to hire more guards to meet the growing tensions among inmates. Violence, he confessed, was likely in the circumstances. Staton conceded similar points and, in a revealing exchange with Taylor, he offered his own, and perhaps the board's, response to the rehabilitation claim in *James.* Staton declared that prisoners required "moral" reform. That attitude, which gave little weight to circumstantial causes of crime and placed emphasis instead on the individual's blameworthiness, ultimately explained Alabama's penal policies, whatever the level of financial support from the legislature.[41]

Ralph Knowles pursued another means of bringing the severity of prison conditions home to Judge Johnson; he hired a professional photographer who toured the institutions and prepared an album of photographs to which the plaintiffs' expert witnesses could refer during their testimony. Other judges had been known to visit prisons personally to see for themselves whether conditions were really so bad, but Johnson resisted, ostensibly because he preferred to rest judgment on evidence that would be available to the Fifth Circuit should there be an appeal. Accordingly, Knowles hoped to provide the judge with the next best thing—graphic pictures of prisoners' living quarters. The scheme worked extremely well. At various times during trial, Johnson was seen examining relevant pictures as witnesses were testifying.[42]

The other lawyers concentrated on the expert witnesses who would explain to the judge what the pictures revealed. Segall decided to call Robert Sarver, then on the faculty at the University of Arkansas, but formerly director of the Arkansas Department of Corrections. In the paradoxical fashion of legal proceedings, Sarver's name had been forever attached to the infamous Arkansas prison case, *Holt v. Sarver,* even though he had become the primary defendant in that case after being hired to address the problems identified in court. Roy Haber had worked with Sarver before and urged him on Segall as an experienced professional who would be persuasive to Judge Johnson. In Washington, Myers selected John Boone, then at Boston University and formerly commissioner of corrections in Massachusetts; William G. Nagel, then at the American Foundation and formerly associate superintendent of the New Jersey Correctional Institution; John Conrad, then at the Academy for Contemporary Problems and formerly a research specialist for the Law Enforcement Assistance Administration and the California Department of Corrections; and Norval Morris, dean of the University of Chicago Law School. Taylor and Knowles selected Dr. Carl Clements, a faculty member at the University of Alabama and a member of Ray Fowler's staff, and another local psychologist, Dr. John M. McKee, who had served as a consultant to one of the human rights committees appointed in *Wyatt*. Most of the experts toured the Alabama institutions in August. Curiously, and in this respect his docile attitude *was* injurious to the defense, Lamar did not interview the plaintiffs' experts prior to trial. His failure to do so arguably led him to underestimate the power of the testimony those witnesses would give. In turn, that miscalculation may explain why Lamar listened to so much damaging testimony before conceding defeat.[43]

The tours were often eventful. Professionals had only to pass through the institutions, examine records, and talk to prisoners and staff to conclude that conditions in Alabama were much worse than any they had seen elsewhere. The experts were not dismayed by what they saw; they were shocked. After visiting the deplorable punishment cells at Fountain, Clements found it impossible merely to take notes for future reference. He pressed Myers to write an angry letter to Lamar, complaining that he had found as many as five men confined in a single cell—when nearby cells were empty. The letter insisted that Sullivan be notified immediately and that something be done to "rectify [the] situation administratively." The lawyers were alarmed as well and none more than Ira DeMent, who took up David Tanner's cause when he initiated his independent lawsuit in early summer. The results of the experts' tours demonstrated that the situation at Mt. Meigs was deteriorating just as rapidly as Sullivan maintained. Johnson's response was to appoint DeMent amicus curiae "with full rights of a party" in the *Tanner* case. The U.S. attorney now worked even more closely with Taylor and Segall, developing evidence useful to all plaintiffs and permitting his office in Montgomery, only one floor above Judge Johnson's courtroom, to serve as a base of operations for lawyers in town for the cases.[44]

At approximately the same time, DeMent attempted something more dramatic. Concerned with the problems developing in local jails, now overflowing with prisoners bound for Mt. Meigs, he attempted to squeeze state authorities from both directions at once. Even as he and the others attacked Sullivan and the Board of Corrections for crowding at the state penitentiaries, DeMent attempted to challenge the conditions in local jails in a single, class action lawsuit in Judge Johnson's court. He proposed to expand the plaintiff class in *Adams v. Mathis,*[45] a pending case involving only the Houston County Jail in Dothan, to include every jail prisoner in Alabama and, in an even more dramatic maneuver, to name all the state's sheriffs as defendants. The sheriffs, for their part, actually approved DeMent's action, understanding that they were sued only as a matter of form and that the real targets of the plan were state officials who controlled the state prisons and the distribution of state funds—badly needed locally. Judge Johnson, however, decided that it would be inappropriate to entertain a single lawsuit touching so many facilities at once. Although it was widely conceded that most jails were at least crowded, the judge could not assume that they were so similar in other respects that evidence regarding some could be taken as evidence regarding all. Accordingly, Johnson appointed DeMent as amicus in *Adams,* but he refused to permit that lawsuit to cover all 200 of Alabama's local jails. In consequence, DeMent, and several Justice Department lawyers, among them Steve Whinston, were forced to litigate in Alabama on a jail-by-jail basis. They focused their attention on *Adams* and another case, *Thomas v. Gloor,*[46] involving the Jefferson County Jail. Elsewhere, private attorneys and the ACLU carried the load.[47]

All this proved too much for L. B. Sullivan, who resigned in late July. In one motion, the board agreed to Sullivan's request to be appointed deputy commissioner for the remainder of the year and appointed the current deputy, Judson Locke, Jr., to succeed him as commissioner. On the same day, Attorney General Baxley assailed the legislature for failing to respond to Sullivan's request for funds. Echoing Larry Newman's earlier statement, Baxley warned that, if something were not done soon, his staff would be unable to defend the prison system at the upcoming trial. As to Sullivan, he was sympathetic. Six months later, the former commissioner joined Baxley's staff as an investigator. Sullivan remained at the Board of Corrections only long enough to testify in *Pugh* and *James* and to make one last plea for a larger budget. He was addressing the legislature on the day the trial opened at the other end of Dexter Avenue.[48]

The prisoners' lawyers met in the U.S. attorney's office for a strategy session on August 6. DeMent gave the impression that he had talked to Johnson and understood that the judge was prepared to "do something." Here again, the recurring suspicion that DeMent had Johnson's ear encouraged the other lawyers. They discussed the witnesses that each would call at trial, the bits and pieces of evidence that still remained to be collected, and a few important assignments of responsibility. DeMent promised to send FBI agents to Mt. Meigs to gather last minute information on the assault rate there and to contact Norman Carlson, director of the U.S. Bureau of Prisons, to ensure that no federal penal authorities would testify for the defense. Bronstein agreed to prepare a draft motion for immediate relief in anticipation that the plaintiffs might wish to demand some instructions to state officials promptly on the conclusion of the trial. He also agreed to prepare a draft motion to name the members of the Board of Pardons and Paroles and the Alabama State Board of Education, the state treasurer, and the comptroller as additional defendants. If Lamar raised the familiar excuse that the penal system lacked the money needed to make improvements, the prisoners' lawyers would be prepared to broaden their net to reach authorities who controlled the state's purse strings.[49]

It remained only to file pretrial briefs to delineate the issues on which evidence would be supplied. Segall stated his thesis very much in the way he had previously.

> Incarceration is the punishment established by law. Correction officials are not entitled to add to that punishment more than what, as a practical matter, are necessary concomitants of incarceration. Certainly, then, to place a prisoner in an environment where reasonable care will furnish him not even a likelihood of protection and safety from his fellow inmates, in and of itself, constitutes cruel and unusual punishment.

Segall concentrated on the circumstances bringing about violence, steering clear of anything that might be construed as an attempt to second-guess penal policies in general. "For purposes of injunctive relief," he declared, "the only question for this Court to determine is whether conditions at Atmore constitute cruel and unusual punishment." To make that determination, Johnson should consider evidence with respect to crowding, classification, staffing, and various other matters, including the "lack of rehabilitation programs." In sum, the plaintiffs in *Pugh* should win if prisoners' living of conditions, taken in cumulative effect, produced a pattern of violence against which inmates were constitutionally entitled to protection.

Taylor took a different route in *James.*

> [I]t has been the plaintiffs' contention throughout this litigation that the real issues go much deeper than correction of inadequate plumbing, though that must be done, or improvement in education, vocational, and counselling programs, though that, too, needs to be made. Reformation of the entire system must be made to eliminate all conditions which cause a deterioration of those persons who enter the system.

The basic proposition was, of course, the idea that Judge Johnson had accepted in the blueprint opinion a year earlier. Taylor claimed that inmates were constitutionally entitled to improve themselves if they chose to do so; prison conditions that frustrated self-improvement and, indeed, caused deterioration could not be sustained. This contention, like Segall's, focused attention on a rigorous investigation of conditions at each of Alabama's institutions, with success under the Eighth Amendment turning on just how bad prisoners' circumstances actually were.

The restraint evidenced in the memoranda filed by Segall and Taylor was in contrast to the pretrial brief offered by Bronstein and Myers for the National Prison Project, which took responsibility for raising more dramatic contentions that all the lawyers on the plaintiffs' side of the cases wished to put before the court. By agreement, Bronstein and Myers bowed steeply at the outset to Johnson's blueprint opinion, extracting from it several overlapping claims on which the plaintiffs were entitled to relief. They cited a hopelessly inadequate system for classifying prisoners, the absence of facilities for elderly and emotionally disturbed inmates, the assignment of prisoners to housing units in which they were subjected to violent assault, and unreasonable restrictions on visitation between inmates and their families and friends. Then came the heart of *James*—the Eighth Amendment argument that prisoners were entitled to living conditions in which self-improvement was possible. First, Bronstein and Myers promised Judge Johnson evidence that the conditions in Alabama's prisons were intolerable, as measured by any reasonable standard. In this, they reiterated the offers of proof made by Segall and Taylor. Second, however, Bronstein and Myers condemned other aspects of the prison system.

> Almost all of the prisoners in Alabama are incarcerated in large, rural prisons, subject to a maximum amount of regimentation and a minimum amount of independence, far from family and friends, far from the com-

munity to which they will inevitably return, and forced to spend the over-whelming majority of their time idle, living in large dormitories with no privacy and in constant fear of assault.

[M]erely improving [these] conditions will not be sufficient to rem-edy the Constitutional violations of the rights of the plaintiff class. The fundamental issues raised . . . will not be resolved by simply improving the sanitary conditions, or the quality of medical care, increasing the number of vocational, educational, social and psychological programs and remedying the overcrowded situation in the major prisons in Ala-bama. The problems inherent in incarceration in [Alabama's prisons] necessitate fundamental changes in the Alabama prison system.

This went well beyond Segall's contention that prisoners were enti-tled to protection and beyond Taylor's argument that prisoners were entitled to an opportunity to improve themselves. The National Prison Project proposed precisely what Judge Johnson hesitated to undertake: a judicial inquiry into underlying penal policies adopted by Sullivan and the Board of Corrections. The point was explicit: "The very exis-tence of the present Alabama prison system is what is being chal-lenged. . . ." This surely was an occasion, and an important one, on which lawyers acting on behalf of prison inmates served notice of a frontal assault on Alabama penal practices taken as a whole. This liti-gation, they declared, was meant to produce a judicial decree that would order state authorities to abandon reliance on incarceration in large, rural, secure prisons and to develop alternative responses to crime.

Lamar and Newman answered with a memorandum of their own, which moved quickly through the issues raised by Segall and Taylor, conceding deficiencies on occasion but denying that any conditions dipped beneath the constitutional floor. Then the defense lawyers turned to the National Prison Project's arguments and met them squarely.

[T]he battlelines of this case will be drawn along an attack not merely on the prison system in Alabama, but upon the traditional American sys-tem of incarcerating people for crimes. . . .

Rehabilitation may be a purpose of a prison, but it is not the only purpose, and society, through its elected officials, has the right to deter-mine what it shall do about those who steal, murder, main [*sic*], rape and rob. It is not a province of a Court to say that because traditional incar-ceration does not rehabilitate prisoners, traditional incarceration should be abolished. . . .

Even assuming that alternatives to incarceration would more effec-tively achieve the goal of rehabilitation, the Courts have no authority

under the Constitution to decide what methods the State should use in
accomplishing its corrective goals and purposes.

Lamar and Newman meant to protest an explicit inquiry into the advisability and efficacy of Alabama penal policy. If the National Prison Project turned the litigation in that direction, they hoped, first, to convince
Johnson of their clients' attempts to make improvements and, second,
to underscore the risks of judging the wisdom of policies unrelated to
the physical conditions of confinement.

After more than a year of preparation, the *Pugh* and *James* cases were
ready for trial. The lawsuits presented conflicts on three levels. First,
the parties were fiercely divided on the essentially political question
whether penal authorities could shift responsibility for poor conditions
to the legislature. While the plaintiffs contended that neither Sullivan's
alleged good faith nor the board's inadequate budget was relevant to the
legal issues at bar, the defendants insisted that Judge Johnson must
acknowledge that many of the system's deficiencies could and would be
remedied voluntarily if sufficient funds were available. The debate at
this level, initiated in *Newman,* promised to extend well beyond the
present context and to influence events and behavior for years. Second,
the parties were just as sharply divided over the extent to which Segall
and Taylor could write the propositions in their two cases into the
Eighth Amendment. Segall's argument that poor conditions produced
violence and Taylor's contention that prisoners could not be denied an
opportunity to rehabilitate themselves were problematic as matters of
policy. The plaintiffs' project to establish them in constitutional law was
still more vexing. The apparent conflict between the parties on the third
level, the dispute over the propriety of examining the wisdom of Alabama's penal policies apart from the physical conditions in the state
prisons, was in large measure misleading, even false. Notwithstanding
the grand manner of the National Prison Project's brief and the sweeping vision it called forth, any suggestion of altering state penal policy so
fundamentally had already been rejected in Judge Johnson's blueprint
opinion. Viewed realistically, the attempt to set the court's sights
higher, albeit prior to the opening of trial, was already too late. Events
immediately following demonstrated as much. All the rhetoric, all the
imagination, all the emotion embedded in that pretrial brief were subordinated at trial to the pedestrian effort to establish the deplorable
physical conditions in the prisons. Once the litigation was focused on
physical conditions, larger aspirations receded into insignificance—not
to be explicitly revived.

4

Denouement

Judge Johnson presided at trial in the firm style for which he was famous. Anyone in the room must be vitally concerned with the business at hand; marshals instructed spectators to stop talking and put aside newspapers. The judge peered down at the proceedings over glasses that seemed to slip lower as the hours passed. Occasionally, he rose, stood behind his chair, or walked back and forth behind the bench—perhaps to encourage circulation, perhaps to register disapproval. Johnson showed no favorites. He was severe with all the lawyers, intending, as he had throughout his career, to strike an intimidating posture in order to foster the appropriate decorum in his courtroom. By contrast, he was extremely cordial to witnesses. Johnson understood that the expert witnesses had inconvenienced themselves to testify and made it clear that he appreciated their efforts. If anything, the judge was even more sensitive to the prisoners whom Taylor and Segall brought to Montgomery. Unlike other judges, who preferred to maintain tight security when prison inmates were in court, Johnson allowed no distracting precautionary measures. During trial, Worley James and another named plaintiff in the *James* case, William Campbell, were in the custody of federal marshals. Yet there were no handcuffs, no chains. At recesses, James and Campbell joined everyone else in the corridor outside. Inmates called to testify were also well treated. In was inconceivable that anyone, even a convicted felon, would dare disturb proceedings before Judge Johnson. The marshals anticipated that prisoners would behave themselves, and they did.[1]

The gallery was typically crowded. Many employees of the Board of Corrections were in attendance. And, of course, the press was represented in strength. Local newspaper and television reporters were eclipsed at times by camera crews from the national networks and special correspondents for the *New York Times* and the *Wall Street Jour-*

nal. Public opinion regarding the testimony was important to both sides. To ensure that reporters accurately registered the significance of the proceedings as they progressed, Steve Suitts and Al Bronstein routinely made themselves available at recesses. This was the formal test of the case against the Alabama prison system. Future events were ever affected by the testimony at this lengthy trial, the strategies chosen by the two sides and, certainly, Judge Johnson's judgment and injunctive order, which followed the trial by six months.[2]

When proceedings opened on Wednesday, August 20, Segall's first witness was Horace C. Sutterer, one of several inmates and former inmates whose shocking testimony established emotional momentum in the trial's early hours. Sutterer had been convicted of minor drug offenses and had served only a year in prison. Yet he had been assigned to most of the institutions in the system. Now a college student in Birmingham, he was able to reflect on his experience in a credible, convincing manner. He recalled that designated inmates, called "strikers," were given supervisory authority over other inmates in the agricultural fields adjacent to G. K. Fountain and that, when recalcitrant prisoners refused to work, the "strikers" assaulted them with "hoe handles," "broomsticks," or "home-made knives." Other prisoners, called "flunkies," had responsibility for breaking up fights in the dormitories. The guards, according to Sutterer, dared not enter large dormitories at night and preferred to rely on armed flunkies to keep order. That, in turn, allowed flunkies to have their way with other prisoners afraid to challenge them on their rounds. The influence of money in the system was dramatic. It was possible, according to Sutterer, to purchase virtually anything—drugs, weapons, women. Prisoners responded to the need for funds by developing ingenious schemes to earn it. Sutterer himself had ghostwritten term papers and taken tests for some guards. There were other things, gruesome things. Sutterer said that a rat had once been found in a vat of food, that sexual violence was common, and that most prisoners he knew carried makeshift weapons for self-protection.

Another inmate-witness, Jimmy Mason, confirmed most of Sutterer's testimony. Under questioning by Taylor, he said he had seen rapes and other episodes of violence at Mt. Meigs, worked in the fields at Fountain under the eyes of mounted guards with shotguns, and spent several weeks in the punishment cells at Holman. These last, according to Mason, were much like the cells in the doghouse at Draper; that is, there were no beds, no mattresses, no lavatories or toilets. Prisoners sat naked on the floor in tiny cells opened only once each day for a meager meal. Later, Mason had been placed in the "lockup" at Holman, where he was kept in a "cage cell" for twenty-four hours a day, with one hour a week free for exercise in an adjacent yard called the "sun parlor." He had been transferred to Fountain after violence broke out in the Holman lockup, and he had witnessed guards beating the inmates responsible. There, in midwinter, the windows had been broken in the dormitory, and there were no blankets. He slept on a concrete slab, and at night saw rats "as big as cats." From Fountain, Mason had been sent to a "road camp" at Troy, Alabama, where he had narrowly escaped being stabbed in the back, to Mt. Meigs again, and then back to Fountain— where he finally was stabbed by another inmate. He recalled being awakened on another occasion by an inmate pleading for his life as he was chased around Mason's bunk.

It is questionable whether these "horror stories" from prisoners were effective. Segall speculates that Judge Johnson may have discounted inmate testimony entirely or, at least, preferred to rest on evidence given by others. In particular, the judge may have doubted the testimony of a third inmate-witness, whose explosive testimony caused such concern even to the lawyers that he was asked to pass a polygraph test before taking the stand. Known in the prison system as "Big John," the witness acknowledged that he was one of the flunkies or strikers described by Sutterer. Armed with a knife, he had patrolled the dormitories and supervised inmates in the fields. Big John described routine violence of all kinds—assaults by some prisoners on others and beatings at the hands of other flunkies or the guards themselves. He accused one warden of ordering him to keep frightened prisoners in their cells and to "knock the shit out of" anyone found out of his cell. He accused another of threatening to kill George Dobbins the night of the riot at Fountain and of permitting the guards to club prisoners after the melee that took Dobbins' life. And he accused still another of using him as a household servant, sometimes grilling beef stolen from the institution kitchen. This testimony, if believed, made explicit what earlier evidence had only suggested. Men with important administrative positions in the Alabama prison system were now associated with the deliberate, in some instances criminal, mistreatment of inmates in their charge.[3]

Judge Johnson was almost certainly moved by the testimony of a fourth inmate, a 20-year-old prisoner whom the parties conceded to be "mentally retarded."[4] This inmate had been found and prepared to testify by Ira DeMent. Now, in open court and in time for the afternoon headlines, the prisoner delivered the most gripping testimony of the trial. Convicted of burglary and sent to prison for three years, he became a victim on the very day he arrived at Mt. Meigs.

DEMENT: Would you tell the court, please, what happened?

WITNESS: Well, I—when I was sent to my cell . . . there was a black male came up there . . . and asked me where I was from and that he wanted to talk to me . . . and asked me will I come down to his cell. . . . So I went to his cell . . . he started talking about having sex with me, and I said no. And he said well, we are going to have sex with you anyway, and I said no again. Then I left and went back to my cell. . . .

DEMENT: Where were the guards?

WITNESSES: I don't know. . . . Well, after I went back to my cell there . . . another guy came up there, what they call Conversation . . . grabbed ahold of my wrist and led me to the next cell. And inside the cell there was an older black male, inside the cell there, and asked me to pull off my clothes and I say no. . . . And the one they call Conversation said that he had a knife and he wouldn't mind using it on me. So, naturally that scared me a little bit more so I pulled off my clothes.

DEMENT: What occurred then?

WITNESS: Then they continued to rape me.

DEMENT: How many of them raped you?

WITNESS: Four. . . .

DEMENT: Where were the guards all this time?

WITNESS: I don't know. . . .

DEMENT: Now, were you ever beaten up . . . ?

WITNESS: Yes, sir. . . . By a white inmate . . . started beating on me and said that he don't like fuckboys and snitches. . . .

DEMENT: Where were the guards at that time?

WITNESS: I don't know. . . . And then he tore part of his cover off his blanket, . . . put it around my neck, was going to hang me . . . tore it down like that in a strip, . . . put it around my neck. . . .

DEMENT: Where did he put the other end?

WITNESS: Around the bars.

DEMENT: Did he pull it tight?

WITNESS: Yes, sir. . . . And that's when the other guy . . . said don't
           do that, you know, don't . . . hang him. . . . [A]nd then [he]
           was talking about making some money off of me right
           there in that cellblock and that they would take care of
           me. . . .

DEMENT: How were they going to make money off of you?

WITNESS: Selling me . . . sell my ass. . . .

DEMENT: Did you ever talk to the assistant warden out there about
           this?

WITNESS: Yes, sir. . . . He made a sarcastic question to me. He asked
           me did they get a little pussy. . . . I didn't, I didn't know
           what else to say to him but yes. And then he said there is
           nothing I can do. . . .

The courtroom was unusually quiet during and immediately following
this testimony. Participants and observers who had not previously been
touched personally by the evidence now felt the dread, and the utter
hopelessness, of a young man thrust into intolerable circumstances with
no recourse, no hope of rescue. There was nothing to be said. Lamar
tried unsuccessfully to get the witness to recall the name of the officer
who had been so callous, but he waived cross-examination. The other
lawyers sat in stunned silence. Then, slowly, they shuffled back to the
work at hand. Bronstein called the next witness and the trial continued.

The presentation of expert witnesses was for the most part successful and according to plan.[5] Their testimony placed in the record the
great body of evidence on which Judge Johnson based his findings of
fact. Under Segall's questioning, Sarver condemned the prison system
in blunt language. Fountain, he said, was "[v]ery, very dirty and unbe-
lievably overcrowded." Prisoners there existed in a "veritable jungle,"
living on food he could not "attempt" to eat himself. The officials with
whom he spoke were "defensive" and seemed to consider inmates
"something less than human." Black prisoners were routinely called
"niggers" by the guards. Conditions were not merely bad in Sarver's
telling. They were "terrible." Especially in the dormitories, where most
prisoners were held, Sarver found nothing to satisfy even minimal standards of decency: "The mattresses were old and filthy. The bedding was
filthy. The floor was dirty. It was a very unwholesome, demoralizing,
degrading and debilitating place to house human beings."

Crowding was an overriding concern. Sarver declared that every prison inmate should be allotted between sixty and eighty square feet of living space. Accordingly, dormitories at Fountain could accommodate approximately eighty, instead of 200 beds. Crowding contributed, in Sarver's telling, to the incidence of violence in the dormitories. Starved for privacy, prisoners hung sheets and towels down over lower bunks, making it impossible for guards to monitor what was happening in and behind those bunks. Even if that practice were banned, according to Sarver, the current system for maintaining order could not hope to be successful. Guard stations were few and poorly placed. On the day he visited Fountain, two officers had responsibility for supervising nearly 1000 prisoners. Verifying the testimony given by Sutterer and Mason, Sarver reported that the number of guards dwindled at night and that, for their own safety, those who were on duty did not venture into the dormitories after dark. At a minimum, Sarver told Judge Johnson, there should be two guards inside each dormitory, reinforced by other officers just outside the door and at other strategic locations.

Even if crowding in the dormitories were eliminated, Sarver went on, fundamental structural flaws would remain. Dormitories, he said, enjoyed no support within the profession: "It's a bad system. It's just cheap; cheap warehousing." The only safe use of dormitories, in his view, was for carefully screened prisoners who posed no risk of violence. Alabama had no rational program for the classification of prisoners and certainly had not screened the inmates assigned to dormitories at Fountain—or anywhere else. Prisoners were simply thrown together and left to settle among themselves the rights to a bed, a blanket, or a place in line for the rare urinal or toilet that would still flush. The only exceptions occurred in administrative segregation, where prisoners were held apart from the general population by their own request or for "mental problems." On his tour of those cells, Sarver came up on a teenaged prisoner whom he understood to be "badly mentally retarded." The young man had been there for some time, but had no idea why. For the run of prisoners, there was very simply no classification at all. Sarver was blunt: "There is no classification; there is no segregation; there is no maximum; there is no minimum in this system. They all do time side by side."

Beyond crowding and inadequate classification, Sarver complained about faulty plumbing and poor food. The kitchen at Fountain was particularly shocking; Sarver said he could not "imagine human beings trying to eat in that situation." His account of the Fountain version of the doghouse was sobering. Sarver had found five black prisoners in a cell not large enough for one. Once again, prisoners in punishment cells had no mattresses or bedding, no running water, and no toilet beyond a hole in the floor that a guard could flush from the outside. They were allowed to shower only once in eleven days. The captain of the guard actually seemed to be "proud" of that. In the end, Sarver said that the conditions in these cells were the worst he had ever seen, until he visited the doghouse at Draper.

Forced idleness, Sarver maintained, could not but cause inmates to deteriorate psychologically. Some prisoners, to be sure, worked in the argricultural fields in season; others were employed in clerical, janitorial, and similar capacities within the institutions; and a comparative few were enrolled in grossly inadequate educational and vocational programs. In the main, however, prisoners in the Alabama prison system were asked to do, and did, nothing—day after day, year after year. Prisoners were like "caged animals." Theirs, Sarver insisted, was a "demoralizing, debasing, degrading and ultimately destroying existence." To reduce the incidence of violence, the system should, at a minimum, provide prisoners with something to do, something to occupy their time and to keep them from dwelling on the fact of their incarceration.

Commenting more generally on the prison system in response to questioning by Myers, Sarver decried the way in which "aged and infirm" prisoners were housed in an upstairs dormitory at Draper, the absence of adequate educational, vocational, and recreational programs there, and the "negative attitude" of the staff. He insisted that 60 to 70 percent of the Alabama inmate population should not be in prison at all but should be housed in minimum security facilities in the community. He conceded that dangerous offenders must be kept apart from society; but he pointed out, by way of illustration, that murderers rarely repeated their crimes and posed no significant threat to the community on release. Finally, Sarver explained that rural whites recruited from small towns near the major institutions made poor supervisors for black prisoners and that the board should hire more black guards.

Carl Clements was equally effective. He had worked closely with Knowles in preparation for testimony that would explore conditions in the prison system in more detail than could be achieved through Sarver or other out-of-town witnesses who had spent only a short time in the institutions. Moreover, Clements could draw inferences from his own evidence and, like Sarver before him, give Judge Johnson his professional opinion about the effects of those conditions on inmates forced to endure them. Clements described shocking crowding in the dormitories and idleness relieved only by occasional assignments to the agricultural fields. That work was hard, and some prisoners escaped it by enrolling in bible-reading courses at the chapel—typically the only clean room available. Occasional rehabilitative programs were set apart from the "mainstream" of prison life and operated as "satellites," affecting few prisoners. A professional psychologist from Mobile was on the payroll, but he spent his limited time with emergency cases. And, of course, inmates seemed always to be heavily armed. As one prisoner explained to Clements, it was better to risk being caught with a weapon by a guard than to chance being caught without one by another prisoner.

Clements did praise Draper Prison's association with the J. F. Ingram Trade School, where some prisoners took vocational training. The number of inmates enrolled in that program was small, however, and Clements judged the enterprise grossly inadequate. He expressed the same view of the "token programming" at Holman Prison. The formal classification system at Mt. Meigs, developed by a former staff member, Hugh Swafford, was tolerable in design but frustrated in practice. Clements was astonished that prisoners' "adjustment" to life in the notorious North Dormitory was taken to be a fair measure of their ability generally to live peaceably with others. Relying heavily on that kind of information and little else, classification teams ignored their own procedures in a rush to move prisoners through the system. When Clements was there, the new director of classification, John E. Nagle, told him that forty men had been processed in only two hours—hardly long enough for deliberative decision-making. Classification touched on Clements' field of expertise and, to capitalize on that point, DeMent revived a maneuver he had used successfully in the *Newman* trial. He sent his deputy up to establish that, if asked, the Center for Correctional Psychology could design a classification scheme for the penal system— thus placing in the record at least one possibility for addressing the classification problem.

Other witnesses contributed important details. Walt Lindsey, a former classification officer, explained that Swafford had resigned when he was placed under the authority of the warden at Mt. Meigs, and, thereafter, Nagle had made classification a "rubber stamp" for the predilections of wardens. The warden at Frank Lee Youth Center, concededly the best institution in the system, now had authority to select prisoners for assignment to that facility. John McKee, a consultant to the Bryce Hospital human rights committee appointed in connection with *Wyatt,* reported that the facilities for "aged and infirm" prisoners at Draper reminded him of the "worst" of the wards at Bryce prior to the *Wyatt* order. John Boone gave a graphic description of the doghouse, and Bill

Nagel insisted that Alabama's prisons would be vastly crowded even if their population were reduced to what state authorities maintained was their "design capacity." Norval Morris and John Conrad blamed outrageous conditions on poor management and urged the appointment of a professional administrator to institute reforms.

More powerful testimony came from a surprising source. Theodore Gordon, a public health officer from the District of Columbia, delivered crushing blows to a prison system already reeling from the testimony of earlier witnesses. Gordon had no expertise in penal policy or mental health; he was a professional inspector of institutions who relied on standards established by the U.S. Public Health Service, supplemented by a widely followed handbook prepared for the U.S. Bureau of Prisons. He had toured each of the institutions in Alabama and now reported a laundry list of health and safety hazards throughout the system. Crowding, faulty wiring, inoperable plumbing, and inadequate waste disposal could only breed disease. Filth and vermin were everywhere. Aside from ubiquitous flies, Gordon reported mice in the food storage areas at Fountain and Draper, a bug "as big as a half dollar" being stirred into food at Draper, and roach infestations everywhere. There was never enough hot water to keep the institutions, particularly the kitchens, clean and free of disease. Prisoners had no eating utensils at Fountain, slept on the floor near leaking toilets at Draper and Mt. Meigs, and languished in their own feces in isolation at Draper and Holman. Poor lighting damaged prisoners' eyesight; poor ventilation promised airborne diseases; dirty mattresses guaranteed fungus diseases. Gordon wasted little time. In just the way he might have written a report in Washington, he ticked off hazard after hazard. Asked in the end for his conclusions regarding the institutions he had described, he was blunt. If he found facilities of this kind in the District of Columbia, he would have them closed as "unfit for human habitation." He frankly doubted whether the older structures, Fountain and Draper, could ever be brought up to minimal public health standards.

In planning a defense to the powerful case against the Alabama prison system, Bob Lamar was realistic. The plaintiffs' witnesses were effective, and he had no hope of rebutting their testimony regarding the physical conditions under which prisoners lived. Indeed, he had stipulated to some of the most damaging points prior to trial. The important issue now was the scope of the relief that would be awarded. Perhaps in consequence of that focus, Lamar's cross-examination of the plaintiffs' experts was rarely thorough, often inartful, and occasionally actually damaging to the defense. Even when he identified weaknesses in witnesses' testimony, those same witnesses were often able to convert unfriendly questions into opportunities to make points valuable to the plaintiffs.[6]

For example, Lamar forced Sarver to acknowledge that the institutions for which he had had responsibility in Arkansas also housed prisoners in dormitories, that, at the time, the Arkansas system had no classification officers at all, that he, too, had used primitive cells to discipline recalcitrant inmates, and that violence had been a serious problem in Arkansas just as it was still in Alabama. On this last point, however, Sarver embroidered his testimony with a description of "creepers"—Arkansas inmates who "creeped up on" other prisoners and stabbed them in their sleep. To avoid creepers, prisoners developed a defense—"catching the bars." They came to the front of the dormitories and stood there all night, grasping the bars in view of the guards. "It's not wise," Sarver said, "to sleep in one of those barracks if you have been threatened." Stories of this kind hardly undermined Sarver's testimony that prisoners should not be housed in dormitories. Similarly, Lamar established that Clements subscribed to the basic tenets of behavioral psychology popularized by B. F. Skinner and suggested that he faulted Alabama's "Christian" theory of penology only because it was inconsistent with his indiosyncratic perspective on good penal policy. The tactic was frustrated, however, when Judge Johnson himself asked whether rehabilitative programs were linked to prisoners' psychological state. That question permitted Clements to explain that human motivations for self-improvement could be frustrated by the absence of such opportunities, thus neatly tying the availability of prison programs to the theory in *James*.[7]

Judge Johnson interjected with his own questions on other occasions. For example, when Jimmy Mason described a dormitory at Fountain, Johnson pressed the inmate for the precise number of prisoners held there. On other occasions, Johnson interrupted to steer counsel in the direction he wished the trial to move. At times, he complained only of repetition. For example, when Myers asked Sarver whether the conditions at other institutions were similar to what he had seen at Fountain, the judge urged him to move on. Even in this, there was substantive significance. It was critical to the plaintiffs that Johnson should conclude that conditions were poor in all the prisons so that any relief awarded could reach the entire system. By cutting off questions touching other institutions, Johnson did not so much frustrate Myers' attempt to prove what he had to prove; the judge signaled that the evidence already offered was sufficient.

In still other instances, Johnson interrupted to foreclose counsel's attempts to explore issues that, in their judgment, were vital. Notwithstanding that he permitted Sarver to criticize the use of rural white guards to supervise urban black prisoners, the judge bristled at questions linking the location of the state's major insititutions to poor visiting opportunities. That line of questioning, he declared, would not "get [Myers'] Eighth Amendment case." The comment was ambiguous. Yet it suggested, once again, that Judge Johnson was not prepared to second-guess the state's policy of incarcerating offenders in large, rural prisons. He was interested primarily, perhaps exclusively, in the physical conditions of life *in* the institutions the state had chosen to employ. Johnson reacted in a like manner when DeMent and Bronstein ranged into sentencing and parole policy in their interrogation of John Conrad. When Bronstein replied that plaintiffs' counsel might yet name the Alabama parole authorities as defendants, Johnson nonetheless refused to hear testimony about what might be accomplished if parole policy were changed. In due course, he rejected Bronstein's motion to involve the parole board, and that body never assisted significantly in the drive to reduce Alabama's prisoner population.

Lamar also lost ground when he summoned John Braddy, now the prison system's planning coordinator, to explain to Judge Johnson that the highway department's decision to close the old road camps had exacerbated crowding in the prisons. Johnson showed interest in that issue and asked pointedly whether some of the camps might be reopened. In describing the work that would have to be done to refurbish the camps, however, Braddy mentioned that the National Advisory Commission on Criminal Justice Standards and Goals, appointed by President Nixon, had recently suggested that prisoners be accorded a minimum of eighty square feet of living space. Lamar recognized the danger and quickly asked Braddy whether floor space devoted to showers and recreational activities was included. Braddy read directly from the text, which referred explicitly to single rooms "with a floor area of at least eighty square feet." The judge gave his interpretation of that language on the spot: "That's talking about personal space."

With respect to other defense witnesses, Lamar's strategy was devoted to persuading Judge Johnson that the difficulties in the prison system did not warrant a sweeping judicial order to force change. He offered evidence calculated to assure the judge that the men in charge of the prison system were capable, responsible public officials who could be relied on to make needed improvements on their own, but with additional financial support. Lamar thus chose as his first witness the system's highest-ranking black administrator, Courtney B. Crenshaw, then directing a work release center for female offenders. The tactic was transparent and ultimately counterproductive, largely because Lamar asked Crenshaw about his earlier involvement in the employment of prison system employees. That opened the defense witness to a withering cross-examination, which demonstrated that those programs were fundamentally flawed. On direct examination, for example, Crenshaw said that new employees must now have a high school diploma, that he had attempted to recruit black applicants for prison jobs, and that a new training program promised to produce "correctional counselors" badly needed in Alabama's institutions. On cross-examination, he was forced to concede that current employees were exempted from the new educational requirements and that only ten percent of the staff held high school diplomas, that his efforts to recruit blacks had been largely unsuccessful, and that "correctional counselor" was only a "high sounding name for a guard." Most important, Crenshaw acknowledged that most of the new training program was devoted to law enforcement skills unrelated to work in the prisons. Indeed, he confessed that much of the instruction was a "waste of time."

Lamar's similar strategy regarding another defense witness, John Nagle, was equally unsuccessful. Nagle attempted to portray his classification program as basically sound, but overburdened. It was true, he said, that many prisoners were passed through without the screening that Swafford's plan envisioned. Yet Nagle insisted that his staff could do no better in the crowded circumstances at Mt. Meigs and that prisoners were properly classified after they reached long-term institutions. On cross-examination, however, he was forced to concede that most prisoners were automatically classified "maximum security" on entry to the system, that inmates of all custody grades were mixed together in living quarters at long-term institutions, and that line personnel at those institutions usually decided what work, if any, prisoners should be assigned to do. Finally, in a revealing exchange with Bronstein, Nagle acknowledged that the system was so desperately crowded that most staff would welcome a judicial order forbidding the acceptance of more prisoners.

Lamar's best witness was L. B. Sullivan, who tried, as he had in *Newman,* to blame others for the many problems besetting the prison system. Sullivan said the prisons were poorly maintained because he had been forced to use scarce funds to purchase food, clothing, and medical supplies. He ascribed prison violence to inadequate custodial staff and declared that by his own calculations he needed 700 guards to supervise the 4000 inmates for whom the major institutions were designed. At present, he had fewer than 400 guards to contend with a population of more than 5000. During the last year, the prices of the goods and services the prison system must purchase had risen sharply. Yet the budget established by the legislature was insufficient to fund the system as it was currently operating. Certainly, Sullivan insisted, there was no money with which to make improvements. If, indeed, the population of the prisons could be reduced to "design capacity," he would still need more than $26 million per year simply to meet operating expenses—apart from the funds needed for capital construction. As it was, he was allotted only about $12 million. Sullivan claimed that he had tried to make changes. He took credit for Swafford's classification system, although he confessed that crowding had frustrated Nagle's efforts to use it. He embraced the system's scattered educational and vocational programs, all of which, he pointed out, were financed by the Alabama Department of Education. And he boasted of the work release centers in several communities.

After Sullivan, the defense called only three wardens. Bill Long denied that he controlled Nagle's classification decisions and that he had ever ordered Big John to assault prisoners. He conceded, however, that crowding and violence were problems at his institution and that he himself would not enter the North Dormitory without guards to protect him. Bill Gilmore, warden at the Frank Lee Youth Center, denied that he exercised a veto over assignments to that institution. He explained that only first offenders under 23 years of age and serving sentences of ten years or less were eligible for Frank Lee. Under cross-examination, Gilmore conceded that the prisoner population there was predominantly white. Finally, Marion Harding denied that strikers and flunkies were given authority over other inmates or instructed to assault other prisoners. He specifically denied significant parts of Big John's testimony about the George Dobbins incident, including the allegation that he had allowed guards to beat prisoners thought to be involved, and blamed prison violence on "revolutionaries" within the inmate population. Lamar recalls that he offered this testimony from the wardens because Long, Gilmore, and Harding were the state's best—to show Judge Johnson that the prisons were in the hands of reliable administrators. The testimony the wardens actually gave, however, is consistent with the view taken by opposing counsel—that the three testified to respond to allegations that, if unrebutted, might have threatened personal liability for the mistreatment of prisoners.[8]

As the defense witnesses were giving evidence, decisions being made outside the courtroom were rapidly bringing the trial to an end ahead of schedule. The critical point was Wednesday evening, August 27, just after the plaintiffs had rested their case. The prisoners' lawyers were confident now of victory. They believed that Judge Johnson had been convinced by their evidence and that for the remainder of the trial he would merely "go through the motions" to accord the defendants their "day in court" before deciding in the plaintiffs' favor. On that supposition, it seemed timely to ask for a preliminary order regarding a range of pressing issues. Bronstein drew up a motion asking the judge to appoint a "Receiver or Special Master" to make dramatic changes in the prison system, including the elimination of dormitories housing more than sixty minimum security prisoners and the renovation or abandonment of the system's older facilities.[9]

Also on Wednesday evening, Lamar organized a defense strategy session at Bill Long's home across town. In contrast to the plaintiffs' assessment, Lamar, Sullivan, and Baxley reached the judgment that all was not lost, that defense witnesses to date, particularly Sullivan himself, had been effective, and that their original objective in the litigation might yet be achieved. The idea was not to avoid an injunction altogether, but to limit the breadth and specificity of the decree that Judge Johnson seemed certain to issue. Having attempted to establish that the prison system was in responsible hands and that the real blame should be ascribed to inadequate funding by the legislature, the defense team hoped that the judge would concentrate on financial support instead of on matters that, in the defense view, touched on penal policy. Specifically, they hoped that the judge would not specify the space that must be allotted to each inmate or the number of guards that must be posted at particular places within the institutions. They hoped instead that he would order the expenditure of much larger sums of money on various facets of the system and that the new commissioner, Mr. Locke, would be able to take the decree to the legislature and succeed with a judicial order where Sullivan had failed without one.[10]

Lamar had expected to offer his own expert witnesses. Yet one possibility, Dr. George J. Beto, formerly director of the Texas Department of Corrections, had refused him, and others failed in the end to appear. Accordingly, the group at Long's home chose an alternative tactic. They would put the three wardens on the stand the next morning, and then they would concede that the plaintiffs had proved their case. It was possible, of course, merely to rest the defense and end the trial. Confessing a constitutional violation was a superior stragegy for three related reasons. First, it would demonstrate that Sullivan, Locke, and the others fully appreciated the gravity of the problems in the prison system. The chances of persuading the judge to trust the ability and good faith of state officials might, accordingly, be enhanced. Second, a concession might permit the defense to choose the theory on which the cases would be decided. Lamar might be able to avoid a decision resting on the theories proposed by Segall and Taylor and guarantee one relying more concretely on the system's physical conditions. Lamar anticipated, in this vein, that he could couch the concession in a way that would make it difficult for Johnson to recognize any "right to rehabilitation" in these cases. Finally, a concession would focus attention on the scope of relief. In light of the defendants' willingness to admit sins of the past, the judge might accept their pledge to do better in the future and thus enter a narrowly drawn order.[11]

Next day, Lamar met Bronstein in the hallway during a recess and told him that he was ready to concede. Bronstein was cautious. He asked Lamar bluntly whether Baxley had agreed to this move. Lamar responded that he was, in fact, acting on the attorney general's "instructions." When the last defense witness, Harding, was finished just before noon, Bronstein asked a marshal to notify the judge that the attorneys requested a conference. Johnson invited them to meet with him immediately after lunch. It was then that Lamar informed the judge of the decision to acknowledge defeat. Memories are in conflict regarding the plaintiffs' reaction to this unexpected development. Bronstein recalls that everyone agreed that acceptance of Lamar's concession would at least protect a favorable judgment from reversal on appeal. While Lamar remained free to object to the relief Johnson might issue, his concession would presumably bar an appeal regarding the threshold determination that conditions in the prisons were unconstitutional. For that reason, the plaintiffs should welcome the defense decision. Others report that the concession was raised, made, and accepted so quickly that serious discussion of it did not occur. Segall recalls that a newspaper reporter informed him of Lamar's decision to "give up" only a few minutes before Segall returned to the courtroom after lunch. Whatever the better recollection of events, no one saw reason to enter an explicit objection.[12]

The conference with Judge Johnson was brief but memorable. Lamar formally announced his position immediately:

> Your honor, . . . we are able to put on more testimony. Most of it will be cumulative and, frankly, we don't see any point in going on. . . . I have talked it over with the other lawyers in the case. . . . At this point the

> Board of Corrections and Attorney General's Office feels that a totality
> case has been made out. We do oppose, and I think the testimony has
> shown that we deny, certain . . . theories on which the plaintiffs are seek-
> ing relief. But we think that relief is appropriate by any conscionable judg-
> ment on the evidence under a totality concept, and that's it.

Lamar purported to speak for the Board of Corrections and, accordingly, board employees such as Sullivan and Locke, and for Baxley. He
did not mention Governor Wallace, a named defendant in the *James*
case. Moreover, Lamar apparently meant to embrace only the broad
proposition that the "totality" of the conditions in the Alabama prison
system constituted cruel and unusual punishment in violation of the
Eighth Amendment. He did not mention rehabilitation; nor did he concede that any particular aspect of prison life was unconstitutional. Nor,
indeed, did he articulate the more precise Eighth Amendment theories
on which the cases had been litigated by Segall and Taylor. No one
probed beneath Lamar's statement, however. Judge Johnson, for his
part, seemed only to be concerned that Lamar repeat it in court, so that
the public might hear that the officials responsible for the prison system
now agreed that conditions there were unconstitutional and, accordingly, that the court had authority to act.[13]

Johnson turned next to Bronstein's motion. He said he preferred
not to "piecemeal" relief in cases of this kind and, for that reason, he
refused to deal early with most matters. Yet he warned that some things
could not wait. In a revealing statement, Johnson made clear his immediate and ultimate intentions and, in so doing, invoked the precedent
that had lurked in the background of the prison cases from their
inception:

> [T]here's no question but that the plaintiffs . . . are entitled to
> relief. . . . They are entitled to wide-scale, long-term relief. Now, . . . what
> constitutes immediate relief depends upon whether you're in one of these
> isolation cells or . . . down here in an air-conditioned courtroom. . . . I'm
> going to issue . . . a far-reaching injunctive order designed to eliminate the
> Eighth Amendment violations and give the plaintiffs the relief to which
> they are clearly entitled, and designed to put the defendants in a better
> position insofar as securing the means through which they can comply.
> We are in the same position in this case that we were at the close of the
> evidence in the *Wyatt-Stickney* case, precisely the same position.

Then and there, Johnson gave oral instructions that, effective immediately, disciplinary cells must measure at least forty-five square feet in
area and must be equipped with working toilets and hot and cold run-

ning water. Prisoners must be provided with basic toiletries, fed three times a day, and permitted regular showers, visitation, and exercise. Inasmuch as the cells in the Draper doghouse measured only thirty-two square feet, they must be closed.

Johnson hesitated to order the state to cease accepting new prisoners. He said that he wished to avoid the perception that he was "trying to run around" Judge Hand, who was scheduled to consider a similar decree in the *McCray* case next day. Accordingly, Johnson said he would talk to Judge Hand. With that, the conference ended. The judge and the lawyers went back into the courtroom for Lamar's public statement. When it was in the record, Johnson gave the lawyers a schedule for post-trial briefs and adjourned the proceedings. Counsel on both sides gathered for cocktails and more talk. The trial of the Alabama prison cases was over.

The next day, Johnson joined Judge Hand in a decree enjoining state authorities from "accepting or permitting the acceptance" of new prisoners into the system until the population of the four major institutions was reduced to the "design capacity" of those facilities. In a separate order, Johnson granted a motion to transfer Big John to an appropriate federal prison to serve out the remainder of his sentence. Johnson denied a similar motion regarding the young man who had been raped at Mt. Meigs because prison authorities assured the judge that the inmate would be protected from reprisals within the Alabama system. A few days later, Sullivan filed an affidavit with the court, declaring that the Draper doghouse had been closed and that all the prisoners still being punished were in cells meeting the specifications that Johnson had fixed during his conference with counsel.[14]

Press accounts of the trial had reported witnesses' testimony in great detail and, as the proceedings wore on, many newspapers offered editorial conclusions. The *Alabama Journal* lamented that the "most telling commentary" on the prison system was that reporters could sit through hours of "horror stories" and "shrug it off with a so-what-else-is-new attitude." It was plain, and it had been plain for a very long time, that the state's prisons were the sites of "pervasive fear, violence, and degradation." Now, with what the *Montgomery Advertiser* called a "dramatic admission" from the defense, the local press pushed hard for immediate action—from someone. Penal authorities still blamed the legislature. In a prepared statement, Lamar insisted that "this unfortunate situation" might have been averted if the legislature had heeded Sullivan's pleas for assistance. He pronounced it a "sad day" for state government "when a federal court has to step in and take control of an entire state agency" because elected officials refused to appropriate sufficient funds. The national press was also disturbed that judical action was necessary in Alabama, but equally resigned to reliance on the court in the face of intransigence from state government. The *Washington Post* worried that federal judges had only "blunt" tools with which to effect social change, but insisted that those tools must be used in situations the Constitution could not tolerate.[15]

Myers' post-trial brief pored over the testimony taken at trial and matched it to factual findings the plaintiffs hoped Johnson would make. Inasmuch as the National Prison Project's pretrial brief had treated the legal issues in some depth, the post-trial brief touched only lightly on the theories put forward earlier, spotlighted Lamar's concession, and concentrated on the particulars of an injunctive decree that would bring the prison system into compliance with the Eighth Amendment. Myers reviewed the history of the *Holt* case in Arkansas, in which Judge Henley's failure to issue a detailed order in the first instance had apparently delayed necessary improvements and generated years of additional litigation over compliance into the bargain. The point was clear. Johnson should not be taken in by Lamar's strategy; the state officials responsible for the Alabama prison system would not act without an order specifying precisely what they must do.[16]

Most of the things the judge was asked to do now had been noted in Bronstein's earlier motion. Johnson should make permanent the preliminary orders he had already issued placing a "cap" on the system's population and fixing minimum conditions in segregation. In addition, he should order a number of changes, some to be effected immediately and others within specified periods of time. He should order the defendants to hold no more than a single prisoner in a cell, to ensure that any new cells measured at least eighty square feet, to house only "minimum security" prisoners in dormitories, to ensure that each prisoner assigned to a dormitory was accorded at least sixty square feet of "personal living space," to hire sufficient guards and other personnel to staff the prisons according to national standards, to establish educational and vocational programs sufficient to allow every willing prisoner to participate, to establish employment programs sufficient to give every willing prisoner an opportunity to work, to create recreational programs and facilities adequate to accommodate all inmates on a regular basis, to improve mail service and visitation for prisoners, to enter a contract with the Center for Correctional Psychology to "implement" a proper classification program, to establish sufficient "community facilities" to house all offenders found to be "eligible" for work release or similar programs, and to prepare a plan for renovating or closing the four major institutions and Tutwiler, the institution for women. Finally, Johnson should appoint a "Receiver or Special Master" to "implement" his order and, perhaps, a "panel of experts" to develop the plans for refurbishing the system's physical facilities.

Lamar's response conceded that the prison system was "besieged with a number of problems and shortages," but argued that "deficiencies" were a function of crowding. The system had too many prisoners, too few guards, and too little money to reduce the numbers of the one or to increase the numbers of the other. Lamar said he had conceded "only" that the "totality" of conditions in the prisons constituted a violation of the Eighth Amendment and intimated that, with the infusion of more funds, the system would meet constitutional standards apart from the other matters the plaintiffs had asked Judge Johnson to address. He reiterated the state's refusal to recognize any "right to rehabilitation" and condemned most of the plaintiffs' other ideas as attempts to change "penal philosophy" better left to the board.

For the moment at least, the lawyers' work was finished; they now had only to await Judge Johnson's judgment. Others, by contrast, were immediately affected by the action the judge had already taken. Jail prisoners and county sheriffs were the first to feel the impact of the cap on the prison system's population. Criminal offenders newly sentenced to prison terms could not be shipped to Mt. Meigs but must, instead, be kept at local jails, exacerbating crowded conditions in those facilities. With more crowding came not only human suffering but additional expense. Baxley's office declared that the state treasury was responsible for the costs of housing sentenced prisoners in the jails, but the funds actually received from the Board of Corrections rarely compensated local authorities fully. Commissioner Locke admitted that local officials were in "serious trouble" and that the problem of backing sentenced prisoners up into the jails could only become worse. City and county officials echoed his sentiment with vigor. Sheriff Pearson in Lee County complained that Johnson "just didn't realize the problems he was creating." Pearson and others did what they could, often converting offices into sleeping quarters, but in the end there was no coping with the press of more and more bodies.[17]

The consequences of crowding in the jails were not all bad. Judges tended in some instances to be freer with bail (thus reducing the number of pretrial detainees with whom the jails must contend) and to sentence more offenders to probation (thus reducing the number of sentenced prisoners to be incarcerated). There was even talk that the state's sen-

tencing policies might be changed to eliminate imprisonment as a routine penalty for "victimless" crimes. Sheriff Robert Turner summed
things up bluntly: "We've got to save . . . space in the county jails for
those who are a threat to society." From statements of that kind it was
a short step to more controversial remarks such as those offered by Fred
Simpson, the district attorney in Huntsville: "Today, it takes a minor
miracle to put someone in prison. . . . It is disheartening to know even
before you go to trial that if the man is judged guilty he still will not go
to prison." In response to statements of *that* kind, Chief Justice Howell
Heflin of the Alabama Supreme Court urged judges to maintain the sentencing policies they had always employed, and Governor Wallace proposed legislation actually to lengthen many criminal sentences. Fortu-
nately for the Board of Corrections, Wallace's bill died without action
in what remained of the 1975 session.[18]

When the public debate turned more realistically to the prison system's genuine needs, it was vexed by the intermingling of penal objectives and, as always, cold economics. Locke requested $70 million in
the next fiscal year, to be spent on road camps, a new prison for women,
and a "trusty barracks" for "minimum security" inmates at Draper.
Those projects were not disturbing in themselves, but they implied a
response to the *Pugh* and *James* cases precisely the opposite of what
reformers hoped to see. It seemed that Locke meant to deal with crowding in state prisons not by reducing the population in existing institutions, but by building new facilities. Representative Robert M. Hill
voiced reformers' objections to such a scheme. It was time, he said, for
state authorities to "come up with some alternatives" to long-term
incarceration. Wallace agreed to sponsor a special bond issue which, if
approved by the voters in an election scheduled for January 1976,
would bring the Board $6 million for additional construction. Reform
groups like the ACLU opposed the bond issue on the ground that the
money would be ill-spent on new prisons. The voters approved the governor's plan, but by then the order in *Pugh* and *James* had been issued,
and it was quite clear that the availability of a few hundred more beds
would not suffice.[19]

Judge Johnson observed events from a distance. When he spoke,
his message seemed oddly mixed. In mid-November, he disposed of
several lawsuits filed by prison inmates claiming damages for the very
unconstitutional crowding that he and Judge Hand had identified in
late summer. Johnson insisted that violations of the Constitution would
not be tolerated in his court, but he found it inappropriate to make
prison authorities pay money damages for their failure to respect min-

imum standards. At the same time, he took the opportunity of a speech at the University of Alabama Law School to repeat his admonition to anyone who cared to hear.

> With the legislature having clearly expressed its intention to once again abdicate its authority, it is now left to the federal court to work out a solution which will protect the constitutional rights which incarcerated citizens still retain.
>
> This is one responsibility the court would gladly relinquish to those who were elected to do it. . . .
>
> A state is not at liberty to provide its citizens only those constitutional rights it feels it can comfortably afford. . . .[20]

The budget approved for the Board of Corrections for the next fiscal year was the same as for the current year. "It's a status quo budget," said John Hale. "It's just exactly what we spent this year." That was not enough, and everyone knew it. "[T]he Governor and his Legislature were happy," said the *Advertiser,* "to let the prisoners stack up until there was no breathing space left inside the stone walls." "The state is neglecting its responsibility," said the *Birmingham News,* "but the federal courts won't let us get by with it for long." The *Post Herald* took the same view: "The legislature talked a lot about the problems, but ended up doing nothing. . . . Meanwhile, city and county jails are filling with convicts the state refuses to accept." The only political pressure truly felt in Montgomery apparently came from the citizens of Mt. Meigs, Alabama, who complained that the bad publicity given the institution near their town, and named for it, had depressed property values in the area. The legislature responded with a bill changing the name of the Mt. Meigs Medical and Diagnostic Center to the Kilby Medical and Diagnostic Center in honor of the former governor, Thomas Kilby. Legislation with a price tag was not, however, forthcoming. The time for action had come and gone and, as one reporter put it, prison officials were now "waiting on the edges of their seats" to see what Judge Johnson would do.[21]

The judge issued his opinion and order on January 13, 1976. His conclusions tracked most of the arguments the prisoners' lawyers had urged on him at trial and in their briefs. He declared that the four principal institutions were "horrendously overcrowded" and found crowding to be "primarily responsible" for the system's "other ills." Yet he went on to identify those ills with particularity: poor plumbing, substandard sanitation, inadequate recreation and visitation, and various other deficiencies. Johnson accepted Gordon's testimony that the pris-

ons were "unfit for human habitation" and warned darkly that if
Draper and Fountain were not properly renovated he would order them
closed. He concluded that Alabama had "no working classification system" and that prisoners were assigned to institutions "on the basis of
available space." In the absence of adequate staff to maintain order,
prisoners were left to fend for themselves in a "jungle atmosphere" in
which violence was "rampant." The conditions in punitive isolation
were, he said, "indescribable."

Relying on his own decision in *Newman,* the *Holt* case in Arkansas,
and other decisions handed down in recent years, the judge said he had
a "clear duty" to hold that there were "massive" violations of prisoners'
constitutional rights in the Alabama prison system—demanding sweeping injunctive relief. His conclusion, in the main,[22] was that the totality
of the conditions in the prisons constituted cruel and unusual punishment in violation of the Eighth Amendment. He referred to Lamar's
concession, but said nothing to suggest that he felt bound by the limitations that Lamar had hoped to build into his statements in court.
Indeed, Johnson clearly embraced the more imaginative arguments put
forward by Segall and Taylor:

> Prison officals are under a duty to provide inmates reasonable pro-
> tection from constant threat of violence. . . .
>
> The defendants in these cases have failed to carry out that duty. The
> evidence establishes that inmates are housed in virtually unguarded,
> overcrowded dormitories, with no realistic attempt by officials to separate
> violent, aggressive inmates from those who are passive or weak. The ten-
> sion generated by idleness and deplorable living conditions contributes
> further to the ever-present threat of violence from which inmates have no
> refuge.
>
> The evidence . . . also establishes that prison conditions are so debil-
> itating that they necessarily deprive inmates of any opportunity to reha-
> bilitate themselves, or even to maintain skills already possessed. While
> courts have thus far declined to elevate a positive rehabilitation program
> to the level of a constitutional right, it is clear that a penal system cannot
> be operated in such a manner that it impedes an inmate's ability to
> attempt rehabilitation, or simply to avoid physical, mental or social
> deterioration. . . .

Judge Johnson was not blind to the controversy his judgment
would generate. Thinking, perhaps, of the press coverage his action
would receive, he insisted that criminals were not to be "coddled" and
that prisons were not to be operated as "hotels or country clubs." State
officials, however, "including the Alabama Legislature," could not be

permitted to maintain prisons that were "barbaric and inhumane." Prisoners must be free from unconstitutional punishment, and that, in turn, meant that they must be protected from violence and accorded living conditions that permitted self-improvement and did not, instead, cause deterioration. After months of work, Segall and Taylor had carried their burden of proof and established the substantive rights outlined in their amended complaints.

The injunctive order accompanying Johnson's opinion revealed his choices among the various options for attempting to cure the constitutional flaws he found in the prison system. True to earlier indications, he declined the National Prison Project's invitation to order changes respecting the root elements of Alabama penology: long-term incarceration as the penalty for most criminal offenses; large, rural penitentiaries; and restrictive parole practices. Johnson would not use the *Pugh* and *James* cases as vehicles for establishing policy he himself thought was superior to that chosen by state penal authorities. Nor did he follow Lamar's suggestion that he focus attention entirely on the need for additional funding and leave choices regarding the expenditure of additional money to state officials. In this instance, as in the past, the judge had reached the conclusion that state authorities would not respond readily and must, therefore, be given explicit commands. Johnson's focus was where he had said it would be. He held state authorities to a series of specific directions, most of which touched on the conditions of daily life in the prisons.

Judge Johnson thus specified what must be done to meet constitutional standards. On first glance, he appeared to blur any distinction between conditions that constituted cruel and unusual punishment on the one hand and the entitlements that must be accorded to inmates to render the system constitutionally sound on the other. Indeed, he set forth a list of things to be accorded to inmates and identified them as the "Minimum Constitutional Standards for Inmates of [the] Alabama Penal System." That label was misleading, however. Johnson's holding was that the "totality" of circumstances in the prison system violated the Eighth Amendment, not that particular prison practices, taken in isolation from other conditions, were independently unconstitutional. Still, the effect was the same. Whatever the theoretical justification for the particulars of the order, and however those particulars were characterized, the fact remained that state officials were ordered to make explicit changes in the prison system. Certainly, the system would not be considered constitutionally viable until those changes were made.

Johnson was, indeed, explicit. New prisoners were not to be

accepted at any institution until the population of that facility was reduced to "design capacity"; prisoners were not to be housed together in cells intended only for one; any cells used for segregation must be properly equipped. At present, isolation cells could be small, measuring forty square feet in area, but all cells must measure at least sixty square feet within six months. Prisoners assigned to segregation for "administrative" purposes must be released unless they voluntarily chose to remain. Older prisons, Draper and Fountain, must be refurbished forthwith—meeting minimum standards established by the U.S. Public Health Service by the end of the year. Newer facilities, Holman and what was now Kilby, must meet the same standards by the end of 1977. Johnson gave the defendants only three months to present him with a plan for the classification of prisoners and only until mid-August to use that plan to classify all inmates in the system. The judge expected prisoners to be classified not only on the basis of their propensity for violence, but according to their mental and physical condition, their educational and vocational needs and, importantly, their qualifications for "community-based" facilities. He ordered the establishment of enough "community" programs to accommodate all the prisoners who might appropriately participate. Johnson said that inmates requiring care available only in facilities for the mentally impaired and handicapped must be transferred to institutions of that kind; prisoners needing only "mental health care" must be given such care within the penal system. To make the scheme work, the judge ordered the defendants to hire at least the "mental health professionals and support personnel" recommended by Dr. Fowler's earlier study.

The judge said that "reasonable efforts" must be made to identify and segregate violent prisoners, that only "minimum security" inmates could be assigned to dormitories, that frequent "shakedowns" must be conducted to discover weapons, that a "scrip system" must be substituted for the use of currency, and that guards must be stationed in all living areas. With respect to this last, he specified at least one guard inside and one guard outside each dormitory at all times. New guards must be hired in sufficient numbers to staff the prisons in the manner that Sullivan had said was necessary. There must be a plan for attracting new personnel whose presence would reduce "the racial and cultural disparity between the staff and the inmate population," and all personnel must be given "appropriate and effective training" for employment in the prisons. The authorities must cease using prisoners to guard other inmates and must, in future, keep accurate records of prison violence to facilitate monitoring the new scheme's success.

Moving to living conditions in general, Johnson said that prisoners must receive specified clothing, linens, storage lockers, and other personal items, that the institutions must be cleaned regularly, and that living quarters must be equipped with specified numbers of toilets and urinals. Each prisoner must have a "bed off the floor" and "a minimum" of sixty square feet of "living space." All prisoners must be given three "wholesome and nutritious" meals each day; to ensure as much, a registered dietitian must be hired to plan menus and supervise the storage and preparation of food. There were other things, new rules for visitation, recreation, and correspondence. Then, coming to "rehabilitative" programs, Johnson ordered that all prisoners must have "meaningful" jobs and a chance to enroll in "basic" education courses, "vocational training programs," and "transitional" programs "designed to aid in [their] re-entry into society." Finally, Johnson allowed the authorities six months in which to submit a "comprehensive report" setting forth their "progress" and the "reasons for the incomplete implementation of any standard" in the order.

The problem of monitoring compliance with the many parts of the January 13 order presented familiar options. The prisoners' lawyers pressed Johnson to do in these prison cases what he had declined to do in *Wyatt* and *Newman*. Primarily, they asked the Judge to appoint a "master" to serve as his surrogate in the implementation stages—to review reports from Locke and others, to hold hearings on the progress toward compliance, and to consult periodically with the judge should problems arise. In some sense, such an agent would serve as an assistant to Johnson himself, performing delegated judicial tasks in these particular cases. In the alternative, the prisoners' lawyers proposed that a professional penal administrator should be appointed to assume direct responsibility for operating the Alabama prison system in accord with the order. Such a "receiver" would not merely monitor state authorities' progress, but would displace Commissioner Locke and the board entirely, taking charge of the Alabama prison system until it could be brought into compliance. Lamar, of course, objected to both those proposals and insisted that state officials were competent to make needed changes on their own.

Judge Johnson steered an independent course. He introduced two outside agencies into the prison system to operate under his authority. First, accepting in this respect a suggestion made by the plaintiffs, he ordered Locke and the Board of Corrections to contract with Fowler's Center for Correctional Psychology "to aid in the implementation" of the classification plan. Second, Johnson established yet another Human

Rights Committee (HRC), similar to those he had formed in *Wyatt,* and assigned it to "monitor implementation" of the standards fixed by his order. In view of his determination that the standards developed in *Newman* had not been respected, he gave the new HRC the "authority and duty" to "monitor implementation" of that earlier order as well. He authorized the HRC to inspect facilities and records, interview prisoners, and review any plans developed by the defendants "to ensure that they comport" with the requirements of the order. At its discretion, the HRC could hire "independent specialists" and support personnel to assist in this work. Those employees and a "full-time" consultant would be compensated by the board, the latter at a salary commensurate with that of the commissioner.

Initial reaction to the January 13 order ranged from jubilation on the part of the plaintiffs to outrage on the part of some local critics. John Conrad praised Judge Johnson's "courageous and human decision"; Al Bronstein said it was the "most sweeping" order "ever entered"; Steve Suitts proclaimed that it marked the end of a century of "corruption, mismanagement, and inhumanity" in the Alabama prison system. Others, particularly the editors of smaller newspapers in Alabama, attacked the order and the man who issued it. The *Livingston Home Record* complained that criminals had "more rights than their victims"; the *Centerville Press* insisted that Johnson was "again . . . messing around with something about which he [knew] little, giving prisoners the 'red carpet, soft pillow treatment'"; the *Montgomery Independent* declared that inmates would now be "better situated and more secure than hundreds of thousands of people . . . trying to make do outside prison without committing crimes"; the *Opp News* compared prisoners' "nice living facilities" to college dormitories at Auburn University. One columnist, Ruby Folsom Austin, said she could not "work up a good cry over thugs and murderers not having cake and ice cream"; another, Tom Johnson, labeled the order "flummery"—the work of a man driven by an apparent "obsession with cracker crumbs and peanuts."[23]

Some observers recognized that the prison system was in need of improvements, but objected that change should occur at the insistence of a single judge instead of through the ordinary political process. Locally, the *Opp News* insisted that the "judicial body" was intended to be the "equal" of the other branches of government, "not their master"; the *Eufaula Tribune* reported that a local attorney had said "[w]e might as well dissolve the legislature and appoint Judge Johnson"; the *Eastern Shore Courier* asked rhetorically: "[H]ow far can judges go in running our country?" That theme was repeated in an otherwise favorable national press, which once again began to speculate that Judge Johnson was the "real" governor of Alabama. Occasional reports linked the order to prison conditions elsewhere, generating admonitions that other federal judges might deal just as harshly with penal institutions in their states. That, of course, was precisely the message the National Prison Project hoped would come from the Alabama cases. Having obtained a sweeping order from Judge Johnson, Bronstein and Myers moved quickly on to further litigation before Judge Pettine in Rhode Island— lest the public write Johnson's order off as "just Alabama."[24]

Most state officials responded with caution. Lamar said it was "too early to tell" whether Judge Johnson's demands could be met within the time allotted and pointed out that, however quickly changes could come, "whopping sums of money" would be required. Locke acknowledged that most of the improvements mentioned in the order were desirable and pledged a "good faith effort" to comply. Governor Wallace, by contrast, viewed the order as "just another example of the federal court trying to run our state." In a news conference held both to condemn Johnson's action and to announce his intention to appeal, Wallace initially said that if the appeal proved unsuccessful he would comply with the order. In a later campaign speech in Massachusetts, however, he hinted that he might never bend. Wallace complained that Johnson had prescribed a "hotel atmosphere and catering service" for prison inmates. He said that he had tried to improve conditions but had found the "burden" "too great." During the battles over segregation in the 1960s, Wallace had called Johnson "an integrating, scalawagging, carpetbagging liar." Now, he said that "thugs and federal judges" had "just about taken over society." Asked whether he thought the prison order would affect his presidential campaign, he said that "a vote for George C. Wallace might give a political barbed wire enema to some federal judges. . . ." The governor's calculated rhetoric forecast his immediate intentions with respect to the January 13 order. He would keep his commitment to pass revenue sharing funds along to the Board of Corrections and would ensure that the board obtained its share of the monies generated in the new bond issue, approved by the voters on the day of his press conference. He would resist, however, easy compliance with the specifics of the order—just as he had resisted court orders of the past. Wallace assumed he could count on the public's lack of sympathy for criminal offenders to distract attention from the evidence adduced in court. Johnson's order posed no obstacle to this campaign;

like his desegregation decrees, this new injunction provided a rallying point. The enemies in the governor's campaign were no longer "integrationists" and "liberals"; they were federal judges and the "thugs" about whom those judges were concerned.[25]

Wallace's response to Johnson's order invited the national press to understand the clash over prisons as another in a series of conflicts between the governor and the judge. The future must depend, then, on the dedication of the two men to the disparate courses they had taken. This appraisal was fueled by Johnson's introductory remarks to the new Human Rights Committee. Standing at the podium from which the lawyers had interrogated witnesses six months earlier, Johnson told the HRC that its work would "not be easy." He urged the committee to "take the high road" and to deal with penal authorities with "dignity and courtesy" as well as "firmness and resoluteness," with an eye always on the "pole star"—the elimination of the "barbaric" conditions in the prisons. Johnson admonished the committee not to be misled by criticisms of the January 13 order: "I say to you," he said, that "the elimination of conditions that will permit maggots in a patient's wound . . . does not constitute the creation of a hotel atmosphere." Nor, he insisted, did the "elimination of other physical and mental indignities" create a "hotel setting. . . ." Comments of this sort, plainly intended to respond to Wallace without mentioning the governor directly, fed speculation that, in truth, the controversy over Alabama's prisons was another joust between two strong-minded men.[26]

That superficial understanding played better nationally than locally. Within Alabama, particularly among the reporters who had covered the trial, the matter was seen in a different, more substantive, light. This was certainly a repeat performance. Yet it was not merely another round in a personal rivalry between Wallace and Johnson but, instead, another instance of default on the part of state government in meeting its responsibilities—calling forth another effort by a federal court to force state authorities to do what they had a duty to do. Thus the state's best newspapers published articles and editorials refuting contentions that the prisons were less grim than Judge Johnson's opinion made them seem and urging state officials to accept the January 13 order without complaint and set about meeting its demands. The *Post Herald* insisted that officials forego the "momentarily popular denunciation of Judge Johnson" and, instead, "find solutions" for the problems he had identified; the *Alabama Journal* found "echoes of the old Wallace" in the governor's response to the order—and warned the public against Wallace's hyperbole "when all Johnson ordered was a measure of humanity in the treatment of prisoners." A few legislators dared to take similar public positions. Representative Lynn Greer acknowledged that the state had ignored the prisons and that it was now time to "face up to" the problems identified in court, and Bob Hill again blamed the "executive branch" for the failure to address prison issues earlier.[27]

Still, it would be misleading to suggest that Governor Wallace's rhetoric misfired or that moderate voices in Alabama convinced the public that prison reform was overdue. The world in which the January 13 order must exist was more complex than that. Wallace's message was powerful; it rang true to the citizens of Alabama he knew best. Other politicians had seen this same strategy succeed on countless prior occasions, and few were prepared to assume the political risks of a different posture. Instead, they treaded softly round the perimeter of the ground the governor had marked off for himself and waited patiently for the state's powerful political forces to sort themselves out.

The trial of the Alabama prison cases was at an end. Counsel for the defendants had conceded defeat. Judge Johnson had found the relevant facts, determined the pertinent legal issues, and entered judgment for the plaintiffs. He had issued an injunctive decree ordering state authorities to make numerous changes in the prison system in order to eliminate unconstitutional conditions. In a more traditional lawsuit, such an order would have been the end, or nearly the end, of the litigation. If the defendants balked, they would be forced to comply and, in due course, the plaintiffs would have satisfaction. These cases, however, were different. The January 13 order was not the victory the plaintiffs had sought for so many months. It was an initial assault on the fortress of state government, which would not be taken without lengthy siege. Events in the next year demonstrated to anyone who remained in doubt that the Alabama prison system would not be changed easily. The resistance was immediately evident on two fronts. Politicians seized on the strategy of placing blame for poor conditions on Commissioner Locke and the Board of Corrections—reviving in the process an idea not widely expressed for a half century but nonetheless part of a primitive creed to which state officials unanimously subscribed. Prisons and prisoners should not need public funding; they should support themselves. At the same time, Governor Wallace and Attorney General Baxley went back to court in an attempt to overturn, or at least to dilute, the order that Judge Johnson had issued.

5

Intransigence

No one doubted that the January 13 order faced massive political difficulties. The sheer cost of implementation was formidable, and efforts to develop a reliable projection of that cost underscored the political complexity of the enterprise. Early on, the legislature commissioned Dr. Frank Toohey and the University of Alabama's Center for Business and Economic Research to study the question. With help from Dr. Fowler's Center for Correctional Psychology and the National Clearinghouse for Criminal Justice Planning and Architecture at the University of Illinois, Toohey marshaled the variables and reported that no "fixed sum" estimate was possible. The expenses that would be incurred to comply with the court order depended on the penal policies adopted in Alabama in the near term. For example, if the state chose to incarcerate fewer offenders for shorter periods of time, and certainly if the state chose to house prisoners in small, relatively cheap facilities near employment opportunities instead of in large, relatively expensive, rural prisons, the cost of complying with the order might be kept down. If, however, the state chose to continue present policies, the very policies that had caused the inmate population to become bloated and operational expenses to soar, the cost would be much greater. At a minimum, according to Toohey, physical improvements at the major institutions would require an outlay of $79 million over and above the prison system's current budget.[1]

Apart from the expense to the state treasury, moreover, Johnson's order touched on state politics at a personal level. It was not so much that the public or state officials genuinely believed that the conditions described in Johnson's opinion were justifiable or even, on this occasion, that knowledgeable Alabamians resisted change at the instance of a federal court. Only Governor Wallace put matters in those familiar terms—playing to visceral reactions to crime, criminals, and federal officials meddling in local affairs. More serious political obstacles to reform resided deeper within the personal rivalries generated by Alabama's public life. Penal officials responded defensively to the charge, now widely repeated, that they had mismanaged the prison system, allowed it to deteriorate, and thus embarrassed the state in court. Commissioner Locke and the Board of Corrections were threatened both by the Human Rights Committee, established by Judge Johnson to superintend compliance with his order, and by other state political figures, who attempted to avoid personal responsibility for what had happened by fastening blame entirely on the commissioner and the board. The cause of penal reform in Alabama, now represented by attempts to implement the January order, was thus caught in a complex web of political relationships. Progress was frustrated not by any united front in opposition to change. State officials in every camp routinely clamored for change, albeit with varying degrees of sincerity. Instead, progress was stalled by fierce battles within state government, waged by individual state officials jockeying for position in an omnipresent struggle for political survival and advancement.

To understand what actually occurred in the first year after Johnson's order, it is essential to probe beneath George Wallace's rhetoric and to examine, first, the HRC's efforts to gain the cooperation of penal authorities in the implementation of the order; second, the clash between penal officials and state politicians, particularly Lieutenant Governor Jere Beasley; and, third, the related shadowboxing between and among Wallace, Beasley, and Attorney General Baxley, each of whom used the controversy over prisons as a vehicle for political maneuvers within a long-term campaign for power in Alabama. In turn, these stories relegated two other matters, reduced crowding in the prisons over the course of the year and the ineffectual appeals from Judge Johnson's judgment, to subordinate roles in the larger, and largely unpleasant, drama that was Alabama politics.

Judge Johnson recognized that if the January 13 order was to be taken seriously, it would have to be pressed on state officials in some effective manner. He might have attempted to enforce it promptly—by calling Locke and the board into the courtroom, holding them in contempt and, perhaps, coercing action by imposing fines on individual state officials or jailing them if they failed to cooperate. Yet that was not Johnson's way. His experience in the school desegregation cases suggested that it would be more fruitful to be patient, to give state authorities time and opportunity to make improvements, and then to prod them periodically until they completed their task. Moreover, the *Wyatt* and *Newman* cases suggested that the judge should not attempt to keep abreast of developments himself, but should establish agents in the field to monitor events and act on his behalf. Johnson's primary tool in this instance was the Human Rights Committee.

After the fashion of similar committees created in connection with *Wyatt,* the new HRC enlisted a large number of respected citizens not only to galvanize public opinion in support of prison reform, but to make it their business to bring the order to the attention of state authorities with the duty and capacity to effect change. Judge Johnson hoped the HRC would fashion a working relationship with penal authorities and that the January order would be implemented, in time, through a relatively informal cooperative effort—without, and this was critical, significant further court action. In a real sense, therefore, local people, state officials and public-spirited citizens alike, would resolve this most troubling of the state's social problems. To ensure that the HRC would be persistent, Johnson added a special catalyst—a particularly aggressive chairman. The man selected for this duty, M. Roland Nachman, had stopped by Judge Johnson's chambers to offer best wishes at Christmas, 1975. The judge, then deeply engrossed in his opinion in the prison cases, surprised him with an immediate and specific request for help.[2]

Rod Nachman was an obvious choice. A respected member of an old Montgomery law firm and an important figure in local and national bar activities, he brought both prestige and political discernment to the work of the HRC. He knew Commissioner Sullivan personally, having represented him in the celebrated libel case, *New York Times v. Sullivan.*[3] And he was familiar with the problems now plaguing Sullivan's prison system. In 1973, as president of the Alabama Bar, Nachman had appointed the committee that later openly criticized the manner in which the prisons were administered and funded. More recently, he had followed the *Pugh* and *James* cases in the *Montgomery Advertiser,* which he served as general counsel. Nachman appreciated the enormity of the task ahead—if he and the HRC were to be successful in achieving reform in the face of the current squalor in the prisons and a new commissioner, Judson Locke, whom Nachman believed would be more obstreperous than Sullivan.[4]

On Nachman's advice, Judge Johnson appointed several former members of the bar committee, among them E. M. Friend, Jr., Thomas Thagard, and Laurie Mandell, to serve on the new HRC. And he asked George Beto, now on the faculty at Sam Houston State University, to serve as the committee's professional consultant. Nachman had once heard Beto address a conference in Texas and had invited him to speak to the Alabama Bar the previous year. The new HRC chairman found in Beto precisely what he wanted—an intelligent, articulate man who could offer sound advice on questions about which Nachman alone could make no confident judgment. Beto was one of the best-known penal specialists in the country. He had administered the Texas prison system, one of the nation's largest, for many years and now was comparatively free to undertake consulting projects elsewhere. Nachman phoned Beto immediately after the order was issued in January. His follow-up letter was explicit: "Judge Johnson and I feel that you are the best qualified person we know to act as . . . consultant."[5]

Beto was flattered, interested, and agreeable. In short order, he flew to Montgomery to confer with Nachman and Judge Johnson. Beto told the judge that he understood the order to have three primary objectives: to obtain meaningful employment for "able-bodied" prisoners, to provide inmates with "basic education," and to ensure safety within the system. Johnson acquiesced in that appraisal, conservative though it was. Moreover, and to Beto's surprise, Johnson acknowledged that some parts of his order, particularly the requirement that cells must measure sixty square feet and the requirement that the system employ the number of guards that Sullivan had requested, were not essential. If Beto had reservations about those points, and he did, Johnson was prepared to make changes. Beto was convinced that Johnson was not a "blazing reformer" but wanted only to achieve a "well-run prison system." Accordingly, the Texan agreed to help put into action Johnson's dominant instruction: "Let's turn this thing around."[6]

However sure Nachman and Johnson were that Beto should be the HRC's consultant, the lawyers for Alabama's prison inmates were frankly annoyed at the prospect. Beto had himself been a defendant in numerous lawsuits attacking prison conditions in Texas and, since his retirement, he had served as an expert witness for the *defense* in other cases around the country. In an Illinois case, he had countenanced holding a teenage prisoner in solitary confinement for as long as seventeen months; in Indiana, he had approved shooting "buckshot" near prisoners staging a sit-in in the prison yard. If critics had dug deeper, they might have discovered that Robert Lamar had asked Beto to testify for the defense in the Alabama cases themselves. There was, then, some substance to the quip that the appointment of Beto amounted to putting "the possum in charge of the henhouse." As a matter of fact, however, Beto had refused to assist Lamar in Alabama because he could not bring himself to defend conditions that, in his view, were worse than what he had seen in other states and tolerated himself in Texas. He was a tough, even hard, man. But he was not without scruples and, more to the point, professional judgment. Matt Myers collected critical information and funneled it to Alberta Murphy, who had been appointed to the HRC and was likely to be sympathetic to prisoners' interests. And in the initial meeting of the HRC, Murphy expressed reservations about the proposed appointment. She withdrew her objection, however, when Nachman explained that Judge Johnson had already made his choice. The motion to retain Beto was approved by voice vote.[7]

Nachman and Beto began their task in three channels. They approached the Alabama legislature in hopes of obtaining needed funding, the Alabama Board of Pardons and Paroles in hopes of generating more and earlier paroles, and the commissioner and the board in hopes of prompting other reforms mandated by the court order. Beto took special interest in the legislature, where he tried to forge personal relationships to serve his purposes. He formed the habit of walking to the capitol building every morning when he was in Montgomery and taking coffee in the Senate lounge with key legislators and members of the press. This was Beto's element. He had experience in the vital business of stroking lawmakers, gradually bringing them round to his views. He was also an effective public speaker before the legislature itself. Beto was enough like the men and women who populated that body to meet them on their own personal and political ground. For this reason, he probably was more effective in his position than the more progressive candidates the prisoners' lawyers would have preferred. What ground was gained for prison reform in the legislature was in no small part the result of George Beto's ability to operate in those circles.[8]

Nachman and Beto labored together with respect to the parole board. Initially, Beto asked the board to end its policy of taking "good time" from prisoners whose paroles were revoked. "Good time" was, in effect, time off for good behavior in custody. The consequence of the parole board's policy was to lengthen the sentences prisoners must serve after their return to prison upon a violation of parole. When the board responded in a letter Nachman found "meaningless," Beto actually raised his sights. He obtained a list of prisoners who were eligible for parole under Alabama law and left it in Judge Johnson's office in hopes the judge would appreciate its significance. Johnson, for his part, recognized the opportunity to make a large dent in the prison population in Alabama in one motion. In a letter to Nachman, the judge acknowledged that "granting or denying parole" was a "discretionary matter." Yet he could only assume that by leaving so many eligible inmates confined in institutions declared to be unconstitutional, the parole board was acting "arbitrarily and capriciously." Johnson recalled that he had passed over an opportunity to bring the members of the parole board into the *Pugh* and *James* cases as parties and that it might be difficult now to insist that they respond favorably to entreaties to parole more inmates. He nevertheless instructed Nachman to approach the parole board "to see if something [could] be worked out . . . in an informal way."[9]

Nachman promptly conferred with Norman F. Ussery, chairman of the parole board, but he and the other board members were unwilling to take the political risks associated with a change in parole policy. In effect, they told Nachman that prison crowding was Locke's problem. The parole board had no intention of exposing itself to public criticism or, worse yet, pressure from Governor Wallace merely to mitigate difficulties it was under no direct judicial order to address. Nachman and Beto attempted to apply pressure of their own, discussing their concerns about the low parole rate in public and raising the issue in legislative hearings. Further efforts, including periodic meetings with the parole board, pleas to sympathetic members for assistance in bringing others round, and coordination with the Board of Corrections, were similarly unsuccessful. Nachman and Beto pressed for a more liberal parole policy until the HRC was dismantled in 1978. Still, there was no discernible effect.[10]

Attempts by Nachman and Beto to work with Commissioner Locke and the Board of Corrections began well but soon collapsed. Immediately after the January order was issued, Dr. Staton invited the HRC to meet with the board and pledged his "cooperation . . . in a mutual effort toward [the] end" of providing prisoners the "best environment possible." Nachman responded enthusiastically, scheduling such a meeting on the day of the HRC's organizational session. The committee met with Judge Johnson in the morning and with the Board of Corrections in the afternoon. At that time, Staton gave the impression that he actually approved Johnson's decision to establish the HRC which, in his telling, would have the political "muscle" the board itself had long wanted. When he and others had gone to the legislature in the past to explain that the "patient," that is, the prison system, had a broken back and needed a "body cast," the legislature had responded with "a few bandaids." Now, Staton said, the situation would be different. Nachman, for his part, seemed to embrace Staton's description of the HRC's role: "We are not and will not become the surrogate administrators of the prison system. . . . [We will] oversee the implementation . . .

[of the order and] make it easier for you." The only note of caution came from Commissioner Locke, who expressed concern about the "inordinate" power of federal judges even as he accepted the order as "the law of the land" and promised, perhaps grudgingly, "to follow it."[11]

Locke's reaction was only to be expected. Staton and the other board members could reconcile the HRC with their role in the prison system. By contrast, Locke could only feel threatened by a man like Beto—summoned to Alabama for the very reason that someone, perhaps everyone, thought that Locke could not handle his own job. One of Beto's early public statements, to the effect that the Alabama prison system needed "[c]reativity and imagination" as well as additional funding, hardly mollified the commissioner's anxiety. Beto disclaimed authority to "tell anybody to do anything" and said that he might finish his assignment within six months. Yet Locke was intimidated and became all the more discouraged as Beto made progress in the legislature, where Locke himself had failed. The *Alabama Journal* summed it up. The board met only a few times a year; Locke must be Beto's figurative "cellmate." The two men were on a "collision course," and Locke, for all his faults, understood well enough that, in the end, he was no match for George Beto.[12]

In truth, Locke soon learned, the chief threat to his position lay not with Beto, but with Nachman. Beto was given to tolerance where Locke was concerned; he was slow to condemn, quick to excuse the younger, less experienced man. By contrast, Nachman regarded Locke as only another in a series of rank incompetents appointed to office by a governor who had no genuine interest in governing. It was Nachman who peppered Locke with complaints, questions, and demands for reports. "We were intrusive," he recalls, because it was necessary to be intrusive. "We had to do more than just point out what was wrong. So much was wrong. There were terrible management problems." Initially, Nachman limited himself to matters of general policy. When he learned, for example, that guards were not periodically searching for weapons, he demanded that Locke establish an effective "shakedown" program and explore the use of metal detectors to locate knives. He also dispatched subcommittees of the HRC, particularly Dr. Nace Cohen's subcommittee on medical care, to monitor Locke's progress. When Nachman received critical reports, he demanded explanations from the commissioner. Later, Nachman took up complaints from individual prisoners, channeled to him through plaintiffs' counsel, family members, and prisoners themselves. He fed grievances to the HRC subcommittees or to Locke directly, always demanding a prompt investigation of an inmate's treatment. In late spring, Nachman hired Laurie Mandell to administer the steady flow of prisoner correspondence, reports, and responses.[13]

The commissioner initially tolerated Nachman's interference and, indeed, accepted the HRC chairman's apparent authority to speak for Judge Johnson. For example, when Locke wished to know whether sentenced prisoners in county jails could be transferred to the prison hospital at Kilby for medical care, he contacted Nachman—to ask, essentially, for a modification of Johnson's order forbidding the acceptance of more prisoners until the system's population had been reduced to "design capacity." Nachman, in turn, granted permission to take prisoners genuinely in need of care that could be provided only at Kilby. Later, however, Locke became more confrontational, refusing to bend immediately to Nachman's demands and probing the limits of the other man's true authority. A report that there were empty beds in some of the system's work release centers provides an illustration. Nachman initially wrote to Locke, stating that he had discussed the matter with Judge Johnson and was "authorized" to advise Locke that the judge expected him to take "immediate steps" to fill those centers to "capacity." On this occasion, the commissioner refused to accept Nachman's instructions standing alone and, instead, directed one of his lawyers, Tom Radney, to approach Judge Johnson with an alternative plan.[14]

Locke was more suspicious of Nachman's authority than he should have been. The record is clear that in this and other instances Nachman acted on instructions from Johnson himself. The judge received copies of HRC correspondence, memoranda, and reports, and often made his reaction known to Nachman. He approved or disapproved proposals for action and also seized on issues in which he was interested and gave Nachman explicit guidance—with respect to matters great and small. For example, when it was reported in the press that the prison system kept Tennessee walking horses for recreational use at one of the rural institutions, Johnson asked Nachman to demand an explanation. And when the HRC subcommittee for Fountain reported that conditions at that facility remained poor, Johnson complained to Nachman that state authorities were showing "callous indifference to the basic requirements of this Court's order." Johnson told Nachman to send copies of the report and his letter to each board member, Commissioner Locke, and the warden at Fountain and to insist on a response within two weeks.[15]

Johnson continued to receive correspondence from individual prisoners as well. He maintained his practice of sending letters raising issues that might be the basis of prosecution to DeMent and Vines. Yet he now relied on Nachman to pursue complaints going only to the enforcement of his order in *Pugh* and *James*. In most instances, the judge merely forwarded letters to Nachman with the notation that he would make no response himself but expected Nachman to ask a sub-committee or the commissioner to investigate. But when Johnson issued affirmative commands, Nachman responded dutifully, precipitating Locke's growing irritation. The paperwork was burdensome; in the nature of things, the exchanges between Nachman and the commissioner gradually became truncated. Weary of detail, Locke offered vague assurances of good faith; weary of generalities, Nachman responded with impatience. In one instance, the HRC chairman protested to Locke that he was "amazed that such simple matters as furnishing eating materials and toilets that work constitute such a problem." On another occasion, Nachman threw up his hands over a further report by Dr. Cohen. To Locke, he wrote simply: "Isn't there something that can be done about this?" In memos to Judge Johnson, Nachman was even more impatient, telling the judge that Locke's failure to repair toilets at Holman was "incomprehensible." In the end, the flow of memoranda between and among Nachman, Locke, and Johnson generated sufficient hostility to sour relations with the commissioner beyond repair, eliminating all hope for a cooperative effort to improve the prison system.[16]

The vacuum in leadership within Alabama's penal system was soon filled by the machinations of Governor Wallace, Attorney General Baxley, and Lieutenant Governor Beasley, who seized on the prison controversy not as an occasion for developing sound governmental policy in trying circumstances, but as an opportunity for furthering their own aspirations for political power. All three saw the potential for demogogic gain at roughly the same time; after that, any advance on this front by one prompted a compensating maneuver from the others. None of the three dared leave the field on pain of finding himself in the background while others commanded the headlines with vote-getting rhetoric about the prisons and the court.

When the January 13 order was handed down, George Wallace was committed to a national campaign for the presidency, while his chief rivals in state politics, Baxley and Beasley, were maneuvering to succeed him as governor of Alabama. Of the three, Jere Beasley had the most to gain from exploiting the controversy surrounding the prisons. He needed public exposure to make himself a credible alternative to Wallace, as long as the governor was on the scene, and to Baxley. Beasley had already enlarged the historically insignificant office of lieutenant governor into a potent political force. He had kept himself and other legislators in Montgomery during the winter of 1975 to address the public issue that always held political promise: efficiency in state government. Now, in the wake of Judge Johnson's order in early 1976, he turned the attention of his Joint Interim Budget Control Committee toward penal affairs. In a series of hearings, Beasley linked the prisons and fears that improvements in them would be expensive to his larger theme of eliminating waste in government. He presented the prison system as poorly managed, even venal, and insisted that better management could effect change without great additional cost to taxpayers. In this, Beasley revived an old and familiar theme in Alabama. He had it that prisons and prisoners should support themselves.

The lieutenant governor kept Locke and other prison officials on a "perpetual hotseat" with questions and observations about their handling of the prison system. Beasley proved to be a master at making headlines with "insinuations of far-flung wrongdoing within the penal system." When Locke responded with appeals for more money, Beasley insisted that deficiencies in administration must be addressed before the legislature would provide more financial assistance to a demonstrably mishandled bureaucracy. In pursuance of this theme, Beasley conducted surprise visits to several institutions in hopes of finding evidence of maladministration with which to embarrass Locke. He accused the commissioner of organizing "dove hunts" on prison lands for senior staff, board members, and their spouses, of keeping the saddle horses about which Judge Johnson had raised questions for use on those occasions, and of serving caviar to his guests. Beasley complained that Locke used an antiquated "barter system" to exchange products from the agricultural program for other goods and services needed to maintain prisoners. In connection with food service, Beasley criticized Locke *both* for grinding the best cuts of beef and pork into hamburger and for feeding steaks and roasts to prisoners. Rarely did Beasley touch on the specifics of Johnson's order. Yet he reacted in his own way to critics who had made the legislature the "whipping boy" with respect to the prisons, and he named a "nonlegislative scapegoat" of his own. Most important, he gained "publicity for a future attempt at higher office."[17]

The commissioner responded only weakly. At times, he "appeared on the verge of an internal explosion." Locke "slouched and twisted in his chair when the questions got tough, spitting out strained, staccato answers that obviously left many thoughts unstated." His performance, indeed, was so disappointing that he narrowly escaped losing his position before the next legislative session even began. After a disheartening trip to Holman and Fountain in late February, Beasley, Nachman, and Beto met for breakfast at Nachman's home and openly discussed the possibility of forcing Locke out. That conversation led to an evening meeting in Wallace's office, attended by representatives of the governor, the Board of Corrections, and key legislators. Wallace himself was out of town campaigning. At that meeting, Nachman and Beasley urged that Locke be fired and replaced by a more able administrator. There was resistance from the board members, particularly Vickers, and the group ultimately accepted Beto's view that Locke should be given more time. Ironically, then, the man whom Locke had initially resented the most was the man who saved him from early dismissal.[18]

When Beasley tired of attacking Locke and the Board of Corrections for political purposes, he stumbled into something with a measure of promise for prison reform. He appointed George McMillan and Brooks Hines to chair a subcommittee to study the problems surrounding the prisons and report to the full budget committee in early summer. The subcommittee, called the Legislative Prison Task Force, allowed its cochairmen to resume their earlier efforts to bring the legislature round to action. The task force held hearings for several weeks and then filed a report endorsing most of the provisions in Judge Johnson's order, quarreling only with the sixty-square-foot requirement, and proposing a series of reform bills, among them an authority to allow prisoners nearing the end of their sentences 90-day furloughs in order to search for jobs, a plan for prison industries to provide employment for inmates with their sentences still ahead of them, and a new "good time" program to give prisoners time off for good behavior if they performed well in the new industries. Those ideas were embraced by the legislature, but another failed to win support—an attempt to remove higher positions in Locke's organization from the state merit system in order to make it easier to dismiss the present occupants. The objective was plain. The men in charge of the prison system had been there for some time and were wedded to the very practices that had brought the system to its knees. Testifying in connection with the bill, Marion Harding conceded as much—referring to his own experience with "about eight persons employed at Fountain" who operated that institution as a "family affair." When Locke's opposition frustrated the bill, McMillan insisted that the commissioner himself should "clean house where housecleaning [was] needed."[19]

Apart from these few reform measures, however, the task force was anything but a progressive force. McMillan said at the outset that "[i]t would be a cold day around" Montgomery "in the summer" before he would vote to appropriate funds to renovate prisons. And, as the hearings progressed, he adopted the same point of view that Beasley had pursued. Even if Locke could explain away the embarrassing matters raised earlier by the lieutenant governor, McMillan and the task force would not be satisfied until he explained something else: why it was that he needed money at all, why it was that the prison system was not self-sufficient. McMillan was impressed that inmates in Texas worked in agricultural fields, in prison industries, and on the Texas Department of Corrections' own internal construction projects. Back in Alabama, he questioned Locke on the strategy for managing the Alabama prison system's vast agricultural lands, marketing the produce, and channeling its revenues into other programs and services.

Self-sufficiency for the prison system, the idea born in the nineteenth century, thus drove McMillan and the task force. It seemed to offer a relatively simple answer to all the problems facing the system and, not coincidently, identified in the court order. Judge Johnson assailed state authorities for permitting penal institutions to deteriorate while punishing prisoners with idleness behind the walls. Commissioner Locke complained that the legislature had not provided funds to maintain the prisons or to establish programs for inmates. The legislature and the public resisted the expenditure of tax revenues for the benefit of criminal offenders. The answer, plain enough to the task force, was to generate funds from inmate labor, satisfying all sides at once.[20]

The scheme failed both because it proved to be impossible to dislodge Judson Locke and other penal officials who knew and defended only what had been done in the recent past and, more fundamentally, because the idea of self-sufficiency was too good to be true. It was one thing to have aspirations, to establish employment opportunities in hopes of encouraging able prisoners to respond favorably. That, after all, was what the National Prison Project had proposed since 1975; it formed the basis for Judge Johnson's requirement that prisoners be given meaningful jobs. It was quite another thing, however, to expect success in a serious fraction of cases. And it was absurd to approach the matter of prisoner employment from the other direction, insisting that inmates be required to work not to provide them with the chance for self-improvement, but to finance the prison system without an additional investment of tax dollars. Such a policy in the 1970s mirrored Alabama's experience with the convict lease system 100 years earlier. Then, the state had generated revenues on the backs of prisoners condemned to the mines, where slave labor was actually profitable. Now, state authorities hoped to make profits in new employment schemes requiring a trained labor force. Alabama established a series of jerry-built economic enterprises that, in turn, demanded a steady flow of inmate workers, however ineffectual, simply to remain viable. Of these, the farms were the worst offenders. In the teeth of expert advice that agricultural lands should be leased to commercial operators or sold out-right, state authorities insisted on sending inmates out to pick butter beans by hand.

Nevertheless, reform-minded observers were hopeful. Judge Johnson himself let it be known that the task force proposals were consistent with his order; Nachman and Beto, who found McMillan's ideas "abso-lutely splendid," began meeting regularly with a new Board of Correc-tions Management and Performance Evaluation Committee, also chaired by McMillan and Hines, charged to monitor the establishment of the prison industries the task force had planned. Indeed, in a further burst of enthusiasm for McMillan's work, Nachman persuaded the Ala-bama senate to ask Johnson to designate a new task force to join the HRC as an additional monitoring body to oversee compliance with the January order. The judge approved the senate's request in an order Nachman drafted for him.[21]

Locke regarded this flurry of legislative activity as another face of Beasley's assault. Responding in angry defiance, the commissioner promised to carry on in a "monumental struggle" in behalf of "correc-tions throughout the country," challenged by "the federal court and now by the [Alabama] Senate." If Beasley were elected governor in 1978, Locke said he would resign without giving Beasley the "chance" to fire him. Members of the Board of Corrections resented both Beas-ley's attempt to shift the focus of public discussion away from inade-quate financial support and Nachman's apparent willingness to be taken in by the lieutenant governor's scheme. When the idea of making the new task force an arm of the court first surfaced, some members, particularly Ricky Robinson, threatened to resign if the plan were accepted. When, however, it was agreed that the task force would not be given actual authority to order the board about, the members who expressed themselves publicly acquiesced. McMillan promised to work with the board "in a spirit of harmony and cooperation"; Vickers said the task force could be a "tremendous help" in keeping the legislature abreast of developments in the prison system.[22]

The board's surface willingness to tolerate the task force was alto-gether prudent. The leadership of the Alabama legislature had little knowledge of, and less interest in, the operation of a prison system. It was unlikely, then, that this new body, another in a series of legislative committees, would interfere greatly with the board's own plans, even if it bore Judge Johnson's imprimatur. Reports of the task force's first meeting supported this appraisal. Having just joined in an extraordinary offer to solve the prison system's many problems, one of the key members of the task force, House Speaker Joe C. McCorquodale, said he had no idea what to do next and proposed that the task force approach the judge again for clarification of its duties. When McMillan scheduled a meeting, however, McCorquodale failed to attend, and Judge Johnson declined to provide specific instructions in any event. The task force operated through the remainder of the year and into the next, conducting investigations and holding hearings with primary focus on the prison system's inability to support itself financially. McMillan and Hines retained two investigators and occasionally loaned them to Nachman for following up complaints. Beyond assisting the HRC in that way, however, the task force had little influence on the prison system's meager efforts to comply with Judge Johnson's order.[23]

If the task force was ineffectual, the Board of Corrections was plainly inept. Stung by criticism from Nachman and Beasley, three members of the board went directly to Judge Johnson in an attempt to persuade him that they were not the incompetent hacks they were portrayed to be. The judge received them, but revealed in memoranda to Nachman and to his personal file that he doubted the success of the meetings that ensued. In early June, for example, Johnson told Dr. Staton that "lack of good management practices was a large part of the problem" and that Staton should retain a consultant "from outside the State of Alabama" to advise the board on the way in which to "put the Alabama Penal System on a sound, business-like basis." Staton and the board insisted, however, that Judson Locke had the "professional expertise . . . to see [the system] through this period of crisis. . . ." Reverend Vickers declared that he would no sooner look beyond Alabama for a penal administrator than for a "doctor, preacher, or lawyer." The board did commission faculty at Auburn University to study the prison system's agricultural holdings, but no major shifts in management occurred for some time. An exchange with Ricky Robinson was even less productive. Robinson phoned to ask whether the January order prevented the board from installing coin-operated pool tables in the prisons to generate revenues. Johnson was candid: "I told him there was nothing in the order [about it]. . . . However, I strongly suggested that the Board spend its efforts in getting educational programs and work programs available to all prisoners . . . [before] fooling around with pool tables." Robinson convinced the board to approve the pool tables, but he suffered merciless criticism in the press for placing "gambling devices" in the prisons.[24]

Pressed to offer more substantive proposals, Commissioner Locke put forward plans on two fronts. First, he presented the legislature with a budget ranging millions beyond what the prison system had received in the past. Nearly half the money would go, he said, for three new institutions, including the "trusty barracks" at Draper and a similarly unpopular work release center planned for Huntsville. If additional funds were not forthcoming, Locke warned, he would be forced to abandon those construction projects and would have to close one of the existing prisons. The response was predictable. Beasley derided Locke's ideas, insisting that McMillan's task force had "more ability in its little finger" than Locke and his cronies had "in their whole bodies." Governor Wallace said he would rather discuss "the victims in their graves sleeping closer together than the prisoners."[25]

On a second front, Locke followed Beto's advice and announced a "three-point program" for reducing the population in existing institutions by 700 men. He planned to identify prisoners approaching the end of their sentences, restore "good time" credits to those who had lost them previously as punishment, and release eligible inmates ninety days early under the new law sponsored by McMillan's task force. This plan was promising, if for no other reason than that it did not depend on the willingness of others to take action that might prove politically unpopular. Indeed, on the very day Locke announced his proposal the parole board declared it was "taking a new, get-tough stand on parolling convicted robbers." Still, the scheme was resisted. Governor Wallace insisted that the prisoners to be released early must be carefully screened, and other officials raised sufficient concerns that Locke was forced to give broad assurances regarding the men affected. In turn, that led to conservative judgments about the danger presented by particular inmates. In the end, fewer prisoners were released than Locke originally envisioned.[26]

Conditions in the prisons improved nonetheless. Even without the release of additional prisoners, the inmate population steadily declined as a result of Judge Johnson's order forbidding the acceptance of new entrants until the state's facilities held only their "design capacity." That welcome change came, however, at the price of ever-increasing crowding in the jails—where conditions continued to deteriorate. Now more than ever, local sheriffs complained that they were being forced to operate maximum security prisons without adequate facilities and staff, county commissions and city councils complained that they were being asked to pay the costs of housing prisoners rightly the responsibility of the Board of Corrections, and prosecutors complained that they were being forced to skew their exercise of discretion in criminal cases in order to allot scarce space in local jails to the most dangerous offenders. In Montgomery, indeed, Judge William Thetford explicitly limited jail space to persons convicted of serious felonies. Once again, there were those who applauded the shift from incarceration to probation for minor offenses. Yet as the population of felons mounted, no one could defend the consequent conditions to which prisoners assigned to the jails were subjected.[27]

Attempts by local authorities to obtain relief from these difficulties in the state courts led to conflicts that Judge Johnson was forced to resolve. Convinced that Locke had authority to shift prisoners between and among local jails as he saw fit, Judge Thetford ordered him to transfer a number of inmates from the jail in Montgomery to another in Dallas County. In response, Judge Edgar P. Russell in Dallas County forbade the sheriff there to accept prisoners from another jail. Caught between the two state judges, Locke asked Johnson for "instructions." Earlier, of course, Johnson had ordered the commissioner to reduce the population at the Houston County Jail, where conditions were being challenged by DeMent and the Justice Department. Now, Johnson issued another order reiterating that Locke could make what transfers he thought appropriate to spread the pain of jail crowding evenly across the state. The judge was not mindlessly rigid. He continued to allow Locke to accept prisoners needing special attention and, when the jail in Lauderdale County was destroyed by fire, he allowed inmates there to be brought to Kilby. He steadfastly refused, however, to relax the "cap" on the population of the prisons in order to alleviate crowding in the jails.[28]

As the pressure in the jails mounted, Locke and the board renewed their efforts to enlarge the prison system's capacity, primarily by constructing new "minimum security" institutions in the northern area of the state. That policy was not chosen in response to reform advocates, who insisted that "community-based" programs were less brutal and less expensive than the large prisons on which Alabama had historically relied, but because community opposition tended to be less vigorous with respect to work release centers than with respect to maximum security penitentiaries. The same local forces that had frustrated L. B. Sullivan's plans for new construction surfaced again, however, and the idea of building in the north collapsed. The Huntsville City Council, individual officials at all levels, and private organizations united in the effort to keep north Alabama free of *any* penal facilities. Sites in Madison, Morgan, Lawrence, and Limestone counties were identified, discussed, and then rejected in the face of local opposition. When it sometimes seemed that the board might dare go forward without local approval, Lieutenant Governor Beasley and Governor Wallace forced penal officials to withdraw. Beasley typically repeated his charge that new institutions would not be needed if the prison system were well administered.[29]

Finally, for their own protection, Locke and the board disclaimed interest in building penal facilities anywhere against the wishes of nearby residents. That disastrous policy barred new construction even in Elmore County near Montgomery, where the board already operated four institutions. And it produced precisely what might have been expected: three extraordinarily poor sites where local authorities *wanted* prisons to generate economic activity. Now, in a paradoxical reversal of the pattern in the north, officials in Heflin, Wadley, and Union Springs, small communities in the depressed rural south, actively campaigned for penal facilities near their homes. There being money for only one new institution, the Board of Corrections took time to make its choice. Union Springs was not selected until the end of 1978 and, even then, construction was frustrated by demonstrations staged by the Alabama Prison Project, an affiliate of the Southern Coalition on Prisons and Jails, which, like the ACLU, hoped to discourage the board's "brick and mortar" policy. The project was ultimately derailed, and no significant new capacity was created in the Alabama prison system until much later when, under the direction of Governor Fob James, the state built several architecturally flawed facilities.[30]

So went prison reform at the hands of Commissioner Locke and the Board of Corrections. An extraordinary meeting of the HRC, held at the end of 1976 in the senate chamber and attended by all the principals, produced only more charges and countercharges. In speeches before the Alabama Bar Association and the legislature, Nachman and Beto focused attention yet again on "mismanagement" and seemed, to most observers, to join Beasley's campaign to saddle Locke and the board with primary responsibility for the problems at hand. Locke, at any rate, understood his critics in that way and responded in kind, suggesting in an interview that Nachman and Beto were not genuinely concerned about improving the prison system.[31]

Frustrated in his efforts to gain ground with Locke and the board directly, Nachman turned public attention to Governor Wallace, who had been largely silent for months. Linking himself all the more tightly to Beasley, Nachman said that the HRC would have been much more successful thus far if it had received from the governor the kind of cooperation it had been given by the legislature, and specifically McMillan's task force. In a contemporaneous memorandum to Judge Johnson, Beto said he had tried to cooperate with the board and with Locke but had come to the conclusion that his counsel was "not welcomed." Now, he intimated, someone else must take action. The media agreed. The *Montgomery Advertiser* declared that it was within Wallace's "domain to demand reform—not to sit about and whine when a federal judge [had] to step into the vacuum the Governor [had] allowed to exist." The *Birmingham News* complained that the men in authority had "formed a circle, with everyone pointing a finger at someone else."[32]

Since Governor Wallace had appointed all the members of the Board of Corrections, his practical influence on state penal policy was unquestioned. In theory, however, the board was an independent body. Wallace often disclaimed any official responsibility for prison conditions and, indeed, insisted that he was an improper defendant in *James*. In the wake of Beasley's success in using the prisons for political advantage, Wallace reexamined his posture and substituted two disingenuous tactics calculated to make it seem that he was taking charge in an emergency while at the same time preserving his ability to forestall serious action. First, the governor insisted, at once, that he still had no direct authority with respect to the prisons and thus could not be held responsible for them *and* that he genuinely wished to have such authority and intended to press the legislature to abolish the Board of Corrections and hand the administration of the prison system over to his office. As long as his proposal to eliminate the board was not enacted, and it was not, the governor had the best of two worlds—disclaiming blame for the prisons and appearing to seek authority to institute reforms.[33]

Second, Wallace startled a joint session of the legislature with a proposal to raise taxes to pay for improvements in the prison system. Here again, duplicity. The governor explained that he did not mean to renege on his longstanding pledge never to raise taxes "without a vote of the people." In this instance, Wallace proposed an increase in the state income tax, the rate of which was fixed by the state constitution. No such rate increase could be achieved, accordingly, without a constitutional amendment requiring a two-thirds vote of the legislature and approval by the electorate. No serious observer anticipated that a proposed tax for the benefit of prison inmates could clear either hurdle. Once again, Wallace sought political benefits from conflicting initiatives. By proposing new taxes, he enjoyed the appearance of leadership;

by choosing a tax that could not realistically be increased, he avoided actual demands on the taypaying public. Moreover, his proposal shifted the problems of the prisons back to Beasley in the legislature, whom Wallace could blame should the new tax not be approved. In the unlikely event that the legislature acted favorably on the plan, the governor could rely on the public to reject it. He then could cite the vote against new taxes to justify his own continued refusal to devote state resources to prison reform.[34]

Despite its brilliance, Wallace's scheme was freighted with risk. Jere Beasley seized on the governor's proposal for a revenue measure as a political self-inflicted wound. Beasley, too, appeared before a joint session of the legislature and admonished the public: "Don't hold your breath until that tax passes." The lieutenant governor condemned Wallace as simply "ill-advised" and promised to campaign against the tax if by some "miracle" it was approved in the legislature. Posturing himself as the protector of the public treasury against this new threat, Beasley encouraged citizens to "contact their local representatives and senators and let them know how they feel about new taxes. . . ." Throughout the remainder of the legislative session, Beasley alternated criticisms of the governor with further attacks on his own selected scapegoat, the hapless Judson Locke. In this, the lieutenant governor, too, was duplicitous. On the one hand, Beasley assailed Wallace for proposing unnecessary taxes—knowing that the governor would be forced to tolerate attacks his own proposal had generated. On the other, Beasley insisted he could improve prison conditions without larger appropriations simply by dismissing Locke and recruiting a manager who would make the prison system self-sufficient—knowing that the Board of Corrections would defend Locke precisely because it was Beasley, not Wallace, who called for his head. In the end, Beasley reaped enormous political profits, political blame fell on others and, of course, nothing of substance was done to improve prison conditions for which, skeptics observed, neither Beasley nor Wallace had any genuine concern.[35]

The next clash of political interests grew out of the new "good time" program sponsored by George McMillan's task force. Under that plan, the Board of Corrections was authorized to reward well-behaved prisoners by deducting as many as two days from their sentences for every day served. Thus the board was able to shorten many prisoners' sentences and to release them early, whether or not the parole board acquiesced. Several objectives for the new scheme were advanced. George Beto said it would encourage discipline by giving prisoners an incentive to behave themselves. McMillan himself explained that the plan was designed to work in tandem with new prison industries. Special "good time" credits were to be the reward for prisoner labor in the manufacturing plants the board would shortly establish. In McMillan's telling, this second objective accounted for the decision to enact a new "good time" law while leaving in place another statute, enacted years earlier, that already authorized sentence reductions for good behavior apart from participation in employment programs. By contrast, others discerned a quite different purpose. The district attorney in Mobile, Charles A. Graddick, condemned the "good time" plan as a ruse for the "wholesale release of prisoners" in order to reduce prison crowding and to provide space for more inmates now in local jails. Governor Wallace took essentially the same view. He vetoed the "good time" bill when it reached his desk, proclaiming that if it were to become law, "there [would] be rejoicing in the prisons . . . [c]ooperate and graduate [would] become the motto of every inmate." Still, at McMillan's behest, the legislature overrode the governor's veto, and the new "good time" program became law.[36]

Nachman and Beto promptly pressed Locke to recognize that the new law "could result in a substantial reduction of the prison population." The commissioner took the hint. He asked Baxley for a formal opinion on whether "good time" credits could be awarded for good behavior exhibited prior to the date on which the new statute took effect. There was method in this. Locke did not ask whether the new law *required* the award of credits "retroactively"; he asked whether it *could be* applied in that way. He plainly hoped not only to reduce sentences in a gradual way, crediting well-behaved inmates with three days for every one served in the future. He meant to take account of inmates' good behavior in the past which, under the new law, might justify a dramatic and immediate reduction in eligible prisoners' terms. The request for an attorney general's opinion was a bureaucratic device. Under Alabama law, state officials could not be held personally liable for actions taken under the authority of such an opinion, and it was common practice for administrators to pass questionable policies through Baxley's office, where they tended to win approval for the very purpose of insulating the officials concerned from attack should their conduct generate litigation. In this instance, one of Baxley's assistants, G. Daniel Evans, accommodated Locke in short order. The retroactive award of "good time" credits, Evans said, "could only further the intent and effectiveness of the statute."[37]

That authority in hand, Locke instructed his staff to identify prisoners with "exceptional" records and to award them "good time" cred-

its "retroactive to beginning date of incarceration." Publicly, he proclaimed that at long last he had found a way to "relieve the congestion"
both in the prisons and in the jails. Locke was cautious. He insisted that
the "good time" law would not be used to release prisoners "wholesale";
only the "cream of the crop" would have its benefits. At the same time,
he and his staff estimated that hundreds of state prisoners would be discharged within a few weeks. Indeed, under an arrangement permitting
local sheriffs to determine the eligibility of sentenced prisoners, it was
possible to release inmates directly from the jails—having served their
terms, reduced by "good time" credits, without setting foot in a state
prison. Within a month, approximately 600 inmates were, in fact,
released. Finally, something substantive had been done about prison
and jail crowding in Alabama. Ricky Robinson summed it up: "It's the
greatest thing we've done in a long time." And it was. By December,
the population in the prisons was down to "design capacity," and Judge
Johnson issued an order allowing Locke to begin accepting new prisoners from the jails.[38]

Yet short-run success bred political repercussions. McMillan now
declared that he had never intended that the "good time" law would be
applied "retroactively"; Graddick and other prosecutors complained
that Locke was assuming an effective power to commute sentences duly
established by the courts; and there were reports that due to mistakes
in the computation of "good time," some prisoners being released were
ineligible even under Evans' reading of law. Beasley blasted Locke for
misreading the statute, for relying on a plainly incorrect opinion from
Baxley's office, and for discharging large numbers of inmates in the
teeth of the laws fixing criminal sentences in the state. Other politicians,
McMillan and Brooks Hines among them, quickly joined in the criticism. Norman Ussery insisted that the parole board had nothing to do
with the "good time" law and pointed out in passing that the Board of
Corrections was actually discharging prisoners before they were eligible
for parole. Once again, Locke and the board were caught in a political
cross fire from which they could not escape. While knowledgeable
observers understood the desperate circumstances that had produced
the "wholesale" release of prisoners, no one would assume responsibility for that action. Locke himself now expressed doubts, recalling that
he had told McMillan before the new statute was enacted that it was
"too liberal." He and Vickers claimed that Nachman and Beto had
forced them to use the "good time" law to reduce crowding in the prisons. Nachman issued a denial, and so the debate ran, every principal
blaming another for what now had become an embarrassment. The law
was changed perfunctorily in the next legislative session.[39]

In the meantime, Bill Baxley found the temptation to redeem himself irresistible. In a startling reversal, he called a press conference and issued a second opinion on the "good time" law. He blamed McMillan for a pernicious public policy, proclaimed his own opposition to that policy, and then located what he himself described as a "technicality" on which to rest a new judgment. Conceding that he was "grasping at straws," Baxley recalled an obscure article of the state constitution, which required that the content of legislative bills be identified in their titles—the better to inform legislators of the substance of bills on which they were asked to vote. Inasmuch as the bill proposing the new "good time" law had not referred expressly to retroactivity, Baxley declared that aspect of the law invalid. This was a curious position to take. Baxley did not contend that Evans had mistaken the meaning of the statute. Nor did he suggest that the entire statute must be discarded. Only the aspect of the law that had caused such embarrassment, and of which he personally disapproved, must be rejected. Even at that, he was inconsistent. He said that the prisoners already released, ostensibly in violation of the state constitution, should not be recaptured and made to serve out their terms. On the contrary, Baxley insisted that the state's resources would better be spent on managing inmates not fortunate enough to be illegally discharged. The result was intellectually chaotic, but politically expedient. Baxley staked out his own defensible ground near Wallace and Beasley. He avoided any confession of error, declared his personal opposition to the release of prison inmates, blamed others for what had happened, and took credit for putting a stop to it. At the same time, however, he preserved for Locke and the board the little ground they had gained by taking advantage of Evans' opinion for the two months it was viable.[40]

On the day before Thanksgiving, as many as 200 prisoners who had already been processed for release were sent back to their cells and dormitories, some to serve years longer as the direct result of Baxley's action. Litigation was inevitable. Baxley himself confessed that his new position might not "stand up" in court. Several lawsuits were filed; one, supported by the ACLU, provoked opinions from both Judge Johnson and the Alabama Supreme Court. In the end, however, the attorney general's turnabout was sustained. Baxley had survived, the damage to his professional reputation offset by the fortification of his political position with respect to his chief rivals, Wallace and Beasley.[41]

The appeals from Judge Johnson's decision in *Pugh* and *James* provided an occasion for still further political posturing. Governor Wallace immediately announced his intention to appeal, notwithstanding Lamar's concession that prison conditions in Alabama were unconstitutional. When Attorney General Baxley seemed unwilling to handle the legal work involved, Wallace retained a private attorney, Thomas S. Lawson, to ask the Fifth Circuit Court of Appeals to overturn Johnson's decision. The January 13 order had been widely reported, and an appeal was "an attempt to grab back some of the headlines the order took away." Still, Johnson found the governor's repudiation of Lamar's confession to be duplicitous and, in response, required lawyers representing Wallace in future cases to produce written authority to act on his behalf.[42]

Attorney General Baxley was formally responsible for representing Alabama's interests in court; indeed, his assistants, including Lamar, had defended Locke and the board at trial. Yet Baxley initially chose not to appeal and, instead, attempted to "negotiate" with Judge Johnson regarding some aspects of the order, namely the requirement that the board contract with the Center for Correctional Psychology to assist with the classification of inmates and various space-per-inmate standards. Baxley's primary request was for relaxation of the requirement, stated firmly in the January 13 order, that cells housing single prisoners must measure sixty square feet in area. He pointed out that the prison system had only sixteen cells measuring sixty, a few dozen measuring fifty, and hundreds measuring forty square feet. He insisted that it was infeasible to enlarge those cells to meet the requirement that Johnson had fixed and that, if the sixty-foot standard were not modified, the board would be forced to abandon as many as 384 cells at a cost of millions of dollars. Accordingly, Baxley asked for permission to continue using forty-foot cells in existing facilities and to construct fifty-foot cells in prisons to be built in the future. He supported his request with a memorandum prepared for McMillan's task force by faculty members at Auburn University in Montgomery, among them Darrell Schlotterback and Dr. William E. Osterhoff, which argued that forty-foot cells met accepted standards in the field.[43]

At first, Judge Johnson was adamant. He amended the January 13 order in some respects—allowing the board to obtain expert advice on classification from someone other than Dr. Fowler and loosening a few other standards. Yet he refused to change the space requirement for individual cells—for present or future prisons; however, when Baxley's representatives assured Johnson that the cell-space issue was the only question on which the attorney general could not compromise and that he would not appeal if his request were granted, the judge relented. For if only the sixty-foot requirement stood in the way of a bargain that would end the attorney general's resistance to the January order and undercut the governor's appeal into the bargain, that aspect of the order could be sacrificed.[44]

On a day when George Beto was scheduled to address the Alabama legislature on the limited progress toward meeting Judge Johnson's demands, he stopped by Johnson's office to ask for advice. When Beto said that he was about to venture once more into the "lion's den," the judge handed him a new order to be issued that day. "Well," Johnson said, "maybe this will help you." The order, issued on May 20, 1976, declared that Johnson had never meant that all the cells in the prison system must actually measure sixty square feet, but that each prisoner must have that much living space, in either a cellular or dormitory unit. If the door to a forty-foot cell were kept locked, that sixty-foot requirement would, of course, be violated. If, however, a smaller cell were not locked and the prisoner were permitted to move in and out at will, *that* would suffice. Thus a prisoner might well be assigned to a forty-foot cell in which to sleep and to store personal items, provided that his total accessible space was at least sixty feet. Johnson reaffirmed his insistence that cells in future prisons must measure sixty square feet, but his acceptance of unlocked forty-foot cells in existing institutions plainly solved the most pressing problem of which Baxley complained.[45]

Beto took the new order with him to the legislature, where it was received with enthusiasm, and for a brief time it seemed that the differences between Judge Johnson and Baxley, if not between Johnson and Wallace, might be resolved. The bargain, however, failed to materialize. Baxley accepted the success he had won in his negotiations with Johnson. Yet spurred by fears that the Wallace appeal would prove politically advantageous to the governor and that his own failure to participate might be taken as timidity, the attorney general soon joined in the governor's effort to overturn the January order. From Judge Johnson's standpoint, Baxley reneged on his agreement to forego an appeal in exchange for a relaxation of the order's space requirements—repeating in this respect his performance in *Wyatt*. The attorney general's willingness to keep commitments to the court was tempered now and always by political expedience.[46]

Having decided to join Governor Wallace in asking the Fifth Circuit to reverse Judge Johnson's decision in *Pugh* and *James,* Bill Baxley reconciled himself to the theoretical arguments that Wallace pressed on the appellate court. Lawson developed those arguments in an elaborate brief in which he acknowledged the dreadful conditions in Alabama's prisons but insisted that the manner in which those institutions were administered was a matter of state policy not subject to judicial oversight. Failing even to mention Lamar's concession that prisoners in Alabama were suffering cruel and unusual punishment, Lawson denied both that conditions in the prisons were unconstitutional and that Judge Johnson had authority to issue such a detailed injunctive order requiring prison reform.

Juxtaposing Johnson's treatment of these cases to Judge Hand's disposition of similar complaints about the Alabama prison system, Lawson highlighted three aspects of Johnson's work as particularly disturbing. Judge Johnson's own protestations to the contrary, Lawson contended that the judge *had* recognized a "constitutional right to rehabilitation," that Johnson had formulated a list of "minimum constitutional rights" that actually represented only enlightened penal policies, and that he had effectively taken control of the prison system through the HRC. Lawson's arguments on each front were tied to a consistent theme. Johnson had ranged beyond what was appropriate for a court charged with constitutional adjudication and had assumed responsibility reserved for other branches of government. In Lawson's telling, Johnson had acted "more like a legislator or administrator than a judge" and, accordingly, had improperly divested the citizens of Alabama of their opportunity to choose, through ordinary political channels, the penal policies they wished to pursue. Finally, Lawson raised a series of technical arguments, among them the claim that the Eleventh Amendment prohibited these lawsuits to the extent they sought federal judicial relief against the state of Alabama or the Board of Corrections as corporate entities. The contention that prisoners could not sue the state itself or one of its agencies, like the argument that Governor Wallace was an improper defendant, made no practical difference. Here again, it was clear that Commissioner Locke and the individual members of the board *could* be sued. Yet the claim was theoretically sound and in Lawson's mind worth making for at least symbolic value.[47]

There were two briefs urging the Fifth Circuit to affirm Judge Johnson's work. Inasmuch as the appeal by Wallace and Baxley implicated not only Johnson's order in *Pugh* and *James,* but his earlier decree in *Newman,* Steve Whinston offered arguments on behalf of the federal government, which had always taken the lead in the medical care case. Then, in another brief prepared by Bronstein and Myers, the prisoners' lawyers met each of Lawson's arguments in turn. They denied that Johnson's order established an affirmative "right to rehabilitation," insisted that the order's specific requirements were amply supported by the evidence at trial, and portrayed the HRC as an entirely reasonable mechanism for ensuring compliance. They met Lawson's more technical arguments as best they could and dismissed his complaint that Judge Johnson had assumed administrative control of the prison system on the ground that the circuit court had previously approved the same kind of judicial behavior in *Gates* and in its earlier treatment of *Newman.* Some had doubts. Taylor thought that Wallace's legal responsibility for the prisons was sufficiently remote that the governor should be voluntarily dismissed as a defendant; Nachman worried that the brief did not defend the Human Rights Committee adequately and, indeed, left the HRC "naked to our enemies." In the main, however, the arguments in support of Judge Johnson appeared strong and were strengthened again by other developments just before the Fifth Circuit's decision.[48]

In this instance, as in the original appeal in *Newman,* the appellate treatment of Johnson's work was colored by eleventh-hour decisions in other cases. After the briefs were filed, the Fifth Circuit handed down an opinion in *Williams v. Edwards,*[49] yet another prison case involving the Louisiana State Prison at Angola. In *Williams,* the circuit court explicitly embraced the theory on which Judge Johnson had relied in the Alabama cases, namely that if the totality of conditions in a prison system amounted to cruel and unusual punishment, a district judge could issue a detailed injunctive decree redressing a series of shortcomings no one of which would have been sufficient to establish an Eighth Amendment violation standing alone. The *Williams* decision thus provided Johnson's order in Alabama with new support. Controversial items in that order, the space-per-prisoner requirements, for example, could be defended in light of the overall conditions in the Alabama prison system, even if the same requirements would not have been justified if the prisons had been clean and structurally sound. A second new case, *Jones v. North Carolina Prisoners Labor Union,*[50] decided by the United States Supreme Court, was much less supportive. In yet another opinion by Justice Rehnquist, the Court held that the federal courts should defer to the policies established by state penal administrators and thus suggested a revival of the hands-off doctrine. Both *Williams* and *Jones* figured in the appellate treatment of *Pugh* and *James,* although *Jones* proved to be less significant than *Williams.*[51]

The three-judge panel scheduled to hear argument in the Alabama cases included Judge James P. Coleman, whose strong personality all the lawyers expected to control the court. Coleman was more politician than judge. He had held several elective offices in Mississippi, including the governorship, and had long been perceived as an opponent of civil rights lawsuits. He was of the Old South, a courtly gentleman known for a personal warmth that concealed a determined commitment to a way of life that had been under attack since the 1960s. In addition, Coleman was widely understood to regard Judge Johnson as a rival. Bronstein worried that Coleman might take the opportunity provided by the Alabama prison cases to frustrate the work of a man whose national reputation and prestige dwarfed his own. At the same time, Judge Coleman was an intelligent man, willing to check his political instincts with legal analysis. Appointed to the federal bench by President Kennedy, he could be expected to side with civil rights groups at least on occasion. Coleman had been on the panel that decided the *Williams* case and might well find the circuit's judgment there compelling in these similar cases. Finally, he might find it most comfortable to affirm Judge Johnson, the better to polish his own image by association with a man he professed publicly to admire.[52]

Judge Coleman did control the court. He asked probing questions when Bronstein and Lawson appeared in New Orleans to argue orally, and he wrote the court's opinion. His primary perspective was not, however, that of the doubtful jurist or the disgruntled rival. In examining these prison cases and Judge Johnson's elaborate order, Coleman relied heavily on his personal experience with the administration of prisons when he was governor of Mississippi. On the one hand, he was concerned that Johnson had taken so much authority away from Commissioner Locke and the Board of Corrections—both by issuing a highly detailed order and by giving Nachman and Beto wide-ranging functions. Coleman resisted the implication that state authorities were incompetent to operate prisons without federal judicial supervision and regarded Johnson's interference with suspicion. On the other hand, he was persuaded that the authorities in Alabama had failed to meet their responsibilities. Conditions were plainly very bad, and precedents on the books, including *Gates* and *Williams,* authorized just the kind of injunctive relief that Johnson had ordered. Indeed, Coleman was unimpressed even with developments that Johnson accepted as welcome. As governor of Mississippi, he had discarded any attempt to make prisons pay their own way, and he now scoffed in private at the suggestion that Alabama could be successful in that vein. In the end, Coleman was convinced that Johnson's actions were justified in the main. Only the language in his opinion, rendered in the spring of 1977, was cause for concern.[53]

Judge Coleman began favorably enough, confirming that prison authorities could not withhold from prisoners the "basic necessities of life" and rejecting "legislative inaction" as an excuse for failure to maintain acceptable living conditions. He described Judge Johnson as "very able" and "highly dedicated" and, indeed, said that Johnson's efforts to "put an end to unconstitutional conditions in the Alabama prison system" warranted "high commendation." Accordingly, Coleman approved most of the provisions in the January 13 order. At the same time, however, he disparaged the very idea of "rehabilitation" in prison, declaring that prison inmates *did* deteriorate and that "no power on earth" could prevent it. Coleman also complained that by creating the HRC Johnson had turned "the administration of the prisons over to" an outside agency when he might "more properly" have appointed qualified "monitors" to observe state officials' efforts to comply with the order and to make periodic reports. Finally, Coleman agreed that Governor Wallace had no direct authority for the prisons and thus was an improper defendant.

Lawson took Coleman's opinion as a rejection of his most important arguments. The discharge of Wallace as a defendant was only a matter of form; Locke and the board remained as appropriate parties to be given the responsibility of implementing Judge Johnson's order. The elimination of the HRC was more important, but that had no effect on the reforms that state officials were still required to achieve. Coleman's remarks about rehabilitation were equally unavailing. Indeed, the only genuine accomplishments Lawson could count from the appeal touched on minor matters: Coleman set aside some of the rules regarding the treatment of inmates' family and friends during visits to the prisons, discarded the one-person-per-cell rule, and directed Judge Johnson to reconsider the sixty-foot rule for new facilities. Lawson was disappointed, moreover, that Coleman had ignored his Eleventh Amendment contention. He decided, then, to ask the court to reconsider its judgment; failing that, he resolved to seek further review in the U.S. Supreme Court.[54]

The prisoners' lawyers were less certain where their interests lay. Bronstein's primary concern was not the substance of Coleman's opinion; he, like Lawson, thought the appellate court had made very few changes in Judge Johnson's order. Bronstein thus asked for reconsideration primarily in hopes of obtaining a second opinion without so much disparaging rhetoric. The Justice Department was unsure whether even Coleman's language was troubling. Steve Whinston suggested that the government join Bronstein's request for reconsideration, but Walter W. Barnett, Whinston's superior in Washington, summed up what was in many minds. Judge Coleman's product was "difficult" to "characterize." The opinion was a "dog," and the "question" was whether it would be a "sleeping one." Newspaper headlines reflected a

similar ambivalence. Some reported that Coleman had upheld Judge
Johnson; others understood quite the opposite. In time, Barnett's
appraisal proved sound. The circuit court denied both requests for
reconsideration, leaving the Alabama prison cases where Judge Coleman had put them, and Judge Johnson treated Coleman's opinion as
affirming his work. In the end, any damage done by the appeal was held
to a minimum.[55]

Still, there was the Supreme Court. The drive to vindicate state prerogatives caused Lawson to seek review in Washington. At this point,
the Prison Project's national perspective came to the fore. Some members of the project's steering committee urged Bronstein also to seek
Supreme Court review in an effort to supersede Judge Coleman's opinion. Others argued against risking a palatable circuit judgment before
justices who, having just decided *Jones,* might be even less sympathetic
to litigation over prison conditions. Even if Coleman's opinion were
viewed as unfavorable, it was at least confined to the Fifth Circuit and
had not yet been given the national moment of a Supreme Court decision. Of course, the Supreme Court had historically sustained Judge
Johnson's decisions virtually without exception, particularly in civil
rights cases. In addition, Chief Justice Burger admired Johnson and
once had suggested that President Nixon name him to the Supreme
Court. Still, by 1977 the Court had come to be dominated by other
Nixon appointees who shared neither the Warren Court's enthusiasm
for civil rights lawsuits nor Burger's special regard for this district judge.
After a vigorous debate, the committee chose a strategic middle ground.
Bronstein did not affirmatively ask the Supreme Court to review the
circuit's judgment. Nor did he wait to see whether the Court granted
Lawson's request for review. He immediately filed a statement telling
the Court that *if* Lawson's request were granted, the justices should consider not only whether the Fifth Circuit had given prisoners too much,
but whether the circuit had undercut Judge Johnson's order, in word or
deed, and thus had given prisoners too little.[56]

These elaborate tactics were wasted in the end. Late in the year,
and without accepting formal briefs or hearing oral arguments from the
lawyers, the Supreme Court disposed of the *Pugh* and *James* cases in a
summary order declining to consider most of Lawson's contentions.
The justices treated only the long-neglected Eleventh Amendment
claim and, on that issue, held that neither the state itself nor the board
could properly be ordered to comply with the January 13 injunction.
That formalism aside, the Court's treatment of the Alabama cases came
to naught. The circuit judgment, described in Judge Coleman's opinion,

became the law of the *Pugh* and *James* cases. Following instructions, Judge Johnson dismissed Governor Wallace, the state itself, and the board as defendants, diluted the rules regarding visitation, dissolved the HRC and, in an abundance of caution, limited the sixty-foot rule to penal facilities already in existence. He plainly implied an understanding, however, that his January 13 order had been sustained in all other respects.[57]

Judge Johnson had not pressed for full compliance with his order while the appeals were pending. Far better, he thought, to "tread water" until his work was vindicated. The resulting delay carried risks. Johnson was under consideration for several prestigious appointments and, by the fall of 1977, knew that President Carter meant to name him director of the FBI. Anything he hoped to accomplish in the Alabama prison cases must be achieved promptly or be left to someone else. Nachman understood as much and informed his committee members that the "attempted appeal" should not "deter or delay" the HRC's efforts to enforce the January 13 order. Judge Johnson's concerns about the appeal, however, were paramount. To underscore his resolve, the judge told lawyers on both sides that he would take no important actions in the short run and that he "or some other judge to whom the cases will be assigned" would proceed only after hearing from the appellate courts. Indeed, during the period in which he was distracted by the FBI appointment, Johnson transferred formal responsibility for the prison cases to Judge Pittman in Mobile. Uncertainty regarding his health ultimately caused the judge to decline the FBI post and to resume control of *Pugh* and *James* the following spring. In the interim, of course, Alabama penal officials and public figures responded to the January 13 order in their own, politically charged manner.[58]

The sole exception to Johnson's pause pending appellate review was the classification of inmates. Everyone, including Johnson, considered classification to be critical to genuine change in the Alabama prison system, and the judge insisted that an effective classification program be established and completed on an emergency basis. To that end, the Center for Correctional Psychology was ushered into the system to do what Locke's staff had failed to do. The center's experience, however, proved to be yet another lesson in Alabama politics. In a real sense, it was the frustration of the Prison Classification Project that signaled that efforts to implement Johnson's order faced a long and bitter campaign against myriad forces seeking to derive only political benefits from the tragedy at Alabama's penal institutions.

6

Recalcitrance

By all accounts, the classification of prisoners was central to the task of reforming the Alabama prison system. At the basic level of the theory in *Pugh,* it was essential to identify violent inmates in order to remove them from the dormitories which, pursuant to the January 13 order, could safely house only "minimum security" offenders. At the further level of the theory in *James,* it was necessary to discover prisoners' needs and desires so that candidates for educational and vocational programs could be assigned accordingly.

In form, Alabama had been committed to classification since the nineteenth century, when rehabilitation emerged as an objective of confinement. The practice of herding "together the boy and the man, the beginner in crime and the hardened sinner" was officially condemned as inconsistent with the object to "reform" either. The lease system substituted its own brand of classification. Penal authorities separated "dead heads" from prisoners who could be made to work and, within the class of working inmates, they distinguished "first class" from "second class" hands. Yet the objective then was not to identify the employment to which a prisoner should be assigned for his own good, but to fix the price that could be charged for his services. The original, rehabilitative purpose of classification resurfaced with the inauguration of the old Kilby Prison. Convicts were interviewed by "trained experts," who determined the course of their "reformatory treatment." Once again, however, classification for the benefit of prisoners was short lived. The press of numbers and persistent demands that the prison system pay its own way resulted in the assignment of prisoners to whatever space was available and to whatever work needed to be done.[1]

The circumstances had not changed markedly decades later when, in January 1975, Hugh Swafford developed an innovative scheme for classifying incoming prisoners at Mt. Meigs. Under Swafford's program, new prisoners submitted to intelligence and psychological testing, underwent physical and mental examination, and met with classification teams charged with assigning them appropriate "custody grades" and "rehabilitative programs." On its face, the plan was promising, but in practice it was not followed. Swafford resigned after only four months when he lost direct access to Commissioner Sullivan and was told to report to Bill Long. Swafford insisted that he could not function properly under the direction of a line officer and that he feared classification would revert "back to the old system." That, it later became clear, is precisely what occurred.[2]

After Swafford's departure, classification deteriorated into the intolerable state of affairs presented to Judge Johnson at the trial in *Pugh* and *James.* Prisoners still were classified according to whether they presented "maximum," "medium," or "minimum" security risks. Yet arriving inmates were routinely assigned the "maximum" label and thereafter were expected to demonstrate their fitness for some less secure status. Rehabilitative programs such as work release could accommodate relatively few inmates. In general, prisoners were assigned to any institution, any living quarters, and any program where space was available. Most flowed into the open dormitories at the four major prisons where visitors could distinguish "maximum" from "minimum" security prisoners only by checking institution records, and a move up or down in an inmate's security status had no discernible effect on the level of supervision he received. As Judge Johnson put it, there was no "working" classification program in the Alabama prison system.[3]

On the assumption that other elements of the January 13 order could not be addressed until prisoners were classified, Johnson made classification the first priority. Even though his temporary "cap" on the prison system's population had now dammed the flow of new inmates, the task of reclassifying existing prisoners was still heroic. Johnson doubted that state authorities could be successful working alone and, accordingly, summoned Dr. Fowler's Center for Correctional Psychology. That action may have been defensible as a reasonable means of establishing a rational classification program and making it operate quickly in trying circumstances. The events that followed, however, rendered the success of a "crash" classification program involving University of Alabama faculty and students modest at best.[4]

Difficulties surfaced immediately and continued in phases. At the outset, confusion and conflict over the precise role that Fowler was to play delayed the classification process for several critical months. Johnson deliberately obfuscated this point in his order, requiring state officials to formulate a plan for classification and then to "contract" with Fowler's center not actually "to implement" the new scheme as the National Prison Project had requested in brief, but "to aid in the implementation" of the plan. This in hopes that relations between Fowler and state authorities could be sorted out informally. Ambiguity bred disagreement, however, and much time was lost in a series of confrontations over the question of authority. Moreover, by the time Judge Johnson resolved doubts by placing Fowler in formal charge of the classification effort, wounded feelings on both sides frustrated future cooperation. Yet cooperation was essential. The barriers presented by bureaucratic routine, inertia, and rank incompetence in the prison system doomed any effort on the part of outsiders to effect change without the support of the officials concerned.

Not only the conflict that developed between Dr. Fowler and state authorities, but the means by which antagonisms were addressed, caused continuing difficulty. Early on, Fowler turned to Nachman and the HRC for help in winning acceptance among state officials. Nachman responded, but a new series of letters purporting to speak for Judge Johnson only aggravated Commissioner Locke's irritation with Nachman's tendency to act as a surrogate for the judge. The informality of that practice, moreover, provided state authorities with an issue for their appeal from Judge Johnson's order. Later, Locke, Fowler, and key members of the Board of Corrections abandoned attempts to resolve their differences by dealing only with Nachman and turned to the lawyers who had represented state officials and prisoners in *Pugh* and *James*. That action proved to be even more frustrating, because the lawyers lacked relevant expertise and could scarcely advise Judge Johnson on the way in which classification should proceed. They could perform, and did perform, only as problem-solving advocates. They initially contrived an interim peace between Fowler and state officials but, inasmuch as that plan failed to resolve underlying tensions, it proved ineffectual. Then, the lawyers simply faced off as adversaries and "settled" remaining conflicts through arms-length negotiations and formal litigation.

In fact, prisoners were classified in the end, most of them according to criteria and procedures that Fowler's center developed. Yet few permanent reforms were effected. After Fowler's departure, evidence of his having operated in the Alabama prison system for more than a year disappeared with barely a trace. The experience with classification was thus a lesson, and an early one, in the monumental barriers faced by any outside agent introduced into an ailing state penal system to make changes opposed by resentful, recalcitrant state authorities.

The choice of Dr. Fowler's center was natural enough. The University of Alabama was itself a state institution, Fowler and many of his faculty and staff members were Alabamians, and the center had previously worked with the Board of Corrections in the development of the master plan and the study of the prison system's mental health programs. Dr. Clements' testimony at trial, albeit on behalf of the plaintiffs, established that the center could assist in new classification efforts and, most important, Ira DeMent assured Judge Johnson that Ray Fowler was a man on whom the judge could rely. As soon as the January 13 order was issued, Fowler and Dr. Brodsky assembled a group of graduate students to anticipate what lay ahead and collected materials on classification from other sources, notably the Federal Bureau of Prisons. They also contributed their estimates of what classification would cost to the university group organized by Dr. Toohey to predict the potential expense of implementing all aspects of the court order. Toohey accompanied Fowler and Brodsky to Montgomery in early February to discuss classification with Nachman and Beto.[5]

Unfortunately, the hoped-for cooperation between the center and penal authorities failed to develop. Shortly after trial, Commissioner Locke employed Dr. Kenneth Warren, a practicing psychologist in Montgomery. Warren was an intelligent professional, albeit of modest experience, whose presence lent credence to Locke's insistence that his staff was capable of classifying prisoners without interference from the outside. In ordinary times, the decision to retain Warren might have been taken as a hopeful sign. Now, it was evidence that the prison system would not suffer lightly a court-ordered agreement with Fowler. Equally important, Fowler and Brodsky brought to their relations with state authorities a surprising, and dysfunctional, bellicosity. These were insightful men, who understood that success would depend on their ability to reassure distrustful state officials. Yet they revealed in their private memoranda and in their relations with Locke, Warren, and others that they regarded those officials with suspicion and understood themselves as having a commission from the court to bring more enlightened thinking to the Alabama classification program.[6]

Locke's resistance to the center was reflected in Attorney General Baxley's motion in late February, asking the judge to lift the requirement that state authorities enter a formal contract with Dr. Fowler. Johnson explained in response that he was adamant only that the state have some source of expert advice with respect to classification and, in fact, was indifferent whether Dr. Fowler's center or some other "comparably qualified and willing" group supplied what was needed. When, however, Baxley proposed the four faculty members at Auburn University in Montgomery who had prepared earlier memoranda on the prisons, including the statement criticizing Johnson's sixty-foot space requirement, the plaintiffs objected vigorously. Bronstein collected statements from knowledgeable professionals in the field, insisting that Fowler and his staff were far superior to Schlotterback, Osterhoff, and the others Baxley named. For example, John Conrad said that employing the AUM faculty, none of whom enjoyed a national reputation, instead of Fowler's prestigious Center for Correctional Psychology, "would be like using a local high school football team . . . when the Pittsburgh Steelers [were] available." Judge Johnson attempted to satisfy all sides by ordering Locke to work with both the University of Alabama and the AUM groups, with Fowler serving as chairman of the joint "panel of experts." That compromise did little to ameliorate tensions. Fowler and Brodsky failed to involve the AUM faculty significantly in the process. And, for their part, Locke and his staff exploited any remaining ambiguity regarding Fowler's authority.[7]

Continuing conflict was evident in still further skirmishing prior to Fowler's arrival. On the apparent assumption that Fowler was to assist in the "implementation" of a new classification plan and not in the development of such a plan in the first instance, Locke and his staff formulated a new scheme and presented it to Johnson within a few weeks after the January order. On first blush, the plan seemed sound. It tracked the Swafford program in the main, departing from it on occasion to take account of guidelines that Johnson himself had mentioned. Dr. Fowler and others in Tuscaloosa were unimpressed. The plan's very plausibility evoked concern that Locke might not mean to carry through with it. Fowler's center might be drawn into an unworkable arrangement with state authorities and the AUM group and, when the joint effort failed, might suffer the blame. A memo from Carl Clements warning that the center should not be allowed to become the "fall guy" for the Board of Corrections underscored Fowler's trepidation. His reaction was predictable. If he was to bear responsibility for classification in the Alabama prison system, he wanted an opportunity to review, and perhaps to modify, the plan with which he would work. In succeeding days, Fowler consulted with Taylor and Knowles on the contents of Locke's plan and, in reliance on Fowler's advice, Taylor filed a motion asking Judge Johnson to delay approval of that plan until the "panel of experts" had an opportunity to examine it. Johnson granted the motion, setting the stage for Fowler's initial efforts to gain control of classification at all levels, from the formulation of the basic framework through the making of actual classification decisions regarding particular prison inmates.[8]

Only now did Fowler make contact with the commissioner—three and one-half months after the January order and only two and one-half months before the classification of inmates was to be completed. His manner was contentious. He wrote to Locke, stating that he understood that he was to have responsibility for classifying prisoners, that he intended to employ the AUM faculty and others to assist in the project, and that it would be "helpful" to have a list of "classification experts" already employed by the prison system who might be "assigned to work in the classification program." He proposed a meeting to be held in early June at the university's office in Montgomery and asked Locke and his staff to attend. Fowler sent copies of his letter to Nachman and Judge Johnson; Nachman then sent Locke a letter of his own, stating that the judge had directed him to inform the commissioner that he was in "complete accord" with Fowler's suggestions and desired that they be "carried out as rapidly as possible." In these circumstances, Locke could hardly refuse even to meet with Fowler, but he did insist on shifting the meeting place to his own office and inviting not only staff members concerned with classification, but Lawson and David Flack, another attorney recently retained to protect state interests in the litigation. The participation of counsel gave the meeting an adversary flavor that, in turn, magnified the mutual suspicions already in evidence. Brodsky's notes are revealing.

> Our first meeting with Judson Locke . . . in his office. It's an ambush.
>
> There are 17 people there: a number of attorneys, six faculty members [from AUM], and the higher level staff in charge of professional services. . . . Every time I've gone to the Board of Corrections headquarters for a meeting, the strategy has been to bring as many people as they can to outtalk, outnumber, overwhelm. It's an ambush, all right.[9]

Other notes taken by Brodsky suggest that Fowler struck a conciliatory posture, that he praised Locke and his staff whenever possible and minimized the extent to which he and the center would alter arrangements already in place. Fowler's own rendition of the meeting presents a different picture. In a follow-up letter to Nachman, plainly intended to memorialize understandings reached in the meeting, Fowler recalled a "frank exchange of information in a generally cordial atmosphere." When Lawson asked that commitments not be made to potential staff members, Fowler "informed" him that he could delay only for two weeks but then would need to employ "several people to begin work in July." In response to questions from the AUM group regarding the existing classification plan, Fowler said that plan was "seriously deficient" and that he intended to submit a "revised plan" that would "specify the steps to be taken to implement each provision of [the January 13 order] with regard to classification." Fowler said that he was willing to develop the revised plan "cooperatively," so that the Board of Corrections might "stipulate its acceptance of the plan and its willingness to proceed immediately toward its implementation." But he made it plain that he would submit his own scheme if agreement proved to be "impossible." Locke's follow-up letter to Nachman ignored Fowler's specifics and reported only that the University of Alabama group would coordinate with Warren in the "evaluation of the techniques to be employed" in the classification program.[10]

Fowler, Brodsky, and the other university faculty had little respect for Locke or, by extension, those associated with him. Brodsky's notes reflect their attitude.

> Judson Locke slouches for a long time and then sits up in his chair. It may be that his chair is just too large for him and the seat is too low. Perhaps his desk is too high. In any case, he appears to be nowhere big enough to fill the seat.[11]

Locke, for his part, found the center's involvement in the prison system irksome, something to be tolerated but hardly embraced. The initial meeting thus left the gap between the principal players wider even than it had been previously. Hovering in the background, Nachman voiced impatience. "I hope," he wrote to Fowler, "that you will be able to impress upon those charged by law with the administration of the Alabama corrections system" that the adoption and implementation of a proper classification plan "is an absolute imperative and must be accomplished forthwith." That impatience was warranted. Still, there was no acceptable plan for classification; still not a single prisoner had been classified.[12]

Fowler understood that time was of the essence and thus quickly developed a "modified" classification plan in two phases. First, he and a small staff would devote the month of July to Draper alone. They would not only reach classification decisions for the prisoners there, but would use the experience to develop and hone standards and procedures for use in the rest of the system. Second, beginning in early August and reaching into the fall, more personnel would be hired, trained, and charged to classify inmates at all the other institutions. This "modified" plan was little more than a timetable, at most an outline, for what Fowler meant to do; the affirmative policies he would pursue and the procedures he would employ were not indicated. A timetable, however, was all that Fowler could muster in the circumstances. He presented his "modified" plan to Locke as a fait accompli.[13]

Locke agreed to submit Fowler's plan to the board for approval, but Fowler would not wait. He went directly to Judge Johnson's chambers. His private description of his conference with Johnson not only illustrates again his attitude toward the work at hand, but reveals Fowler's perception of the judge.

> The Judge as one might expect, sits behind a very large desk placed in the exact center of the far end of a long room. The walk to his desk is long. The urge to bow on reaching his desk is overwhelming. The Judge was in fine spirits. He smiled, shook my hand, greeted me warmly, and obviously had no idea what I was doing there. I told him that I had brought the response to his request for a revised classification plan, and everything immediately clicked into place.
>
> He began to talk about classification with great intensity. He said that classification was the key to the entire prison problem, and that he was convinced that nothing could ever be done to improve the situation until the classification system was developed. He thanked me for taking on the responsibility, opened the envelope, and began to thumb through the material rapidly.
>
> After about a minute, he said, "Do you need any court orders on this?" Raw power!
>
> I had a mad impulse to ask him to make Stan Commissioner of Corrections, but, instead, I told him that I thought everything was going all right. . . .
>
> When I told him that the classification would require eleven months, his reaction astonished me. He was not indignant, as I had feared, or resigned, as I had anticipated. Instead, he said quietly, "Couldn't you do it just a little faster?" He reminded me that the case was under appeal, and said that, whatever happened, "I'd sure like to know that at least the classification has been accomplished."
>
> Well, what do you say to a federal judge? I told him that we would move as rapidly as possible, and make every effort to complete the classification. He seemed pleased.
>
> He wrote some notes, apparently reminding himself to read and to respond to the plan on Monday. He said, "I'll look this over carefully and see if any judicial action is necessary."[14]

Three days later, Johnson issued an order rejecting the defendants' earlier plan and accepting Fowler's "modified" plan in its stead. And in new language that seemed to sink Fowler ever more deeply into the business of classification, the judge ordered state authorities to implement the "modified" plan "through" the Center for Correctional Psychology and the AUM group.[15]

Fowler now had an approved plan of his own making and instructions to carry it out, but he lacked immediate financial support. Instead of losing more time wrangling with Locke about expenses, he persuaded the University of Alabama to underwrite his work through the summer, with the expectation that the Board of Corrections would reimburse the university when a new fiscal year began in the fall. Although it seemed that some students would participate, Fowler's program was not presented as a teaching or research project. Another agency of state government simply could not, or would not, pay the bill for immediate action required of that department by a federal court. Yet university officials agreed, in the same spirit in which they had responded to the legislature's request for assistance in estimating the cost of implementing the January order. Not only did Fowler's project seem to be worthwhile, but it offered the university another opportunity to preserve its special relationship to state government generally. In short order, Fowler received permission to establish a Prison Classification Project (PCP), operating directly from the office of the president of the University of Alabama with Toohey as project director.[16]

Fowler and Brodsky now assembled a staff for Phase I. They held orientation meetings in Tuscaloosa, then moved the team to Draper Prison. When the PCP began work in July, the group numbered approximately twenty faculty and graduate students. The project shared "cramped, poorly ventilated, and overheated quarters" with a local junior college, which offered basic education courses to selected inmates. Fowler and Brodsky divided the staff into three-member "classification boards" to interview inmates and make recommendations regarding appropriate "custody grades" and program assignments. The boards began with few guidelines, leaning heavily on factors mentioned in Johnson's order. They identified elderly and emotionally disturbed or retarded prisoners who needed special treatment or transfer to more appropriate facilities, and they located other inmates who might safely be assigned to work release centers in the community. Within the category of prisoners properly held at Draper, they separated potentially violent offenders from those appropriate for the dormitories. The criteria at this early stage were rough: age, offense, criminal record, mental stability, and aptitude. The process for making judgments was also simple. Prisoners were first provided with an explanation of classification and its objectives, this in hopes they would see their own interest in cooperation. Then they were given a battery of tests, their files were examined, and they were interviewed—once by a single member of the staff and then by a classification board. Finally, either Fowler or Brodsky reviewed the board's recommendations.[17]

The work progressed deliberately. A few decisions had been reached by the end of the first week and, by the end of the month, several classification boards were operating simultaneously and turning out reasoned judgments in which Fowler and Brodsky had substantial confidence. Yet there were drawbacks. Institution records proved to be inaccurate and incomplete, prisoners misrepresented the facts, and the boards occasionally reached inconsistent conclusions in similar cases. Those difficulties were overcome slowly, as experience permitted the staff to sharpen substantive criteria and improve procedures. In general, inmates were given the least restrictive custody grades and program assignments consistent with serious security concerns. Prisoners came to trust and appreciate the work being done, and staff members enjoyed a measure of satisfaction that something worthwhile was being accomplished. The primary source of concern at this early point was the arduous pace of decision-making, which Fowler and Brodsky wished to make as reliable as possible.[18]

Early success bred its own problems. Now that at least some prisoners were being identified as dangerous and, accordingly, inappropriate for dormitory housing, it was necessary to place them in single cells, cells generally unavailable at Draper. At the other end of the scale, promising inmates were being selected for educational and vocational programs—also in short supply. Fowler and Brodsky refused to take the number of single cells and places in rehabilitative programs as given, such that the boards could assign to those cells and programs only the number of prisoners that could be accommodated under existing circumstances. The psychologists made their decisions in the abstract, based on each individual prisoner's needs, and then expected Locke and the Board of Corrections to respond by making suitable situations available in the quantity required. With every prisoner given one of the PCP's three custody grades signaling some potential for violence ("maximum," "close," or "medium" security prisoners) the pressure on the system's scarce single cells began to build. The demand was even greater for opportunities appropriate for prisoners assigned to "community" custody—educational and vocational programs and, in particular, work release.

The result was more conflict, on two levels. First, at the personal level, the assignment of numerous prisoners who had previously been considered "maximum" security risks to community facilities in which they would be loosely supervised underscored the arbitrariness of the classification scheme the PCP supplanted. Warren and Nagle were incensed that their own work should be jettisoned in favor of recommendations from inexperienced students. Second, at the systemic level, the new assignments threatened to accomplish what Judge Johnson had explicitly refused to order—the restructuring of fundamental penal policy in Alabama. State authorities were presumably entitled to operate secure prisons in which inmates were kept in cells and dormitories, so long as those institutions met minimal public health standards. Yet the classification judgments being made by the PCP contemplated that large numbers of prisoners would not be confined in that way and would, instead, be channeled to community facilities that state authorities wished to reserve for the privileged few. Fowler and Brodsky disclaimed any authority to use classification to thwart Alabama's sentencing laws. Indeed, they worried aloud over the risks their judgments portended for the public at large. Nevertheless, they persisted in making classification assignments consistent with sound criteria. The result was that convicts who previously would have languished in prison were slated for transfer to less secure facilities.[19]

Warren in particular regarded Fowler and Brodsky as interlopers—rivals for control of matters he had been appointed to oversee. He understood that Judge Johnson's order had brought Fowler into the system to assist in classification and that state officials now must work *with* the PCP in some fashion. Still, Warren considered that fundamental responsibility for the enterprise was his and that he was called on only to cooperate with Fowler as he, Warren, performed under his own mandate. Warren repeatedly challenged Fowler, always searching for opportunities to demonstrate his own, independent authority and testing the full measure of Fowler's support from the judge. Some tactics were successful for a time, then backfired. For example, Warren insisted that his own staff of classification officers was occupied at Mt. Meigs, now the Kilby Medical and Diagnostic Center, where escapees, parole violators, and other prisoners whom Judge Johnson had exempted from the "cap" order were being classified. As a result, Warren's officers were not regularly available to work with Fowler's group at Draper. By denying

Fowler essential staff, Warren not only underscored the point that he controlled his own employees and, with them, the major share of the classification process throughout the prison system. He also severely restricted the pace at which the Draper project could progress. At the same time, however, Warren had considerable influence with the men and women who answered to him and could have an impact on classification assignments made by PCP boards in which they participated. When he kept his staff away from Draper, he lost the opportunity to affect that work and, as a practical matter, rendered it more likely that PCP boards, constituted by temporary psychologists and students working alone, would reach decisions Warren found unacceptable.[20]

Warren was under pressure from wardens to retain stringent custody grades for most prisoners. "Hell, Doc," one warden said to him, "if they got a number, they're maximum." Thus when it became clear that the absence of his own staff from PCP boards effectively silenced his voice in the classification process at Draper, Warren shifted to a new and more effective strategy. At least in Fowler's perception, Warren identified those members of the permanent staff who tended to agree with Fowler's personnel and kept them at Kilby most of the time. Others, who were less sympathetic to the Fowler group's views and more receptive to Warren's influence, were sent to Draper with increasing frequency. If Fowler now had a larger staff from which to constitute his classification boards, he also must contend with a group of permanent staff working at cross-purposes with his own people. This tactic, too, may have backfired. For as much as Warren may have hoped to vindicate prior classification decisions and to pacify wardens by insisting that most prisoners receive "maximum," "close," or "medium" custody grades, his effectiveness in that vein necessarily prevented prisoners from being given "minimum" or "community" assignments. It was one thing to shun the "community" label—and thus to avoid the need to find more places in the system's oversubscribed work release programs. It was quite another to resist the "minimum" designation-- and thus to limit the number of prisoners who, consistent with Judge Johnson's order, could be housed in dormitories. Paradoxically, any success in keeping Fowler's group from declaring arguably undeserving prisoners to present only "minimum" security risks actually undercut state officials' overarching interest in finding the dormitories suitable for most prisoners.[21]

Conflicts also arose directly with respect to the custody grade and program assignments the PCP selected for particular inmates. Anticipating disagreements, Fowler agreed to forward PCP recommendations to Warren and Nagle and to consider any "objections" they might have. If they raised objections, he agreed to meet with them in an attempt to reconcile their positions with his own. The plan was simple enough and consistent at one level with the threshold understanding that classification was to be a joint effort. Yet the scheme also formalized the contentious nature of the enterprise and, moreover, produced delays. Fowler charged that Warren did not work fast enough after receiving files and, indeed, deliberately held files longer than necessary in order to postpone final decisions and, ultimately, the need to find placements for prisoners in the programs to which they were assigned. Warren, for his part, maintained that he could not devote immediate attention to files sent to him and that Fowler frustrated his attempts to keep pace by sending large numbers of files at once.[22]

Warren and Nagle raised objections in two forms. Occasionally, they complained merely that mistakes had been made regarding individual prisoners. Fowler and Brodsky often agreed to modifications but, in some instances, they resisted in order to prove their resolve, and their authority, in "test" cases. When, for example, a 17-year-old prisoner pleaded desperately for an assignment preventing the authorities from returning him to Holman, where he had previously been assaulted, Brodsky telephoned Locke to demand assurances that the prisoner would not be removed from Draper and kept the inmate near his office while he waited for a reply, to ensure that the man was not shipped to Holman that very afternoon. If Locke did not respond by day's end, Brodsky planned to contact Nachman; if Nachman could not help, Brodsky intended to approach Judge Johnson directly. Locke did return Brodsky's call, and it seems the commissioner settled the matter to Brodsky's satisfaction. In retrospect, however, the episode reflected a program debilitated by mutual suspicion, personality conflict, and an outsized tendency toward the dramatic.[23]

In addition, Warren and Nagle insisted on several blanket policies applicable to all cases. First, in response to the system's general emphasis on security, inmates were to be assigned at least to "medium" custody if they presented a risk of escape. Prisoners with "detainers" (notices from other states informing Alabama authorities that the prisoners were wanted in those states after they completed their Alabama sentences) automatically were to be considered escape risks. Second, on the theory that work release was a "transitional" program, only prisoners within eighteen months of their release dates should be assigned to placements in the community. Third, on the ground that the Frank Lee Youth Center was reserved for the system's most corrigible inmates, prisoners who committed infractions of the rules there and were sent to any of the state's other institutions, even for a short time, should never be reassigned to Frank Lee. This out of concern that prisoners with experience elsewhere might corrupt the state's best penal facility. Fourth, "aged and infirm" prisoners were not to be given "extended furloughs" amounting, in actual effect, to permanent release from custody. Finally, and most important, Warren and Nagle insisted that changes in custody grade could be employed as penalties for misconduct. Custody assignments made by the PCP at Draper thus could be countermanded by wardens and the penal system's own classification teams at Kilby.

Fowler objected to each of these policies in turn. His criteria for selecting custody grades placed emphasis on prisoners' potential for violence, the better to identify those who might harm others in the dormitories or in the community, and subordinated evidence that inmates might attempt to escape. Fowler refused, moreover, to assume that every prisoner subject to a "detainer" was for that reason an escape risk. He insisted on probing further to determine whether the basis of "detainers" in particular cases actually gave prisoners an incentive to flee. Fowler flatly rejected the eighteen-month limit on work release. Conditions in the major institutions being what they were, he refused to credit the argument that prisoners who presented no serious danger to others should nevertheless be denied work release assignments. Fowler also rejected the rigid rule governing assignments to Frank Lee. While he conceded that prisoners should be selected for that facility with care, he made no sense of an unbending prohibition on giving any inmate a second chance. He could find nothing in the controlling statute fixing time limits on "furloughs" and found it perfectly appropriate to use that law to release elderly and disabled inmates into facilities more appropriate to their needs.

The use of custody grade changes as penalties for the violation of prison rules presented, in Fowler's mind, the most flagrant disregard of the classification program he hoped to establish. This was the "old system" revived, the system in which wardens and other line personnel undercut rational distinctions among prison inmates in order to maintain their own severe, militaristic, often petty brand of discipline. The character of an inmate's behavior was, to be sure, relevant to the custody grade that should be assigned to him and, in that light, a prisoner who harmed another inmate might well see his custody grade stepped up. Yet in Fowler's judgment it was the inmate's violence, not the coincidence that his violent behavior ran afoul of prison rules, that justified the change. Of course, it was completely unacceptable that Warren and Nagle should be able to trump PCP assignments, even if it was to enforce discipline. If embraced, that proposition would render the PCP meaningless, frustrating Judge Johnson's original order as well as more recent orders that, in Fowler's view, gave him ultimate authority regarding classification.[24]

Finding himself at impasse with state officials, Fowler took his troubles to Roland Nachman, who conferred with Judge Johnson and then dictated a series of letters to both Fowler and Locke, supporting Fowler's authority with respect to classification and insisting, in gradually escalating rhetoric, that Locke and his subordinates must cooperate with the PCP and get on with classification forthwith. In July, Nachman wrote that Fowler had "final responsibility" for classification assignments and that state authorities had no "veto power" over the PCP. In August, he decried "this lamentable situation," reiterated that Fowler had "sole responsibility" for classification, and declared that the judge wanted PCP classification assignments "put into effect immediately." On the authority of Nachman's letters, Fowler wrote equally strident letters of his own to Locke, demanding fuller cooperation in individual cases and an end to the blanket rules on which Warren and Nagle had been insisting. Both Nachman and Fowler challenged the commissioner to complain to Judge Johnson himself if Locke objected to what they, as Johnson's agents, called on him to do with respect to classification.[25]

Locke, Warren, and Nagle would have none of this. They, too, were perplexed by their continual conflicts with Fowler; their proposed solution was, however, quite different. Locke initially approached George Beto with a proposal to end the stalemate by returning responsibility for classification to Warren. Beto was sympathetic, but stayed his hand when it became clear that, at least for the moment, Nachman was adamant that the PCP should remain in charge. Next, the commissioner accepted the challenge to complain to Judge Johnson directly. He was furious that Nachman and Fowler should meet with the judge in private and then purport to speak for him by letter. Locke had begun his relations with Fowler two months earlier with counsel present, and he now once again summoned Danny Evans and Gary Maxwell, the young lawyers Baxley had assigned to assist him. With their help, the commissioner framed a letter to Nachman, professing disbelief that Johnson intended the Board of Corrections to "abdicate" responsibility for classification, asserting that he intended to "maintain overall authority and control" of classification until "the Bench" notified him to the contrary, and declaring his intention to "seek a formal clarification" of the matter "as soon as possible." Nachman responded with a note to Judge Johnson, joining Locke's request for clarification, because, in Nachman's telling, the "attitude and directions of the Commissioner . . . and his subordinates" had "seriously handicapped" Fowler's effort.[26]

The disputes between the PCP and the prison system's permanent personnel could no longer be contained within the informal framework Judge Johnson had devised for superintending compliance with this vital aspect of his order. Fowler could not achieve essential cooperation alone, and Nachman, Johnson's chief agent in the field, had also apparently failed. Accordingly, the judge agreed to receive Evans and Maxwell in chambers. Inasmuch as lawyers would be present to represent Commissioner Locke, the judge invited Ralph Knowles to attend the conference on behalf of the prisoner-plaintiffs in the *Pugh* and *James* cases. Nachman also appeared, but neither Locke nor Fowler was present.[27]

The meeting offered little more than an opportunity for Locke's point of view to be heard. Evans and Maxwell asked the judge to disclaim Nachman's letters and to leave "final authority" for classification with the permanent staff. Johnson refused on both counts. By contrast, he gave the state's lawyers what they apparently demanded—confirmation from his own lips that Nachman was acting on his instructions. Johnson expressed concern, moreover, that Warren and Nagle were holding PCP assignments without action and reaffirmed his desire that the classification of all inmates should proceed promptly. To that end, the judge embraced a "compromise" procedure under which Warren and Nagle would notify Fowler of any objections to assignments within five days of receiving them. Then, the two sides would have an additional fifteen days in which to negotiate a settlement. If negotiations failed, Johnson would resolve disputes himself.[28]

Johnson declined to memorialize this new procedure in a formal order, perhaps because he thought Nachman's letters, now personally reaffirmed, were sufficient. It is also possible, however, that Johnson hesitated to embellish the record with still further decrees that might attract attention in the Fifth Circuit. The judge was concerned about classification, concerned enough to press Fowler for speed and, in this instance, to subordinate the views of state authorities to the success of the PCP. At the same time, he thought classification might prove to be a troublesome issue on appeal. The less said formally about it, the better. Johnson's failure to issue an order, however, left the lawyers free to record the conference in the way most favorable to their own interests.

Evans and Maxwell wrote a follow-up letter, which recalled that the judge "expressed the strongest desires [sic] that the Board of Corrections remain the controlling authority over the prison system." Another follow-up by Knowles made no mention of that, but did say that Johnson was "emphatic" that he "did not expect to receive numerous appeals" from PCP decisions and that the judge "stated plainly" that his orders "superceded [sic]" any administrative policies that were "inconsistent with, or an impediment to, the ordered classification process." Evans and Maxwell failed to mention those points.[29]

The new procedure, worked out by the lawyers in the absence of their principals, still could not resolve tensions. The board's most active members, Staton and Vickers, were convinced that they could dispense with the PCP if they, and not the young lawyers that Baxley sent to speak for them, could cut through to the judge himself and explain the situation to him. Johnson had received board members before with respect to other issues, notably the legislature's failure to appropriate adequate funds, and it seemed appropriate now to seek him out again. Staton phoned the judge in early August to defend the way in which Warren and Nagle were behaving. A week later, he and Vickers joined in a letter to Johnson that attempted to justify the administrative policies that, at least according to Knowles, Johnson had already overridden. Staton and Vickers did not act entirely on their own; Warren was present when Vickers' share of the letter was drafted. Yet the sense of these two men that they must communicate personally with the judge permeated the episode. Staton, indeed, went home to type his share of the letter on his own typewriter. It was hardly coincidental, moreover, that the two board members acted at the very time Johnson was embracing the Legislative Prison Task Force as a mechanism for ensuring compliance with the January order.[30]

Johnson agreed to a meeting. When Staton and Vickers arrived for it, they brought their own motion requesting an end to the PCP and return of the classification function to the permanent staff—the very idea that Johnson had rejected two weeks earlier. Consistent with their belief that the judge did not fully understand the circumstances, the two board members contended that the prison system had always had a classification program similar to Fowler's, but that the scheme had not been presented to Johnson because of a "misunderstanding." They had in mind the suggestion that Locke had previously put to Beto. Phase I of the PCP was coming to an end at Draper and, according to Staton and Vickers, it made sense for the Board of Corrections to employ additional permanent staff to undertake Phase II at other institutions. This proposal came at a critical juncture. Fowler might not have the capacity to employ sufficient numbers of temporary employees, train them adequately, and then send them off to do so much work in so little time. Fowler himself and several other PCP members had to return to campus for the opening of the fall academic term. Moreover, Toohey's revised estimate of the cost of Phase II, if carried out according to present plans, far exceeded anything that Fowler had anticipated. Judge Johnson's primary concern continued to be speed. In January, he had ordered the classification of all inmates in the system to be completed by mid-August. Now it was mid-August, and the PCP had not reached beyond Draper. Both the judge and Nachman were growing impatient with Fowler, whose personality conflicts with state officials had apparently contributed to so many delays to date. It was tempting, then, to accept these board members' promise to take "immediate and energetic action" to hire more personnel and to proceed with classification promptly.[31]

Judge Johnson knew better. His experience with the Alabama prison system told him that he could achieve results only by independent means. And the means he had already chosen, the PCP, promised the best chance of success notwithstanding its sluggishness. The judge scheduled a hearing on the proposal put forward by Staton and Vickers, but he did not conceal his doubt that he could be persuaded to sack Dr. Fowler. "[T]he time for generalizations [had] now passed," he said. State authorities had been given one chance to present an "acceptable classification plan" and had "failed to do so." "In order to justify a hearing at this stage," he would expect evidence of the number and qualifications of the staff members Staton and Vickers would employ, a "precise timetable," and "detailed proposals" for the assignment of all prisoners to the "minimum custody . . . consistent with security. . . . "[32]

Johnson fixed the date of the hearing for September. In the interim, Fowler and Brodsky hired additional staff, expedited their procedures, and pressed the PCP on to other institutions. By the first of the month, classification boards were operating at Holman and Fountain, and it seemed possible that all prisoners in the system could be classified by the end of November. Warren, meanwhile, developed a new "special classification plan" he hoped would displace the PCP well before that. Under Warren's plan, as many as thirty-eight prison system employees, some of them guards, were to be reassigned to finish the classification of all prisoners within eight weeks. In a real sense, the two warring camps were now in a race to determine which would survive to complete the task their quarrels had frustrated for so long.[33]

In the midst of preparations for the scheduled hearing, those quarrels continued apace. Selected notes that Fowler and Brodsky had been keeping on their experiences suddenly appeared in an article published in the *Monitor*, the journal of the American Psychological Association. The notes had been developed for a book that Fowler and Brodsky were planning and had been furnished to the *Monitor* for use in an introductory article on the PCP. Fowler had explained to the editor that the notes were "raw material" that might never "see the light of day." They were passed along merely to give the editor a "feel" for what he and Brodsky were doing. The editor nevertheless misunderstood. When the article appeared, its uncomplimentary descriptions of Locke and his staff were devastating. Notes on Judge Johnson, while hardly critical, also undercut the professionalism on which the University of Alabama psychologists depended. Fowler offered written apologies to both Commissioner Locke and Judge Johnson, but the critical damage was done. During the hearing in September, Tom Radney quoted at length from the *Monitor* article in an apparent effort to embarrass and discredit Dr. Fowler and, through him, the PCP.[34]

The hearing gave Dr. Warren an opportunity to explain what he hoped to do and allowed board members, particularly Ricky Robinson, to assure Judge Johnson that they were committed to the program that Warren outlined. Radney also produced an expert witness, Allen Ault from Georgia, to endorse the view that, except in extraordinary circumstances, classification should be in the hands of state authorities. None of this testimony was compelling; Ault's comments, indeed, seemed to undermine the state's case—it being plain that the circumstances in Alabama *were* extraordinary. Johnson listened patiently, then disposed of the issues orally from the bench. He emphasized that he had introduced the PCP into the Alabama prison system only because he viewed the proper classification of prisoners to be an "emergency" and said that he saw no reason at this late date to shift authority for classification back to the Board of Corrections. In a maneuver reminiscent of his handling of the AUM group, he ordered that the permanent staff that Warren proposed to use in his program, other than guards, should be made available to the PCP. With a greatly enhanced staff, Fowler should be able to finish the classification task within six weeks. Then, Johnson assured the defendants, the PCP would "phase out." Classification would proceed pursuant to PCP rules and procedures. Other policies proffered by state authorities, including the administrative rules over which Warren and Fowler had been fighting for weeks, must give way.[35]

The new arrangement, like others in the past, failed to mollify personal relations now beyond repair. Warren and Nagle worked with the PCP grudgingly, yet they plainly did not function as Fowler's subordinates. Minor disagreements were inflated into serious disputes; personal slights degenerated into vitriolic charges and countercharges. The administrative policies that Johnson had overridden continued to generate friction. Staton complained publicly that only the views of the "University of Alabama" seemed now to count in classification and that the board's views were "not very pertinent." Vickers said that the board was "over a barrel"; Robinson charged that Fowler's refusal to adhere to the eighteen-month rule for work release was filling community facilities with "questionable" prisoners. More important than rhetoric, however, was substance. In October, Fowler told Nachman that he had never been "officially informed" that a "single inmate" classified by the PCP had actually been physically moved into the custody grade and programs assigned to him. In Fowler's view, state authorities were simply ignoring the product of his labors. Of all the dilatory tactics Fowler had seen in the past, the simple failure to *do* anything with respect to PCP decisions was by far the most vexing—and potentially successful.[36]

Nachman received the bad news with mixed feelings. On the one hand, he was angry that state authorities should persist in their recalcitrance. Thus he demanded that Locke respond to Fowler's "grave charges." He pointed out that there were empty beds at many work release centers and "honor camps" and warned the commissioner that "Judge Johnson [expected those facilities] to be filled to capacity." On the other hand, Nachman was all the more impatient with the PCP's continued inability to get the classification job done. Thus he told Fowler frankly that he did not "believe . . . that repeated and piecemeal confrontation" with Locke and the board could "produce the most worthwhile results."[37]

Fowler reported in early November that the classification of inmates was "complete." By that he meant that the PCP had developed custody grades and program assignments for all prisoners. The physical transfer of prisoners was quite another matter, of course, and Warren and Nagle might yet enter formal objections to the PCP's work in hundreds of cases still stacked on their desks. Therein lay the last frustrating stages of what Judge Johnson had hoped would be a "crash" program to classify prisoners in the Alabama prison system. As the year wound down, Warren and Nagle gave the press to believe that they had resumed responsibility for classification and that as soon as they could attend to final details, the book on the PCP could be closed forever. While they explained that they meant to employ roughly the rules and procedures used by the PCP, they nonetheless made it unmistakably plain that there would be changes. "The PCP," Warren and Nagle insisted, "was responsible to the Federal Court." They, by contrast, were "responsible to the Board of Corrections." That meant, it soon became clear, that action on PCP assignments would be delayed indefinitely and that Warren and Nagle would formally object to many more such assignments than anyone had expected. On the former point, another of Locke's attorneys, Scears Barnes, filed a contemporaneous report with Judge Johnson, asking for additional time in which to find or establish more places in crowded work release centers. On the latter, David Flack gave Johnson the names of several prisoners for whom the PCP on the one side, and Warren and Nagle on the other, could not choose mutually agreeable classification assignments.[38]

Fowler protested that under the arrangement established in August any disagreements over PCP assignments were to be discussed with him before being passed along to the judge. Now, however, no one in the state system was prepared to deal with Fowler any longer. The working assumption in Montgomery was that the PCP had run its course and that any vestige of the state's experience with that project must now be treated in court. Flack filed formal "motions to resolve disagreements" in Johnson's office on two further occasions in October and November. Then, in mid-December, Johnson held a hearing to consider the cases identified in those motions.[39]

At the outset of the proceedings, Judge Johnson called the participants to the bench and asked whether the ten cases identified in Flack's motions were "all [they were] going to have." He said he did not wish to "do this piecemeal" and would prefer to postpone the consideration of any case until he had all before him for decision. Barnes excused himself to telephone Warren, then returned with startling news. Objections were anticipated in 400 other cases. That figure, moreover, took no account of an additional 400 files that Warren and Nagle had not yet reviewed. The implications were staggering. In effect, state authorities proposed that an extraordinarily large percentage of the cases handled by the PCP had resulted in irreconcilable differences with the permanent staff and that the task of resolving those differences would require an enormous expenditure of judicial effort—a particularistic examination of hundreds of prisoner files. Johnson's face showed a "moment of controlled rage," yet his apparent anger "passed as easily as it came." The judge "almost smiled" and then "calmly" postponed further proceedings until more efforts at reconciliation could be made. He ordered negotiations regarding the existing 400 cases to begin the following day and fixed dates for objections and negotiations regarding the other 400 later in the month. He said he intended to resolve any disputes that came to him as quickly as possible and established a schedule for a series of "implementation reports" state officials must file to describe the pace at which they actually placed the prisoners concerned in assigned programs.[40]

With Judge Johnson's evident impatience as a spur, Warren and Nagle now proved more receptive to discussions with Fowler, and the number of disagreements was pared to just over 100 by the end of the year. Still, the sheer number of individual cases indicated that Johnson would have to devote a large amount of time to their resolution. Instead of stealing that time from his other duties, the judge referred these remaining classification matters to M. Lewis Gwaltney, a long-time associate who served as federal magistrate in the Middle District. Gwaltney often handled relatively minor matters arising in Johnson's cases, saving Johnson's own time for more demanding duty, and for that reason his appointment on this occasion was unexceptional. Still, the decision to delegate responsibility for the matters at hand surely revealed Johnson's view that the parties were making too much of the assignments to be given to individual prisoners and his general exasperation with the morass that classification had become. If, he seemed plainly to be saying, the "experts" were so disaffected that they could not do what he had asked them to do, and these last cases had to be resolved judicially, he would leave the task to an assistant instead of spending his own time on it. That implication was supported by Flack's contemporaneous concession that in virtually all remaining instances the basis of the two sides' inability to agree was Warren's insistence on, and Fowler's resistance to, the same administrative policies that had divided the two sides since August—the eighteen-month rule for work release, the "no reassignment" rule for Frank Lee, the rule that furloughs granted even to "aged and infirm" inmates could extend no longer than ninety days, and the rule that custody grade changes could be used for punishment.[41]

Proceedings before the magistrate provided the occasion for still more skirmishing, both between the PCP and state officials and among state officials themselves. The catalyst was Gwaltney's decision that the administrative rules Flack mentioned were in conflict with Judge John-son's previous orders and must be jettisoned. Most of those policies could be discarded without grave concern; the elimination of the eigh-teen-month rule for work release, however, proved to be explosive. The political implications of housing convicts in community facilities had previously been subordinated to the concrete task of making those assignments in the first instance. Now it seemed that large numbers of prisoners with lengthy terms yet to serve might be permitted to live under loose supervision, able to walk the streets during working hours. That spectre generated both concern and activity.

First, Locke and the board understood that any prisoner whose classification assignment had been in dispute because of Warren's adherence to the eighteen-month rule must promptly be placed in a community facility. Accordingly, dozens of such prisoners were, in fact, transferred to work release centers. Attorney General Baxley, by con-trast, insisted that Gwaltney's rejection of the rule only eliminated the length of a prisoner's sentence as a selection criterion for work release and that community assignments might still be resisted on a case-by-case basis. Gwaltney and Johnson acquiesced in Baxley's understand-ing, and just over forty prisoners who had been "mistakenly" sent to work release were promptly returned to prison. Second, when Knowles (representing prisoners) and Barnes (representing state penal officials) met with Fowler, Brodsky, and Warren to discuss cases that the rejec-tion of blanket rules did not resolve en masse, they fought for hours before reaching settlements. Fowler and Brodsky typically agreed to delay, but not to forego, community assignments for inmates they thought were deserving; Warren typically accepted such delays as short-term protection against inmates he believed to be dangerous.[42]

Then, when the negotiators presented the results of their labors to Gwaltney, there was conflict on yet a third level. Larry Newman, who had not participated in the classification process earlier, came forward on behalf of Attorney General Baxley and condemned the assignments on which the others had finally agreed as "the most disgusting thing [he had ever] seen." That outburst provoked Scears Barnes, who *had* par-ticipated in the negotiations as Locke's legal representative, to criticize both Newman and Baxley for interfering with the good faith efforts of state penal authorities to respond to Judge Johnson's orders respecting these last classification cases. Once again, Alabama officials were pub-licly at odds, each blaming another for what was fast becoming yet another embarrassment in the press. The major newspapers carried pic-tures of the inmates to be assigned to work release under the new arrangements—complete with lurid descriptions of the crimes they had committed. Gwaltney was unmoved. He waited a few days, then issued an opinion formally embracing the agreements reached between the Fowler and Warren groups. Judge Johnson confirmed that judgment the following day and, at last, all prisoners in the Alabama prison system had classification assignments.[43]

Implementation was another matter. Pursuant to Judge Johnson's earlier order, Barnes and Flack filed several subsequent reports on the extent to which prisoners were actually moved into the programs to which they had been assigned. Yet "head counts" at the prison system's less secure penal facilities belied any suggestion that prisoners were actually having the benefit of the negotiations just completed. Indeed, Nachman reported to Johnson in early April that more than 100 beds were vacant at Frank Lee, the Red Eagle Honor Farm, and the Cattle Ranch. Despite the volatile backlog of state prisoners in local jails, moreover, Locke and his staff had allowed the total population in the state prisons to fall more than 400 below "design capacity." Incensed, Johnson issued an order demanding a written explanation of the current situation, together with weekly accountings to Nachman for future empty beds. Barnes filed a response in due course, which put most of the difficulty down to tuberculosis quarantines at both Fountain and Holman and delays associated with a new classification program inaugurated by Warren on the PCP's departure. Behind the scenes, this new confrontation produced yet another round of blistering correspondence between Nachman and state authorities, further reflecting the disastrous state of their relations. Nachman, for his part, insisted that he had reported the facts to Johnson out of duty and that he would "not blink at noncompliance." Vickers said in response that he could only regret Nachman's "total lack of confidence" in the board.[44]

The circumstances called for some objective monitoring mechanism. Ira DeMent discussed the matter with Fowler, who enthusiastically agreed to develop a program. Nachman, too, saw the need for monitoring, but his impatience with Fowler was now such that he resisted any scheme contemplating a continuing role for the PCP. Nachman was insistent on this point, telling DeMent that he could not support a plan that would have the PCP "administering the prison system" long after the "emergency" that brought it into being had subsided. It was not that Nachman meant to ignore the valuable experience gained by the PCP; indeed, he ultimately recruited two of Fowler's graduate students to assist with monitoring. Instead, Nachman simply wished to be rid of Fowler himself and preferred another expert who would report to his own HRC. Nachman's choice was Dr. Wiley R. Boyles, a member of the HRC. Boyles was on the faculty at AUM, but he had not been associated with previous efforts by members of that faculty to become involved in the prison system.[45]

Commissioner Locke shared Nachman's sentiment that Dr. Fowler had served his purpose. The wounds were now too deep to heal; state authorities preferred to deal even with Nachman, no favorite in their eyes, instead of tolerating any further interference from the University of Alabama. On a deeper level, however, Locke objected to any plan for continued oversight from the outside. He thus complained to Judge Johnson when Nachman proposed to introduce Dr. Boyles to serve as monitor. It was this final dispute over the advisability of a monitoring mechanism, whether involving Fowler or not, that finally encountered the danger of which Judge Johnson had been concerned for months: the possibility that the drawn-out business of classification would trouble the appellate court, which now, in the wake of oral argument, was coming to its decision in New Orleans.[46]

Judge Johnson scheduled a hearing on Nachman's proposal for mid-July. Next, something altogether unexpected. In a letter received in the interim, the court clerk in New Orleans asked the parties in *Pugh* and *James* to answer three specific questions touching classification. The court of appeals wished to know whether the "University of Alabama group" was "continuing to classify" prisoners, involving itself in "inter-prison transfers" and "matters of discipline"; whether Fowler's decisions were "binding" on state authorities; and whether there were any "specific plans" for the withdrawal of the PCP and the return of classification to "duly constituted Alabama prison authorities." It was impossible to know what motivated the court to ask such questions, particularly these questions. Yet it seemed safe to assume that at least one of the judges on the three-judge panel found the PCP sufficiently troubling to warrant a departure from normal procedures in order to expand the record respecting classification. In any case, when the hearing on Nachman's suggestion for a monitoring device opened in Montgomery a few days later, Johnson and the lawyers were no less concerned with events in New Orleans and the fair and proper answers to the appellate court's questions, than with the issue immediately at hand.[47]

Participants in the hearing spoke explicitly to what was on everyone's mind. When Larry Newman mentioned in passing that classification had been "taken out of the hands" of state authorities, Judge Johnson interjected that responsibility for classification had now "been put back." That exchange led into a more general discussion of the PCP and whether Johnson had yet entered a formal order dismantling Fowler's group. There was some uncertainty on the point, grounded undoubtedly in the technical nature of the issue. Everyone knew that the PCP had finished making classification assignments the previous December and that the remaining conflicts with Warren and Nagle had been resolved before Gwaltney in May and June. Still, no formal order had yet been entered. In the end, Johnson conceded as much, but then met the substance of the matter forthrightly. "Well," he said, "let me give you my reaction to the entire thing. The Prison Classification Project is concluded is [sic] my understanding . . . it is over." That understanding was underscored by a contemporaneous letter from Dr. Fowler, stating flatly that the PCP's work had been concluded.[48]

In the wake of the hearing, called to dispose of the monitoring question but used as an occasion for clarifying the status of the PCP, the lawyers answered the appellate court's questions according to their own perspectives. Lawson reported that PCP classification assignments were "binding" on state authorities. Then, reviewing events at the hearing and Fowler's letter to Johnson, he suggested that the PCP's withdrawal was both timely and potentially brief. Two things might happen. Johnson might approve Nachman's monitoring plan, and classification might come yet again under the supervision of outsiders. Now the "expert" in charge would be Boyles, not Fowler, but the employment of former PCP staff members invited a program similar to the PCP but with a "different name." In the alternative, the lawyers for the prisoner-plaintiffs might file a motion for a monitoring device of their own. If Johnson granted such a motion, the same result might flow, but by another route. Lawson meant, of course, to suggest to the appellate court that Johnson's intrusion into classification, by way of the PCP or some similar entity, was far from ended, notwithstanding his statements at the hearing and Fowler's letter—both of which, Lawson implied, constituted well-timed attempts to diffuse the issues surrounding classification on appeal. Answering for the prisoners, Bronstein emphasized that state authorities had acquiesced in most of the classification assignments made by the PCP and then negotiated with Fowler on the disposition of other cases. Gwaltney and Johnson had only approved bargained-for settlements. As to the current status of the PCP, he reported Johnson's statements at the hearing and insisted that "neither the Human Rights Committee, nor any of the parties . . . [had] requested that the classification function be removed" from state authorities "at the present time."[49]

Bronstein's account apparently persuaded the circuit court. Judge Coleman's opinion, handed down two months later, acquiesced in Judge Johnson's position with respect to classification. Coleman read the answers the court had received from the parties, together with the record of the hearing in July, to confirm that "the University of Alabama group" was "no longer functioning." Accordingly, the PCP was of no further concern. While Coleman explicitly said that the court would have "no comment" on what Fowler and Brodsky had done, he volunteered his understanding that classification would in future be in the hands of state authorities, subject to appropriate monitoring by Johnson "to see that constitutionally required classification standards, if any, were observed by . . . prison authorities in the exercise of a function which is fundamentally theirs." When, after the appellate opinion appeared, Segall filed a motion requesting the appointment of a classification monitor, Lawson notified the circuit in hopes of persuading Coleman to reopen the classification issue. Now, of course, the implication was that Segall had deliberately delayed his request for further outside interference until the circuit court had acted on the assumption that such interference had been terminated. That argument failed, along with all others, when the circuit refused to grant rehearing. Nachman's plan for a monitoring program under the aegis of the HRC died with the HRC itself. Segall's motion regarding a classification monitor merged with larger efforts to identify the kind of monitors that Coleman's opinion allowed Johnson to appoint. And the classification phase of the litigation over the Alabama prison system ended in much the way it had begun more than a year earlier. Confusion, controversy, and friction had followed the PCP from its birth and now accompanied it to its much-delayed demise.[50]

A year later, in preparation for his testimony in the first thorough compliance hearing to be held in the Alabama prison cases, Carl Clements visited the classification programs then in place at the state's major institutions. He was more saddened than shocked by what he found. The rules and procedures developed by the PCP were no longer in use. Classification teams or, in some instances, individual classification officers, made recommendations without reference to any fixed criteria or procedural framework. Custody grades were "systematically more restrictive" than necessary, largely because those in charge, Warren, Nagle, and the wardens, consistently rejected recommendations they considered too lenient and because custody grade changes were again being used as punishment. Once again, prisoners were often treated the same regardless of custody grade; most were housed in dormitories with nothing to occupy their time. Once again, assignments to rehabilitative programs were made on a "space available" basis. There was, in sum, little trace of the work that Fowler, Brodsky, Clements, and the others had done. The PCP did, of course, channel many inmates into more tolerable living conditions than would have been their lot at the hands of penal authorities acting alone. Yet the academicians achieved no long-term systemic change. The prison system's omnipresent bureaucracy, with its own norms and practices, closed in to fill the hole left by the PCP and, very shortly, eliminated all evidence that the intruders had ever come to Draper.[51]

This is not to say that the introduction of competent outsiders was flawed from the beginning. Judge Johnson had no reason to believe that state officials were capable of formulating an adequate plan for classification or implementing such a plan in a responsible fashion. The evidence, indeed, was to the contrary. When the prison system had developed a sound program under Hugh Swafford's direction, other senior staff, particularly wardens, had frustrated its objectives at every turn. Yet classification was critical to the successful enforcement of the January 13 order. Johnson had to ensure that this first step would be taken, and he was given to understand that Dr. Fowler would get this vital job done, and that he would do it well and quickly. It made some sense, then, to involve the Center for Correctional Psychology. Moreover, Johnson did not displace state authorities altogether, but attempted, through ambiguous language in his orders, to encourage cooperation. Fowler and Brodsky had worked with Alabama penal authorities in the past; it may, indeed, have seemed genuinely tactful to call on them again in this new, coercive context. Conflicts with Locke, and certainly Warren and Nagle, were inevitable. But the speed with which personal bitterness developed and the great depth of state authorities' recalcitrance could not, perhaps, have been anticipated.

When matters did not go well, the judge hesitated either to withdraw Fowler in the nature of an early retreat or to slide immediately to the other extreme and to give outsiders the very decisive authority he had deliberately failed to accord them initially. Johnson's middle course was intelligent and entirely understandable in the circumstances, constituting an attempt both to retain the benefit of Fowler's expertise and to account for penal authorities' wounded pride. Still, the absence of an early order from Johnson himself channeled the players to other ostensible sources of assistance: Nachman, certainly, and to a lesser extent Beto. Nachman's accelerating impatience, first with Locke and then with Fowler himself, and Judge Johnson's attempt to speak through Nachman to the combatants, generated still more confusion, frustration and, in the end, open anger. Locke's resolve was tightened proportionately as Nachman's letters enhanced Fowler's apparent authority in what was, in this instance, an understandable yet damaging gradualism. Still, the controversy in the Fifth Circuit over the PCP and the manner in which Judge Johnson dealt with both Nachman and Fowler was paradoxical. The judge encountered criticism from the appellate court not because he determined the way in which prison inmates should be classified and forced state authorities to conform to his judgment immediately, but because he encouraged Locke and the board to make use of available expertise in the field and attempted to sort through difficulties informally, through agents, instead of continually haling state officials back into his courtroom for further formal proceedings.

Attempts to gain advantage or, at least, clarity regarding power relations by drawing the lawyers into the fray were dissatisfying at best. All sides turned that way at some point, but with little enthusiasm. Nachman and Fowler challenged Locke to follow letter instructions or seek formal judicial override but, at the same time, obstructed the path to the court by means of their special access to the judge. Locke approached the judge only as a last resort; Staton and Vickers joined that effort only after failing in their own, personal attempts to undercut Fowler in the privacy of Johnson's chambers. When the lawyers were introduced, they wished to avoid further litigation of the issues dividing the principals and, instead, pressed for a negotiated end to each confrontation in turn.

The unfortunate experience with classification notwithstanding, the generally favorable treatment of Judge Johnson's actions in the appellate courts revitalized hopes that the other requirements in his order might yet be met. When, however, the focus shifted to the enforcement of public health standards, space requirements, and similar provisions, it soon became clear that the way would be strewn with still more barriers. Steve Suitts warned that the Board of Corrections would respond to further pressures by building more prisons and that, if that disastrous course was to be avoided, it would be necessary to set about enforcing compliance with the court's order in a way that channeled scarce resources to better uses. Certainly, he maintained, carefully groomed and concerted efforts to make a success of the litigation must begin immediately. For when "bulldozers [began] moving dirt and contractors [began] putting ajax on the floors in Atmore," it would be virtually impossible to "redirect" the state's "energies and resources" toward "more sane" policies. The time, then, was critical. And principal players on all sides looked forward to the new year with both hope and trepidation.[52]

7

Déjà Vu

The opening days of 1978 were a time to take stock. The Fifth Circuit had now sustained most of the provisions in the January 13 order, but it remained unclear whether, in the final analysis, Judge Johnson would actually enforce that order in its particulars. Locke and the Board of Corrections hoped the judge would reassess the need for some requirements in light of the changes that had taken place over the previous two years, during which time Johnson had hesitated to press for compliance (apart from classification) because of the pending appeal. State authorities explained, for example, that the population of the prisons had been reduced to "design capacity" and that, to make room for still more prisoners, they would shortly open a new facility adjacent to Draper. This new prison, to be named the Thomas F. Staton Correctional Center, coupled with the three planned institutions at Wadley, Heflin, and Union Springs, would expand the system's capacity to house most of the sentenced prisoners backed up in local jails. In this light, Locke asked Johnson to relax some of the space requirements in the order, to allow the commissioner to accept more prisoners from the jails in the near term while he planned for the prison system's future. Specifically, Locke wished to be free of space-per-prisoner standards at the Kilby receiving center.[1]

Lawyers for the prisoners, by contrast, argued that the judge should neither change requirements already established nor take satisfaction in plans for new construction but, instead, should now enforce all the standards in the January 13 order. They, too, were vexed by the backlog in the jails. Indeed, conditions there presented an ethical dilemma; prisoners held in the jails were not bystanders, forced to suffer in local facilities so that the litigants in *Pugh* and *James* could be accorded the living space that Johnson had decreed should be theirs. Jail prisoners, too, were plaintiffs in the prison cases and thus were entitled to be housed under conditions specified for state facilities. Still, Segall, Knowles, and the other lawyers resisted proposals to dilute the January order so that their clients in the jails could be spared current suffering. To surrender living standards established for existing prisons because the price, measured in jail crowding, had become too high was to risk the ultimate success of the campaign to reform those institutions begun nearly four years earlier. To acquiesce in the construction of similar prisons in the future was to abandon more ambitious hopes to alter fundamental penal policy in Alabama. Indeed, Segall and Knowles dared hope that if the January 13 order survived intact and if new construction were by some means avoided, the situation in the jails might generate, at long last, more enlightened answers to the pressing question of space. Plaintiffs' counsel resolved, then, to stand fast, focus Johnson's attention on the future, and hope that pressure from the jails would not frustrate long-term benefits from the prison litigation.[2]

Johnson met with the two sides in February, then ordered Locke to file a "complete and detailed compliance report" reflecting the aspects of the court's order, "if any," to which he and the board had thus far responded, identifying "areas of noncompliance," and describing "plans for achieving compliance" in the near future. The commissioner produced an optimistic report, the prisoners' lawyers objected, and the judge scheduled a hearing to determine the truth—and thus to decide how and when he should enforce the January order and whether, if at all, he should relax its standards in light of changed circumstances. The *Pugh* and *James* cases, in short, must be litigated all over again. Events in the months to follow were colored by the approach of the hearing, which promised to channel the future course of prison reform in Alabama. Lawyers for the prisoners negotiated with state authorities regarding the backlog of inmates in local jails in hopes of resolving that problem in advance of the hearing. When negotiations collapsed, the prisoners' lawyers invested enormous resources in the hearing itself, developing ample evidence that the prison system was still woefully short of the goals fixed by the January order. Then, as the parties awaited new orders from Judge Johnson, the judge unveiled a genuine surprise. He appointed a newly elected governor in Alabama to serve as the prison system's "temporary receiver" and thus placed *his* hopes for the future in the hands of state authorities.[3]

When Judge Johnson scheduled the new hearing, the prisoners' lawyers set to work developing evidence revealing the prison system's many remaining flaws. Knowles sought information from the Legislative Prison Task Force, Myers arranged new surveys of the prison system's medical care facilities, and Bronstein commissioned the American Foundation to study staffing levels. Occasionally, these efforts produced evidence favorable to the state. After Bill Nagel toured the prisons in June, he reported that he was "impressed" by the "not . . . insignificant" accomplishments in the two years since he had last been in Alabama. In the main, however, the evidence showed conditions that had improved only marginally. Classification had actually deteriorated since the end of the PCP, medical and mental health care was still sorely inadequate, sanitary conditions remained substandard, and violence was still routine. Even Scears Barnes acknowledged that the board would not be able to "provide facilities and programs" required by Johnson's order "at any time in the foreseeable future. . . ."[4]

The state's preparations, meanwhile, were distracted. Bill Racette, an employee whom Locke had recently discharged, alleged that the board had made a "deal" with key legislators to hire Wheeler Foshee, state senator E. C. "Crum" Foshee's brother, as Locke's deputy in exchange for increased appropriations. Racette's charge was startling, and the more so inasmuch as both the Foshee brothers currently faced trial on federal mail fraud indictments. The matter was confused still further by allegations from Alvin Holmes, one of the few black legislators in Alabama, to the effect that one board member, W. F. "Buddy" Hamner, had promised to appoint a black administrator to the post assigned to Wheeler Foshee and that Foshee would be given Deputy Commissioner Bennett's position. The possibility that Larry Bennett might be dismissed was hardly a surprise. The former Methodist minister had formed close ties to John Vickers, himself a Methodist pastor, and it was widely believed that Locke considered Bennett to be a rival. In early June, Locke transferred him away from the board's central offices in downtown Montgomery.[5]

In these circumstances, there was reason to think that Judge Johnson would not wait for the hearing, now scheduled for September, before taking further action. Initially, he considered appointing yet more outsiders to serve as interim "monitors" on the model suggested by the Fifth Circuit. Indeed, he solicited the names of nominees from the parties in mid-July. In the end, however, Johnson rejected both Bronstein's suggestion (that a person of national reputation be given sweeping powers to gather evidence, file reports, and make recommendations) and Barnes' counterproposal (that Darrell Schlotterback or some other local person be appointed). Later, the judge took forthright action. In response to reports that local jails were riddled with fire hazards, he issued a new order requiring state authorities to meet fire safety standards in the jails—putting even more pressure on local authorities desperately attempting to contend with the overflow of sentenced prisoners. And in response to a report from the State Examiners of Public Accounts indicating that the prison system's agricultural lands should be leased to private operators or sold outright, Johnson demanded descriptions of the system's landholdings giving rise to speculation that he might order the board to dispose of real estate in order to obtain revenues for improvements in the prisons.[6]

The most pressing issue was, of course, crowding, in both the prisons and the jails. If the state prison system as a whole was no longer overflowing, particular state facilities were. At Kilby, prisoners awaiting classification were held for as long as five weeks in cells measuring only forty square feet. The trickle of new inmates accepted from the jails, moreover, hardly dented the great backlog of prisoners still held in local facilities. Early in the year, Locke acknowledged that the number of jail prisoners, 2800, nearly matched the number of inmates, 3400, housed in the state's long-term institutions. Now there were more instances in which local officials took matters in their own hands. Shelby County constructed a new jail, and city officials in Birmingham adopted a resolution against routine detention for public intoxication. More often, city and county officials looked to Montgomery for assistance. Several new grand jury reports blamed the Board of Corrections for conditions in local jails, and the Alabama Sheriffs' Association discussed a lawsuit to force the board to take action.[7]

More powerful pressure came from other federal lawsuits respecting individual jails. By now, all the state's larger jails were in litigation. Ralph Knowles and Jack Drake sued Tuscaloosa County officials over conditions there and, after a week-long trial in the fall of 1977, Judge Sam Pointer issued an order drastically limiting the number of prisoners that could be held in the jail. A few months later, Pointer issued a similar order with respect to the Jefferson County Jail in Birmingham. Still more orders were entered by Judge Robert Varner and Judge Hand regarding jails in Montgomery and Mobile. Locke responded to each new order by moving prisoners from the jail concerned to some other jail that, while undoubtedly crowded, was not yet subject to a similar federal court order. Stop-gap tactics were not successful for long. Judge Pointer ultimately held local and state officials in contempt for failing to comply with his orders in Tuscaloosa and Birmingham. He levied fines for noncompliance and, in a controversial ruling, required part of the money exacted in Birmingham to be paid directly to the prisoners affected. Judge Varner proved firmer still. He ordered Montgomery

County officials to *release* a number of inmates whom Varner himself, on Sheriff Butler's advice, decided were not dangerous. The spectre of discharging sentenced prisoners before the expiration of their terms lent new urgency to the problems presented by the state's crowded prisons and jails. Things had seemingly come to a head. The state's very authority to incarcerate criminals was now in question.[8]

Judge Johnson's contemporaneous actions in the Houston County Jail case, for which he had responsibility, only aggravated these tensions. While the judge had refused to permit Ira DeMent to expand that case into a vehicle for attacking conditions in all the state's local facilities at once, Johnson had always responded favorably to claims touching only Houston County--establishing population limits at that jail and enjoining Commissioner Locke from "failing or refusing to forthwith transfer State prisoners from the Houston County Jail into the State penal system." Locke reacted in this case as he had in others; when the population of prisoners in Houston County slipped above the limit, he made short-run adjustments to meet Johnson's requirements. Soon, however, the commissioner bristled at being sandwiched between Johnson's orders regarding the prisons and this single jail. To gain breathing space, he asked the judge for "clarification" of what seemed to be his conflicting obligations. That maneuver put the matter of jail crowding and its relation to *Pugh* and *James* squarely before the man whom many in Alabama held personally responsible for pressing the state's local facilities into service to house sentenced prisoners.[9]

Johnson identified the challenge for what it was—and responded to it in a new order in *Pugh* and *James*. Unfortunately, he chose language that only further confused an already unsettled state of affairs. He said that upon consideration of the circumstances in the prisons and in the Houston County Jail, he had decided to "rescind" his previous orders in the prison cases to the extent they prevented Locke from "taking all state prisoners into the Alabama Penal System" and implied that state authorities were "authorized by this Court to house state prisoners for any length of time in various county and city jails. . . ." On first blush, the new order seemed to Locke to be a godsend. Johnson had evidently realized at long last that the commissioner could not hold the population in the state prisons to "design capacity" and, at the same time, accommodate new prisoners from the jails in the numbers necessary to meet the demands of orders regarding individual local facilities. Something must give way, and Johnson had apparently decided that it should be his "cap" on the prison system's population. On closer examination, however, other observers developed doubts. It seemed implausible that after adhering to the "design capacity" rule for more than two years, notwithstanding crowding in the jails, Johnson would now lift the "cap" and risk an immediate return to the dreadful conditions in state prisons that had motivated his original order. That result would amount to an admission that state officials had won the battle over space and that all the anguish concerning crowding since the summer of 1975 had come to naught. Telephone calls to Johnson's office soon elicited a resolution of the puzzle.

The week following the controversial order "rescinding" previous decrees regarding space in the prisons, the judge instructed his secretary to answer inquiries about it by reading from a prepared statement. In guarded language, the statement explained that the order had not changed the "cap" decree at all, but had merely called on Locke to reduce crowding in Houston County. The judge had only meant to make clear that "state prison officials cannot continue to use this Court's order [capping the population in the prisons] as an excuse . . . for keeping state prisoners backed up in the . . . jails." If, Johnson insisted, Locke and the board left sentenced prisoners in local facilities, it would not be "by virtue of this Court. . . ." Johnson had no intention of jeopardizing ground gained in the prisons, whatever the impact on local jails. He meant to maintain pressure from both directions, hoping to force Locke and the board to contend more realistically with the great number of state prisoners, wherever confined.[10]

Prior to the confusion over the order in the Houston County case, the prisoners' lawyers in *Pugh* and *James* had been content to confer with the lawyers handling individual jail cases, offer assistance, and thus develop a loose network of attorneys whose sympathies and ultimate objectives, at least, were consistent. Now, Johnson's clarifying statement suggested the way in which jail crowding might yet make (or break) overarching efforts to effect penal reform in Alabama. Ralph Knowles fashioned a formal request for further relief in *Pugh* and *James,* grounded in familiar theory. Since prisoners in the jails were members of the plaintiff classes in *Pugh* and *James,* they were entitled to be housed under the conditions specified in Johnson's original January 13 order—whether they were physically in the custody of Commissioner Locke and other state authorities or, for the moment, backlogged in local jails. If, then, it could be established that conditions in local jails did not meet the standards fixed for the state prisons, Johnson should issue a new injunction requiring the commissioner to "remove all state prisoners from all city and county jails" and to "confine them, if at all, in facilities meeting constitutional standards."[11]

The difficulty, of course, was that Knowles lacked the resources required to demonstrate that conditions in *all* the state's jails were as bad as he alleged. While anyone connected with penal institutions in Alabama would concede privately that very few jails met the standards in the January 13 order, formal proof (witnesses and documentary evidence) could be produced only by heroic efforts. That, after all, had been Judge Johnson's primary reason for refusing to permit Ira DeMent to expand the Houston County case into a statewide class action. To meet these difficulties halfway, Knowles proposed to concentrate on the jails in Tuscaloosa, Mobile, Montgomery, and Birmingham. The independent lawsuits regarding those jails had already generated substantial evidence and, indeed, several injunctive decrees from other federal judges.[12]

Knowles' strategy was not without risk. Pressing state authorities with respect to the state's largest jails while at the same time insisting on adherence to the original order in *Pugh* and *James,* most important the "cap" on population in the prisons, might leave the commissioner and the board with no politically feasible escape route. To be sure, Judge Johnson himself had already ordered Locke to reduce crowding in Houston County without breaching the "cap" decree. Knowles' motion proposed essentially to multiply the effect of Johnson's order fivefold. Yet the risks seemed worth taking. If Knowles and the others delayed or merely continued in their strategy of nourishing, but not joining, litigation regarding individual jails before other judges, the commissioner and the board might win time in which to pursue their proposals to further desiccate the January 13 order. The better tactic, or so it seemed, was to meet the jail crowding issue forthrightly, underscore Johnson's firm action in Houston County, and hope that such a devastating assertion of federal judicial power would not precipitate a confrontation from which prison reform in Alabama could not emerge victorious.[13]

With matters in this posture, Locke and the Board of Corrections adopted positions on two tracks. Publicly, they responded to crowding in local jails with renewed efforts to expand the capacity of the state prison system. The new Staton facility was constructed in short order and was immediately filled with minimum security inmates. This new structure was much cleaner than the system's older facilities, yet its design posed the threat that Knowles and his colleagues had dreaded for months. Staton was truly a human warehouse: a drab building constructed of concrete blocks, with four dormitories holding just over 100 men each. Plans to construct similar units at other locations indicated that the authorities meant to build such dormitory-style facilities as cheaply and quickly as possible, with no attempt to provide anything beyond the minimum space per prisoner that Judge Johnson's order prescribed.[14]

On a more private track, however, Locke and the board were willing to discuss the solution to jail crowding that Knowles and the others hoped to achieve—the release of nondangerous prisoners. In a routine meeting in the U.S. attorney's office in Montgomery, Barnes and Lawson, the latter representing Governor Wallace, conceded that the only realistic answer to the problems in the jails was to discharge some prisoners who seemed not to threaten public safety. Lawson astonished Knowles and Segall by proposing that all the 2800 sentenced prisoners in the jails could be released over the next sixty days. Larry Newman, speaking for the attorney general, opposed any such radical action. Yet even Newman acknowledged that some prisoners had to be released. Of course, the practicalities had to be considered. Locke and the board found it politically infeasible to be publicly associated with any scheme for the release of prisoners en masse. It would be essential that the judge order that action, albeit state authorities would receive such an order with (private) acquiescence. In Knowles' telling, state officials would "oppose release in open court" but would "concede that there [was] no other solution" and would in reality "hope" that a release order from Johnson would "wake the people and the legislature up" so that money would be allocated for the prisons.[15]

Matters rested there for some time. No immediate conference with the judge was held. Indeed, Johnson never ruled on Knowles' motion. Judson Locke resigned in mid-July, explaining that it was impossible to cope with both crowding in the jails and the ceiling on the prison system's population. The extent to which pressure to release prisoners contributed to Locke's decision to leave is unclear. His position as commissioner had never been solid, and other recent difficulties, including his differences with Bennett, had begun to weigh against him within the board. At all events, the board seized the occasion of Locke's departure both to appoint Bennett to succeed him and to introduce Andrew L. Cooper, a Birmingham parole officer, as the prison system's first black deputy. In the end, the long-rumored shifts among the system's high-ranking officials occurred after all, although with an unusual twist. Locke, like L. B. Sullivan before him, left office on the eve of a hearing in Judge Johnson's court that promised to bring the prison system under yet further judicial orders for reform. He was retained in the system in a less accountable capacity until he was dismissed by a subsequent commissioner in 1979. Cooper served only a bit longer. Like his predecessor, Wheeler Foshee, Cooper was convicted of criminal activities and ended his career in penology as a prison inmate.[16]

As commissioner, Larry Bennett, too, resisted public association with any plan to release prisoners. He put the system's continuing difficulties down to insufficient funding and devoted his early months in office to a campaign for another bond issue for capital construction. Behind the scenes, he pursued the scheme that Locke had failed to carry out. Only days after Bennett's appointment, Barnes told Knowles that prisoners within one year of the expiration of sentence might be released on "leave" and in such numbers that the jails could be "emptied." A bit later, he explained to Segall and Taylor that Bennett was prepared to release short-term prisoners "in waves" as soon as Warren's classification teams could identify those least dangerous to the public. The only condition, now as in the past, was that the judge must order the commissioner and the board to take this action. If such an order could be arranged, then at least the crowding question could be diffused before the scheduled hearing on the general level of compliance thus far.[17]

Neither Knowles nor Barnes was confident that Judge Johnson would cooperate. From the outset, the judge had resisted anything that smacked of a judicially inspired change in the state's penal policies and had concentrated, instead, on coercing improvements in prisoners' living conditions within existing prisons. The only chance of success, then, lay in bringing Johnson a plan on which the parties had already agreed and presenting it as the commissioner's freely chosen response to his constitutional obligations. Then the judge might attach no great significance to incorporating the agreement into a decree. To this end, Knowles and Barnes actually rehearsed their lines before meeting with Johnson in chambers. Unfortunately for their scheme, Judge Johnson cut short the lawyers' performance before its meaning could be made plain. As soon as Knowles mentioned the release of sentenced prisoners, Johnson interjected. "Mr. Knowles," he said firmly, "I just want to make one thing clear. It will be a long time before this court will order the release of duly convicted felons from prisons in the State of Alabama." When Barnes heard that, his position changed radically. He could now assume that Johnson would not do the one thing that promised actually to reduce crowding in the jails. That being clear, Barnes abandoned the plan he and Knowles had developed. The conference ended a few minutes later with nothing further having been said about releasing inmates—the matter the lawyers had sought the meeting to discuss. And there was no court order for the mass release of prisoners while Frank Johnson was on the district bench.[18]

The participants offer differing interpretations of these events and the failure to obtain a release order in the summer of 1978. Bennett recalls that he was ready to accept such an order only as part of a larger settlement intended to make the scheduled compliance hearing unnecessary. When it seemed that Knowles and his colleagues would not compromise regarding other aspects of the January 13 order, the incentives for an agreement on releasing prisoners were drastically reduced. At that point, Bennett and the board declined to engage the public criticism that a release order would have provoked. Myers and Segall share this rough assessment. Knowles, by contrast, believes that only Johnson's statement foiled the arrangement with Barnes and Bennett.[19]

The collapse of negotiations meant that the compliance hearing would be held on schedule. The prisoners' lawyers had "done [their] homework" and anticipated that the hearing would be only a "formality." When they met to map strategy in the Prison Project's offices in Washington, they set their sights high: to obtain compliance with "all aspects" of the January 13 order, remove sentenced prisoners from local jails, "[p]revent the construction of additional secure facilities," and establish an "adequate monitoring system." They also resolved to prove that state authorities had never met the standards Johnson had fixed for medical care in 1972. There was reason to be optimistic on that question. In a pretrial conference a few days later, the judge told Barnes that if the system were shown not to be in compliance with the *Newman* order, he might hold the responsible officials in contempt. State authorities, for their part, resigned themselves to an embarrassing proceeding in which the prisoners' lawyers meant to have a "show and tell."[20]

The four-day hearing in September was precisely that. Knowles put Judson Locke on the stand initially and drew from him a frank admission that the prison system was not in compliance with Johnson's order and could not be brought into compliance without significant new funding. The environmental engineer, Ted Gordon, ticked off the public health hazards remaining in the system and pronounced most facilities still to be "unfit for human habitation"; expert witnesses described deficiencies in the medical and mental health care programs. Some testimony was graphic. Carl Clements said he had found one inmate "who had human waste smeared all over him." The prisoner "said he had no water," and while Clements watched, "dipped his bowl in the toilet, which had not been flushed in some time, and drank it. . . ." Another inmate-witness described routine violence in the dormitories. He himself had been raped by one inmate and then "another took his turn." The assailants threatened to kill the witness if he "snitched." Repeated sexual assaults "went on for four or five days in a row."[21]

Judge Johnson listened to the testimony with some impatience. Early on, he interrupted to acknowledge that the situation in the prisons was "still critical." And when a defense expert, Fred Wilkinson, took the stand, the judge wanted to know why the authorities in Alabama had not been able to do better. Johnson peppered Wilkinson with questions, concentrating on the state's failure to keep inmates busy. "I've been trying," the judge said, "to get them to put the prisoners to work in meaningful jobs for three years, and they are still not working in significant numbers." The larger issue, of course, was mismanagement, about which Nachman and Beto had always complained. After the hearing, Bennett said there was a "good chance" that Johnson would now order prison officials to "turn loose" sentenced inmates overflowing the jails and to spend millions to refurbish the prison system. In truth, the judge had no intention of ordering the release of prisoners, but he *had* finally concluded that the Alabama prison system could be improved only by taking the reins away from men such as Judson Locke, Larry Bennett, and the members of the Board of Corrections.[22]

Whatever happened next in the *Pugh* and *James* cases, it was clear in the fall of 1978 that the litigation had outrun the staying power of many individuals who had played key roles earlier in its history. By the time of the compliance hearing in September, Ira DeMent had been replaced as U.S. attorney by Barry E. Teague who, while less colorful than DeMent, promised continued support for the prisoners' cause. Teague was joined increasingly by Steve Whinston, drawn into *Pugh* and *James* by the resurrection of *Newman,* in which the Justice Department had always taken the lead. George Taylor's role had been declining for some time, leaving Knowles and Segall with primary responsibility. That arrangement shifted yet again during the year, when Knowles left his law practice in Tuscaloosa to become associate director of Bronstein's program, and John Carroll, an attorney with the Southern Poverty Law Center, replaced Joe Levin as one of the attorneys for the *Pugh* plaintiffs. When Matt Myers left the Prison Project some months later, the full weight of the Alabama cases fell to Knowles, Segall, and Carroll.[23]

On the defendants' side, Larry Newman had begun to lower his voice after moving to the attorney general's Birmingham office in March, and Thomas Lawson formally withdrew from the prison cases just before the hearing. This left only Scears Barnes to speak for all state officials, at least in the near term. Not only had the Board of Corrections exchanged Locke for Bennett, but the board itself had changed in recent months. Two new members, Hamner and a Birmingham attorney, J. Louis Wilkinson, promised to cut an important figure in state policy in the coming months. Indeed, by some accounts, they had already engineered Locke's ouster.[24]

More important than any shifts within the penal department, however, were the changes in the state's political leadership. In a hotly contested primary conducted only the week following the hearing, Forest "Fob" James, a former football player at Auburn University who had made a fortune manufacturing plastic-coated exercise equipment, defeated Bill Baxley for the Democratic gubernatorial nomination. Neither candidate had made the prisons a campaign issue, and it was unclear whether the election of James, who presented himself as a conservative businessman, would produce a different perspective on penal affairs. It was plain, however, that the candidate who captured the Democratic nomination in Alabama would be elected. In November, James easily defeated his Republican challenger. If nothing else, Judge Johnson now had a new, untested and largely unknown, chief executive with whom to deal. George Wallace, who had been barred by law from running again, was gone, albeit temporarily. Finally, Baxley's campaign for the governorship had made way for Charles Graddick, the district attorney from Mobile, to win election as attorney general. Graddick had long opposed reforms in the state's prisons and had criticized actions by the Board of Corrections which, in his view, wasted state revenues for the benefit of the undeserving. He had made "hard line" criminal justice policies in general, and enthusiastic support for the death penalty in particular, the keystones of his campaign. His rhetoric—Graddick once proposed "frying" [convicted murderers] "until their eyes pop[ped] out"—made him seem not merely "tough on crime," but rabid regarding crime and criminals. If Bill Baxley had been resistive to genuine reform in the prisons, Charlie Graddick promised to be contumacious.[25]

Everyone familiar with the evidence presented in the September compliance hearing expected Judge Johnson to conclude that very little progress had been made over the past three years and, accordingly, to issue an important new decree. Knowles and Myers composed an elaborate post-trial brief, that listed the many respects in which the prison system remained out of compliance and urged Johnson to write a lengthy opinion—the better to fend off criticism if there were an appeal. For if the appellate courts were once again asked to review Judge Johnson's work in the prison cases, it would be essential that they be made to understand that conditions remained intolerable, notwithstanding the defendants' claims of marginal improvements. Encouraged by Johnson's recent actions and comments at the hearing, Knowles and Myers again urged the judge to appoint a "special master" to superintend further efforts to comply with the January order or, as an alternative, to appoint a "temporary receiver" with power to "operate" the prison system, to take "whatever" steps were necessary to bring it into compliance—including, if necessary, the sale of agricultural lands to raise funds. In any case, the prisoners' lawyers asked Johnson for more stringent timetables. If, for example, the older facilities, Draper and Fountain, could not be refurbished within ninety days, those prisons should finally be closed. Prisoners backed up in the jails should be removed within six months and confined thereafter, "if at all," in "constitutional facilities." Scears Barnes offered a perfunctory response, but Bennett told the press to anticipate "new deadlines," both for meeting standards fixed for the prisons and for attending to the jails, and, at the least, the appointment of a "monitor."[26]

Those prospects apparently moved the Board of Corrections to fasten blame on the new commissioner. Bennett insisted that the board would hardly sack him after only a few months in office. Yet rumors were circulating as early as November; in December, the board divided over a proposal to solicit applications from would-be successors. Carroll and Hamner were prepared to fire Bennett immediately; Vickers and Staton supported him; the new chairman, Louis Wilkinson, agreed to accept applications in order to compare Bennett with possible alternatives in early January. In the meantime, Bennett's detractors sought George Beto's advice regarding a replacement. Beto leaped at the chance, finally, to help choose a professional to administer the prisons. He recommended Robert G. Britton, a member of the first graduating class at the school for corrections specialists at Sam Houston State University and now a midlevel penal administrator in Arkansas. Carroll, Hamner, and Wilkinson brought Britton to Alabama at year's end and left him with the impression that he would shortly be offered the commissioner's job.[27]

With his future at risk, Bennett announced his intention to spend the monies generated in the new bond issue on capital construction. The prisoners' lawyers complained immediately, and Judge Johnson obliged them with an order prohibiting any action until the judge had seen and approved a sensible plan with "consensus" support within the board. Given the divisions there, no such "consensus" could be obtained easily. Bennett himself thought the Wadley, Heflin, and Union Springs sites were ill-advised and that new facilities should be located near Birmingham or in the Tennessee Valley to the north. Yet the commissioner's principal supportors on the board favored the sites previously chosen, while his detractors bitterly opposed them. If Bennett failed to support those projects, he stood to lose his job. In the end, he bowed to the board's internal politics and proposed a plan featuring the three sites of which he personally disapproved. Carroll, Staton, and Vickers approved that scheme. Wilkinson, who opposed it, nevertheless conceded that it had "consensus" support, and Barnes so represented it to Judge Johnson. In this way, construction projects opposed by the plaintiffs, the commissioner, and at least two board members were presented to Judge Johnson as the programs on which the board meant to spend scarce funds.[28]

The administration of the Alabama prison system was now disintegrated. Most participants and observers hoped that the board's new plan, born of confusion and general irresolution, would not be carried out and that, instead, some alternative would yet emerge—to avoid the perpetuation of failed policies. Judge Johnson said at the time that he could ask only for a plan supported by the board "as presently constituted," but that "we may have a new ball game in this thing, come January." And it soon became clear what he meant. Extraordinary negotiations backstage of the drama being played out within the Board of Corrections were about to be revealed, with the result that the board would be stripped of the responsibilities it so plainly had been unable to meet. The plaintiffs would have their receiver, but it would not be one of the professionals they had proposed, but Fob James, who would personally "operate" the Alabama prison system.[29]

As early as October 1978, when James had obtained the Democratic nomination, he discussed the prisons with George McMillan, long an advocate of change in the prison system and now the Democrats' candidate for lieutenant governor. McMillan advised James to abandon the defensive posture that Wallace had assumed and to cooperate with Judge Johnson in bringing administrative order to the prison system. Then, the judge might stay his own hand, for a time, and allow the new governor to prove that he would implement the January order. James warmed to McMillan's view. The new governor was a businessman who genuinely believed that most state problems could be solved through better administration and little else. Accordingly, he asked McMillan to approach the judge on his behalf. Johnson received McMillan and met with James himself just after Thanksgiving, by which time James had been elected. While Johnson's own experience in Alabama caused him to doubt that James could be successful, the judge found the new governor's blunt style refreshing and accepted James' commitment to act decisively at face value. Once again, the judge disciplined himself to give elected officials in Alabama an opportunity to act before taking action himself.[30]

Over the holidays, James held further meetings with McMillan and Speaker McCorquodale at a retreat on the Gulf Coast. The three evaluated several options, including legislation that would abolish the Board of Corrections and a motion, within the framework of *Pugh* and *James,* asking Johnson to appoint James himself as "receiver." Back in Montgomery, and on McMillan's advice, James sought help from Roland Nachman, who favored asking the judge to put James in charge through a federal order—roughly in the fashion that Johnson had earlier appointed the Legislative Prison Task Force to monitor compliance by the board. The tactic was curious inasmuch as Governor James could gain control of the prison system simply by persuading the legislature to change the relevant state statutes. Indeed, the notion that a sitting state chief executive should choose to displace a state agency through federal judicial power instead of through ordinary, legislative means was shocking to many observers. Nachman, however, thought it wise to approach Judge Johnson in this way, the better to convince the judge, and others, that James' objective was finally to bring the long-standing, burdensome, and bitter litigation over the state's prisons to an end.

Nachman phoned Judge Johnson, then attending a conference in Florida, and put the idea to him. The judge agreed to make the appointment but only on condition that James state explicitly that the Alabama prison system had not been brought into compliance under the supervision of the board and that the governor himself would now implement the January 13 order as soon as possible. Recalling past occasions when commitments made by one state officer were ignored or rejected by others, Johnson also demanded that McMillan, McCorquodale, and Attorney General Graddick join with James in such a statement. The governor agreed to those terms and assigned Nachman to prepare a petition to be filed in late January—at the very time the prisoners' lawyers and state penal authorities were distracted by the board's plan for prison construction. Nachman responded with alacrity. Banished from the field some months earlier when the HRC had been abolished, he now seized the opportunity to build his often-stated views directly into state policy—then to be given Judge Johnson's own imprimatur. He produced a ringing document that acknowledged the very charges against the prison system that Governor Wallace and the board had long denied. Nachman conceded that the evidence in the compliance hearing had demonstrated "indefensible" conditions in the system, maintained that the primary reason for those conditions was "inadequate and inefficient management," and insisted that nothing short of the dramatic relief requested by the plaintiffs—the appointment of a receiver—would achieve genuine change. Then, he recited all the ways in which the system remained deficient and James' commitment to cure each. On the critical question of administration, Nachman committed James to appoint "able" and "experienced" people to manage the system effectively and constitutionally. That, of course, spelled the end for the Board of Corrections. Other men might have balked at this point. But Fob James was a maverick, a novice in political circles who genuinely believed he could make good on the promises Nachman's draft made for him. Accordingly, he signed the petition, as did McMillan and McCorquodale. Graddick also signed, albeit reluctantly.[31]

Within hours, Judge Johnson issued an order appointing "Fob James, as Governor of the State of Alabama" to be "temporary receiver of the Alabama prison system" and ordered the Board of Corrections to "transfer" all its authorities and functions to the governor. At the same time, the judge issued an explanatory memorandum, which borrowed from the opinion he had been preparing in the wake of the September hearing. Now buoyed by James' concession that conditions in the prison system had not greatly changed, Johnson declared that the "overwhelming weight of the evidence" established that "what was true in 1972 and 1976 [was] still true. . . ." The "very fact of confinement" in the Alabama prison system violated the Constitution.

> Time does not stand still, but the Board of Corrections and the Alabama Prison system have for six years. Their time has now run out. The Court can no longer brook non-compliance with the clear command of the Constitution, represented by the orders of the Court in this case. . . . It is clear that the Board of Corrections is incapable of effective leadership. Difficult as the Board's position was made by the lack of adequate funding, the Court finds that the Board could have ameliorated the conditions confronting it, but instead contributed to the gravity of the situation by its indifference and incompetence. . . . The extraordinary circumstances of this case dictate that the only alternative to non-compliance with the Court's orders is the appointment of a receiver. . . .[32]

The message was, then, the same message Johnson had sent on so many prior occasions. He insisted that he was acting only because of default on the part of state authorities. In this instance, however, what was formally an order divesting state officials of their authority under state law was paradoxically a most deferential decree, turning over an important state executive function to the state's chief executive officer. Thus the substantive effect of Johnson's action was merely to allocate authority within state government and, even then, only on the request of the state's political leadership. Johnson insisted later, and all conceded, that he would never have placed anyone other than Governor James in the receiver's position.[33]

Judge Johnson *did* give the new governor a chance to prove himself. Three days after making the appointment, Johnson wrote to counsel on both sides, informing them that he considered James' appointment to give the plaintiffs "a substantial portion, if not all" they had requested in their post-trial brief. To underscore that the "ball game" genuinely had changed, the judge also excused James from any duty to comment on the board's plan for spending the bond monies. James, for his part, moved quickly to meet Johnson's challenge. Appointed on Friday, he summoned Bennett to his office the following Monday and demanded to know what the commissioner proposed to do in the new administrative environment. A few weeks later, and notwithstanding Bennett's attempts to offer genuinely promising plans, James dismissed him in favor of Beto's protege, Robert Britton.[34]

Judge Johnson also rejected an attempt by the prisoners' lawyers to test James' resolve in the early going. Knowles, Myers, Segall, and the others were pleased that someone in state government was now willing to admit the prison system's faults and to commit to immediate, serious action. Yet they were not at all sure that Fob James would actually carry through on the course that Nachman had charted for him. James' willingness to appoint a professional to administer the system was to the good, but the choice of Britton was disappointing. Whinston's office quickly confirmed that Britton had been cited by Judge Henley in Arkansas for using unreasonable force with an inmate. Governor James' political conservatism suggested, moreover, that he might hesitate to spend funds genuinely needed and, certainly, that he might balk at the particular uses of money that the plantiffs wished to promote. Lurking beneath doubts that James would prove willing to act was the suspicion, shared by other observers in Montgomery, that the governor vastly underestimated the political difficulty of doing anything of substance with the prisons. Experience with Alabama politics counseled pessimism, and the plaintiffs hardly wished to lose even more time waiting for this new politician to show his true colors to a judge who, in the plaintiffs' view, was again deferring to state authorities when he might be taking decisive action of his own.[35]

Johnson, however, rejected a motion by the prisoners' lawyers, filed in April 1979, seeking James' removal as receiver. The judge acknowledged the lawyers' concerns. He knew, by now, that the conservative new governor had instituted a "hiring freeze" throughout state government and that, in consequence, new guards were not being hired to meet staffing requirements in the prisons. He also knew that James had refused to propose significant increases in the prison system's budget. Yet Johnson was not prepared to abandon hope so soon. Rod Nachman, now serving as James' legal advisor with respect to *Pugh* and *James,* vigorously supported the governor, and that in itself may have influenced the judge to give James additional time. More fundamentally, Johnson thought he had no other choice. Any attempt to appoint someone other than James had little hope of success. The prison system was now, had always been, and in future would be in the hands of state authorities. The only serious chance for reform lay in the possibility that with the passing of George Wallace and the elimination of the Board of Corrections, a brash newcomer, willing at least to promise change, would finally make a difference.[36]

This implicit message was Johnson's last in the prison cases. A month later, he took a position on the Fifth Circuit Court of Appeals, the appellate body that had so often reviewed his rulings. He assigned the Alabama prison cases to Judge Varner, a man whose reputation was no match for Johnson's own and from whom, it was widely believed, Johnson had long wanted to protect the inmates of Alabama's prisons and jails. It was no secret that Judge Johnson had been offered a circuit judgeship and that, in contrast to prior occasions on which he had hesitated to leave the district court, he regarded this opportunity with some favor. Now 61 years of age and troubled by a heart condition that had threatened his life a year earlier, the judge might reasonably seek a respite from the rigors of trial work in the less demanding atmosphere of the appellate bench. Yet some had understood that, should he leave the district court, he might take the prison and mental health cases with him. There was precedent for such action in important, long-standing litigation of this kind, and Johnson might hesitate to release cases in which he had invested so much effort. Commissioner Britton, who had visited Johnson on his arrival in Alabama, had come away with the impression that the judge intended to retain the prison cases. Segall, Johnson's former law clerk, was astonished to hear that the judge meant to give them up. On reflection, however, most observers concluded that Johnson had grown no less weary of these cases than others on his docket. When, indeed, Nachman later expressed regret that the judge had not kept the *Pugh* and *James* cases, Johnson said that it was in part to be rid of the problems in the prisons and the schools in Alabama that he departed the district court. Whatever the explanation, Judge Johnson did leave his great civil rights cases behind him. As a local reporter told the story, Johnson finished a final round of routine trials in Dothan and celebrated the conclusion of his twenty-four-year tenure on the district bench with a drive downtown for a butter pecan ice cream cone.[37]

8

Ambivalence

The appointment of Governor James as receiver was a milestone in the history of the *Pugh* and *James* cases. The shift from Judge Johnson to Judge Varner was of even greater significance. The lawyers representing prison inmates in Alabama had invested themselves in the prison cases only because they believed that Johnson would be sympathetic to the cause of prison reform. Whatever ground had been gained thus far was plainly ascribable to Johnson—as a judge and as a man. Varner was quite another matter. If he had been presiding in 1975, it is most unlikely that Segall and Taylor would have been appointed to represent the prisoners or, certainly, that they would have developed their cases into major class actions for the purpose of thoroughgoing reform—and more unlikely still that Ira DeMent and Al Bronstein would have devoted the resources of the United States and the National Prison Project to such an effort. Now, four years later, with the prisons in roughly the same condition and with local jails jammed with overflow inmates, faced with a new governor and commissioner and denied the hope generated by an extraordinarily able and compassionate judge, the prisoners' lawyers found themselves committed to litigation with little promise of success.

Bob Varner was a Nixon appointee whose confirmation in the Senate had been delayed because he had not paid thousands of dollars in inheritance taxes. His reputation in civil rights matters was mixed at best. He had chaired the notorious Macon County School Board, and he had been accused of racism on the bench. It was alleged, for example, that he had once asked DeMent to strike black jurors from criminal trials because white jurors might refuse to dine with them. Certainly, there was no reason to think that Varner would be sympathetic to the interests of prison inmates. While he had held that conditions in the Montgomery County Jail were unconstitutional, his concern was less that inmates there were suffering cruel and unusual punishment than that they might sue local officials for damages. Consistent with this emphasis on economics, Varner embraced the view, long pressed by state officials, that the real cause for the prison system's inadequacies was the legislature's failure to provide funds to refurbish dilapidated facilities or to build new ones.[1]

For all his faults, however, Varner evidenced some attributes of apparent value to prisoners. Where Judge Johnson had conceived of his task as cooperating with state authorities in hopes of achieving reform over time, Varner considered it his duty to force change more quickly. He would never have issued the January 13 order; that was plain enough. Yet the order was now in place, and Governor James had admitted that its requirements had not been met. Varner, accordingly, took the very steps that Johnson had refused to take. Previously, Varner had ordered officials in Montgomery County to release prisoners to keep the population in their jail at tolerable levels and to prompt some legislative recognition of jail crowding. Now, in new release orders directed to state penal authorities, Varner demonstrated, paradoxically, that a comparatively unimaginative and, indeed, unsympathetic federal judge could bring even greater coercive power to bear on state authorities than his more cerebral and sensitive predecessor.[2]

Still, it was late in the day for anything so dramatic. If Johnson had been willing to order the release of convicts in 1976, or even in 1977, he might have forced state officials to act responsibly instead of diffusing prison issues in personal politics. Judge Varner's release of prisoners in 1981, appraised in light of the patterns of behavior that had developed over the years, was a surprising and jarring tactic that failed in short order—underscoring the great power of settled arrangements to resist reform. An understanding of these events requires, first, an examination of Governor James' inability to satisfy the January 13 order, primarily by constructing new prisons, and the consequent issuance of yet another order fixing deadlines for further action; second, an appraisal of the circumstances surrounding Judge Varner's orders to release prisoners and the concomitant quarrels between James and Attorney General Graddick; and, third, a discussion of attempts, by both James and Graddick, to confound Varner's actions by appealing to higher courts.

Having survived the plaintiffs' attempt to remove him as receiver, Fob James now set about to exercise his power, relying on Commissioner Britton for details. The legislature was glad to oblige; a bill formally eliminating the Board of Corrections and creating a new *Depart-*

ment of Corrections directly under the governor's control passed both houses without discussion. At the same time, James pursued his general objective of reducing the size of state government and, in that vein, holding the budgets of state agencies to a minimum. The governor forced his new commissioner to make ends meet in the first year with the same allotment that Bennett had found inadequate. When, moreover, James revealed the policies he meant to follow with respect to criminal justice, it was apparent that the consequence would be even more difficulty in the prisons. The governor proposed to broaden the range of criminal prosecutions by changing the age at which youths could be tried in adult courts from 16 to 14 years and to lengthen sentences in general by reducing the credits available under the "good time" law. Britton, for his part, signaled change of *some* sort. He discharged a number of holdover officers, including Kenneth Warren and Judson Locke, and appointed in their stead administrators and wardens of his own choosing, among them Joseph Hopper from Georgia. Yet Britton hesitated to criticize James' criminal justice policies in public, albeit he told James privately that more sentenced offenders with longer terms could only aggravate crowding, thus jeopardizing the governor's ability to keep his promises to the court.

Specific plans for the near term were presented to Judge Varner in a midsummer compliance report featuring Britton's appointment. Having dismissed Dr. Warren, the new commissioner now proposed to solve the classification problem by contracting with Allen Ault and Herbert Eber, consultants from Atlanta and Dallas, for the development of a "computerized" system for assessing inmates' characteristics and selecting an appropriate custody grade and work assignment for each. This new system promised faster results at a lower cost in comparison to plans employing psychologists to interview prisoners. Responding to criticisms that James' hiring "freeze" would prevent the acquisition of sufficient guards to keep order in the dormitories, Britton said he was consulting with specialists regarding the number of "correctional counselors" needed to superintend the prisons and intimated that he intended to ask Varner to reduce the number of guards required under the January 13 order. Britton said he would carry out Bennett's plan to contract with a private company for medical, dental, and psychiatric care.

Finally, on the vexing question of crowding, Britton abandoned the three construction sites that had been the subject of so much debate within the board and proposed, instead, to find a site in Jefferson County, near the homes of prisoners from Birmingham. Of course, penal authorities in Alabama had agreed for years that new prisons should be located in the north; Bennett had taken that position only a few months earlier and, in fairness, Locke and L. B. Sullivan had made similar proposals in the past. The same difficulties faced by past commissioners presented barriers to Britton: local citizens objected to prisons near their homes. On this occasion, however, Fob James' brash manner produced different results. When Britton met resistance to a site in St. Clair County just north of Birmingham, James engaged the political risks of forcing a community to accept a new prison for the good of the state as a whole. After time-consuming litigation both in the state courts and before Judge Varner, Fob James finally had his way. The prison was constructed and, when it was opened in 1982, it provided important new space for the prison system's ever-expanding population. On the basis of the precedent set in St. Clair County, moreover, James and Britton later overcame opposition to new facilities in Jefferson and Limestone counties.[3]

The prisoners' lawyers were dismayed. Knowles, Segall, and the others had hoped that their efforts would not produce only more penitentiaries on the traditional model. A new governor had proved willing finally to act, but his action had been in precisely the direction the plaintiffs had wished to avoid. The only tactic seemingly available now was to persuade Jude Varner that long-range construction projects of the kind state authorities planned were insufficient to respond to *current* needs and that, accordingly, Varner should order the immediate release of nonviolent inmates. There was evidence that penal officials could not contain the growing prisoner population: guards gunned down an inmate alleged to have jumped off a truck on the way to the fields, and Deputy Commissioner Hopper shot and killed an honor farm escapee. Neither the commissioner nor the governor conceded anything to these points. In answer to the charge that present conditions foreclosed waiting for new prisons, they converted little-used space at Kilby and Draper into temporary dormitories, refurbished more road camps, and housed scores of prisoners in metal equipment buildings adjacent to Draper. They proposed a new "housing facility" at the cattle ranch, considered abandoned schools for use as shelters, and explored the acquisition of temporary space at Bryce Hospital.[4]

Three days after the governor announced these last plans in February, the prisoners' lawyers gathered in Bronstein's office in Washington to discuss strategy. This, in Ralph Knowles' words, was a "crucial point" in the prison reform movement. Governor James had now had a "reasonable time" in which to show results and, in the plaintiffs' view, had failed to keep his commitments of a year earlier. Still, neither Teague nor Segall, who knew Judge Varner best, thought that Varner would relieve the governor. At most, the judge might force James' hand by fixing timetables for compliance with the most important aspects of the January 13 order. Then, if the governor failed to meet new deadlines, Varner might take more drastic action, even requiring the release of prisoners. To that end, the lawyers began preparing for yet another hearing in the fall.[5]

The prospect of more trial work was daunting. George Taylor voiced an attitude that others were rapidly developing: "I'm hanging in there on the suit, but I'm ready to do or die in October. Six years is a long time." Still, and however wearily, the prisoners' lawyers set to work, just as they had for the original trial in 1975 and for the compliance hearing in 1978. In a real sense, this new hearing would be the third time they had been forced to prove the constitutional case against the Alabama prison system. Once again, Ted Gordon, Carl Clements, and other veterans of prior evidentiary hearings toured the facilities in preparation for testimony; once again, Scears Barnes was forced to admit that conditions in the prisons fell short of established federal requirements. The prisoners' lawyers reported the results of their work to Judge Varner in June. Governor James, they said, had been receiver for eighteen months, yet the prisons remained "seriously out of compliance with almost every provision of the 1976 Order." If James were not removed, they argued, he should be given firm new deadlines.[6]

In responding to these contentions, the governor was both aided and influenced by George Beto and Roland Nachman, who took James' election and appointment as receiver as the occasion for shifting their earlier posture as critics of state penal authorities. Beto insisted that the backlog of prisoners in county jails must be reduced and warned Britton that, with respect to the jails, Varner's patience, "like that of our Lord in the fig tree episode, may have an end." Yet on other issues, such as staff levels, classification, and medical care, Beto applauded Britton's success in making so much progress. . . in so short a time." With that encouragement, Britton and his legal counsel, Scears Barnes, developed confidence that any new hearing before Judge Varner might be less embarrassing than the one before Judge Johnson two years earlier. There was reason to think that Varner might accept Beto's testimony that modest progress had been made in the past year and that Varner might, indeed, take James' demonstration of "good faith" regarding some matters as justification for softening other, more demanding standards established by Judge Johnson.[7]

Nachman, however, had a different perspective. While he was committed to protecting James in the short run, perhaps to vindicate his own participation in the arrangements that had put the governor in his current position, Nachman retained his long-range objective to effect genuine reform in the prison system. He did not want to square off against the prisoners' lawyers in open court, matching expert against expert and pleading with a more conservative judge to dilute standards that Nachman himself had attempted to enforce as chairman of the HRC. On the contrary, Nachman hoped to develop new arrangements that would pacify the plaintiffs for the moment and give Britton time in which to make the changes required by Johnson's order. Nachman's strategy, then, was to negotiate on this occasion precisely what Knowles and Barnes had failed to achieve in the fall of 1978—a settlement that would abort formal proceedings in court.[8]

Nachman's attempt to orchestrate the situation along these lines was fortified by the governor's desire to avoid direct, personal confrontation with the prisoners' counsel. It may be that James was worried that if he were called to give evidence, before or during a formal hearing, he would be asked questions for which he had no answers and, in the end, would be embarrassed publicly. There is evidence to suggest, however, that the governor's reservations about subjecting himself to interrogation were traceable to a distaste for the particularistic formality of lawyers and legal proceedings. Fob James was ill at ease among attorneys; he could not understand them and their ways and felt threatened by them. He took their attacks on his performance personally and was mystified that they did not concede to him the good will he insisted he had exhibited. The governor was an active manager of affairs, a man who genuinely believed he was doing a good job and would succeed if only the lawyers would suspend their tendency to put form and process ahead of substance. The very character of the man who had become governor of Alabama thus played a primary role in the final month before the hearing was to open.[9]

The prisoners' lawyers were questioning a number of prison system officers, Britton among them, and were working toward a session with the governor. Nachman asked Judge Varner to prevent it but, when Varner refused, Nachman scheduled a meeting with James to discuss the likelihood that it would be necessary to sit for interrogation *and* the possibility of a settlement. In this, James' anxiety over being placed on the witness stand was linked with the chance of a negotiated agreement. No direct questioning would be necessary if the governor acquiesced in enough of the plaintiffs' demands to avoid a hearing altogether. The prisoners' lawyers were aware of the meeting between Nachman and James and the possibilities it presented. They scheduled another meeting of their own with Nachman and Barnes for the following day to learn the results. Knowles admitted at the time, however, that in his view there was "no chance that the talks will be productive."[10]

Yet Nachman *was* successful with James. On the morning after his meeting with the governor, he presented Knowles with a proposed settlement scratched out on a half sheet of paper. The offer focused primarily on crowding and contemplated, in that vein, the construction of several new prisons on a fixed timetable. Knowles was unimpressed. He explained to Nachman that the plaintiffs were prepared to negotiate, but only if the governor would discuss all aspects of the January order. Certainly, given the plaintiffs' hopes to *discourage* the construction of more prisons, any proposal that relied primarily on "bricks and mortar" was unacceptable. Nachman was slowed, but not halted by Knowles' reaction. So intent was he on the idea of settlement that he suggested that Knowles draft a counteroffer to be taken back to James. Knowles agreed and, after discussions with his colleagues that afternoon, typed a draft order on a typewriter in Teague's office. After a few more hours of bargaining, during which Nachman shuttled back and forth between the plaintiffs' lawyers and Governor James, the parties reached agreement on the essentials of Knowles' draft. All the lawyers then gathered with Judge Varner in a jury room near his chambers, and the judge agreed to build their settlement into a consent decree issued on October 9, 1980.[11]

Varner expressed little interest in the contents of the agreement. He assumed that the lawyers for the two sides had protected their clients and was disinclined to challenge them when their efforts would allow him to escape another time-consuming evidentiary hearing. That was a fair appraisal of the circumstances. Whatever Britton and Barnes may have thought about the chances of impressing Varner in open court, Nachman and James clearly wished to avoid such a confrontation, and they were prepared to pay a high price to do it. It is difficult to say that the October 9 order favored the plaintiffs unduly; mainly it tracked the standards previously imposed by Judge Johnson's January 13 decree. Still, inasmuch as some provisions of that original order had been criticized, namely the sixty-foot requirement and the prescribed number of guards, this explicit reaffirmation was of no small consequence. Knowles was careful, moreover, to specify precise deadlines. By the terms of the October 9 decree and an accompanying statement incorporated by reference, the governor agreed to reduce the number of sentenced prisoners in local jails in stages—1000 within three months, another 1000 within a month thereafter, and so on until all such prisoners were removed from the jails by September 1, 1981. Different deadlines were established for other matters, but James agreed to bring the entire prison system into compliance as soon as possible and, at the outside, within one year.

These timetables were not chosen arbitrarily; they corresponded to projected dates for the opening of the new prisons in St. Clair and Jefferson counties. Yet no one familiar with current conditions in the prisons seriously believed that the governor could keep such a tight schedule without varying his current policies. Regarding crowding in the jails, the prisoners' lawyers expected James finally to concede that new facilities could not be built soon enough and to turn instead to the release of nondangerous prisoners on a plan similar to the one that Bennett and Barnes had been willing to discuss two years before. The governor, however, was not familiar enough with the facts to grasp the implications of his new commitments; Nachman, too, may have underestimated the significance of the bargain that Knowles had struck with him. The inevitable shortfalls occurred, leading to the next seismographic development in the long history of the Alabama prison cases. Pressed to enforce the deadlines in the October 9 decree, Judge Varner did with the prisons what he had previously done with the Montgomery County Jail. He ordered state authorities to release prisoners outright.[12]

Genuine progress was slow, far slower than the timetables fixed by the October 9 decree would permit. Meanwhile, the population of inmates in the prisons and jails climbed to record levels. By common account, crowding was exacerbated by Attorney General Graddick, whose public criticism of the Alabama parole board for alleged leniency reduced the rate of paroles during this period by more than half. Before long, Britton reported to Varner that he would need an additional $30 million to meet the requirements in the order and conceded in the press that time was too short to be successful even if that much money were currently in hand. The contract for the St. Clair facility had only just been signed, work had barely begun on another project in Marion County, and the planned institution in Jefferson County was still in the "preliminary stage." Fearing that Varner might interpret patience on their part as an invitation to allow James and Britton additional time, the prisoners' lawyers promptly complained that the deadlines in the order were not being met and promised additional requests for judicial action if progress were not made immediately.[13]

Then, in the eleventh hour, the financial circumstances of the state of Alabama, typically listed among the nation's poorest, changed dramatically. Coastal areas were opened to development by petroleum companies, and Alabama received $450 million for offshore mineral leases. Every agency of state government immediately looked to the windfall to resolve problems long neglected for want of adequate revenues. The essential political question was familiar—how to divide a fixed pie among competing uses. But in this instance the pie had suddenly become larger, presenting special opportunities for the prisoners' lawyers, who claimed that the constitutional imperatives in the prisons entitled the Corrections Department to an especially large slice. Knowles conferred with his former law partner, Jack Drake, who still served as counsel in the *Wyatt* mental health case, and together they developed a joint motion, to be filed both with Judge Varner and with Judge Myron Thompson, who had taken responsibility for *Wyatt* on Judge Johnson's departure. The lawyers urged the two federal judges to order state authorities to set aside the money necessary to comply with the orders in *Pugh, James,* and *Wyatt* before any revenues from the oil leases could be channeled to other uses. To ensure that such orders could be effective, the lawyers once again asked that the state comptroller and the state treasurer be brought into the cases as additional defendants.[14]

Notwithstanding the convenience of catching the state at a time when resources were particularly ample, the plaintiffs' request for federal orders coercing specified choices in the expenditure of state funds raised monumental questions regarding the scope of federal judicial power. Knowles and Drake referred Varner and Thompson to the Supreme Court's decisions in the Arkansas prison case and *Milliken v. Bradley,*[15] a recent school desegregation case in which recalcitrant state officials had been held in contempt and given jail terms and heavy fines to coerce compliance with federal court orders. If those extreme measures were available, the plaintiffs' lawyers insisted, then their less "draconian" request for an allotment of state funds was entirely reasonable.[16]

Both Varner and Thompson postponed action on the motion, hoping that the threat of new orders requiring oil lease revenues to be spent on prisons and mental hospitals would pressure the legislature into authorizing funds on its own. Thompson was successful; on the last day of its current session, the legislature allotted an extra $20 million to the mental health system. Varner, by contrast, actually lost ground. At the same time that the legislature increased the Mental Health Board's budget, it *reduced* the budget for the prisons by $7 million. The evidence is that the Alabama legislature surrendered to the implicit threat of an order from Judge Thompson, a bright, young, black judge who might well reach into the state treasury for funds needed for mental hospitals, but called Judge Varner's bluff—anticipating that the older, more conservative man would balk at forcing state expenditures directly.

Varner did balk. But he made it plain that he was not happy with the situation. He scheduled a prompt hearing, at which Thomas Lawson, who had formerly represented Governor Wallace, appeared on behalf of the comptroller and the treasurer. Varner pressed Lawson to suggest what might be done to relieve prison and jail crowding in the face of insufficient funding and asked pointedly whether he should not order the release of prisoners. When Lawson acknowledged that a release order was a possibility, the future course of the *Pugh* and *James* cases became clear. Judge Varner was not prepared to touch the state treasury directly. Nor was he inclined to hold James and Britton in contempt and thus jail or fine them for their refusal to comply with the October 9 order. His target was the Alabama legislature. Having failed to affect the legislature's behavior with an implicit threat, Varner now saw promise only in the extraordinary action he had taken in Montgomery County. At the conclusion of the hearing, he instructed Nachman to prepare a list of prisoners approaching the expiration of their sentences, unlikely to pose a threat to the public if released early and, accordingly, "least deserving incarceration."[17]

James and Britton actually seemed to welcome the prospect of a release order. Their efforts to mitigate crowding in the jails lagged; deadlines at the jails in Birmingham and Mobile were allowed to pass without action. The commissioner spoke openly in the press about an impending order and acknowledged that his staff was "working overtime" to identify more than 1000 prisoners who might safely be released before their sentences expired. In response to Graddick's charge that "rapists and murderers" were on the list, Britton insisted that no one convicted of a violent crime would be discharged. Still, public anxiety, fueled by Graddick's rhetoric, developed by the day. People interviewed on the street expressed concern and, predictably, yet another citizens' group, the March Against Crime, presented the attorney general with a petition signed by thousands of Alabamians opposed to the release of prisoners. Newspapers published editorials urging state authorities to forestall a mass release. The occasion was now ripe for politicians to oppose a release order. Fall campaigns were beginning, and it was suicidal to be on the "wrong" side of a controversial issue so early in the season. Ideas were cheap. Graddick asked the governor to mobilize the

Alabama National Guard to supervise excess inmates wherever they could be held. George McMillan, who still hoped to be elected governor, said that overflow state prisoners should be shipped temporarily to federal facilities.[18]

Finally, Governor James abandoned his acquiescent attitude and joined the crusade to avert the release of prisoners at all cost. James had not yet decided whether to seek reelection, but he could ill afford to let his position on such a volatile issue make the decision for him. It was only a matter of time before George Wallace and Bill Baxley, who clearly were candidates again, would capitalize on any false step. So James sent Britton to the legislature to request funding for prefabricated "modular" buildings, which could be shipped by rail to several sites in the state and used temporarily to house as many as 500 minimum security prisoners. Each inmate would have only thirty-five square feet of living space, and his bunk would occupy most of that. The cost was staggering—nearly $500,000 for the buildings and another $500,000 for sixty-five new guards to be hired, trained, and assigned to duty in the new structures within a matter of days. Even if it were feasible to throw up the modular units in short order, and there were grave questions about that, it was patently obvious that prisoners assigned to them would not be accorded the living conditions promised in the October 9 order. The metal buildings would contribute only another layer of unconstitutional treatment to an already intolerable prison system. Governor James maintained only that the modular units were better than existing prisons and jails and hoped that Judge Varner would permit them to be used while more appropriate facilities were under construction. Even at that, the governor acted more in response to Graddick's machinations than in any genuine belief that the construction of the buildings was sound policy.[19]

Knowles immediately drafted a motion for an "emergency" order enjoining the use of state funds for the project and sent it off to John Carroll to be filed with Judge Varner on June 16. Varner received Carroll in chambers and scheduled a hearing for the following day. By evening, however, matters had taken a new twist that threatened to frustrate any plan then in the minds of the plaintiffs or Judge Varner to effect the release of prisoners. The afternoon newspapers on June 16 were filled with reports of a new decision, *Rhodes v. Chapman*,[20] in which the Supreme Court had held that prison inmates could constitutionally be confined, two prisoners to a cell. And early next morning, Judge Varner postponed the hearing he had just scheduled in order to allow the parties, and himself, time in which to study the new precedent. When the lawyers met with Varner a few days later, however, he seemed to be satisfied that *Chapman* had little bearing on the *Pugh* and *James* cases. The Ohio prison involved in *Chapman* was comparatively new, and the Supreme Court's decision in that case was apparently limited to cells that were only small—not dirty, dark, or unventilated in the manner of the cells and dormitories at Fountain and Draper. Indeed, to underscore the context of the "double-celling" rule announced in *Chapman,* the Supreme Court explicitly distinguished the Alabama cases, which involved poor conditions well beyond insufficient space, in a critical footnote. Given that the *current* issue with respect to the acceptability of the proposed modular units *was* primarily one of space, as opposed to other deficiencies, Attorney General Graddick insisted that Varner should read *Chapman* to mean that the metal buildings met constitutional standards. Yet Judge Varner was apparently persuaded that the situation in *Chapman* had been different. He told the lawyers that he intended to order the release of 400 prisoners on Britton's list.[21]

Varner had reason to act. At the very moment he was considering a release order, the press carried frightening reports of similarly desperate circumstances in other states. In April, Judge William Wayne Justice had issued a decree requiring fundamental changes in the massive Texas Department of Corrections, where George Beto had held so much influence for years. Perhaps in light of the unfortunate experience with state authorities in states such as Alabama, Justice immediately named an experienced outsider to serve as "master" while the court's standards were implemented. Other states seemed ripe for similar judicial action. In early May, prisoners had rioted at the Southern Michigan Prison near Jackson. Many of the prisoners at that facility were being held in temporary metal buildings similar to those proposed in Alabama, and it was rumored that guards there were considering a strike to force Michigan authorities to make needed changes, including the elimination of crowding. Two days after the Michigan disturbance, the Michigan Supreme Court upheld an extraordinary state statute that automatically reduced all prisoners' sentences by ninety days whenever the prison system's population exceeded a fixed ceiling. In Massachusetts, guards at local institutions staged a strike when long-delayed wage increases were stalled in the Massachusetts legislature. And after years of hesitation, the Fifth Circuit Court of Appeals ordered the consolidation of a series of jail suits in Louisiana, so that a single federal district judge could "assist the state legislature" in managing crowding. Finally, on the morning of July 15, the day that many expected to bring Varner's order, an apparent argument over a poker game at the

Reidsville prison in Georgia set off a major riot in yet another institution already subject to an unenforced federal order to reduce crowding.[22]

Judge Varner would wait no longer. He discussed the situation with Governor James one final time, then issued writs of habeas corpus requiring the release, by July 24, of 400 prisoners whose names were listed in an appendix. He also ordered state authorities to accelerate the parole eligibility of an additional fifty prisoners, named in a second appendix. Varner was clear that he was not ordering the prisoners on the second list to be paroled at any fixed time; he meant, however, that the inmates on that list were good candidates for early release and that state parole authorities should not wait until their normal eligibility dates to make decisions. In this, Varner meant to guide state officials in what they might do in future to maintain the prison population at a tolerable level. Britton should identify more prisoners whose records suggested that they might safely be released and should funnel their names to the parole board, which should give those inmates early consideration for parole. Action of that kind would constitute a dramatic turnabout from recent practice. Yet it offered some hope for the resolution of the system's crowding difficulties without further intervention by the court. That, at all events, was Varner's strategy—to demonstrate in his own order what state authorities genuinely concerned with crowding could do to end it.[23]

As soon as the order appeared, Nachman telephoned Knowles to explain that Governor James would not contest it on appeal. James acknowledged in private that there was nothing else to do in the near term and, now that Judge Varner had accepted responsibility for this drastic action, the governor thought he was insulated from political attack. James held a news conference at which he expressed regret that he had not been able to meet the deadlines agreed to in October, and he blamed Charlie Graddick's attack on the parole board for diminishing the rate of paroles and, accordingly, increasing crowding during the very period in which the governor had attempted to reduce it. Graddick, for his part, immediately condemned James for acquiescing in Varner's action. Convicts "aren't school children," Graddick insisted, "We are talking about bad people." The attorney general resisted the release of prisoners notwithstanding the governor's posture and assurances from Britton that only inmates with "good conduct records" would be involved. Judge Varner's dramatic order, accepted however grudgingly by a governor who had grown weary of his own failure to keep his commitments to the court, thus only set the stage for another series of appeals to higher courts—at the instance of a new attorney general who had not been involved in the *Pugh* and *James* cases previously and who flatly refused to accept the consequences of Alabama's failed penal policies.[24]

The remainder of the summer was yet another time of transition. Britton revealed his intention to take a position with Prison Management Systems, a Birmingham firm that had recently won a contract to provide medical care to Alabama prison inmates, and Governor James promptly named Joe Hopper to succeed him. Meanwhile, not only the emergence of Attorney General Graddick as a primary player in the prison reform story, but the virtual disappearance of Steve Whinston reflected deeply rooted political developments. Graddick's attitude was predictable; he was only one in a series of Alabama public officials who found political advantage in demagoguery. Whinston, by contrast, had been a vigorous advocate for the rights of prison inmates in Alabama. The spring of 1981, however, brought Ronald Reagan to power. The new president's legal advisors, Edwin Meese and William French Smith, announced changes in the government's policies with respect to prison litigation. Meese characterized the ACLU as a "criminal lobby"; Smith promised a review of pending cases to ensure that lawyers like Whinston were not "asking the states to do more than the Constitution requires." According to Al Bronstein, the change in administrations "created a . . . new mood" in Whinston's office; "people began leaving." The new assistant attorney general for civil rights, William Bradford Reynolds, made a personal trip to Texas in an attempt to "settle" the prison litigation there without the participation of the staff lawyers who had handled that case. Whinston was given to understand that he no longer had authority to fashion policy regarding the Alabama cases, but must obtain approval of his actions from Reynolds himself. The times, in short, had changed since the summer of 1972, when men like David Norman and Jesse Queen had dispatched Gail Littlefield south to help with the *Newman* case and, indeed, since 1975, when the Justice Department had supported DeMent's involvement in the more ambitious litigation in *Pugh* and *James*. From the perspective of prison inmates in Alabama, the times had not changed for the better.[25]

Notwithstanding his belated proposal to house prisoners in the modular units as an alternative to releasing convicts early, Governor James greeted Judge Varner's order to discharge selected prisoners with equanimity. An aide put it simply: "We are not going to stand in the prison house door." James assured reporters that Varner was "doing everything possible" to enforce prior orders "while not endangering the public in any way." The prisoners on the list were approaching their ordinary release dates anyway, and their names would be announced a week before actual release in order to permit comment from the public.[26]

Attorney General Graddick's reaction was quite the opposite. Within hours, Graddick instructed two assistants, Rosa G. Hamlett and Philip C. Davis, to find some legal basis for challenging the court's action, first before Varner himself and then, if necessary, in the appellate courts. The tactic they developed was extraordinary, even for litigation in which unusual maneuvers had become commonplace. On the day following Varner's order, Hamlett and Davis filed a motion by which Graddick proposed formally to intervene in the *Pugh* and *James* cases as an additional party defendant, on his own behalf as the state's chief law enforcement officer and as the representative of "all law abiding citizens" of Alabama who were the "potential victims" of the convicts scheduled to be released. The motion explained that Graddick had previously assumed that Governor James would offer "reasonable alternatives to the release of convicts." Now, however, the attorney general felt compelled to step in. Graddick insisted that circumstances had changed since the last compliance hearing in 1978 and that Varner should "reopen" the *Pugh* and *James* cases and determine anew whether, in light of the *Chapman* decision, the conditions under which prisoners were now living justified any federal judicial order. In the alternative, Graddick declared that if the prisons *were* still substandard, Varner should allow state authorities to use the modular units or tents borrowed from the National Guard to accommodate overflow prisoners in the short run. At all events, Graddick contended, Varner should stay the release order pending a new hearing on current conditions in the prisons and jails and plans for reducing crowding.[27]

Hamlett and Davis also filed a motion requesting that Governor James be joined as an additional defendant in the *Pugh* and *James* cases. In one sense, this was only a legalistic detail. No one doubted that Fob James spoke for the "defense" in the prison cases, albeit his formal status was as court-appointed receiver. Certainly, no one believed that the governor operated as an arm of the court, to be instructed by Varner in the way that Nachman, as chairman of the HRC, had once been instructed by Judge Johnson. Still, George Wallace's name had been struck from the list of defendants in these cases; accordingly, the new governor could not succeed to the party status of his predecessor in office. And while the legislature had abolished the Board of Corrections and given the governor responsibility for the prisons, no formal action had ever been taken on that basis to name James as a defendant. It was thus possible to argue, although no one had, that only Commissioner Britton, or Commissioner-elect Hopper, was a formal party defendant—as the linear successor to Sullivan, Locke, and Bennett. If, then, Graddick wished Judge Varner to issue an order to James compelling him to take action as a defendant, a formal motion identifying the governor in that capacity seemed necessary. In another sense, however, Graddick's motion to join James as a formal defendant carried substantive weight. It drove a wedge between Alabama's chief law enforcement officer, Graddick, and the state's chief executive. Divisions between and among state officials were not new, of course, but the spectre of a latecomer like Graddick launching a federal legal attack on James, who had volunteered to deal with the prisons, struck many observers as a substantial step beyond previous attempts by Wallace and Baxley to disclaim actions by other state officers.[28]

Graddick's action was all the more anomalous in that he, the attorney general, was already a formal defendant even if Governor James was not. Graddick's predecessor in office, Bill Baxley, had been named as a defendant in the original *Newman* case, which had been consolidated with *Pugh* and *James* in 1976. And when Baxley had appealed from the January 13 order, he had acted as a defendant. While Baxley, like Wallace, might have obtained an order of dismissal at the time, he had not done so. His name had been carried on the prison cases ever since, and now Graddick, as Baxley's successor, automatically inherited party status. His new motion to intervene, then, was out of order. Graddick did not need to become a defendant; he was a defendant. And a curious kind of defendant at that—one who was doing his best to shift blame to Governor James, who was *not* formally a defendant at all.

Graddick quickly made his convoluted scheme public, declaring in a news conference that it had become "incumbent" on him "as attorney general" to "sue our governor." In Graddick's telling, James had come to the idea of using modular buildings too late and had refused to acknowledge that Texas authorities had been successful with tents as makeshift housing. "If tents are good enough for the military," Graddick insisted, "they are good enough for prisoners." The attorney general said he was "just trying to keep 400 prisoners behind bars" and that he was surprised that Governor James had not joined him in an attempt to "keep these people off the streets." The political strategy was self-evident. Graddick hoped to capitalize on public anxiety over the release of convicts and thus to increase his political popularity—both affirmatively, by resisting the release order in court, and negatively, by suggesting that James *favored* the release of felons and contrasting the governor's stance with his own.[29]

This was too much for Fob James, who marshaled all the anger and frustration built up over a year and a half and released it in the direction of the attorney general. Appearing on television with his coat off, his tie askew, and his sleeves rolled up, James fumed that Graddick was "legally incompetent" for filing a motion that was "not worth the paper it was written on." If Graddick thought the governor would approve the "comic book answer" of using "a bunch of pup tents" to house prison inmates, he was "out of his cotton picking mind." If, indeed, the attorney general wished to do something worthwhile, James declared, he should cease his criticism of parole authorities so that they might, once again, grant paroles at the normal rate. Ralph Knowles, too, described Graddick's motion to intervene as "just the latest in a series of irresponsible actions." The *Tuscaloosa News* applauded James for "wisely" rejecting Graddick's plan to house prisoners in tents. James' position on that idea was soon vindicated, moreover, when a riot broke out in the tents in Texas, leaving fifty prisoners injured and causing nearly $250,000 in property damage.[30]

Meanwhile, Judge Varner made his position seem as reasonable and flexible as, in fact, he meant it to be. He received Brooks Hines, Joe McCorquodale, and other legislators in chambers to discuss the situation and answered reporters' questions over the telephone. And he promptly deleted some sixty names from the list of prisoners to be released when Britton reported that they had been included by mistake. Indeed, since many other prisoners on the list were discharged at the expiration of their sentences or on parole before Varner's order became effective, only 277 of the original 400 inmates were actually released by virtue of the court order. Many of those, moreover, were delivered up to authorities in other jurisdictions to serve sentences imposed for crimes in those states. Varner's hopes that the Board of Pardons and Paroles would release the prisoners whose parole eligibility dates had been accelerated were dashed, however, by the attorney general, who persuaded the board to deny parole in almost all cases.[31]

In due course, the lawyers responded formally to Graddick's motions. Rod Nachman, speaking for Governor James, told Judge Varner that the attorney general's attempt to become involved came too late and that the governor, as receiver, *was* formally "an officer of [the] Court" and therefore an inappropriate defendant in the litigation. The prisoners' lawyers recalled that Graddick, too, had joined the agreement on which the October 9 order was based and hardly could argue now that the standards in that order should not be met. The attorney general's "campaign to intimidate" the parole board had frustrated efforts to comply with the October 9 decree; his plan to house prison inmates in tents would only "further exacerbate violations" of that order. At bottom, according to the plaintiffs, Graddick was asking Varner to "ignore the history of this litigation over the last nine years" in a final effort to forestall what everyone else had concluded was essential. Judge Varner soon issued an order routine on its face but devastating to Graddick in its practical effect. Varner acknowledged that the attorney general's motions were entitled to consideration but set them down for hearing on August 6, two weeks after the 277 prisoners were scheduled to be released. Varner refused to stay the release order until after the hearing.[32]

Graddick's only hope now was an emergency appeal. In the interim since the Alabama prison cases had been on appeal in 1977, the Fifth Circuit Court of Appeals had been divided. Alabama, together with Georgia and Florida, was now assigned to the new Eleventh Circuit Court of Appeals sitting in Atlanta, and it was to that new court, staffed by judges who had formerly served the Fifth Circuit, that Graddick took his complaints. Hamlett and Davis requested the formation of a special panel of three circuit judges in hopes that such a panel would hear their arguments on an expedited basis and, perhaps, grant the kind of stay that Varner had refused to issue. If such a stay were obtained, Varner would be forced to postpone the release of prisoners until he considered Graddick's arguments on August 6. If Varner rejected those arguments and reinstated the release order, Hamlett and Davis could appeal yet again. If, however, the circuit court refused to issue a stay, it seemed that the 277 inmates would be released as scheduled—four days from the day on which Hamlett and Davis first approached the circuit court in Atlanta.[33]

Nachman and the prisoners' lawyers had little time in which to respond to Graddick's arguments in the Eleventh Circuit. After Hamlett filed Graddick's motion for a stay on July 22, an emergency panel, led by Chief Judge John Godbold of Alabama, gave the other lawyers only four hours in which to state their arguments. Steve Whinston wanted the Justice Department to oppose Graddick in the appellate court but, in an early indication of things to come, Mr. Reynolds found "insufficient federal interest" in filing a brief in such a short time. Nachman met the deadline by dictating his response to friends in Atlanta; Knowles and Carroll recruited lawyers in the Atlanta office of the

ACLU. In the end, the appellate panel had the benefit of the arguments that Varner had heard before refusing a stay at the district level. Those arguments prevailed; the emergency panel met on the afternoon of July 23 and denied Graddick's motion without opinion.[33]

The Eleventh Circuit's action did not, however, end the episode. Anticipating a negative judgment in Atlanta, Davis was already in Washington preparing to file a request for emergency action in the Supreme Court. As soon as the circuit panel acted, Davis asked Justice Lewis Powell, the justice assigned to entertain emergency motions arising in cases in the Eleventh Circuit, to issue a stay. Nachman, now relying on friends at a Washington law firm, managed to get a response to Powell a few minutes later. And Al Bronstein quickly filed yet another response on behalf of the plaintiffs by sending a messenger to deliver it to one of the police officers assigned to guard the Supreme Court building after hours. If Powell had been in his office, he might have acted on Davis' request that day, July 23. In fact, however, he was en route to his home in Richmond, Virginia. When a clerk reached him, Powell had neither time nor opportunity to read and digest the materials received in Washington. Instead of denying Davis' request, and thus allowing the release of prisoners next day without considering Graddick's arguments, Justice Powell issued a terse stay of Judge Varner's release order, pending a further order from Powell himself or the full Court.[34]

The reaction in Graddick's office was effusive. A spokesperson proclaimed the stay a "major victory," and Graddick's aides made the rounds of Alabama's prisons to ensure that no warden failed to hear the news and released prisoners notwithstanding the stay. At the same time, the *Post Herald* expressed doubt that Justice Powell was "fully familiar" with Judge Varner's reasons for undertaking this "rather mild attempt to get the state moving again" and speculated that when Powell took time to "study the legal briefs" and to trace the history of prison litigation in Alabama, he might "dissolve his order and let the release proceed." That is precisely what happened. The very next day, after reading the relevant documents and composing a short opinion explaining his actions, Justice Powell issued a second order vacating his first. He said that Fob James was responsible for the prison system "in his capacity as receiver in one instance and in his capacity as governor in the other." Since James was "apparently satisfied" that the people of Alabama would suffer no "irreparable injury" from the release of these prisoners and "affirmatively support[ed]" Judge Varner's action, there was no reason to interfere. The attorney general's arguments would be considered, of course, but on an ordinary appellate schedule. Coincidentally, as it turned out, Graddick's contentions regarding this initial release of prisoners in July would be heard at the time the Eleventh Circuit took up his attack on a second release order that Varner would issue in December. For the moment, however, the release of these 277 prisoners could proceed.[35]

Britton telephoned Nachman for instructions, and the governor's lawyer told the commissioner to "get them out" as soon as possible, before Graddick found another way to frustrate the plan. The next day's papers were filled with headlines and stories about the "mass release" of prisoners. There were photographs of inmates marching out of Draper Prison, waving to onlookers, and interviews with freed prisoners about their good fortune. One said he "never should have been [in prison] in the first place," another claimed he "ain't never coming back," and yet another insisted he would have a job by Monday morning. One inmate at Draper, not among those released, was heard shouting over the din near the gate: "Tell Judge Varner to let us all out."[36]

The release of even a handful of prisoners was a cathartic event. Yet serious observers recognized that Judge Varner had no intention of issuing enough such orders actually to solve the crowding problem. The prisons and jails, after all, held 2000 convicted felons more than they could accommodate. Varner regarded the release of a few prisoners, even those who posed little threat to public safety, as an unfortunate but necessary device for spurring action from the Alabama legislature. He wanted more prisons built, and faster. Knowles, indeed, worried that by "getting two hundred prisoners released" the plaintiffs might have "won the battle only to lose the war." The legislature's reaction to the release of prisoners in July was to approve plans to "expand" the new St. Clair and Jefferson county prisons by assigning two prisoners to cells originally designed for one, this with the expectation that the Supreme Court's decision in *Chapman* would permit closer quarters in new facilities.[37]

For Governor James, this was a time for soul searching. The victory over Attorney General Graddick was satisfying, but the wages of James' efforts with respect to the release order were not entirely pleasant. The governor had been wounded politically by his bout with Graddick and, for all his naiveté, James knew it. He also knew that he stood to suffer even greater political losses if the same thing happened again and, again, he acquiesced while Graddick resisted. Then, too, the governor was personally anxious that Graddick might have been right— that Nachman might have misled him into weak policies with respect to the prisons and, worse, that Britton might have fed Judge Varner the names of dangerous criminals. James was haunted by fears that the men released pursuant to the order might harm innocent citizens. When he read a particularly lurid account of a homicide at a Montgomery convenience store, he told one of his aides, Jimmy Samford, that he would never again approve the early release of convicts, lest such a policy lead to more crime. The governor's concerns were unjustified. When the data were collected, Britton's staff reported that the recidivism rate among the prisoners released early was well below average. Still, James was personally unconsoled.[38]

The significant date now was September 1, 1981, when under the terms of the October 9 consent decree all sentenced prisoners were to be removed from local jails. The governor pressed ahead with stopgap measures—the modular buildings and McMillan's idea to place some state inmates in federal penitentiaries. He agreed to spend part of the state's mineral lease monies on the new "expanded" prisons in St. Clair and Jefferson counties, and he pressed the parole board to accelerate favorable parole decisions. The prisoners' lawyers maintained their attack on the modular units. Knowles and Carroll acknowledged that Hopper had succeeded in building a "trailer park prison" at Staton, but the notion that such a facility could actually eliminate crowding according to the terms of the October 9 consent decree was, in their view, preposterous. While James' other ideas for contending with crowding without "the release of more prisoners" had more merit, none of them could succeed soon enough to matter. Meanwhile, tension was mounting among prisoners crowded together in the heat of the Alabama summer. One major riot had already occurred. In late summer, the governor conceded that he needed more time and formally asked Judge Varner not to order the release of more prisoners for another sixty days. Varner, for his part, scheduled a hearing on the governor's request.[39]

Simultaneously, James pursued an alternative strategy with the federal government. Encouraged by the Justice Department's more sympathetic attitude of late, and buoyed, perhaps, by his personal contacts with President Reagan, the governor attempted to persuade Mr. Reynolds and others to side with him in further battles with the prisoners' lawyers and Judge Varner. Toward that end, he had already been to Washington on several occasions to meet with Reynolds, usually outside the presence of Steve Whinston. The impact of James' approach to Washington was obscure, yet Knowles and Carroll feared that any softening in the Justice Department's attitude at this critical juncture would severely damage their ability to persuade an already doubtful district judge to brave yet another release order.[40]

The government's position regarding James' request for a sixty-day reprieve provided a test. An expected memorandum from Steve Whinston was delayed nearly three weeks while he argued with his superiors about what should be said. In the end, the government equivocated. The body of Whinston's memo appeared as vigorous as ever, condemning state authorities for failing to meet court-ordered standards and criticizing ineffectual plans for easing crowding without another release order. If Governor James was serious about avoiding the release of more prisoners, Whinston argued, he and his advisors should abandon the ideas offered to date and develop an alternative program that promised actually to work. On a final page, however, Whinston asked Varner to allow Governor James the sixty days James had requested. This was not Whinston's idea. He endorsed James' request for a postponement only under strict orders from his superiors, who flatly refused to allow him to join the plaintiffs in seeking another release of prisoners. In order to ensure that Whinston adhered to the department's official position in this respect, officials in Washington insisted that he not only present his memorandum for approval, but obtain a transcript of the hearing before Judge Varner—so that senior lawyers in Washington could check his oral statements in court. Steve Whinston, long a valued and trusted ally of the plaintiffs in the Alabama prison cases, was now on a leash held by Justice Department officials in sympathy with the state authorities whose actions the plaintiffs continued to challenge.[41]

The shift in the Justice Department's position figured significantly in the strategy now forged for the plaintiffs by Knowles and Carroll. If Frank Johnson had still been presiding in these cases, it might have been prudent to give ground as the political support for their point of view seemed to be weakening and to trust the judge to position himself to maintain pressure on state authorities. If the prisoners' lawyers had any hope for success before Judge Varner, however, it lay in mounting the most powerful case possible in order to persuade him to act decisively notwithstanding the Justice Department's retreat. The upcoming hearing would have to be, in effect, yet another trial of the Alabama prison cases in which the plaintiffs would spread before the court all the evidence they could marshal to demonstrate that the prison system remained out of compliance with court-ordered standards. If Varner held firm, all would be well; more prisoners might be released to reduce current crowding and force Governor James to abandon hopes of meeting his responsibilities by building more prisons. If Varner waffled, the future might well belong to Charlie Graddick. To avoid that catastrophic course, the plaintiffs would appeal immediately in an attempt to win in the appellate courts what they might be denied at the district court level.[42]

Knowles and Carroll were not sanguine. In July, neither the Eleventh Circuit nor Justice Powell had said squarely that Judge Varner had been right in ordering the discharge of prisoners as a means of reducing crowding. The appellate judges had only refused to take up the merits of that question on an emergency basis, and their failure to issue stays of the initial release order pending consideration of the question in the ordinary course had allowed a handful of inmates to be released. It was by no means clear, then, that the first release order would have been sustained if it had been treated on its substantive merits. Now, particularly in light of *Chapman,* Varner might refuse to issue a second order and if he discharged more prisoners, the appellate courts might reverse. Still, the prisoners' lawyers could argue that the *Pugh* and *James* cases were controlled by the October 9 consent decree. So long as that order was in place, it must be enforced. Knowles and Carroll hoped that Varner himself would see the matter this way and, accordingly, would hesitate to amend the contract embedded in the consent decree by granting Governor James more time. Alternatively, they hoped the appellate courts would direct Varner to enforce the October 9 decree, if necessary, by the release of more prisoners.

Attorney General Graddick and his assistants formulated a drastically different set of contentions. To begin, Graddick argued that, at least with respect to crowding, the state prisons were now in full compliance with *constitutional* standards. While the sixty-foot rule, established in the January 13 order and reaffirmed in the October 9 decree, had never been satisfied, the *Chapman* case put the validity of that rule, if not the "design capacity" standard itself, in doubt. In any case, prisoners could be allotted much less space in the new modular units, which at least met rudimentary public health standards. The same could not be said of local jails; conditions there, Graddick grudgingly conceded, were substandard. Even in the jails, however, Graddick contended that the extent to which prisoners suffered unconstitutional treatment depended on the duration of their stay. The constitutional problem in the present circumstances was not that 2000 sentenced prisoners were backlogged in the jails, but that they tended to be the same 2000 prisoners over time. The attrition rate at the state's prisons did not permit inmates to be moved quickly enough through the (ostensibly unconstitutional) jails and into the (arguably constitutional) prisons and modular buildings. The trick, then, was to shuttle prisoners back and forth between the jails on the one hand and the prisons and modular units on the other, so that no inmate was forced to spend more than a few months in a crowded jail. Such a program would not merely work a sort

of· constitutional equity among individual prisoners. Graddick proposed that it would actually end prisoners' unconstitutional treatment—a brief term of confinement under substandard conditions in a
jail being, by his account, no basis for constitutional complaint. To the
plaintiffs, Graddick's scheme was not only impractical, but silly.
Knowles dubbed it the "MX" plan, after the then-current Pentagon proposal to safeguard nuclear missiles by moving them about on flatbed
rail cars. Nachman, too, thought the idea was unsound. At the hearing
in November, however, two of Graddick's assistants, Walter Turner
and John Lockett, put it forward gravely.[43]

Judge Varner credited the argument that it might be constitutionally acceptable to place prisoners in substandard facilities if the duration of their stay were limited. In this, he drew some support from
Judge Pointer's orders in Birmingham. Local authorities there had been
fined according to the number of days the population of the jail
exceeded the court-ordered maximum. That suggested to Varner that
Pointer, too, attached constitutional significance not merely to the
nature of prisoners' living conditions, but to the period of time inmates
were forced to suffer deprivation. As the hearing progressed, however,
the practical limitations became obvious. Commissioner Hopper confessed that a plan requiring prisoners to be transferred more than twice
a year would be a "logistical nightmare." When Varner considered the
idea of obtaining formal waivers from prisoners left in unconstitutional
circumstances more than six months, John Carroll interrupted to make
explicit what most of the lawyers in the room were thinking. If the
defendants' attorneys would not say it, Carroll would. The MX plan
offered no serious answer to the myriad problems affecting the Alabama
prison system. Within its own terms, moreover, it was flatly infeasible.
If tried, it would be an administrative and financial disaster. Graddick's
assistants had proposed it only because they feared the obvious alternative—the release of more prisoners. Judge Varner was called up
short: "That hurts me," he said, "And I recognize that. But what else
am I going to do with them?" Carroll's answer was predictable: "Let
them out."[44]

That, it later became clear, is what Varner had always intended to
do. When Knowles and Nachman argued over the extent to which the
state's construction plans might solve the crowding problem over the
long term, Judge Varner interrupted: "How many inmates constitute
the overcrowded population right now? I mean, how many are we
above our limitations?" When the lawyers fixed that figure, the judge
turned to Governor James' counsel with the present issue: "And there

is an order that there be no prisoners in county jails by now. . . . What do you propose to do about that, Mr. Nachman? Isn't that just a matter of simple math?" Whinston interjected the position he had been instructed to take, but Varner responded candidly.

> My problem is this: If a Judge orders something that can't be done he is making the Court look bad. I have already done that in this case. I don't want it to look any worse than it has gotten. . . . I have got people before me here today who are nearly all in contempt of court now. . . .
>
> Now, I have released prisoners several times in various cases, and it gets the attention of the public, gets me some nasty phone calls, gives the newspapers something to talk about and releases some people that, when the parole board was functioning, probably [would have been released by the board]. . . .
>
> I am just trying to grope around and find something that will work. And I don't think your plan will work. . . .
>
> Let me say this. I think the Governor has a very tough job and he has got something that I don't have, and that is politics. . . . For that reason I can certainly understand why he would not favor a mass release of prisoners.
>
> My duties are a little different. I have a duty to protect anybody whose constitutional rights are violated. . . .
>
> Don't you think we have exhausted the possibilities short of release? Do you think the Legislature is going to give us any more money? If you do, do you think you can get anything done inside of years? I don't.
>
> I have been sitting on top of this case for years and it is all that Ralph and John . . . and everyone else could do to get a little attention through all these years and get some money when the oil money came in. And it has been like pulling hen's teeth to get anybody to do anything. . . .
>
> I just don't think we can wait. I don't think we can continue to wait. . . . [45]

Turner and Lockett raised one last legal argument—that a new order requiring the release of identified prison inmates could be valid only if supported by formal findings that those very individuals were suffering unconstitutional conditions. This, of course, had nothing to do with the validity of releasing prisoners per se, but spoke to Varner's preference for naming the particular inmates to be discharged. Some prisoners on any list of inmates approaching the completion of their sentences would probably now be found in the state prisons where, according to Turner and Lockett, conditions were no longer crowded or otherwise deficient and from which, accordingly, inmates were not constitutionally entitled to be released. Knowles and Carroll focused their attention on the *number* instead of the *identity* of inmates to be discharged. They would have been satisfied if Varner simply required the release of a fixed number of inmates, leaving the selection of prisoners to Commissioner Hopper. Judge Varner, however, had his reasons for taking it on himself to choose the prisoners to be released. The release of convicts was obviously unpopular, and the judge wanted to spare James and Hopper the political costs that would flow from making decisions of this kind. This had been Varner's attitude in the Montgomery County Jail case, and it had formed the backdrop for the release of state prisoners in July. In a real sense, then, Varner accepted the tendency in Alabama politics, a tendency about which Judge Johnson had complained so often, to shift responsibility for politically unpopular governmental actions to the federal courts.[46]

Two weeks later, Judge Varner asked Hopper for the names of prisoners having less than one year to serve and, on December 14, 1981, he ordered the release of 352 prisoners with "good conduct records" who were scheduled for release within six months in any event. This time around, Varner said the prisoners so released could and should be subject to reasonable "parole conditions." And, again, he ordered an acceleration of the parole eligibility dates of prisoners named on a second list. He explained his action simply: the Alabama prison system remained out of compliance with the October 9 decree, under which crowding was to have been eliminated more than three months earlier, and something must now be done to protect prisoners' constitutional rights.[47]

The new order was headline news across the state, and some newspapers published critical editorials. Governor James was in Japan at the time and thus unavailable for comment, but a spokesperson indicated that there was a "good possibility" that James would join an appeal this time. Graddick, for his part, delivered some of the most acerbic rhetoric to date. Calling the order "obscene," the attorney general accused Judge Varner of "playing Santa Claus to a bunch of dangerous violent people" and "destroying the criminal justice system" into the bargain. Graddick issued a warning to parents: "You can tell your children: when you go to bed it won't be Dancer, it won't be Prancer up on the roof. It'll be a bunch of thugs and criminals released from our state prisons." Indeed, the attorney general actually proposed that prisoners might steal holiday gifts from beneath Alabama Christmas trees. These men, Graddick insisted, were dangerous felons; they were not convicted and sent to prison for "singing too loud in church."[48]

Commissioner Hopper, too, condemned the release order. A spokesperson in his office said that the judge was now reaching down to the "scum" of the prison population and proposing early release for men who had committed violent felonies. Yet in an interview a few weeks later, Hopper conceded that crowding could not be eliminated by the construction of new facilities. Neither the planned prisons in St. Clair and Jefferson counties, nor a third in the Tennessee Valley, would keep pace with the growing population of inmates. On the contrary, according to the corrections department's own projections, the state would need a new prison capable of housing 1000 prisoners every year through 1990 and beyond in order to achieve and maintain adequate space for prisoners. Each such prison would cost $30 million to build and roughly $600 million to operate over its useful life. "When we really get down to looking at economics," Hopper declared, "we cannot afford to lock up all these people." This, of course, was precisely the point the prisoners' lawyers were advancing. Judge Varner responded to questions from the press, but only to explain that the men to be released had "indicated by their conduct" that they were "ready to come out." Summing up, he said he simply had to act to relieve a prison system "bursting at the seams."[49]

Judge Varner postponed the actual release of prisoners until December 22. Graddick promptly filed a notice of appeal and a motion for a stay of Varner's order until the circuit court could review it. The grounds asserted were familiar. The attorney general complained that the release of prisoners was beyond a federal court's power and that the references to parole in the order "usurped" the authority of the Alabama parole board, whose members still were not parties to the litigation. Primarily, however, Graddick rested on the argument that Turner and Lockett had put forward in November. Varner had ordered the release of identified inmates without first determining that the conditions under which those men were living were unconstitutional. Nachman, representing Governor James, joined in the request for a stay, but only on the ground that James needed more time in which to make good on his many promises to find space for overflow inmates pending the completion of the new prisons now under construction. In Nachman's telling, the timetables established in the October 9 order had never been intended to be rigid deadlines, but only the reasonable hopes and expectations of those involved.[50]

Judge Varner called the lawyers in and explained himself once more—for the record and, in consequence, for the appellate court waiting in Atlanta. He embraced the plaintiffs' position that the applicable standards for the *Pugh* and *James* cases were those set forth in the October 9 consent decree—whatever the Constitution, if considered afresh, would require. Conditions in local jails in Alabama did not meet those standards. Judge Johnson had said as much in 1978, and Judge Varner now reaffirmed that assessment. It followed that Varner *could* order the release of *all* the state prisoners backed up in the jails. By contrast, he had ordered the release of inmates who promised little threat to the community. That is why he had worked from Hopper's list and why many inmates among those to be released were, in fact, held in state prisons. Those prisoners were not chosen according to the facility in which they happened to be housed at the moment, but because they were judged not to be dangerous and, of course, because they were about to be released anyway. In Varner's view, it was reasonable to choose the men he had and, by releasing them, to make room for inmates now backed up in the jails to be transferred to more acceptable quarters in the prisons. Varner acknowledged that James had done the "best" he could in a "bad situation." But the dates in the October 9 order were *deadlines* and could not be ignored.

> I think I have looked John Carroll in the face long enough and said, "You can't have it now." I think he has looked his clients in the face long enough and said, "The Court has ordered you out of this county jail by September 1st, 1981, and you can rest assured that what the Court says it will do." And I have reached the end of my patience as to that.

Three days later, Varner formally refused to stay his new release order. Graddick went immediately to the Eleventh Circuit, once again requesting an emergency stay and expedited review. His papers arrived at the court on Friday, December 18, and he was given until midmorning the following Monday to present arguments to each of the three judges on yet another emergency panel, now at their homes scattered along the Florida coast. Inasmuch as the release was scheduled for December 22, all the lawyers assumed that the court would act by noon on Monday, December 21, to allow time for the losing side to petition the Supreme Court. Once again, nearly a dozen lawyers worked furiously through the weekend to prepare motions, briefs, and other documents in hopes of impressing appellate judges who, at the moment, knew nothing at all about litigation that had been before the district court for seven years. This time, Graddick was successful—perhaps because he now had the support of Governor James or perhaps, as Knowles and Carroll speculated, because it was now clear that there would be many release orders in Alabama and many similar appeals until the Eleventh Circuit finally decided whether Judge Varner could force state authorities to take such strong medicine. In a vague reminder of the day five years earlier, when Bill Baxley's shift on the meaning of Alabama's "good time" law prevented the discharge of hundreds of prisoners on Thanksgiving day, a crisp order from the circuit court now forestalled the release of hundreds more within hours of Christmas eve.[51]

There was still time for the prisoners' lawyers to ask the Supreme Court to dissolve the Eleventh Circuit's stay, but that course seemed futile by any account. The justices would probably reject any such attempt out of hand and, if they were to overturn the circuit court's order, the consequence would only be to postpone yet again a decisive determination of the important question at hand. Knowles and Carroll had been wrestling with these problems in the district court long enough. They had persuaded Judge Varner that he must take dramatic action of this kind, and yet it seemed that prisoners would actually be discharged only if the circuit court approved. It was time, then, to accept the further challenge of convincing three more federal judges that the circumstances in Alabama warranted an attempt to enforce earlier orders by releasing prisoners. On this occasion, all relevant issues would be taken up together. The court of appeals joined Graddick's pending appeal from Varner's release order in July, which had been waiting its turn on the appellate docket, for consideration in conjunction with the new appeal, by both Graddick and James, from this, Varner's second release order. Given the time and effort that had been necessary to bring Judge Varner round, the plaintiffs could not be optimistic regarding their chances. Graddick, by contrast, was ecstatic. Invoking his holiday metaphor once again, he told the press that "Santa Claus [had] brought an early . . . [gift] to the people of Alabama. . . . There [would] be no prisoners going home for Christmas this year." Oral argument was scheduled for February 8, 1982, leaving the attorneys just under two months in which to refine the arguments they had drafted in such haste in recent days.[52]

The alliance between Governor James and Attorney General Graddick was provisional and uneasy. The governor's lawyer, Rod Nachman, had little tolerance for Graddick's bellicose attitude toward the federal courts and thus resisted joining the attorney general's brief on appeal. At the same time, Nachman hardly wished to leave the appellate process to others, as he had been forced to do in 1977 as chairman of the HRC. He thus filed his own brief on the governor's behalf, placing emphasis on James' role as the "voluntary receiver" appointed by

Judge Johnson to begin a campaign of prison reform that other state officials, including George Wallace, had been unwilling to undertake. Nachman resisted the release of more prisoners and argued that Varner had exceeded his authority below. Yet he withheld any general argument that release orders were never warranted and, indeed, reminded the court that his client, Fob James, had acquiesced in the first release in July—the better to portray the governor as a comparatively objective public official doing his best and to put some distance between James and Attorney General Graddick.[53]

By contrast, the brief prepared for Graddick was openly confrontational. Hamlett and Lockett insisted that the constitutional standards that Judge Johnson had imposed in 1976 had been eroded by *Chapman* and two other recent opinions from the Supreme Court, both written by Justice Rehnquist, a Nixon appointee who had only just joined the Court when the original order in *Pugh* and *James* had been issued. Writing for the full Court in *Bell v. Wolfish*,[54] Justice Rehnquist had said that "[a]n institution's obligation under the Eighth Amendment is at an end if it furnishes sentenced prisoners with adequate food, clothing, shelter, sanitation, medical care and personal safety." Acknowledging that the federal courts must occasionally issue orders requiring improvements in prison conditions, Rehnquist had warned nonetheless against becoming "enmeshed in the minutiae of prison operations." Judges, he insisted, should not substitute their own judgments for those of state authorities; they should identify minimum constitutional standards, then leave "[t]he wide range of judgment calls" to state authorities. Writing only for himself in another recent case, *Atiyeh v. Capps*,[55] Justice Rehnquist had been even more blunt: "[N]obody promised [state prisoners] a rose garden," he said, "and I know of nothing in the Eighth Amendment which requires that they be housed in a manner most pleasing to them. . . . "

Working from a draft prepared by Elizabeth Alexander, one of Bronstein's staff lawyers, Knowles and Carroll developed a brief with a quite different approach. None of the recent cases regarding the meaning of the Constitution in prison cases was relevant to this appeal— *Chapman, Bell,* and *Capps* included. The *Pugh* and *James* cases were controlled by the January 13 order, which had been substantially sustained on appeal three years earlier, and the October 9 order, from which neither James nor Graddick had taken an appeal. The standards fixed by those orders now established the "law" of these cases; the suggestion that the meaning of the Eighth Amendment had now changed and that, in effect, the Alabama cases must be adjudicated all over again to identify current constitutional standards simply ignored, in the plaintiffs' telling, the history of the Alabama cases to date. Knowles and Carroll insisted that the standards in the October 9 order reflected a bargain, something the plaintiffs had obtained only by surrendering value in return: the opportunity then presented to hold a thorough evidentiary hearing and to demonstrate, on the evidence, that the prison system remained out of compliance with requirements previously established by the court. By this account, Nachman was plainly wrong in characterizing the timetables in the October 9 order as "goals" instead of "deadlines." James and Graddick bargained for those dates, accepted them, and failed to seek review of them; now, they were bound by them.[56]

It remained only to hear from the federal government. By now, John C. Bell, a Reagan appointee, had succeeded Barry Teague as U.S. attorney in Montgomery. Bell had attended the hearing before Judge Varner in December but, having come so lately into the prison litigation, he deferred to Steve Whinston for current strategy. Initially, Whinston drafted a tight, matter-of-fact brief, which traced the Alabama prison cases from their origin down to the October 9 consent decree and then took the plaintiffs' part—both on the question whether the October 9 order, as opposed to the Eighth Amendment, was controlling, and on the question whether Judge Varner could order the release of prisoners as an enforcement device. That brief, however, was never filed. Whinston's draft wound its way to Assistant Attorney General Reynolds, who again found "insufficient federal interest" to warrant Justice Department participation in an appeal from an order to release Alabama prisoners. Whinston implored Reynolds to reconsider. Was there, he argued, "insufficient federal interest" in participating in an appeal in connection with cases in which the Justice Department had been involved "for years," in enforcing a consent decree to which the department was a "signatory," in addressing the circumstances in which a federal court "may order the early release of prison inmates" or, indeed, in "protecting" the constitutional rights of "citizens held in unconstitutional jails"? In Whinston's estimate, of course, there was ample federal interest, and any failure to file a brief would amount to "[d]ucking" the hard issues presented by this appeal. His protest went unheeded, however; the plaintiffs in the Alabama cases could no longer count on the Justice Department as an ally.[57]

Oral arguments were given on schedule before a panel led by Judge Lewis R. Morgan, whom the prisoners' lawyers considered not to have strong sympathies in prison cases, and including Judge Gerald B. Tjoflat, whom the plaintiffs anticipated would hold firm views and, very likely, would carry Morgan with him. The third panel member, Judge Phyllis A. Kravitch, gave the plaintiffs some hope. In the course of the arguments, Kravitch asked several questions suggesting concern for the prisoners' cause. She indicated, at least, that she was familiar with Judge Varner's experience in these cases, state authorities' failure to make improvements over an extended period of time and, most important in the plaintiffs' eyes, the desperate plight of prisoners backed up in local jails. Early in the hour, however, the lawyers were made to understand that this day would belong to Judge Tjoflat.[58]

Nachman had hardly begun his argument when Tjoflat interrupted to "explain" what was "bothering" him and what it was he wanted the lawyers to address. At first, Tjoflat seemed to be persuaded by the plaintiffs' case. He dwelled on the specific requirements and timetables established by the October 9 order, Governor James' agreement to those provisions, and the failure of any party, including Graddick, to seek appellate review of the order at the time. Tjoflat seemed unwilling, however, to take the next step in the plaintiffs' argument. He did not accept that, in these circumstances, Judge Varner could reasonably force compliance by releasing prisoners. Tjoflat was troubled by Varner's failure to employ the tactic approved by the Supreme Court in *Milliken v. Bradley,* the school desegregation precedent on which the prisoners' lawyers relied and, indeed, the tactic used by Judge Pointer in Birmingham. Why, he asked, had Varner not enforced his order by holding state officials in contempt and either fining or jailing them until they met their responsibilities? Tjoflat repeated this same theme when Lockett took the podium to argue on Graddick's behalf and when John Carroll stood to argue for the plaintiffs. It was clear that Tjoflat, at least, was utterly uninterested in any of the arguments the lawyers had meant to make and wanted only to hear their responses to his unanticipated approach.

This, to put it mildly, was unnerving to all sides. The plaintiffs regarded Tjoflat's suggestion with genuine alarm. If accepted, such a theory would mean not only that they would lose on this appeal, but that, back in the district court, they would have no alternative but to ask Judge Varner to hold Hopper, at the least, and perhaps James and Graddick as well, in contempt for failing to remove state prisoners from local jails. That, the plaintiffs predicted, would be futile. It was one thing for Judge Pointer to employ the contempt power to coerce the removal of prisoners from a single jail; it was at least possible for state authorities to respond immediately, if only by transferring overflow prisoners to some other local facility and exacerbating crowding there. A contempt order regarding all the jails at once would leave officials no safety valve. They would have to choose between open defiance and a general release of state prisoners. Varner would not risk confrontation with a man like James when, in his own mind, the fault lay with the Alabama legislature. He might order the release of a few prisoners, but he would not simply back James against the wall and attempt to force the governor to discharge 2000 convicted felons. The very idea of heavy fines, moreover, would offend Varner's sense of proportion. Certainly, he would not insist that these men pay such fines out of their own pockets. And he would see no point in requiring the state to pour scarce state funds into the federal treasury. Nor was it realistic even to contemplate that Varner might imprison the state's chief executive officer or the director of a major state agency even if he concluded that they were in contempt of court.[59]

Nachman was, if anything, even more fearful. Tjoflat was putting words in his mouth—demanding to know why Nachman was not arguing that his client, whom he had attempted to present as a willing public servant, should have been fined or jailed for failing to meet his obligations. Nachman so resisted such a contention that in the last few minutes of his oral argument he actually seemed to support the action that Varner had taken. Contempt was unrealistic, he insisted; Varner could not be limited to that mechanism of enforcement to the exclusion of others, among them, it would seem, the release of prisoners. In the end, Judge Tjoflat's surprising perspective threatened to send the business of prison reform in Alabama into a debilitating stalemate. The lawyers on all sides had come to Atlanta with widely divergent arguments, hoping that the court of appeals would make a vital choice that, in turn, would guide Judge Varner in charting a future course. On that choice rode everything the plaintiffs had gained in more than seven years of litigation. Yet Tjoflat now seemed to be suggesting that the only path open was contempt—something that Judge Varner would almost certainly reject, that none of the parties wanted anyway, and that promised no genuine answer to long-standing problems that now, more than ever, required attention.

There was nothing more to do. The lawyers paused outside the court building to repeat their positions to the press. Carroll again insisted that the only feasible action was the release of prisoners; Graddick threatened to go "all the way to the Supreme Court" to resist. Neither side wished to discuss Judge Tjoflat's questions or the likelihood, now great in their minds, that all the players in the Alabama prison cases would be disappointed in the court's decision. That decision arrived in early August. Judge Tjoflat wrote for a unanimous panel—dismissing Graddick's appeal of the first release order as moot and taking the position that Tjoflat had suggested at oral argument with respect to the second order in December. If James and Graddick objected to the requirements in the October 9 order, they should have raised their complaints at the time or asked Judge Varner to modify that order later. Their failure both to comply with the order and to effect a change in it left them open to contempt. The plaintiffs, however, had never asked Varner to cite the governor or the attorney general for contempt; nor had Varner initiated contempt procedures on his own. Instead, Judge Varner had entertained the plaintiffs' quite different request for yet another injunction, mandating the release of named prisoners. Tjoflat intimated in passing that the release order was also "defective" in that it "involved the court in the operation of the State's system of criminal justice to a greater extent than necessary to remedy the constitutional violation" and "overrode the division of authority between the Department of Corrections and the Board of Pardons and Paroles." In this, Tjoflat suggested that the circuit court might have reversed on some of the grounds that Graddick had raised even if Tjoflat's own perspective on the matter had not been available. Varner's failure to employ the contempt process was, however, decisive.[60]

The plaintiffs were hardly satisfied with this result. They quickly petitioned the Supreme Court for review, insisting that Tjoflat's opinion ignored a host of precedents approving the use of one injunction to enforce another, particularly in class action civil rights cases in which the nominal defendants were highly placed state officials. The principal illustration, was the Montgomery County school desegregation litigation, in which the Court had praised Judge Johnson's "yearly proceedings, opinions, and orders" designed to push state authorities gradually toward compliance with his basic injunction requiring integration. Johnson had not held state officials in contempt; he had kept his contempt power in reserve as a threat, knowing full well that if he once invoked it and still state authorities resisted, he would have nothing else on which to rely. The prisoners' lawyers argued now that Judge Varner should be permitted to behave in the same way. The Supreme Court declined to review the circuit judgment, however, and Judge Tjoflat's opinion became the legal backdrop for further developments in Montgomery.

The impact of the Eleventh Circuit judgment, coupled with the Supreme Court's retreat in *Chapman* and *Bell,* proved conclusive. The message being sent from the appellate courts was that law reform litigation was now out of favor. It was as though Judge Tjoflat and his colleagues yearned for a simpler day when lawsuits were tried, relief was ordered, and losing parties were made to conform forthwith, so that an end to litigation came quickly and confidently. If the Alabama prison cases had thus far been understood in some other way, contemplating much more complexity, flexibility, and patience in the enforcement stages, they had been misconceived and now must be reexamined. It was, however, Judge Tjoflat's perspective that was flawed. The notion that *Pugh* and *James* could be understood in such rigid, simplistic terms was unrealistic in the extreme. The appellate court's insistence that the impossible be attempted translated promptly into a demand that Judge Varner extricate himself and his court from the cause of penal reform in Alabama. Events to follow, taken as a whole, merely played out that theme to its inevitable conclusion.

9

Paralysis

Crowding in Alabama's jails continued apace in the spring of 1982, but Judge Varner now understood that he could no longer "release anybody," and plans to alleviate crowding through more construction remained stalled. Commissioner Hopper opened bidding for the new prison in Jefferson County, but his efforts to locate still another new facility in the Tennessee Valley drew the usual local opposition. Months passed before a site was chosen in Limestone County near Huntsville. The funding needed for construction was even more difficult to obtain. In the short run, Judge Pointer imposed more fines in Tuscaloosa, and Judge Pittman imposed even higher assessments in Mobile. Yet those measures failed utterly to focus serious attention on the penal system's chronic overpopulation.[1]

The overriding fact of public life in Alabama now was the autumn campaign. Candidates were developing their strategies; anything touching the prisons must be approached with the greatest care with an eye on the likely effect of unpopular positions at the polls. Attorney General Graddick warned that if more new space were not developed quickly, there would be "problems" when the state courts channeled "many, many more people into the system" after new criminal convictions. Yet Graddick applauded Alabama's policy of saddling convicts with lengthy prison sentences and promoted other proposals that, if adopted, promised to swell the ranks of prison inmates. Graddick supported Fob James' proposal to permit 14-year-olds to be treated as adults and argued as well that the parole board should notify victims before discharging prisoners with good records in confinement. Bill Baxley was again in the race for the governor's chair, as was Joe McCorquodale, the speaker of the house. Both promised a "toughened" state policy regarding crime and criminal justice. George Wallace, seeking to return to office, revived his "thugs and judges" rhetoric of six years before and proclaimed once again that prisoners were no more crowded than their victims whose bodies were buried in the state's graveyards. Wallace, in fact, pledged that, if elected, he would countermand Fob James' decision to build in Limestone County. Only George McMillan, a liberal by Alabama standards, advocated improvements in the prison system in conformity with the court's orders.[2]

For Fob James, this was yet another time for reassessment. By now, James had decided to withdraw from public life at the end of his term in January 1983. He thus could ignore the political campaigns being waged around him and could concentrate, instead, on preserving a positive image for his record in office. James had sold himself to the people of Alabama as an active manager who could bring hard-minded, businesslike efficiency to state government. Having failed to show impressive results, particularly with respect to the prison system, he wished to vindicate himself, to salvage something from his experience with the prisons that would suggest to the public, to history and, perhaps, to himself that the fault was not solely his. For the last few months of 1982, accordingly, the course of the *Pugh* and *James* cases was dominated by James' efforts to extricate himself from the prison cases with reputation intact. Within those efforts, James' personality, together with his fundamentalist religious faith and his primitive understanding of legal affairs, played primary roles.

When Governor James did leave office, he was succeeded by George Wallace, who regained power in a surprising victory over many younger rivals who had figured in the prison cases over the years. If, however, Wallace wished to resume his former posture with respect to the prison cases, he was limited by yet another provisional agreement among the principals on the eve of Fob James' departure. Rod Nachman labored furiously in the closing hours of the James administration to fashion yet another court-appointed body, the Implementation Committee, to continue efforts to reform Alabama's penal system notwithstanding Wallace's return. That committee, on which both Nachman and Ralph Knowles took seats, was a creative attempt to enforce the court's orders even by comparison to Judge Johnson's HRC in 1976 and the appointment of James as receiver in 1979. After some initial successes, however, the new committee, too, was rendered largely ineffectual. Wallace appointed a new commissioner, who was willing on occasion to take bold steps, at least with respect to crowding. Yet in time the forces resisting change in Alabama proved to be too powerful, the support Judge Varner and the Implementation Committee could summon from the appellate courts too weak. Over the last two years in the life of *Pugh* and *James,* the penal reform movement in Alabama was captured by an inexorable spiral downward into frustration, doubt, and resignation. In the end, those who had persisted in the reform effort despite routine and regular setbacks found it necessary to accept the genuine gains made against unspeakable prison conditions but to abandon hopes that something more, something more enduring, might be accomplished in a future they themselves could foresee.

The catalyst for Fob James' reassessment of his posture in the prison cases was a seemingly unrelated federal lawsuit attacking a new state statute, drafted by James' son, that allowed teachers to lead public school children in prayer. Inasmuch as the Supreme Court had often held that the Constitution prohibited any such practice, it seemed a foregone conclusion that a prompt challenge to the new law, launched by Ishmael Jaffree in Mobile, would be successful. Surprisingly, however, Judge Hand upheld the statute and, in so doing, declared that the Supreme Court's precedents were simply wrong. The root idea in Hand's opinion (that the federal courts had misinterpreted the Constitution to restrict state authority) seemed to charm Governor James. He was a deeply religious man and believed fervently that prayer in the public schools was sound policy. When the Eleventh Circuit overturned Hand's judgment, James went personally to Washington to put his arguments directly to the Supreme Court, only to be turned away by an astonished clerk. Thereafter, James openly encouraged school authorities in Mobile to lead students in prayer in defiance of the Eleventh Circuit's order.[3]

The governor had no serious chance of success in the *Jaffree* case; the Supreme Court ultimately disapproved Judge Hand's opinion summarily. But the litigation over school prayer aroused in James an emotional ferment that spilled over into other matters. If Hand was correct that federal judges had illegitimately commanded local authorities to change important policies with respect to school prayer, and James believed he was, then federal judges might also have erroneously mandated change in other fields, specifically the treatment of mental patients and prisoners. James was troubled by his inability to accomplish with the prisons what he had promised Judge Johnson he would achieve on first attaining office. He had assumed, as he put it, that he could "take the bull by the horns" and simply *do* what needed to be done. Many circumstances had frustrated that scheme, among them James' own penal and fiscal policies, but what was significant now was the fact, not the cause, of shortfall. The governor genuinely believed that the penal system had been improved during his tenure and that the addition of planned prisons would finally bring the system into compliance with the court's orders. Yet his fervor for his own cause was now fused with another, more powerful rhetorical strain that promised some measure of vindication even if he was wrong and others were right, even if he had failed utterly to meet the obligations he had undertaken four years earlier.[4]

James now insisted that the federal courts had no "jurisdiction" to superintend state prisons as Judge Johnson and Judge Varner had done in Alabama. He told law students at the University of Alabama that Johnson had violated his oath of office in appointing James receiver of the prison system and that he, James, had violated his own oath by accepting the appointment. The task now was to end the receivership not merely as the logical consequence of bringing the prison system into compliance with court orders, but as an end in itself: the elimination of illegitimate federal court interference with state penal affairs. There was little time left for any such thing. Yet Fob James, the erstwhile halfback, reminded his audience in Tuscaloosa that "[a] lot [could] happen in the last two or three minutes of a ball game."[5]

The governor's newfound contention that the federal courts lacked authority to entertain suits such as *Pugh* and *James* was plainly frivolous. James, however, hoped that the Justice Department under Ronald Reagan would be receptive, at least to an argument that it was imprudent for courts to become involved in penal administration. This was the sentiment expressed recently in the *Chapman* and *Bell* cases, and it certainly comported with the attitude adopted by Mr. Reynolds in the civil rights division. James and Samford now went more frequently to Washington and spoke openly to the press about the likelihood of forging an agreement with the federal government to resolve the issues remaining in the litigation over both prisons and mental hospitals in Alabama. James contemplated either a negotiated settlement that would remove the Justice Department formally from the fray or a theoretical reorchestration of events, such that the governor might simply declare that his job as receiver was finished and that the *Pugh* and *James* cases should be brought to a prompt conclusion, whatever the true state of the facilities in which prison inmates still were forced to live.[6]

In July, Governor James told Judge Varner that the Alabama prison system was now in "substantial compliance" with the court's orders and that he, James, had fulfilled his commitments. The only serious problem remaining was the backlog of state prisoners in the jails, but the governor insisted once again that new prisons would eliminate that vexing difficulty. While James did not explicitly say that Varner lacked authority to hold the state to account for prison conditions, the governor did say that the progress to date justified a "return of the management of Alabama's prisons to state officials charged by state law to do this job." The prisoners' lawyers immediately reiterated the position they had taken for months. Knowles and Carroll denied that the current crowding problem could be resolved by new construction and insisted, moreover, that much more work on a range of other problems would be necessary to bring the prisons into compliance with *all* the standards in the October 9 consent decree.[7]

To Judge Varner, matters appeared bleak. In his view, the Eleventh Circuit's decision had "missed the point" by stripping him of the most promising tool he had for encouraging the Alabama legislature to appropriate more funds. Now, Varner could no longer order the release of prisoners but could only attempt to enforce the consent decree by holding state executive authorities in contempt. That meant, however, punishing the "wrong people" and *still* failing to effect change. Governor James' new resistance to the federal courts, whatever its source, took full advantage of the situation. Knowing that Varner *could* not order the release of more prisoners, and guessing that the judge *would* not impose heavy fines or put important state officers in jail, James now wished to proclaim victory and to withdraw, despite grave doubts regarding his performance. The governor's posture thus challenged Varner to choose either to press ahead with his contempt power on a course Varner himself thought would be unsuccessful or simply to bow out of the prison reform effort. The other players, meanwhile, took the positions forced on them by Judge Tjoflat's opinion. Knowles and Carroll asked Varner to hold James, Hopper, and Graddick in contempt and to fine the three men ($25 per day per prisoner housed in the jails) and to imprison them (for six months, suspended for thirty days) to force compliance with the October 9 decree. Attorney General Graddick, represented by yet another assistant, Terry R. Smyly, asked Varner to modify the October 9 order—by discarding the sixty-foot rule, paring the number of guards required at existing prisons, relaxing the timetable for removing sentenced prisoners from local jails, and eliminating various other standards that Graddick considered no longer to be constitutionally grounded, including provisions for vocational, educational, and recreational programs.[8]

Varner was quite prepared to *threaten* contempt in these cases, and on several occasions in succeeding weeks he made his threats explicit. Yet he hesitated actually to carry through and thus anticipated that he would inevitably be moved toward Graddick's position. He would be unable to force compliance with the October 9 decree and would have to dilute it. The future, Varner thought, could hold little else. George Wallace was ahead in the polls and would almost certainly win election to a fourth term as governor in November. In the short run, Varner called a meeting with the principals, gave Governor James until September 7, the day of the gubernatorial primary, to develop yet another plan to bring the system into compliance, and postponed consideration of a contempt order until he saw the governor's report. On the street outside after the meeting, Commissioner Hopper admitted that there was nothing that could or would be done in that time. James did file a report a short time later, but it included nothing that he had not advanced before. Wallace *was* successful in the Democratic primary and thus clearly was destined to assume power again after the turn of the year. Until then, the prison cases seemed at impasse.[9]

Into this breach stepped Roland Nachman. As he had on so many occasions in the past, Nachman attempted to further his own ambitions for prison reform through negotiations. In part, perhaps because he now served as Fob James' attorney, but also because he genuinely believed that James had made progress in the prisons, Nachman hoped to do *something* in the next few months that would memorialize James' contributions to change. At the same time, however, Nachman recognized that much more needed to be done, and he despaired of further progress if authority for the prisons came again into George Wallace's hands. Initially, Nachman advocated an early, informal hearing at which Beto and others could testify to improvements wrought during James' tenure. When, however, Knowles and Carroll insisted on a more elaborate investigation of the many flaws remaining in the system, Nachman shifted to a second strategy. He acceded to a hearing in early January, within days of James' departure from office, but immediately initiated behind-the-scenes discussions with the prisoners' lawyers in hopes of coming to yet another consensual arrangement that would abort the hearing and, in addition, safeguard prison reform efforts from Wallace.[10]

The occasion for serious negotiations arrived in October, when John Carroll finally interrogated Governor James in preparation for the January hearing. Now it became clear why the governor had avoided dealing directly with the prisoners' lawyers a year earlier and, indeed, had signed the agreement underlying the October 9 decree in order to avert such a confrontation. James was argumentative, given to sweeping pronouncements about the progress made in the prisons and his honest belief that Judge Varner should now "dissolve the receivership and call it a day." Yet the governor was short, markedly short, on hard evidence to support his conclusions. Nachman could see that and could anticipate the way in which a hearing would proceed—the way Carroll and Knowles would methodically take the governor through the October 9 order, demonstrating at each turn the extent to which the prison system was not yet in compliance, and the way the governor would appear to Judge Varner. It was painfully evident that James knew very little about prisons, in Alabama or anywhere else. Nachman could argue, as he had before, that James could leave the details of penal administration to Commissioner Hopper. Yet the spectre of a withering cross-examination of the governor at the hearing was worrisome, to say the least, both to Nachman and to James himself.[11]

The governor was not rigidly opposed to a settlement, as long as his accomplishments were credited in some fashion and it did not appear that he had agreed to terms only in the face of the plaintiffs' evidence and the threat of further court orders. James frankly discussed the possibility of an agreement with Nachman and Carroll before the latter left the governor's mansion after the interrogation session. The precise positions taken by the two sides were then refined in other meetings and telephone conversations in succeeding days. Early on, Nachman insisted that the prisoners' lawyers should concede that James had solved several of the most serious problems and thus should agree to delete some matters—medical care, for example—from the October 9 decree, thus eliminating further judicial concern for those issues. As to other matters, Nachman suggested that more time should be allowed. Knowles and Carroll, however, were unwilling to dilute the consent decree in any respect. They offered to acknowledge that James had made some progress, but they refused to drop any aspect of prison reform from the formal order, fearing that state authorities, particularly George Wallace, might allow conditions no longer covered by court order to deteriorate. And inasmuch as additional time had never been used effectively in the past, the prisoners' lawyers declined to accept more delay in place of genuine results. There negotiations were stalled until yet another meeting with Judge Varner on November 1, 1982, the day before the general election in which Wallace would be reelected. When the lawyers were crowded into Varner's office for a discussion of procedural issues touching the upcoming hearing, the judge stated flatly that the Eleventh Circuit had left him no choice but to hold Graddick, and perhaps James himself, in contempt. That threat, offered before the hearing scheduled to determine the extent to which the prison system remained out of compliance and on the eve of Wallace's return to power, moved negotiations in a new and more promising direction.[12]

In subsequent discussions with the prisoners' lawyers, Nachman developed yet another option. If there could be no agreement making changes in the substantive standards to be met, or on more time for compliance with existing standards, perhaps a postponement coupled with a new enforcement mechanism could win acceptance. The receivership was now beyond repair, and no other device used previously in the Alabama cases seemed feasible. This was not an occasion for another HRC, which had been useful, perhaps, at the stage when the involvement of ordinary citizens seemed worthwhile. Nor did the idea of a "monitor" hold serious promise. Something innovative was essential. As always, the prisoners' lawyers preferred the appointment of an outside professional who would simply displace James and operate the prison system forthrightly. Nachman, however, had something else in mind: a three-member committee, charged to superintend the final stages of the implementation process. Each side would select a member, and a third would be chosen by agreement.[13]

Knowles and Carroll were skeptical. The plan would have to be memorialized in a document to be approved by the court in the manner of the October 9 consent decree. That drafting task would be difficult; the prisoners' lawyers would want strong language acknowledging the prison system's remaining deficiencies, and Nachman would prefer to downplay the work still to be done. Even if those problems could be solved, Judge Varner might regard the arrangement as a transparent attempt by the plaintiffs and Governor James to tie George Wallace's hands with respect to the prisons on the lip of the transfer of power to the new chief executive. Such an interpretation would be all the more obvious if Nachman himself were named as James' nominee to the new committee. Nachman responded with characteristic candor. His plan was, and was meant to be, a final effort to allow Fob James to emerge from the prison litigation having achieved something of value and to protect the ground gained thus far from Wallace. It was essential, in Nachman's view, that he be named to the committee and thus be enabled to continue his personal efforts to bring prison reform to Alabama. These, then, were the ideas under discussion in the final days of 1982. The negotiations took place, as usual, against the backdrop of preparations for a formal hearing. Indeed, some of the most productive talks occurred on the day the parties met in open court to sort through still more procedural matters on the brink of trial. Nachman and Knowles joined each other in a vacant jury box for further conversations. Afterward, they continued in one of the U.S. attorney's rooms upstairs. At day's end, there was still no firm agreement. The essential idea, however, was in place and would mature.[14]

Nachman conducted the negotiations in the strictest confidence. Only he and Samford, the governor's personal attorney, participated on behalf of state authorities. Neither Scears Barnes nor any attorney for Graddick was aware of the undertaking. Nor, more importantly, was George Wallace involved, notwithstanding that he designated a new legal advisor, Kenneth Wallis, and a new commissioner of corrections, Freddie V. Smith, shortly after the election. Nachman, indeed, understood that the governor-elect had no interest in participating actively until after his inauguration. Nachman also excluded the federal government. He had never participated in James' efforts to obtain Reynolds' support in the prison cases and saw no reason now to involve the Justice Department in what he thought should be local negotiations. The department's ambivalence in the Alabama cases had by now largely incapacitated its representatives in any event.[15]

Steve Whinston, for his part, continued to consult with the plaintiffs. He and another staff lawyer, Mitchell W. Dale, joined Knowles, Carroll, and the others for an important strategy session in Washington in early December. Yet while Whinston assured the plaintiffs of his personal support, he could not persuade his superiors to take an aggressive stance. Intermediate-level officers in the Justice Department did not pass Whinston's recommendations along to Reynolds until the first week in January and, by that time, Reynolds had formed his own impressions of the situation in Alabama, primarily on the basis of conversations with Samford and Governor James himself. Reynolds sympathized with the governor, but he could identify no prudent way to assist him. In the end, then, neither the prisoners' lawyers, who trusted Whinston but not his superiors, nor Governor James, who could get no commitment from Reynolds, had any substantial confidence in the Justice Department's support. The only promise of an agreement lay with Rod Nachman, who had in mind neither to commit state authorites voluntarily to a future course nor to give effect to Justice Department policies regarding state institutions, but to bind a potentially unwilling and always irascible new governor to an agreement that would leave important authority with respect to Alabama's prisons in the hands of others.[16]

The hearing opened on January 3, 1983, two weeks before Wallace's inauguration. Judge Varner mentioned in passing that he had invited Kenneth Wallis to attend, and Wallis was in the gallery on the first morning of trial. The actual participants were familiar in one respect and notable in another. These were the same lawyers who had represented the principals in previous conferences. Yet few of them had been in court five years earlier, when Judge Johnson had conducted the last thorough hearing on conditions in the prisons. Terry Smyly, now representing Graddick, had been actively involved in the prison cases for less than a year; Mitch Dale, appearing for the United States, had been on the federal payroll less than two months. Others, to be sure, were more experienced. But only one, Ralph Knowles, had been before the bar when the *Pugh* and *James* cases were originally tried in 1975. The very age of the prison cases and the tendency of lawyers to move in and out of them over the years combined to make this new hearing an inefficient, frustrating, and ultimately ineffectual affair for as long as it lasted.[17]

From the outset, the lawyers wrangled not only over current conditions in the prisons, but over the historical course of the *Pugh* and *James* cases to date. On one occasion, when Knowles and Carroll posited that prisoners were entitled to sixty square feet of living space, Smyly surprisingly insisted that Judge Johnson's orders of May 20, 1976 and September 6, 1978 had discarded the sixty-foot rule. Judge Varner was perplexed. He *thought* the sixty-foot rule was among the standards he was bound to enforce, but he was not sufficiently confident to reject Smyly's argument out of hand. Knowles, then, was forced to lead the participants back through the orders in question, explaining at each juncture wherein Smyly had gone wrong. The order in May 1976 had concerned only single cells (and then had permitted the use of small cells only temporarily); the order in 1978 (issued in the wake of Judge Coleman's opinion for the Fifth Circuit) had merely accepted the appellate court's ruling that the sixty-foot rule could be applied only to facilities in existence at the time of the original trial. On another occasion, Smyly contended that inmates confined in the jails were not, after all, members of the plaintiff case in *Pugh* and *James* and thus were not entitled to the living conditions mandated for the state prisons. Once again Judge Varner was taken aback, but he was unprepared to dismiss Smyly's contention without yet another trip through the files in search of an order that would clarify the status of jail prisoners. Again, Knowles' superior experience carried the day. The relationship between prisoners confined in local jails and the lawsuits challenging conditions in the prisons was controlled, first, by the description of the plaintiff class in the prison cases early on and, second, by Judge Johnson's reference to the jails when Governor James was appointed receiver in 1979.

Even after the parties agreed on what standards were in place and what prisoners were affected, there was still further debate over the extent to which Judge Varner should rigidly enforce the standards and, of course, over the bearing of the Supreme Court's recent decisions. Nachman's witnesses, Beto and Hopper, offered vague assertions that the prison system was now "substantially" in compliance with standards fixed by the October 9 order *and* the Constitution. On cross-examination, however, Beto admitted that he had never seen the October 9 consent decree and was relying on his memory of Judge Johnson's order of January 13, 1976—the original order with which he and Nachman had worked in the HRC. And after Knowles took him through each of the provisions in the more recent decree, Beto was forced to retract his generalizations about the state of the system's current compliance. Hopper also conceded self-evident deficiencies, but he attempted to subordinate them to renewed promises about the future: new prisons, more paroles, and gradual improvements over time.

Only Governor James' own testimony broke this familiar pattern. The governor delivered himself of a soliloquy during which he read aimlessly from Judge Coleman's appellate opinion and brandished his own efforts to achieve prison reform. His declarations were wildly hyperbolic. At one point, he insisted that the level of violence in the Alabama prison system "ranked in the top five per cent of the nation," by which he apparently meant that prisons in his state were among the country's safest. Later, however, he acknowledged that he had no data to support that proposition. James was persuaded in his own mind that violence had been diminished, and the "five per cent" figure was only his inartful, and misleading, manner of expressing that conviction. This was a man prepared to believe what could not be proved—what, in truth, had been disproved time and again. He simply wanted the prison system to be better and therefore pronounced it so notwithstanding the evidence.

The gap between James' own grip on the proceedings and the impressions of others was particularly evident in his concluding remarks. The governor turned to Judge Varner and said that he believed "with all [his] heart" that the prison system no longer "violate[d] the Constitutional rights of its inmate population by any stretch of the imagination," that he now had "serious reservations" about the court's "jurisdiction" in these cases, and that, given his responsibility to "uphold the laws of the State of Alabama and the Constitution of the United States," he must "resign as the Federal Receiver" with the completion of his testimony. At that, James rose from the witness chair, walked around the bench to Varner, and handed the startled judge a resignation letter. The scene may have been meant to be dramatic, portraying both the governor's satisfaction with his own performance and his defiance of further judicial intervention in state affairs. In reality, James appeared awkward and foolish. The lawyers were at a loss both to understand what the governor intended by his display and to gauge the import of his resignation. For a few moments, indeed, they worried that he might be attempting to avoid a contempt citation by extricating himself from the cases unilaterally. That possibility was quickly diffused; James was now presumably a proper defendant in the cases by virtue of his statutory responsibility for the prisons and, at all events, he said he would "volunteer" to be a party for the remainder of his term of office. That being the case, the governor's curious behavior on the witness stand came to nothing.[18]

It was, then, a day of confusion compounded, and by late afternoon Judge Varner was exasperated. He called the lawyers to the bench for a private conference, indicated that the evidence tended to show that the prison system was still woefully short of the standards established by the October 9 order, and again threatened to hold James and Graddick in contempt. Both state officials had not only failed to improve prison conditions but had actually contributed to continuing difficulties— James by pressing the legislature to lengthen criminal sentences (thus exacerbating crowding in the prisons) and Graddick by intimidating the parole board (whose more conservative decisions had also increased crowding). The time for "cursing the darkness" was over, Varner said, and the "defendants had better light some candles." The judge recalled that James and Graddick had protested his orders to release prisoners. Now they "had better start" releasing prisoners on their own. If they did not, Varner said he would be forced to take the only action left to him.[19]

Still, Varner's tough talk failed to produce results. Neither the prisoners' lawyers nor Nachman believed that Judge Varner would actually take severe measures. If he did resort to contempt, moreover, it seemed that the consequences would be minimal at this late date. James was leaving office, and Varner would hardly impose harsh penalities on him now. Graddick, perhaps, was more vulnerable, but a contempt citation naming the attorney general would be futile. For all his maddening antics, Graddick had no managerial authority with respect to the prisons and could do nothing to effect change, whether he was held in contempt or not. Accordingly, when Nachman and Knowles resumed efforts to negotiate, it was not because Nachman genuinely feared that his client was about to be held in contempt, but because both he and the prisoners' lawyers doubted that the hearing now under way could produce worthwhile results. Nachman spent the evening with Samford and James at the governor's mansion and then presented Knowles with an offer the next morning. There was no time to seal an understanding before the hearing began again, so the lawyers went back to the courtroom to continue formal proceedings. The morning was devoted to arguments from Smyly, who still was excluded from the negotiations. When Smyly finished at noon, Judge Varner canceled the afternoon session because some expert witnesses had not yet arrived in Montgomery. That left more time for face-to-face bargaining.[20]

The prisoners' lawyers held a strategy session just after lunch to which they invited Whinston and Dale from the Justice Department. This proved to be one of the most wrenching such meetings in the long history of the *Pugh* and *James* cases. As advocates, Knowles and Carroll rebelled from a settlement now, when they had begun an evidentiary hearing and state authorities were, as Knowles put it, "on the ropes." The plaintiffs were winning; a compromise at this point would amount to an admission that the federal court was no longer capable of providing satisfactory relief, that the campaign to change the lot of prisoners had outlived the court's endurance and, sadly, that prison inmates in Alabama were better served by the terms of an agreement the essentials of which had been chosen by lawyers for state officials. Yet Varner's unreliability, Tjoflat's simplistic opinion, and a host of similar considerations generated this singular conclusion. If the plaintiffs took this hearing to judgment, the result could at best be more of what they had seen in the past and, then, some day next year or the year after, yet another ineffectual hearing like the current one. It was time, then, to pull the prison cases back from the court once again. Dealing from strength, the plaintiffs could demand that the settlement reaffirm the specifics of the October 9 order, acknowledge explicitly that the prison system was not yet in compliance with that order, and fix new priorities and deadlines for further improvements.[21]

Nachman's plan for a three-member oversight committee was appealing, but the composition of the new group was troublesome. Nachman still wished to serve himself and had suggested that either Knowles or Carroll should also be named for balance. That arrangement was agreeable, but Nachman's proposal to name Beto to the third position raised serious concerns. The plan would hardly succeed if the new committee proved willing to accept slow progress by a two-to-one vote, and it could be assumed that Nachman and Beto would find themselves in agreement in most instances. The prisoners' lawyers considered proposing John Conrad as a substitute for Beto, but then developed another alternative with greater promise. To be genuinely successful, a body such as this must not be divided at all, but must operate by consensus. It would be better, then, to name a four-member group that, without a clear "swing" vote in the middle, might tend to resolve issues in a manner satisfying to all. In the end, the plaintiffs agreed to propose a committee composed of Nachman, either Knowles or Carroll, Beto, *and* Conrad.[22]

Once the prisoners' lawyers had determined to accept these general terms, the march toward a firm settlement was relentless. Steve Whinston was relieved. He could not be sure that the Justice Department would approve. Indeed, he had not yet learned Reynolds' reaction to his recommendations and feared the worst—explicit instructions from Washington to shift the federal government's position in the direction of Governor James. If, however, James agreed to a negotiated settlement establishing a committee to oversee further compliance, it seemed likely that Reynolds would acquiesce. Nachman and Samford went over the plaintiffs' proposals with James and Hopper and, after another long evening of more drafts and redrafts, the governor and the prisoners' lawyers found the common ground Nachman had been seeking since October.[23]

Next came Graddick. Samford invited the attorney general to his home in the evening, showed him the proposed agreement, and asked him for his reaction. Graddick declined to respond immediately, but next morning he asked Samford, Barnes, Knowles, and Lawson to discuss the plan with him in his office. The attorney general was not pleased. He insisted that the agreement should state that prison conditions were no longer unconstitutional, and he wanted to drop Nachman from the proposed committee. Graddick held Nachman responsible for James' acquiescence in the first release of prisoners and now flatly refused to endorse an arrangement that would give the governor's attorney continuing authority in the prison cases. There the matter rested, not to be dislodged. Both sides understood that the committee was not an ordinary institution whose membership could change without altering its mission. This proposed settlement was deeply grounded in the judgment, or at least the hope, that certain individuals, all of whom had been involved in the *Pugh* and *James* cases for years, could finally see the prisons in Alabama on their way to compliance with federal court orders. Graddick would not agree to place Nachman in such a role; Knowles and Carroll would not consent to the omission of Nachman, on whom the future of prison reform in Alabama might now depend.[24]

Two days later, Nachman and Knowles reported to Judge Varner that they, at least, had reached agreement. Varner was pleased in the main, but expressed concern that neither Graddick nor Governor-elect Wallace had endorsed the settlement. He offered the floor to Mr. Wallis, who explained that the new governor would consider the plan when he took office and that he might well sign an agreement much like the one before the court. Yet Wallis found it "inconceivable" that Varner would accept this settlement now, without the approval of the governor-elect and only twelve days before his inauguration. In a letter delivered to Varner a few days later, Wallis, now joined by Lawson, declared that Wallace would consider it an "insult" if Varner were to approve the plan before the new governor took office. Judge Varner was unmoved. He was seriously concerned that Wallace was not involved and would have preferred that the new governor had acquiesced in the settlement at bar. Yet Varner had never expected Wallace to join in any sincere effort to improve the prisons. At all events, Fob James was still formally in office, and Varner could justifiably deal with him alone in the short run. Having allowed Wallace's advisors an opportunity to be heard, Varner refused to let their views alter his judgment.[25]

Graddick's objection to the settlement was of a different order. The prisoners' lawyers recalled that Graddick had never been a proper party in the *Pugh* and *James* cases and urged Varner to dispose of his interference once and for all simply by dismissing him from the litigation. To that end, Knowles and Carroll formally withdrew their earlier request that Graddick be held in contempt. If, in the alternative, Varner allowed Graddick to participate further, the prisoners' lawyers insisted that their agreement with Governor James did not require Graddick's approval. The settlement could be embraced, and the attorney general could press his attempt to dilute the October 9 order independently. Judge Varner, too, had his "doubts" that Graddick had "any business as a party in these cases," but the judge decided it was too late to drop the attorney general from the cases summarily. At the same time, Varner hardly wished to continue the hearing with Graddick alone. Accordingly, the judge allowed the attorney general to remain as a party, but denied his request to modify the October 9 order on the theory that Graddick, for lack of administrative responsibility for the prisons, was an *inappropriate* party to seek such changes. Graddick, for his part, immediately appealed from that judgment.[26]

A few days later, Steve Whinston finally received permission to tell Judge Varner in writing that the United States did not "oppose" the agreement, and Varner promptly built the settlement into yet another consent decree issued on January 18, 1983—George Wallace's first day in office. The differences between the parties were accommodated in the document in the ordinary manner of lawyers who desire a bargain notwithstanding disagreements and who hope that the march of events will resolve or moot continuing disputes. Thus James and Hopper were said to "contend" that the prison system was significantly improved, while the prisoners' lawyers were said to "maintain" that there were still "substantial and serious failures to comply with the court orders and the Eighth Amendment." The new Implementation Committee was charged to "monitor compliance" with the court's orders, taking as matters of priority the backlog of prisoners in the jails, care for the mentally ill, and the conditions in disciplinary segregation. No term was established for the committee itself, but each of its four members was to be appointed for two years. Press accounts were largely favorable, although the *Post Herald* warned that the new arrangement bore the "seeds of failure" inasmuch as it had been forged over the new governor's objections.[27]

Nachman was named to the committee expressly, as was Knowles, whom the plaintiffs agreed would now surrender his representation of prison inmates. The other two members, Beto and Conrad, were then formally chosen by Nachman and Knowles under the terms of the prior agreement. It was, perhaps, the measure of the difficulty that lay ahead that this new plan was even more irregular than the gubernatorial receivership it replaced. Two committee members, Nachman and Beto, had initially been involved in the prison cases as Judge Johnson's agents in the field. More recently, they had been aligned with the state's chief executive. Now, they would exit and re-enter in costumes reminiscent of their former roles. A third member, Conrad, had previously served as one of the plaintiffs' favorite expert witnesses. Now he would assume a more prominent, authoritative position. And yet a fourth, Ralph Knowles, would turn a legal arabesque unequaled even by Nachman and Beto.

Superficially, the achievement of the *Pugh* and *James* cases to date seemed to be the transformation of Knowles, the indefatigable advocate for prison inmates in Alabama, into an arm of the federal court with instructions to superintend the enforcement of standards he had won for his clients in the court room. The mind-numbing spectacle of such a development forecast its fate. This new committee would be no more successful in bringing tangible reform to the Alabama prison system than any of the previous schemes hatched by the parties and the court. Meanwhile, the relentless horror of prison life continued. During the week that Varner's new order was issued, inmates rioted in Virginia, New York, and Florida, and two local prisoners, arrested for parole violations, hanged themselves in their jail cells. Relatives of one man explained that he had vowed never to return to prison in Alabama.[28]

George Wallace's choice for commissioner of corrections was one of the more cerebral young administrators the corrections department had attracted in the wake of *Pugh* and *James*. Born and reared in the same rural area of the state that had produced Worley James, Fred Smith was a graduate of Auburn University and held one masters degree (in criminal justice) from Auburn and another (in counseling) from Northwestern State College in Louisiana. He had been initiated into corrections in the military and had joined the department in Alabama in 1975, when L. B. Sullivan appointed him to supervise a new guard training program for which Smith himself had obtained federal funding. Smith recognized the value of data collection within the prison system and presently situated himself to monitor operations and functions against the background of relevent demographic trends. He soon was named director of research and later, under Governor James, became the system's first associate commissioner for research, monitoring and evaluation. More than anyone else in the department, Smith had command of the raw data concerning sentencing policies, population levels, economic conditions, and related matters bearing on prison operations. Thus he was an obvious, nonpolitical choice to shape state penal policy for the next four years.[29]

Shortly after the election, Wallace peremptorily called Smith to his home and asked him bluntly whether, if he were appointed commissioner, he could operate the state's prisons in a "constitutional manner" and keep prison problems "off" the governor. Smith readily promised to "end the federal court order." His strategy was not, however, actually to satisfy the demands of the January 13 and October 9 orders. Smith understood that the Alabama prison system was still well short of straightforward compliance and privately conceded that Fob James had only put "bandaids" on the system's wounds. The better strategy, in Smith's mind, was to pursue Graddick's claim that the prisons could be "constitutional" notwithstanding their failure to meet court-ordered standards. In his first weeks in office, the new commissioner attempted to convince the Implementation Committee to be content if the Alabama prison system were brought into compliance with *current* federal law, as illustrated by the Supreme Court's decisions in *Chapman* and

Bell, regardless of what Judge Johnson and Judge Varner might have ordered in the past.

If, however, the objectives that Commissioner Smith and Attorney General Graddick had in mind were in this sense consistent, their methods could hardly have been more different. Graddick made a series of post-election speeches in which he promised to "keep on being the same Charlie Graddick." Freed from any immediate concern that he might be held in contempt, the attorney general renewed his attacks on the parole board, whose decisions, he said, were "unconscionable." In a similar vein, Graddick proposed to abolish the insanity defense, mental illness being, in his view, "no excuse" for crime. And he once again asked the legislature to permit juveniles to be tried as adults. Both these ideas, of course, promised to add to the prison system's crowding difficulties. Fred Smith, by contrast, decried the very policies that Graddick endorsed. In the commissioner's telling, the reduction in the rate of paroles was doing nothing to eliminate crime in Alabama and much to frustrate meaningful prison reform. Smith's diagnosis of the state's troubles was simple enough: "Too many people [were] being sent to prison for property crimes" and held there far too long.[30]

Reformers found the commissioner's initial attitude toward new construction to be a hopeful sign. Smith acknowledged that "some people" seemed to think that "building more cells" was the answer, but he insisted that the construction of new prisons simply would not "work." Indeed, he maintained that the state's willingness to imprison criminal offenders seemed to gain strength with the availability of space in which to house prisoners. "The more beds you build," Smith complained, "the more people you incarcerate." Alabama already had an incarceration rate far exceeding that of most states. And this when Alabama's inmate population was still growing twice as fast as the national average. In the short run, Smith said, he would complete the new institution in Limestone County, assuming that Wallis could find no way to rescind the construction contract there and thus to keep the governor's campaign promise to scuttle the project. But the Limestone County prison would be the department's last. Other ways of contending with crime, aside from incarceration, must be found. The commissioner mentioned requiring offenders to make restitution to victims and announced that he had revived a moribund Criminal Justice Advisory Committee to propose other possibilities for the future.[31]

In more private communications with the Implementation Committee, however, the commissioner seemed potentially resistive. As the first order of business, Smith "urgently" requested that the committee state explicitly what provisions in the October 9 decree were thought to be *constitutionally* grounded, such that they must be satisfied before the prison system could be freed of judicial supervision. On the surface, the request seemed only fair. A new commissioner would naturally wish to know what shortcomings in his institutions were thought still to be unconstitutional and, certainly, what would be required of him to end the federal court's involvement in state penal affairs. Yet both Knowles and Nachman were suspicious of Smith's attempt to distinguish between constitutional and court-ordered standards and of his suggestion that any remaining flaws in the prisons could simply be listed for his convenience. Specifically, they worried that Smith might conceive of his task as taking particular deficiencies in the system one at a time and coming to the committee periodically to insist that he had done enough to justify the elimination of individual standards from the court's orders. By contrast, Knowles and Nachman hoped that the commissioner would work toward *general* amelioration of the totality of prison conditions, so that Judge Varner might eventually survey all improvements at once. Beto and Conrad approved that approach, and the committee's first formal action was to deny Smith's request for guidance.[32]

Inasmuch as Knowles had represented prison inmates in Alabama for so long, it was hardly unexpected that he should distrust Commissioner Smith from the outset. Nachman's attitude was more surprising perhaps, but only on the surface. Although Nachman had only recently made arguments similar to Smith's, his role change carried with it a radical shift in perspective. Now Nachman was back to the posture he had assumed as chairman of the HRC. Indeed, his adversary was, again, George Wallace, for whom Nachman had no respect. This was the man, after all, who had long resisted the very reforms that Nachman had hoped to achieve in the prison system. The Implementation Committee, dominated by Knowles and Nachman, meant to maintain the court's orders in full until state authorities showed results across the board. The committee's relationship with the commissioner, accordingly, deteriorated over time. Smith contended that the committee's refusal to give him more specific guidance evidenced a desire to retain power and authority in the prison system regardless of the improvements the commissioner was able to make. The committee, for its part, regarded the commissioner's insistence on explicit instructions as an attempt to trap the committee into whittling the October 9 order away bit by bit.[33]

In the near term, both Smith and the committee approached the parole board for assistance with the vexing crowding problem. The commissioner brought board members to his office for regular breakfast meetings at which he pored over statistics in an attempt to explain the difficulties the board's restrictive attitude regarding parole had made for the prison system. The committee held a single meeting with the board in early January. Nachman and Beto were, of course, experienced in this; they had lobbied parole authorities vigorously in 1976, when the parole rate, low as it was, was still much higher than at present. Attorney General Graddick was equal to the challenge, however. He telephoned the chairman, Elon M. Lambert, just prior to the board's meeting with the committee to warn him against a more liberal parole policy. The meeting then proved unproductive. The board members acknowledged that more paroles were warranted, but insisted that they could not endure the political assault Graddick threatened to launch if they granted paroles more freely.[34]

Not to be deterred, Smith promptly proposed the functional equivalent of an increase in the rate of paroles. Larry Bennett and other former commissioners had employed the state "prerelease discretionary leave" (PDL) statute on a small scale, allowing nondangerous offenders to leave confinement a few months before the expiration of sentence in order to seek housing and employment. Smith now proposed to enroll nearly 1200 "property offenders" in a special PDL program, under which promising inmates would be released as much as two years early. This was a bold scheme. Realistically viewed, the plan was much like Judge Varner's previous orders; it identified prisoners who seemed not to threaten public safety and who were about to be released anyway and discharged them before they completed their sentences. Smith recognized as much and anticipated that the program might evoke complaints from familiar quarters. Accordingly, he dressed his plan in new clothing. At an Implementation Committee meeting in March, Smith linked accelerated PDL with the "restitution" ideas about which he had been talking in the press. Prisoners released early under the PDL law would participate in what the commissioner called the Supervised Intensive Restitution (SIR) program. They would live and work in the community under the guidance of supervisors hired by the Department of Corrections and would send a portion of their earnings to their victims.[35]

The SIR plan made good sense as a matter of penal policy. Conrad recalled that other states had been successful with such programs as an alternative to long-term incarceration in property crime cases. More-over, the plan made very good sense as a political matter. Smith could and did present SIR as an effort to reduce costs, reimburse innocent victims, and reduce crowding—in a single stroke. This plan, coupled with the opening of the St. Clair facility in June, would remove enough prisoners from existing institutions to permit all remaining sentenced inmates in the jails either to be released themselves on SIR or to be moved to a long-term prison—by July 1, 1983. Initial press accounts of SIR were discouraging. The *Tuscaloosa News* labeled the program a "mass convict release" contemplating that prisoners would "pay . . . victims and go free"; the *Birmingham News* reported that Smith pro-posed the "largest mass release of Alabama prisoners in state history" in order to satisfy "inmate complaints." Several local sheriffs insisted that the scheme would not reduce crowding in their jails substantially, and one, Sheriff Burgess in Morgan County, dramatized his doubts by establishing a makeshift annex to his jail in an abandoned automobile showroom. Yet, as the commissioner explained the SIR program in a series of public statements and reports to the Implementation Com-mittee, opposition began to fade and support to build. For the moment, at least, neither Wallace nor Graddick voiced complaints.[36]

Best of all, the commissioner's transparent circumvention of the parole board was enormously successful. Within days of the opening of the new prison in St. Clair County, guards initiated a well-orchestrated redistribution of prison inmates throughout the system that resulted in the removal of almost all sentenced prisoners from local jails by Smith's deadline of July 1. No more direct action to reduce crowding had been taken by state authorities since 1977, when Judson Locke had dis-charged large numbers of prisoners under the short-lived "incentive good time" statute. SIR was not perfect. In order to accommodate all prisoners backlogged in the jails, Smith sent more to St. Clair County than that prison had been designed to house—even as the plans had been revised to contemplate two inmates to each cell. And nearly 300 prisoners remained in local jails after signing waivers. The com-missioner nonetheless proclaimed victory and was surely entitled to do so.[37]

Having had such success with respect to crowding, Smith turned to other matters and within a few weeks declared that, here again, he had made progress. He insisted, for example, that the medical and mental health care programs now met federal specifications, that a new main-tenance plan had been implemented in all institutions, that regulations governing disciplinary segregation now guaranteed decent living conditions, and that current staff levels were sufficient to ensure protection from violence. These results were undeniably impressive. On the strength of new studies undertaken by Smith's staff, the committee recommended to Judge Varner that he approve Smith's proposal to employ fewer guards to supervise inmates. Beto had always thought that the staffing levels originally ordered on the basis of Commissioner Sullivan's trial testimony were unrealistic, and his view finally prevailed. The committee rejected, however, Smith's characterization of the Alabama prison system as now "the best in the nation" and refused the commissioner what he wanted most—a recommendation to the court that the *Pugh* and *James* cases be dismissed outright. A judgment of that gravity would take more time, Nachman explained, inasmuch as "adversary proceedings" could be concluded only on the agreement of "all sides."[38]

The message was clear. The Implementation Committee approved Smith's efforts, but it was not prepared to rest an ultimate assessment of the prison system on his reports alone. Long experience with the Alabama prison system had steeled men like Knowles and Nachman against optimism where state authorities were concerned. For all his progress and resolve, Commissioner Smith had not yet satisfied the committee with respect to the matters on which the committee had fixed a priority. And beyond priorities, there were still numerous other aspects of the prison system that must meet court-ordered standards. This, moreover, was still a Wallace administration and thus bore watching for some time before its assertions were taken as substantive. Wallace himself was incapacitated during this period—hospitalized in Birmingham for treatment of the paralysis he had suffered since an attempt on his life in 1972. Yet he might at any time regain his old vigor and take a personal interest in the prisons. Wallace's current legislative proposals promised nothing good in that regard; his administration was once again pursuing "anti-crime" bills that would increase the penalties for a range of criminal offenses. While Wallace had submitted a comparatively generous budget for the corrections department, it was far from clear that the legislature would embrace it. Indeed, the governor's assertion that he needed "accelerated revenue sources" in order to fund new prisons threatened to discourage favorable legislative action. The Alabama legislature was no more inclined now to raise taxes to be spent on prison inmates than it had been in previous years. The Implementation Committee thus chose to await further developments before surrendering authority. The committee filed a modest initial report with Judge Varner, praising Smith's accomplishments but withholding final judgment pending further study. More meetings were scheduled for July, and the commissioner was invited to renew his request for the committee's withdrawal at that time.[39]

If matters had rested there, it is likely that the Implementation Committee would have retreated by midsummer. John Carroll thought so, and thus quickly sent the committee a letter insisting that a trial would be necessary before it could be determined that any aspect of the prison system was finally up to standards. Carroll's initiative drew from the committee only a personal note from Conrad, who denied the need for further fact-finding and indicated, at most, a willingness to "continue the Committee" for another six months, during which time it would be necessary to meet only quarterly. The other committee members were of much the same mind. It was late in the day to insist on precise fulfillment of old commitments. Now that Smith was making actual progress, the overwhelming sentiment was to find his work satisfactory, leave well enough alone and, finally, acquiesce in the inevitable. As Conrad explained to Carroll, it was critical to recognize not only the failings that remained in this imperfect system, but the "absolutely dramatic" improvements that had been made. It was, then, a matter of proportion, just as Smith was suggesting.[40]

Yet things did not rest there. Two developments cut short all talk of the Implementation Committee's withdrawal and perpetuated the committee's involvement in the Alabama prison system for another full year. First, Fred Smith lost composure. Speaking to a meeting of the Montgomery County Commission in June, the commissioner declared that the two prison experts on the committee, Conrad and Beto, had concluded that the committee's work was finished and that the lawyer-members, Nachman and Knowles, persisted only to "line their pockets" with the fees they earned for participating. In July, when the committee was scheduled to meet with lawyers for Wallace, Graddick, and Smith himself, the commissioner insisted on a personal meeting in his office. By now, Nachman and Beto, key figures in any move to terminate the committee's work, were angry enough to reject the change in schedule out of hand. Smith then held a news conference coinciding with the committee's meeting with the lawyers and distributed a "final compliance report" to the reporters who attended. Asked about the title, the commissioner was blunt: "You can believe it's a final report," he told the press. "It's the last one they'll get." Playing openly to the media, Smith put place cards carrying the committee members' names opposite empty chairs around his conference table and excoriated all four for "nitpicking" and "trying to come up with something else" (beyond what he had already done) as justification for keeping the prison system "under the courts." The stunt was untimely at best. It offended the committee and undercut the good will that Smith had developed because of his successes. The commissioner's outburst generated calls from the media for more patience, yet another noncomittal report from the Implementation Committee and, perhaps, greater attention within the committee to Knowles' insistence that it was not yet safe to assume that state authorities could be trusted.[41]

The second event was even more debilitating. After an unexplained silence on an issue of such significance to his political program, Charlie Graddick finally launched an attack on the SIR scheme. Inasmuch as this plan was not of the federal court's making, Graddick focused his assault on Commissioner Smith. His vehicle was a lawsuit filed in state court in Montgomery in which the attorney general challenged Smith's use of the PDL law as the legal basis for releasing "dopeheads, thieves, and robbers" without adequate supervision. The action infuriated Smith and most observers but, in this instance, Graddick was on firm legal ground. The commissioner plainly *was* pressing his authority under the PDL law, albeit with justification. In due course, Joseph Phelps, making another appearance in the prison cases as a newly appointed state court judge, upheld Graddick's more conservative interpretation of state law. That, in turn, promised to upset everything Commissioner Smith had achieved. If hundreds of prisoners previously assigned to SIR were rounded up to be returned to confinement, local jails would fill up again with sentenced prisoners for whom there was no space in the state prison system. In yet another parallel with the "incentive good time" episode of 1977, Attorney General Graddick, like his predecessor in office, was threatening to thwart a genuinely effective means of meeting federal standards in the prison system by successfully interposing state law between a willing commissioner of corrections and court-ordered objectives.[42]

In this instance, however, Judge Varner would not allow such a critical program to be frustrated. At long last, he readied the weapon he had refused to use earlier. John Carroll urged Varner to hold Graddick in contempt, and the Implementation Committee endorsed the idea with enthusiasm—complaining that the attorney general's "acts and omissions" constituted a "stark and deplorable departure" from Varner's expectations that state authorities would cooperate in the effort to enforce the court's orders. Where Smith had proposed and implemented the SIR program as a serious, productive response to crowding in the jails, Graddick had engaged in "disingenuous" tactics calculated to' frustrate the commissioner's efforts just as they were beginning to bear fruit. Judge Varner drank this in gulps. He was frankly mortified that the attorney general had defied any sensible solution to the prison system's many difficulties. The judge held a perfunctory hearing, then cited Graddick for exercising "influence" over the parole board in aid of a "very restrictive" parole policy, for "unmitigated arrogance" in criticizing Smith's efforts, and for "wasteful delay" in initiating state court litigation to foil the commissioner's plans. The evidence was clear. Graddick had "by his own admission done absolutely nothing to ease overcrowding in the prison system and bring this expensive lawsuit to an end." There was, in Varner's view, only one course to follow— the course charted by Graddick himself when he appealed Varner's release orders in 1981 and obtained the Eleventh Circuit judgment that forced the district judge to enforce his prior orders with the contempt power. The attorney general had "asked for it," said Varner, and now he would get it—a contempt order requiring him to pay $1 per day for each prisoner held in crowded conditions in any Alabama institution longer than thirty days.[43]

In addition, Varner instructed Commissioner Smith to continue the SIR program for the moment, pending Smith's request that the Alabama legislature enact new legislation eliminating the flaw in current law identified by Judge Phelps. If, in any case, state facilities remained crowded on March 15, 1984, Varner ordered Smith simply to select inmates "least deserving of confinement" and to release them in order to bring the population down to established limits. This release order, Varner reasoned, would satisfy the Eleventh Circuit inasmuch as it was entered in connection with an express order of contempt.[44]

The Implementation Committee was elated with Varner's order and seized the moment for decisive action of its own. At its next meeting in November, the committee suggested that if the revival of the SIR program did not pare the prisoner population in time to meet the March 15 deadline, the legislature should enact a "population cap" statute patterned after the law in Michigan. Legislation of that kind would focus on population levels to the exclusion of any other consideration and would authorize Smith to release prisoners whenever crowding threatened to creep above fixed limits. The idea should have offended professionals concerned with the exercise of judgment in the incarceration of criminal offenders. That it did not, that it, indeed, was put forward by four men with expertise and experience in penal affairs, testified to the desperation of the times. Something, it mattered not what, had to be done to bring the population of the state's institutions under control. In this instance, however, the legislature proved responsible enough to give Smith the authority he needed to renew the SIR program and, in that way, the pressure of sheer numbers was addressed in a reasonable fashion. Funds, as always, were another matter. The legislature rejected Graddick's request for an appropriation with which to pay his fines and allowed Smith only $10 million to support the prisons in St. Clair and Jefferson counties, as well as new construction elsewhere.[45]

Graddick, meanwhile, added an appeal from his contempt citation to the growing list of matters before the Eleventh Circuit. In truth, no one in the state actually believed that the fines would be paid without remission later. If the appellate court sustained Judge Varner, the judge himself would at some point relent, as had Judge Pointer in the Birmingham Jail litigation. In the short term, however, the payments due and owing grew dramatically; Graddick paid over $300,000 within the first two months following the contempt order. The drain on the attorney general's budget was significant, and he soon looked to Commissioner Smith for assistance in making further payments. That strategy, in turn, generated a joint effort to persuade Judge Varner to do now what, it was argued, he would have to do in time anyway—declare that the prison system met constitutional standards, relinquish the court's involvement in the *Pugh* and *James* cases and, of course, rescind the attorney general's fines. Varner scorned each such proposal in turn. To underscore his insistence that jail crowding be ended immediately, he held Fred Smith in contempt along with Attorney General Graddick. Still, most observers now conceded the inevitable. Neither Judge Varner, nor his Implementation Committee, nor, certainly, the plaintiffs any longer had the strength to carry on. The only remaining question was the nature of some new "settlement" that would finally write an end to the litigation.[46]

The Implementation Committee attempted to influence the making of this final peace by encouraging Smith to double the number of inmates assigned to SIR while he completed the new prisons in Jefferson and Limestone counties. Graddick, however, condemned that plan as a means of giving the commissioner "unbridled power" to release criminal offenders at will. The attorney general sent yet another young assistant to monitor the discussions, but maintained for himself what Nachman called his usual, "studied effort" to avoid meaningful attempts to resolve remaining differences between and among the parties. It was as though Graddick knew what others were only slowly coming to appreciate. The prison cases were at an end. Nothing further needed to be conceded. The entire enterprise was about to fall of its own weight. In consequence, the attorney general said he would accept only an agreement that exchanged his willingness to drop the appeal from his contempt citation for an order forgiving all fines paid and payable. A short while later, Smith reconsidered heavy use of SIR to reduce crowding and, instead, announced that he would press 1600 prisoners into the new facility in Jefferson County, a prison originally designed to house 600 inmates and subsequently revised, in light of the *Chapman* case, to accommodate 1000. John Carroll resisted, insisting that prisoners would be herded together in dormitory-style rooms intended to be used for prison industries. Inmates would have nothing to distract them at all and would only be "warehoused" in a manner all too customary in Alabama. The commissioner conceded as much and frankly predicted violence among frustrated prisoners in such crowded quarters. Yet he would offer no other way to meet Judge Varner's new deadline with respect to crowding in the jails and declared he would abandon this last scheme only if a court ordered him to do so.[47]

The Implementation Committee members recognized the folly at hand and, concomitantly, their own failure to avert disaster. Through the spring of 1984, Knowles peppered his colleagues with the distressing facts. In February, he suggested that they report to Judge Varner that in the "current circumstances" the committee could not "function in a very helpful fashion. . . ." In April, he insisted the committee should either "go out of business" or lapse into a "dormant stage," to be revived later if Varner or the parties should come to think that the committee could be of "some benefit." And in August, he threatened to resign unless the committee took stock of itself and managed to find some useful role to play. John Conrad opposed surrender. He complained that Smith's proposals were "diametrically opposed to good sense and [the committee's] recorded statements of principle" and that leaving the field now might be taken as an endorsement of ill-considered policies. "George [Beto] and I have reputations to protect," Conrad insisted. "[W]e cannot allow words to be put in our mouths. . . ." Nachman, too, counseled patience, at least until the Eleventh Circuit ruled on Graddick's contempt citation. If that order were sustained on appeal, Nachman speculated, Judge Varner might yet silence the attorney general and force Smith to see reason.[48]

The circuit decision arrived in September 1984. A lengthy opinion by Judge Paul H. Roney collected all the matters that Graddick had raised on appeal over the preceding year and disposed of each in turn. At the outset, the court seemed to favor the plaintiffs. Roney rejected all Graddick's complaints regarding the consent decree issued in January 1983, at the end of Governor James' term, and frankly approved the settlement embraced in that order, together with the Implementation Committee it established, as the "proper framework" for resolving further questions touching the conditions in Alabama's penal institutions. Yet Roney accepted Graddick's argument that Varner should hold new hearings to consider modifications of previous orders in light of more recent interpretations of the Eighth Amendment. Judge Varner could require the release of more prisoners, Roney made clear, only if Varner did what Graddick had asked him to do for two years—only if he held yet another trial of the Alabama prison cases and determined whether current conditions violated the less-demanding standards articulated in *Chapman, Bell,* and similar recent decisions. Finally, as though to ensure the outcome of events to follow, Roney set aside the contempt citations issued to both Smith and Graddick. The action with respect to Smith was not, in itself, disturbing; for all his rhetoric, the commissioner had made undeniable progress since taking office. Roney's treatment of Graddick, by contrast, carried great symbolic weight.[49]

The fate of the *Pugh* and *James* cases was now sealed. Fred Smith gave the Implementation Committee forty-five days in which to "disband" and threatened to go back to the Eleventh Circuit with still another appeal if the committee attempted to perpetuate itself in the new climate. Ralph Knowles initially confessed that he was "confused" regarding the proper course to take. Then, he urged his colleagues to solicit the parties' views on current conditions in the prisons in order that the committee might fashion some proposed "modifications" that would pacify state authorities without permitting the prison system to "backslide." John Carroll reminded everyone concerned that there had been no evidentiary hearing on prison conditions since the fall of 1982 and declared that he had an "ethical duty" to "investigate" thoroughly before crediting state authorities' allegations of progress. Within days, however, Carroll retreated to a more compromising position. He had no taste for further battles in a war that could not be won. The most he could bring about now was a new trial on the defendants' terms, and he admitted privately that he had little hope of persuading Judge Varner that the prisons fell below the standards fixed by the *Chapman* decision. Even if Varner were convinced, he would undoubtedly hesitate to issue a new decree, knowing that he could neither enter further enforcement orders nor successfully hold recalcitrant state authorities in contempt.

Carroll brought one final consultant to Alabama to tour the facilities in an effort to identify deficiencies on which he might win concessions, then resigned himself to negotiations.[50]

Final bargaining sessions were held in November under the Implementation Committee's auspices. Once more, and for a day and a half, the lawyers quarreled over the extent to which the prison system was improved and what, if anything, remained to be done to make it acceptable to the plaintiffs and the court. By now, however, the relative strength of state authorities was palpable. Issue by issue, Carroll's positions were submerged in the acquiescence that now affected all the participants. In the end, he achieved only two things. First, the settlement to be written into a final court order would not explicitly state that the Alabama prison system was now in compliance with court-ordered or constitutional standards. Instead, it would provide only that the system was in "sufficient compliance" to "permit" the parties to "recommend" that the *Pugh* and *James* cases be dismissed—subject to being reopened if conditions should deteriorate. Second, the Implementation Committee would remain in place for at least three years to monitor events and recommend further proceedings if, in its judgment, the circumstances warranted. Neither of these matters seemed at the time to be significant, however; in effect, the parties simply agreed to end the litigation without committing either side to specified action in future.[51]

When agreement was reached, the participants walked down the street to Governor Wallace's office for the obligatory public announcement. There were attempts to put the best face on the situation. Carroll explained that there had been "substantial movement" toward compliance in recent years and that the time had finally come when state authorities should resume responsibility for the prison system. Beto offered that Smith could take "pardonable pride" in his accomplishments; John Conrad, despite his private reservations, declared that the Alabama system was "very nearly the state of the art in corrections." Smith and his attorneys proclaimed that the Alabama prison system was now in compliance with constitutional standards—and would remain so—even if the settlement did not recognize as much explicitly. Yet the gnawing suspicion that things were not as they seemed permeated the room. There was no guarantee at all that the prison system was now so much better than it had been previously, and much reason to think that the frustrations of decade-old litigation, more than current conditions in the prisons, truly explained this oblique conclusion. The future, moreover, was fraught with familiar danger. "[L]est we forget," warned the *Post Herald,* "the court order is the reason for improved conditions in the prisons." And "the administration that is showing pride in the current situation, the administration that will be responsible for maintaining that situation once the court order is dissolved, is headed by the same governor who was in power when the old penal conditions prevailed."[52]

There were scattered suggestions that something might yet go amiss. Graddick was upset by the perpetuation of the Implementation Committee and threatened briefly to resist that provision of the settlement in court. Yet the common understanding that this really was the end, for the committee as well as the litigation, persuaded him to withdraw the threat of another appeal. Judge Varner issued an order embracing the agreement on November 27, 1984—roughly eleven years after Jerry Lee Pugh and Worley James filed their original complaints. At last, it was over.[53]

The dismissal order was, by this time, anticlimactic. It had been plain for months that the future of penal affairs in Alabama would be charted without significant concern for the federal courts. Still, Commissioner Smith found the short-term continuation of the Implementation Committee useful, if irritating. The committee's mere existence, however formal, provided a foil for Smith's rhetoric in the legislature. At least for the next year or two, he still could enhance his budget by complaining to legislators that he needed more funds to rid the prisons of this last vestige of federal judicial intervention. George Wallace gave Smith a relatively free hand. Indeed, the governor made the enactment of a new statute supporting the SIR program the highest priority in the next legislative session. Freddie Smith, in sum, basked in the glow of his own success. While he readily admitted that Judge Johnson's original order had been necessary, Smith insisted the Alabama prison system had now outstripped the federal courts' ability to foster improvements and could face the future on its own—indebted to litigation that had been a "godsend" a decade earlier but had lingered on too long and now, at last, had been discarded.[54]

The sense of relief among the principal players in the winter of 1984 gave way, however, to the harsh facts of prison life in the spring of 1985. In April, 200 inmates in the new prison in St. Clair County stormed a guard room, occupied several administrative offices, and took the warden, his deputy, and as many as thirty employees hostage for a period of eleven hours. By early reports, the inmates were armed primarily with clubs and knives, but some witnesses said that two pistols and a shotgun were also used. Two hostages were beaten into unconsciousness, one female officer was raped, and three other employees were injured less seriously. The rebels presented Smith with a list of complaints ranging from the use of punitive segregation to the denial of television privileges. The commissioner ascribed the disturbance to the "frustration of incarceration" generally. Other comments to the press confirmed that assessment. The St. Clair facility, now the system's largest penitentiary inasmuch as it housed so many inmates in tiny two-man cells, had become another "tough" maximum security prison. Inmates enjoyed new educational and vocational programs there, and a small minority worked in a few prison industries within the walls. Yet the frustrating monotony and spartan conditions of daily life made occasional violence inevitable. St. Clair, it now became clear, was Holman and Fountain all over again. The very nature and structure of the facility could have produced nothing else. And it was too late to change it. Attorney General Graddick seized the occasion of the riot to attack Fred Smith yet again for being too sympathetic to prison inmates. Speaking to the Victims of Crime and Leniency, Graddick called on the commissioner to resign and promised to "get him gone" if he refused to leave office voluntarily. Smith responded in anger and, once again, a serious crisis in prison administration was submerged beneath a clash of personalities.[55]

The Implementation Committee despaired of its ability to address the St. Clair riot at all and thus attempted no investigation of the disturbance, the circumstances that had given rise to it, or Commissioner Smith's response. Indeed, the committee disapproved John Carroll's attempt to question state penal officials regarding more routine prisoner complaints from other institutions. The consent decree of the previous November had brought an end to formal proceedings, Nachman explained, unless Carroll could demonstrate genuinely "serious" concerns that could be treated in no other way. Even Ralph Knowles acquiesced in this, although he expressed the hope that Smith's staff would cooperate with Carroll in some way. The committee did not meet formally again until the fall of 1985, when the parties were brought together for a "free flowing" assessment of events over the first year following the dismissal order. Carroll complained about a range of deficiencies remaining in the prison system Smith simply renewed his charge that the Implementation Committee was "not needed" and that its members, particularly Nachman and Knowles, wished to continue only to receive fees for their time.[56]

The commissioner was not oblivious to chronic problems. In December, he fired several officers and a former warden for beating prisoners at Kilby, notwithstanding that the men involved had been acquitted of any federal criminal offense in a trial before Judge Varner. Smith did, however, resent what he regarded as the committee's meddling in the affairs of a state department for which he had responsibility. When, for example, Knowles filed fee statements for time spent answering individual prisoner complaints, the commissioner refused to approve payment and, later, negotiated an agreement with the committee under which isolated inmate complaints would in future be referred to a new grievance system that Smith would establish within the prisons. The committee continued to meet irregularly, occasionally expressing concerns that some institutions—particularly Holman and Fountain—might be drifting back into disrepair. Ultimately, however, the committee withdrew into the dormancy to which Knowles, at least, had submitted two years earlier. While it remained formally in place, it served only as a loose monitoring device with minimal influence on the behavior of state penal officials.[57]

Having achieved this much of his first objective, the substantial diminution of federal judicial involvement in the prison system, Commissioner Smith now turned to a second—a reduction in the cost of holding inmates within that system. Under the administration of Fob James, and during Smith's own tenure, the Alabama legislature had (grudgingly) appropriated modest funds for the operation of the prisons—funds that had made it possible to build several new facilities, refurbish older institutions, and expand the educational and vocational opportunities available in all. And Smith hardly meant now to retreat from his established position that a great deal of money was needed to operate the state's penal system in a satisfactory manner. At the same time, the commissioner insisted that costs could be held to a minimum if the legislature could be persuaded to fund prison industries (which would generate revenues from inmate labor) and to support SIR (in which convicts could be accommodated at a fraction of the cost of physical confinement). Tracking in some measure the very reform arguments the plaintiffs in *Pugh* and *James* had made over the years, Smith contended that policies that seemed at first to be desirable primarily from prisoners' point of view were, in fact, advantageous to a state government hoping to conserve its limited resources. Work release programs were to the same effect. The commissioner contended, moreover, that educational and vocational programs for inmates promised future savings notwithstanding their cost in the short run.[58]

Finally, in an effort to capitalize more forthrightly on the often-mentioned conjunction of idle prisoners and public works projects desperate for cheap labor, Smith established community labor crews at several institutions. By the middle of 1986, prisoners were being "loaned" to local authorities to work in parks, on roadways, and in some public buildings. The analogy to the convict lease system was available, of course, but by most accounts these new programs were anything but brutal. Prisoners preferred the relative freedom and accepted the work expected of them with some enthusiasm. Ironically, indeed, the most successful of these ventures proved to be a series of jail renovation squads, which supplied convict carpenters, plumbers, and electricians to city and county officials for the maintenance and repair of local jails that, a few years earlier, had been crowded with the very inmates now employed in their restoration. Nevertheless, and consistent with an Alabama tradition rooted in the nineteenth century, the commissioner of corrections offered his package of labor programs not as an enlightened attempt to facilitate the "rehabilitation" of prison inmates, but as an exercise in economics. If prisons and prisoners could not be made to support themselves, they should at least contribute to their own maintenance.[59]

The other paramount theme regarding Alabama penal institutions for the past century also influenced Smith's operations and plans in the new era. Notwithstanding all the efforts that had gone before, the Alabama prison system remained crowded by any fair measure. Many bunks had been removed from the dormitories, to be sure, but new dormitories were created in space designed to house prison industries at the new West Jefferson facility. Smith confessed that prisoners in the dormitories, and certainly those held in single cells, were denied the space allotment that Judge Johnson had mandated in 1976. Indeed, the system was spared the egregious crowding that Johnson had seen ten years earlier only because the modular units introduced by the James administration in 1981 continued to be used for overflow inmates. Intended originally only as temporary shelters for prisoners vacating local jails, those rapidly deteriorating structures still stood adjacent to most of the state's permanent facilities, both old and new. All the state's penal institutions, moreover, were full to their inflated "design" capacity.[60]

These data vexed the commissioner, who had built his career on the appreciation of vital statistics. The population of prisoners in the Alabama prison system had nearly doubled since the mid-1970s and, given the attitude prevailing among local politicians, promised to rise steadily for the forseeable future. There were now 300 prisoners serving life sentences without possibility of parole and thousands more serving exceptionally lengthy terms, often by virtue of extremely harsh sentencing laws sponsored by Attorney General Graddick. The current "good time" law, enacted in the wake of Bill Baxley's attacks on the erstwhile Board of Corrections, forbade the diminution of sentences for good behavior with respect to any inmate with a sentence of ten years or longer. The Board of Pardons and Paroles was prepared to grant paroles only in a thin stream, and Smith's own SIR program was limited to "property offenders." Then, too, the average age of prisoners entering the system had dropped well below 30 years, posing the real possibility that Alabama's prisons might actually be asked to house individual prisoners for nearly a half century. Smith admonished other state officials that new prisons would invite the state courts to sentence more offenders to longer terms, filling up new bed space and leaving the system with the same crowding problems. Yet the commissioner himself proposed a massive construction program to keep pace with a burgeoning inmate population that threatened the reforms the system had enjoyed in recent years.[61]

Even as the new prison in Limestone County was opening in the north, Smith revived the idea of building in Bullock County to the south, on the very site near Union Springs that he and his predecessors had rejected in the past. The new prison there opened in the fall of 1986, holding 400 minimum security inmates in dormitories and offering space for another 200 prisoners in need of mental health care. Two more prisons were planned for Barbour County, also in the rural south. The way of "bricks and mortar" was not only ill-conceived, in Smith's view and in the view of knowledgeable observers; it was expensive. The commissioner announced that he could not operate the new Bullock County institution unless the legislature held a special session and appropriated an additional $10 million in operating funds. The same financial commitment would be necessary in succeeding years, of course, and similar lavish spending would be required for the Barbour County projects to come. Indeed, if sentencing policies and penal objectives did not change in the near term, the business of corrections in Alabama would be what it had always been—the constant shuttling of inmates from the dormitories, through modular units, to new prisons in a desperate effort at the end of each day to assure that all prisoners for which the prison system was responsible could find an open bed. While Commissioner Smith planned educational, vocational, and employment opportunities at new prisons, the prospect of financing programs of that kind, in addition to the creation of living space, was admittedly bleak. Alabama's prisons promised to be, then, the very human warehouses the plaintiffs had long condemned.[62]

Epilogue

I went back to Alabama in the summer of 1986. I walked through the prisons, talked to officers and inmates, and generally took the measure of the prison system a decade following Judge Johnson's order. And I found change. In 1976, the prisons were "unfit for human habitation." They were filthy, noisy, dimly lit, unventilated, vermin-infested affronts to decency. Pipes and windows were broken, toilets would not flush, and electrical wiring was exposed. There was no regular maintenance program. Prisoners were denied the most basic means of personal hygiene—toothbrushes, toothpaste, shaving cream. Food was prepared in grossly unsanitary conditions, with neither the supervision of trained professionals nor occasional checks by public health authorities. In 1986, a quite different picture was presented. Even the older prisons were markedly cleaner; they were painted, patched, and generally refurbished, such that they appeared on the whole to be in good repair. Genuine efforts were being made to maintain acceptable public health standards, both in prisoners' living quarters and in the mess halls, laundries, and other common areas. Inmates had access to ordinary hygienic tools and now could keep themselves reasonably clean in fresh, starched uniforms. Regular menus were designed by a dietitian, kitchens were supplied with necessary equipment, and state health officers conducted regular inspections.

In 1976, 5000 prisoners were confined in five major institutions and a string of minimum security facilities. The prisons then were horrendously crowded. Most prisoners were housed in tightly packed dormitories, with many inmates sleeping on the floor between bunks occupied by the more fortunate. The system was woefully understaffed. Most guards were poorly educated rural whites drawn from the small towns near the institutions in the southern region of the state. They necessarily concerned themselves with basic security, to the exclusion of the development of rapport with their charges and, at that, they were unable to keep even minimal peace in impossible circumstances. The only training available was instruction in conventional police work. Inmate "strikers," employed to supplement the guard staff, actually contributed to the level of violence. Rapes and assaults were everyday occurrences. Weapons were plentiful, and most prisoners kept them to fend for themselves in the "jungle atmosphere" that prevailed after dark. Gambling, smuggling, and extortion fed on the trickle of money into the prisons from family and friends.

In 1986, the inmate population had more than doubled, but four new prisons and a variety of less secure community facilities had been established to accommodate them. Prisoners were still accorded little living space; many were held in tiny single and two-man cells, while most were assigned to bunks in dormitories. Yet the dormitories were now much more open. There was walking space between beds and a wide path down the middle. No inmates remained on the floor. Staff levels at the prisons had doubled, and many new correctional officers were blacks recruited from Birmingham, Montgomery, and the Mobile area. Now there was a black deputy commissioner, a black regional coordinator, a black warden, and a number of black captains. And more women were employed in the prison system, including a number working as correctional officers. Nearly half the guard staff held college degrees. All officers received instruction in prison work at a special academy established for the purpose, as well as regular in-service training covering subjects such as "stress management" in addition to ordinary security techniques. The notorious "strikers" were no more. The rate of violence had plummeted. Regular "shakedowns" still produced makeshift weapons, and there were routine reports of fights and sexual abuse. Yet prisoners housed in the dormitories consistently reported that they felt safe in their quarters. More officers patrolling the dormitories at night and keeping watch from glass booths overhead maintained a studied vigilance, supplemented by inmate peer pressure discouraging assaults. Money was no longer in use; prisoners purchased nonessentials from the prison stores by drawing on accounts kept by the operators.

In 1976, there was no "working classification system" in Alabama. If penal authorities had known something about the prisoners with whom they dealt, it would have made little difference. There was no choice but to send prisoners wherever space could be found for them. The result was the comingling of dangerous felons with comparatively passive and weak offenders. The system offered no meaningful oppor-

tunities for educational or vocational endeavors. Places in work release
programs were strictly limited. Many inmates in the south were sent to
the agricultural fields; most languished in idleness. Prisoners in need of
medical or mental health care received only the harsh treatment available in badly equipped infirmaries and the notorious prison hospital at
Mt. Meigs. Elderly and handicapped prisoners were held in a dilapidated dormitory upstairs at Draper. There were no organized recreational programs, and the conditions attending visitation actually discouraged family and friends from spending time with inmates.

In 1986, prisoners were classified as they entered the prison system
through the receiving center at Kilby. Classification specialists, relying
both on the Heber computerized system and on interviews, assigned
each incoming prisoner to a custody grade and a long-term institution.
Those assignments were reviewed by a Central Review Board in Montgomery. At some institutions, local community colleges offered a range
of courses for willing inmates, and new prison industries, particularly
at St. Clair and West Jefferson in the north, occupied prisoners in meaningful jobs. Work release centers and the SIR program allowed
hundreds of prisoners some measure of freedom in connection with
their work, and labor crews such as the jail renovation squads employed
still more inmates in projects outside the walls. Medical and mental
health care, now provided under contract by Correctional Management
Systems, was vastly improved; all institutions now enjoyed regular
service from physicians, dentists, and nurses. Older and incapacitated
inmates were housed in a new minimum security unit near the Hamilton work release center. Recreational opportunities were now plentiful, often organized by trained professionals. And visiting opportunities
and facilities were greatly improved.

In 1976, inmates thought to have violated prison rules were summarily removed from the dormitories and thrust into tiny, airless punishment cells indescribable in their brutality. As many as a half dozen
inmates might be found crowded into a single cell, while other cells
stood empty nearby. Inmates in segregation were stripped naked and
left for weeks with no beds, no lights, no running water, and no toilets.
They were fed one meal a day and were permitted to shower once every
eleven days. They were never allowed to exercise, read, write letters or,
indeed, do anything save suffer the torture of their confinement. In
1986, inmates were entitled to a hearing to determine whether they had
violated institution rules and were thus subject to punishment. Those
found guilty could be sentenced to punitive isolation no longer than
three weeks—one inmate to a cell. They were allowed two meals per

day and were allowed to exercise at least forty-five minutes each afternoon. They took showers once in two days. Disciplinary cells were equipped with bunks and mattresses, steel lavatories and toilets, and electric lights. Visitation rights were suspended, but prisoners were allowed books from the prison law library and communication with their attorneys.

Beyond these self-evident changes, there was something else. Wardens and correctional officers with whom I spoke in 1986 exhibited a genuine sense of self-satisfaction. The attitudes they expressed to me, regarding both their work and the prison inmates in their charge, suggested a new sensitivity to the profound fact of human incarceration. No longer did these officers, or most of them, consider themselves to be merely turnkeys; they believed themselves to be "managing," not merely detaining, the inmates of Alabama's prisons. They seemed, in their own way, implicitly to credit George Taylor's claim that prisoners were entitled to an opportunity to improve themselves and Bobby Segall's insistence that imprisonment was punishment in itself—admitting no justification for further punishments *in* prison. They were pleased to have assisted Commissioner Smith in achieving his primary goal, freedom from federal judicial supervision, yet equally proud that the system had earned its freedom by making significant improvements. Guards who had been in their jobs a decade earlier now professed astonishment, and no small pleasure, that the prisons had changed so drastically before their eyes. They shook their heads over the way things used to be, and they were quick to volunteer that Judge Johnson's order had been essential as a catalyst for reform. Yet, in their eyes, the prisons were now institutions in which they and the public could take some measure of pride.

I could not share state officials' view that the Alabama prison system was now affirmatively good as opposed to merely better. For my judgment was colored not only by the apparent progress in the prisons, but by the equally evident shortfalls. The physical facilities were improved, but primarily at the level of housekeeping. Even the new prisons in the north showed signs of wear; in the south, the threat of slipping back to ruin was palpable. The nature of the prisons was, moreover, unchanged. Alabama's penal institutions, old and new, were cheap structures of concrete and steel, surrounded by steel fences topped by razor wire, located in remote areas of the state. Their very character denied the humanity of the inmates they confined. Inside, the constant shouting and the clanging of doors and gates underscored the unremitting presence of coercive force. There was more space per inmate, to be sure, but the prisons still seemed crowded to an outsider. The space requirements fixed by Judge Johnson had never been met. The same forty-foot cells in use at Holman in 1976 were still in use ten years later; the two-man cells at St. Clair and West Jefferson measured fifty square feet, albeit prisoners assigned to them were not always locked in. The stark presence of the modular buildings adjacent to most of the long-term institutions provided a constant reminder that the system managed to house its overwhelming population only by extraordinary means.

The classification process was primitive by comparison to the scheme developed by the Prison Classification Project and, certainly, by comparison to more sophisticated programs developed in other states in the wake of the PCP. An entering inmate saw only a single classification officer at Kilby, who made critical decisions within an hour or two, subject to review by a three-member board that would never interview the prisoner. Once institution assignments were made, prisoners were held in dormitories and modular units at Kilby for four to six weeks, until space could be found for them in assigned facilities. Upon arrival at long-term institutions, prisoners' interest in educational or vocational programs was subordinated to the particular prison's needs. Thus inmates assigned to G. K. Fountain still were routinely sent off to the agricultural fields, in 1986 just as in 1976. Meaningful programs now existed, but they were hardly available to all. Space designed for prison industries at West Jefferson still was used for dormitories; no funds were yet allotted for programs of any kind in Bullock County. Idleness remained pervasive.

Finally, I had only to stand for a moment in one of the spartan cells used for mental patients at Kilby, in one of the stark two-man cells at West Jefferson, or in any of the many punishment cells throughout the system to taste again the cold reality of imprisonment in Alabama. Something fundamental had not changed; men and women were still kept in cages, and long enough to ensure that they could never again function as ordinary citizens. At St. Clair, the huge complex that Fob James once thought would bring an end to the prison system's problems, the official designation for the prison's punishment cells was now "disciplinary segregation." Some officers called those cells "K-Block," after the label they were given on the institution's original blueprint. Older guards, maintaining an Alabama tradition with gripping symbolic significance, had a different name for the ring of tiny cells covered by heavy steel doors. They called it the doghouse.

Notes

Individuals

LB: Larry D. Bennett
RB: Robert G. Britton
SB: Stanley Brodsky
AB: Alvin J. Bronstein
JC: John L. Carroll
ID: Ira DeMent
RF: Raymond D. Fowler
CG: Charles A. Graddick
JH: John H. Hale
FJ: Frank M. Johnson, Jr.
RK: Ralph I. Knowles, Jr.
RL: Robert S. Lamar, Jr.
JL: Judson Locke

GM: George D. H. McMillan
MM: Mathew L. Myers
RN: M. Roland Nachman, Jr.
JS: William J. Samford
RS: Robert D. Segall
FS: Fred V. Smith
SS: Steve Suitts
GT: George P. Taylor
RV: Robert E. Varner
JV: John E. Vickers
KW: Kenneth Warren
SW: Stephen Whinston

Primary Sources

(HRC): Human Rights Committee Files
(JD): Justice Department Files
(NPP): National Prison Project Files
(PCP): Prison Classification Project Files
(US): U.S. Attorney Files (Montgomery)

(RK): Knowles Files
(RS): Segall Files
(GT): Taylor Files

Secondary Sources

AA: *Atmore Advance*
AC: *Athens Courier*
AJ: *Alabama Journal*
AO: *Alexander City Outlook*
AS: *Anniston Star*
BN: *Birmingham News*

MA: *Montgomery Advertiser*
MG: *Manchester Guardian*
MI: *Montgomery Independent*
ML: *Marshall-Dekalb Monitor-Ledger*
MR: *Mobile Press-Register*
NT: *Nashville Tennessean*

BT: *Baldwin Times*
CP: *Centerville Press*
CR: *Clayton Record*
CT: *Cullman Times*
DD: *Decatur Daily*
DE: *Dothan Eagle*
DS: *Daily Sentinel*
EC: *Eastern Shore Courier*
EL: *Enterprise Daily Ledger*
FT: *Florence Times*
HN: *Huntsville News*
HT: *Huntsville Times*
JE: *Jasper Daily Mt. Eagle*
LR: *Livingston Home Record*

NY: *New York Times*
OD: *Opelika-Auburn Daily News*
ON: *Opp News*
PH: *Birmingham Post Herald*
SA: *St. Clair News-Aegis*
SP: *St. Louis Post-Dispatch*
ST: *Selma Times-Journal*
TN: *Tuscaloosa News*
TT: *Tallassee Tribune*
UH: *Union Springs Herald*
VT: *Valley Times-News*
WJ: *Wall Street Journal*
WP: *Washington Post*

Chapter 1

1. Nat. Inst. of Justice, II American Prisons and Jails: Population Trends and Projections 17-21 (1981). See Rich & Barnett, Model-Based U.S. Prison Population Projections, Pub. Admin. Rev., November 1985, at 780.

2. 347 U.S. 483 (1954).

3. AB, 8-17-81.

4. Klan Act, 42 U.S.C. §1983. On the act's revival, Developments in the Law, Section 1983 and Federalism, 90 Harv. L. Rev. 1133 (1977). On class actions, Developments in the Law, Class Actions, 89 Harv. L. Rev. 1318 (1976).

5. On attorney fees, *Alyeska Pipeline Serv. Co. v. Wilderness Soc.,* 421 U.S. 240 (1975); 42 U.S.C. §1988. See Percival & Miller, The Role of Attorney Fee Shifting in Public Interest Litigation, 47 Law & Contemp. Probs. 233 (1984).

6. 325 F. Supp. 781 (M.D. Ala. 1972).

7. On early claims, Hirschkop & Millemann, The Unconstitutionality of Prison Life, 55 Va. L. Rev. 795 (1969). The due process clause of the Fourteenth Amendment denies the states power to "deprive any person of life, liberty, or property, without due process of law."

8. 309 F. Supp. 362 (E.D. Ark. 1970).

9. Bureau of Justice Statistics: Prisoners in 1982, 1-2 (1983); Bureau of Justice Statistics, Prisoners in 1981, 1 (1982). See also National Prison Project, Status Report: The Courts and Prisons (1981).

10. *Procunier v. Martinez,* 416 U.S. 396, 404-06 (1974).

11. D. Rothman, The Discovery of the Asylum (1971); H. Hart, Social Progress in Alabama: A Second Study of the Social Institutions and Agencies of the State of Alabama 62, 15 (1922).

12. Bagby, Executive Message, Senate Journal, 1839-40; Second Bien. Report of the Inspectors of Convicts (1888); Oakes, Report of the State Prison Inspector (1914).

13. Report of the Joint Committee to Enquire into the Treatment of Convicts (1881), quoted in A. Going, Bourbon Democracy in Alabama 172 (1951); Proc. of the Nat. Prison Assoc. 82 (1882); Lee, The Lease System of Alabama, in Proc. of the Nat. Prison Assoc. 105 (1890).

14. H. Hart, supra at 36. On the Kilby facility, AJ, 7-1-77; BN, 7-2-77.

15. See T. Yarbrough, Judge Frank Johnson and Human Rights in Alabama (1981).

16. "Just a judge," BN, 2-20-79. Accord Bill Moyers' Jour., Judge: The Law & Frank Johnson, Part 2, 11 (1980). *Liuzzo,* quoted in W. Douglas, The Court Years 132 (1980). On observers' views, Brill, The Real Governor of Alabama, *New York,* 4-26-76.

17. "In retrospect," BN, 2-20-79; Kohn, quoted in Brill, supra.

18. Johnson, The Alabama Punting Syndrome, The Judges' Journal, Spring 1979, at 4, 6. See McCormack, The Expansion of Federal Question Jurisdiction and the Prisoner Complaint Caseload, 1975 Wis. L. Rev. 523, 538.

19. "Balance of power," Commencement Remarks at Yale, 1980. "Everyone," Bill Moyers' Jour., supra, Part 1, 12.

20. FJ, 4-19-83.

21. 162 F. Supp. 372 (N.D. Ala. 1958).

22. 221 F. Supp. 297 (M.D. Ala. 1963).

23. See *Lee v. Macon County Bd. of Educ.,* 231 F. Supp. 743, 750 (M.D. Ala. 1964).

24. On Doar, Brill, supra. On Davies, FJ, 4-19-83.

25. See O. Fiss, The Civil Rights Injunction 7 (1978).

26. 232 F. Supp. 705 (M.D. Ala. 1964).

27. *United States v. Montgomery Bd. of Educ.,* 395 U.S. 225, 236 (1969).

28. ID, 7-20-82.

29. *Stockton v. Alabama Indust. School for Negro Children,* Civ. Action No. 2834-N (M.D. Ala. 1969).

30. 297 F. Supp. 291 (M.D. Ala. 1969).

31. Id.

32. *Wyatt v. Stickney,* 325 F. Supp. 781 (M.D. Ala. 1972). My version of the meeting with Judge Johnson is based on a telephone conversation with Howard Mandell, then Johnson's law clerk, who was present at the time. Mandell, 4-4-83. It squares roughly with other descriptions of the meeting. E.g., T. Yarbrough, supra at 158-59 (1981) (quoting Mandell); Drake, Enforcing the Right to Treatment: *Wyatt v. Stickney,* 10 Amer. Crim. L. Rev. 587, 596 n. 27 (1972).

33. For the Bazelon cases, *Rouse v. Cameron,* 373 F.2d 617 (D.C. Cir. 1966); *Ragsdale v. Overholser,* 281 F.2d 943 (D.C. Cir. 1960). See Bazelon, Implementing the Right to Treatment, 36 U. Chi. L. Rev. 742 (1969). For Johnson's "procedure" case, *Lynch v. Baxley,* 386 F. Supp. 378 (M.D. Ala. 1974).

34. *Wyatt v. Stickney,* 334 F. Supp. 1341, 1344 (M.D. Ala. 1971).

35. "Foremost," *Wyatt v. Stickney,* 344 F. Supp. 373, 375 (M.D. Ala.

1972). On the establishment of the Center for Correctional Psychology, Fowler memo, 1-25-76 (PCP); RF, 6-23-82.

36. FJ, 4-19-83.

37. On Baxley's appeal, T. Yarbrough, supra at 171-72. See Note, The *Wyatt* Case: Implementation of a Judicial Decree Ordering Institutional Change, 84 Yale L.J. 1338, 1358 & n. 121 (quoting a letter from Johnson to Harriet Tillman, 4-18-74, stating that he would take no action on her proposal to employ a staff until appellate review was completed). See Barnett, Treatment Rights of Mentally Ill Nursing Home Residents, 126 U. Pa. L. Rev. 578 (1978).

38. Bill Moyers' Jour., supra, Part 2, 11.

Chapter 2

1. 263 F. Supp. 327 (M.D. Ala. 1966), aff'd, 390 U.S. 333 (1968).

2. Civ. Action No. 24722, 1-24-69 (unpublished).

3. 329 F. Supp. 196 (S.D. Ala. 1971).

4. The prisoner's true name was Irvin Abbot Gibb. He gave the name "Newman" in his correspondence with the court because he had been convicted under that alias and appeared as "Newman" on the Board of Corrections' rolls.

5. FJ to ID, 10-28-71 (JD).

6. ID to Norman, 10-29-71 (JD); Norman to Turner, 11-12-71 (JD); Turner to Queen, 11-12-71 (JD). On the FBI, ID to Frye, 10-29-71 (US).

7. The FBI report appears in the U.S. attorney files in Montgomery.

8. FJ, 4-19-83. Robert D. Segall, Johnson's law clerk at the time, confirms this explanation of Phelps' appointment. RS, 4-11-82. Cathy Wright, who clerked for Johnson when *Pugh* and *James* were decided, suggests as well that it may have amused Judge Johnson to put Phelps in an unfamiliar position. Wright, 8-17-82.

9. After Braddy stepped down, DeMent offered the tax returns of six part-time physicians serving the prison system. The source of the returns and their relevance to the *Newman* litigation is unclear. It seems likely, however, that DeMent hoped the tax records would show that the doctors did not depend heavily for their livelihood on their work at the prisons. The returns were entered into evidence, but they were neither released to the public nor placed in the clerk's file.

10. ID, 7-20-82.

11. For summary dismissals, *Haskew v. Wainwright,* 429 F.2d 525 (5th Cir. 1970); *Roy v. Wainwright,* 418 F.2d 231 (5th Cir. 1969); *Thompson v. Blackwell,* 374 F.2d 945 (5th Cir. 1967).

12. 404 U.S. 519 (1972). See also *Wilwording v. Swenson,* 404 U.S. 249 (1971) (holding prior to *Haines* that prisoner complaints regarding prison conditions could support a §1983 action).

13. For new circuit decisions, *Campbell v. Beto,* 460 F.2d 765, 768 (5th Cir. 1972); *Hutchens v. Alabama,* 466 F.2d 507, 508 (5th Cir. 1972). See also *Bur-*

roughs v. Wainwright, 464 F.2d 1027 (5th Cir. 1972); *Bowman v. Hale,* 464 F.2d 1032 (5th Cir. 1972). For Johnson's opinion, *Newman v. Alabama,* 349 F. Supp. 278 (M.D. Ala. 1972).

14. Relying on the standards then applicable, Judge Johnson ordered state authorities to pay Phelps' fee, because the named plaintiffs had pursued the litigation for the benefit of a large class of other prisoners. The defendants resisted the attorney fee order, and the matter required independent treatment at the appellate level. It was resolved against the defendants after en banc consideration in the Fifth Circuit.

15. FJ to Caraher, 11-30-72 (US); ID to Caraher, 12-1-72 (US); Mims to FJ, 11-21-72 (US); FJ to Mims, 11-24-72 (US); FJ to ID, 12-5-72 (US). It is likely, of course, that Judge Johnson received negative mail in the wake of the *Newman* order. If letters of that kind were sent, they did not find their way into the files maintained by the clerk or the attorneys involved in the case.

16. I rely here on Littlefield to Thrasher, 1-12-73 (JD). The letter collects Littlefield's notes on the meeting with Vines and Judge Johnson. Quotations in the text are taken from the letter.

17. PH, 1-8-73.

18. "To supervise prisons," *Cruz v. Beto,* 405 U.S. 319, 321 (1972); "iron curtain," *Wolff v. McDonnell,* 418 U.S. 539, 555–56 (1974). Free speech decisions, *Procunier v. Martinez,* 416 U.S. 396 (1974); Wolff, supra. For *Holt,* 309 F. Supp. 362 (E.D. Ark. 1970).

19. 349 F. Supp. 881 (N.D. Miss. 1972).

20. 501 F.2d 1291 (5th Cir. 1974). The attorney fee question appeared in both *Newman* and *Gates.* Yet in *Gates* Judge Keady split it off from the merits by issuing two separate decrees—one holding for the prisoner-plaintiffs on the substance of their claims and the other awarding attorney fees. It was possible, then, for the three-judge appellate panel assigned to *Gates* to review Keady's decree going to the merits while leaving the difficult attorney fee issue for consideration by the full court sitting en banc. In *Newman,* Judge Johnson covered both the merits and the fee issue in a single decree. In order, then, to consolidate treatment of the fee issue in both cases before the en banc court, the panel assigned to *Newman* passed the entire appeal to the full body. At oral argument, counsel for the Alabama defendants focused primarily on the fee issue, neglecting the merits of the case. Thereafter, the full court decided that only the attorney fee issue warranted en banc treatment and returned the merits to the original three-judge panel. By then, of course, the other panel had rendered an opinion in *Gates.*

21. 503 F.2d 1320 (5th Cir. 1974).

22. On the loss-of-life statistic, MA, 2-19-74. On the highway patrol alert, MA, 2-14-74.

23. MA, 2-15-74.

24. MA, 2-12, 14-74.

25. Martin, MA, 2-14-74. Report of the Escambia County Grand Jury, Spring Term, 1974.

26. MA, 1-27, 2-17-74. Judge Webb ascribed the "prisoners cannot vote" statement to Senator Robert Edington of Mobile.

27. Memoranda in the U.S. attorney's office in Montgomery describe these internal activities. For example, FJ to Vines, 3-25-77.

28. FJ to ID, 4-16-75 (US).

29. The correspondence regarding the Justice Department's laborious efforts to prepare the report is voluminous. Littlefield to ID, 8-5-75 (US); FJ to Littlefield, 8-26-75 (US); Littlefield to ID, 9-3-75 (US); FJ to ID, 9-4-75 (US); Littlefield to FJ, 10-1-75 (US); FJ to ID, 1-15-76 (US); ID to FJ, 1-16-76 (US); Littlefield to FJ, 3-10-76 (US). Judge Johnson acquiesces in the link between *Newman* and the other cases as articulated in the text. FJ, 4-19-83. This is not to suggest that the judge meant to retry *Newman* within the framework of *Pugh* and *James*. Indeed, in a November meeting in chambers he made it clear that the lawyers were not to dwell on medical care. MM, 8-19-81. Of course, there was testimony in the new cases touching the issues in *Newman,* and Johnson's opinion and order in those cases acknowledged that the evidence showed that the *Newman* order had not been followed. On the lawyers' lack of attention to *Newman,* GT, 3-8-82; RK, 4-20-83; SS, 5-17-85.

Chapter 3

1. 386 F. Supp. 378 (M.D. Ala. 1974).

2. RS, 4-11-82.

3. RS, 4-11-82.

4. 501 F.2d 1291 (5th Cir. 1974).

5. RS, 4-11-82.

6. RS to SB, 5-24-84 (RS). In a memo to the file, Segall noted that he had identified at least one other potential plaintiff who would testify in aid of the "right to rehabilitation" theory. RS to File, 5-25-74 (RS). He now recalls that he became concerned that if he attempted to establish any such right and failed, the result would be a "bad precedent" that might present an obstacle to the long-run cause of penal reform. That concern, coupled with his lack of success in developing expert testimony, drove him to abandon the idea in due course. RS, 4-11-82.

7. Pretrial Memorandum, 8-11-75.

8. 377 U.S. 533 (1964).

9. GT, 3-8-82.

10. At least some of the personal injuries of which James complained had been suffered some years earlier when he was at Holman Prison in the southern part of the state. He had filed a lawsuit regarding those injuries in the U.S. District Court for the Southern District of Alabama. His claims were evidently dismissed in January 1973. Civ. Action No. 3903-N. In September 1974, after James' personal injuries had been eliminated from the case in which Taylor was

involved, the prisoner filed yet another lawsuit in the Southern District. That complaint was dismissed because the applicable statute of limitations had run. When James attempted to bring the same injuries to Judge Johnson's attention, the judge found his claims barred by the action taken earlier in Mobile. MA, 1-18-75. Later still, James filed yet another lawsuit in Judge Johnson's court, complaining further about inadequate medical care. At that point, Johnson dismissed on the ground that James was a member of the class in *Newman* and entitled to the benefits of the order in that case. A new, independent lawsuit in his behalf was unnecessary. Misc. No. 894, 3-18-77.

11. Ala. Code tit. 45, §188(1)(4). See generally, M. Moos, State Penal Administration in Alabama 175–76 (1942). For court decisions, *Law v. State,* 238 Ala. 428, 191 So. 803 (1939); *Pinkerton v. State,* 29 Ala. App. 472, 198 So. 157, cert. denied, 240 Ala. 123, 198 So. 162 (1940). Supreme Court: *Williams v. New York,* 337 U.S. 241 (1949); *Procunier v. Martinez,* 416 U.S. 396 (1974).

12. GT, 3-8-82.

13. Segall did locate one case close to the mark—*Nelson v. Heyne,* 491 F.2d 352 (7th Cir.), cert. denied, 417 U.S. 976 (1974), in which the Seventh Circuit Court of Appeals had held that involuntarily detained juveniles were entitled to appropriate treatment.

14. GT, 3-8-82. Segall recalls his thinking only vaguely. He may have understood *James* to be only another "conditions suit" and unlikely to produce the bad precedent on the "right to rehabilitation" that had worried him earlier. RS, 4-11-82.

15. GT, 3-8-82; Pretrial Memorandum, 8-10-75.

16. I attended the meeting as an observer in the company of Taylor, Knowles, and Suitts. The recollections in this pargraph are my own, but they do not conflict with the memories of others in attendance.

17. AB, 8-17-81.

18. Responding to encouragement from Suitts, Bronstein had sent a staff member, Arpiar G. Saunders, to Alabama the year before to investigate the allegations being made in *White v. Sullivan,* 386 F. Supp. 292 (S.D. Ala. 1973), one of the cases handled by Judge Pittman in Mobile. Mandell led Saunders through the prisons and offered to serve as local counsel in a lawsuit funded and directed from Washington. The idea foundered, however. See Saunders to File, 1-29-73 (NPP); AB, 8-17-81.

19. There was some further delay before the Prison Project entered *James* formally in November. Order, 11-22-74. To ensure that Bronstein's interest did not flag, Suitts kept up a steady correspondence urging decisive action. For example, SS to AB, 10-12-74 (NPP) (insisting that the Prison Project must soon "fish or cut bait"). Suitts plainly hoped at this early juncture that the Prison Project would assist Taylor and Segall to establish a "right to rehabilitation." His press release, issued when the project was formally admitted, said so explicitly. Press release, 11-26-74. Contemporaneous descriptions of the Alabama cases in Bronstein's own publications repeated the "rehabilitation" theme. For example, Bronstein, Prisoners' Rights, delivered to the ACLU's biennial confer-

ference, 6-74; Litigation Docket, 4-75. In time, however, talk of any "right to rehabilitation" was dropped.

At this point, the participants on what I will call the "prisoners' side" of the *Pugh* and *James* cases begin to multiply. Instead of attempting to be precise (and therefore verbose) in my descriptions to follow, I will often use the generic term "plaintiffs" to include the prisoners themselves, their lawyers, and the amici curiae—the National Prison Project and, later, the United States. I will also use the term "prisoners' lawyers" to include all counsel arguing on prisoners' behalf, not just those attorneys formally appointed to represent inmate-clients.

20. Lamar's appointment was routine. Instead of maintaining a large stable of litigating attorneys to respond to lawsuits against state authorities, Attorney General Baxley preferred to hold his permanent staff to a minimum and to retain private attorneys to handle cases when they arose. Lamar was one of many lawyers used by Baxley's office; his title was intended only to designate him as entitled to speak for the defendants and the state of Alabama in the course of his duties. RL, 8-2-82. I accompanied Taylor to the argument. The recollections in this paragraph are my own. Taylor's memory is consistent. GT, 3-8-82.

21. MM to RK, 7-2-75 (NPP). See also SB to GT, 10-20-74 (GT) (stating that the September 30 opinion "spells out exactly what you . . . ought to do"); AB, 8-17-81.

22. "Right track," FJ, 4-19-83; GT to James, et al., 10-2-74 (GT).

23. Lamar recalls that the counterclaim was Newman's idea. RL, 8-2-82. Johnson, BN, 12-28-74; MR, 12-30-74. The description of the meeting with Judge Johnson rests on Taylor's recollections. GT, 3-8-82. The order allowing the Prison Project to participate was phrased ambiguously. On its face, it seemed to recognize the project as an independent party in the case—able to represent its own interests as well as those of the prisoner-plaintiffs. No one, however, raised any question about the project's designation or the way in which its lawyers participated in the proceedings. When Ira DeMent and the United States entered the cases somewhat later, the same designation was used. According to Judge Johnson, his appointment of the Prison Project and the United States as amici "with the rights of a party" was "deliberate and significant." He fully intended that those entities would have "much broader rights" than amici would ordinarily be accorded. FJ, 4-19-83.

24. BN, 7-29, 9-9-74; TN, 9-10-74; McLaughlin, MR, 4-16-75; Staton, PH, 2-18-75.

25. Sullivan, PH, 1-11-75; MA, 2-27-75; Harding, HT, 2-6-75; MA, 10-6-75; Hale, BN, 1-29-75; MA, 2-23, 3-7-75.

26. Hale, BN, 1-29-75; Mt. Meigs, BN, 2-14, 17-75; Assistant Warden, CT, 2-18-75; Bailey, BN, 2-21, 23-75.

27. Hale, MA, 2-14-75; Long, HT, 6-10-75; Press release, MA, 7-3-75. On the riot, AJ, 7-7-75.

28. PH, 2-21, 25-75; EC, 2-24-75; MA, 7-17-75.

29. BN, 4-12-75; MR, 2-6-75. On the tours, AA, 2-13-75.

30. MA, 11-22-74, 1-8-75; OD, 1-9-75; FT, 1-11-75; HT, 3-4-75; MR, 3-4-75.

31. On Sullivan generally, DD, 2-14-75; Staton, BN, 2-23-75; Sullivan, BN, 6-15-75. See also HT, 1-16-75. For an editorial, BN, 12-30-74 (rejecting the analogy to *Wyatt*). For Sullivan's concession, PH, 6-10-75; Newman, PH, 6-10-75.

32. On the legislative session, BN, 4-11, 22-75; MA, 4-10, 5-6-75. "New awareness," MA, 4-27-75. For the *News* article, BN, 1-30-75. On the committee report, BN, 3-8, 6-10-75; MA, 5-18-75.

33. BN, 4-22-75. See also MA, 4-22-75.

34. GT to ID, 2-13-75 (GT); ID to Pottinger, 2-24-75 (GT). See also AB to Queen, 10-23-74 (NPP) (covering the amended complaint in *James*); MM to GT, 2-11-75 (NPP) (confirming Bronstein's more recent telephone conversation with Queen); ID to Sullivan, 2-18-75 (GT) (forecasting DeMent's opposition to the Cutter Labs proposal); Sullivan to MM, 4-29-75 (NPP) (reporting the board's rejection of the plan); Order, 8-15-75 (appointing DeMent as amicus in both *Pugh* and *James*—with "full rights of a party" in each).

35. I collect in the text attitudes expressed to me by the principals, including DeMent. GT, 3-8-82; RS, 4-11, 5-29-82; RK, 4-20-83; AB, 8-17-81; ID, 7-20-82. On the short-lived proposals to request studies by the Bureau of Prisons and the Environmental Protection Agency, Trial Transcript, Vol. VI, p. 1324. DeMent abandoned the idea of a Bureau of Prisons survey when the defense conceded defeat and insistence on such a study threatened to delay relief. For reasons that are now unclear (Lamar having failed to object), Judge Johnson denied the plaintiffs' motion for an EPA survey just before trial. Order, 8-8-75.

36. MM, 8-19-81; AB, 8-17-81; ID, 7-20-82.

37. 509 F.2d 1332 (5th Cir. 1975). Three cases were involved: *McCray v. Sullivan,* Civ. Action No. 5620-69-H; *McCray v. Sullivan,* Civ. Action No. 6091-70-H; *White & Claybrone v. Commissioner,* Civ. Action No. 7094-72-H.

38. Lauten to MM, 6-30-75 (NPP). See also MM to Lauten, 6-20-75 (NPP)(suggesting arguments and precedents); Lauten to MM, 6-23-75 (NPP)(describing recent developments in *McCray*). Judge Hand recorded Sullivan's concessions. Order, 8-7-75.

39. Lamar and Larry Newman suggested to Judge Johnson that Hand's order barred consideration of similar issues in the *Pugh* and *James* cases. Motion, 8-11-75. DeMent, for his part, acquiesced in that view. Response, 8-13-75; MA, 8-20-75. On the resolution, RS to FJ, 8-13-75 (RS); Order, 8-18-75 (denying the defendants' motion without explanation).

40. RL, 8-2-82. See MM to GT & RK, 6-27-75 (NPP) (recording the division of labor on the prisoners' side).

41. Sullivan deposition, 3-10-75; Staton deposition, 6-16-75.

42. RK, 4-20-83.

43. MM, 8-19-81; AB, 8-17-81. Haber also recommended Dr. Thomas Gualtieri, who had testified for the prisoners in the *Gates* case in Mississippi. Gualtieri, according to Haber, could explain the causes of violence within the

prison environment. RS, 4-11-82; RS to Sarver, Gualtieri & Haber, 7-1-75 (RS) (explaining that *Pugh* had been consolidated for trial with *James* and apologizing for any inconvenience the delay might cause potential witnesses); RS to File, 3-10-75 (RS) (describing the testimony expected from Gualtieri).

44. MM to RL, 6-19-75 (NPP); *Tanner v. Sullivan,* Civ. Action No. 75-178-N, 5-28-75. See Order, 5-28-75 (appointing DeMent in *Tanner);* Order, 5-29-75 *(Geans v. Sullivan, Stinson v. Sullivan & White v. Sullivan)* (consolidating the three unnumbered cases with *Tanner).* See also MA, 5-29-75; AJ, 5-29-75. Judge Johnson's practice of recognizing new complaints filed by different inmates as independent lawsuits but then consolidating them with existing cases in which counsel had been appointed resulted in considerable confusion. Some months before *Tanner* was filed, for example, a prisoner at Holman, Floyd Hartley, had filed a complaint alleging that the state's failure to provide "rehabilitation" programs for sex offenders was unconstitutional. *Hartley v. Sullivan,* Civ. Action No. 74-380-N, 11-25-74. That case was evidently consolidated with *James*— without objection from George Taylor, who had only recently converted *James* into a class action raising the "right to rehabilitation" claim. Gordon to GT, 11-29-74 (GT) (asking for Taylor's reaction to Johnson's plan to consolidate); GT to FJ, 12-11-74 (GT) (expressing no objection). Taylor does not recall doing anything in connection with the additional case; if he represented Hartley at all, it was only in the sense that the definition of the plaintiff class in *James* included someone in Hartley's position. GT, 3-8-82. In later instances, Judge Johnson handled attempts by different prisoners to launch their own lawsuits in a more straightforward and efficient fashion. He dismissed their complaints with the notation that they were already submerged in the pending cases, *Pugh* and *James,* carried on for the benefit of all prisoners in the Alabama system. For example, Order, 7-28-75 (disposing of a petition signed by 200 prisoners at Draper in this manner). Judge Varner, who succeeded Johnson in the prison cases, followed the same practice. For example, *Cooks v. Lee County Jail,* Civ. Action No. 83-17-E, Order, 2-4-83.

45. Civ. Action No. 74-70-S. DeMent had been appointed in the *Adams* case the previous year and had stated publicly, in December 1974, that he had in mind the scheme discussed in the text. On support for the plan, Press release, 3-28-75. DeMent elaborated on his intentions and motivation in an address to the Fraternal Order of Police in Mobile, 4-7-75. Later developments in the case are reported in *Adams v. Mathis,* 458 F.Supp. 302 (M.D. Ala.), aff'd, 614 F.2d 42 (5th Cir. 1978).

46. Civ. Action No. 77-P-0066-S.

47. The *Thomas* case was handled by Judge Samuel C. Pointer, Jr., U.S. District Judge for the Northern District of Alabama.

48. MA, 7-25-75. See also NY, 7-29-75.

49. The description of the strategy conference in the text is based on contemporaneous notes taken by Bronstein and included in his files. The notes were circulated to others in attendance. Cf. RS to MM, 8-8-75 (RS) (mentioning the notes).

Chapter 4

1. AB, 8-18-81; RS, 4-11-82; MM, 8-19-81.
2. RS, 4-11-82; MM, 4-19-81.
3. RS, 4-11-82. The name of the witness is a matter of public record, but I do not repeat it.
4. This witness' name is also in the record.
5. AB, 8-18-81. One minor interruption occurred when Knowles was forced to discontinue his interrogation of Carl Clements so that Bronstein could examine Norval Morris on Monday of the second week of trial. Morris had flown in over the weekend and could not wait until the Clements testimony was finished. A more serious dislocation occurred near the end of the evidence for the plaintiffs and the amici. The Prison Project's last two witnesses, Theodore Gordon and John Conrad, would not arrive until next morning and, to avoid losing the afternoon, Judge Johnson ordered Lamar to begin his case for the defense knowing that he would be interrupted next day when the amicus witnesses arrived.
6. On Lamar's strategy, RL, 8-2-82. The defense interrogation of inmates was based entirely on the prisoners' institution files. Lamar depicted Mason as the source of "agitation" in the prison system. Was he not responsible, Lamar demanded to know, for "stirring up unrest" at the institutions to which he was assigned? Mason's answers were predictably defensive; if Lamar gained ground at all, it was in the form and style of his questions. He asked, for example, whether prisoners themselves were not responsible for damage to the plumbing and whether they did not break windows deliberately in order to obtain glass for more weapons. To undercut the value of Mason's testimony, Lamar characterized him as a "loner" who, by inference, might not be a reliable informant regarding the experience of the majority of Alabama prisoners. Lamar attempted to draw a rough parallel between the prison conditions Mason had described and the witness' prior experience in the Air Force. There, too, Mason had lived with many others in a large barracks, and there, too, he had seen occasional fights. In this, the cross-examination was rather obviously flat. Later testimony from Norval Morris handily distinguished military barracks from prison dormitories. In questioning Sutterer, Newman demanded to know why the witnesses had not notified the authorities when they saw other inmates with weapons. Sutterer explained that "if you wanted to live and be healthy you kept your mouth shut no matter what." Then, in a diversionary maneuver, Newman attempted to reveal that Sutterer had earlier reported to Newman that one of the lawyers for the plaintiffs had offered Sutterer $500 to give false testimony in a different, unidentified legal proceeding. Sutterer refused to confirm the report and explained that he had meant that another inmate had once offered him money to perjure himself. Judge Johnson permitted this line of questioning on the theory that it might uncover evidence tending to impeach the credibility of Sutterer's testimony in the cases at bar. When, however, Newman's interrogation produced nothing substantive, the matter was dropped.

7. The cross-examination of John McKee fared little better. Lamar implied, with little subtlety, that the professionals that McKee insisted were needed in the prison system were not available. In the alternative, Lamar suggested that the testimony McKee and Clements had given was primarily in aid of employment opportunities for graduates of the Center for Correctional Psychology. On the question of work release, Lamar once again did more injury than good for his case. McKee said flatly that as many as half the prisoners in the system could be employed during the day in ordinary community jobs and that sufficient work could be found for that many prisoners. If Lamar was surprised by this, he had only his lack of experience to blame. Anyone familiar with work release programs might have explained to him that private employers were pleased to cooperate in order to obtain a steady supply of unskilled laborers who arrived on time (in prison buses) and left only when the day's work was done. If Judge Johnson had not understood as much when Taylor finished his direct examination of McKee, the judge surely was educated by Lamar's inartful cross-examination.

8. RL, 8-2-82; GT, 3-8-82; AB, 8-18-81.

9. AB, 8-18-81. In the wake of Sarver's powerful testimony, yet before the defense had had an opportunity to respond, some of the lawyers had considered a plan to force some issues immediately. As Friday afternoon was slipping away, it seemed that the time was ripe to ask Judge Johnson for emergency relief regarding the most egregious aspects of the prison system. Levin passed Segall a note proposing an immediate motion for an order closing the doghouse. Levin to RS, 8-22-75 (RS). It appeared to Levin that Johnson would grant such a motion, and prisoners at Draper would be spared another weekend of suffering. Segall, however, was toughminded. He sent Levin a note of his own in which he warned that Johnson was in "no mood" to entertain such a motion so early and that the chances of success in such an effort would be improved if the motion were postponed until Monday, after Clements, too, had described the doghouse. RS to Levin, 8-22-75 (RS). Levin acquiesced, but sent Segall a third note: "Those guys in isolation might not understand our sophisticated reasoning." Levin to RS, 8-22-75 (RS). Even as Levin was abandoning the idea of an immediate motion, DeMent and Vines were hatching a similar plan at their table. When Johnson proposed to recess the trial for the weekend, Vines stood up with the very motion that Levin had decided not to pursue. Acting not only as counsel in these cases, but as an "officer of the court," Vines asked Johnson to issue a temporary restraining order requiring Sullivan to release any prisoners then in the doghouse pending a determination of the merits. As Segall had predicted, Johnson was surprised by this sudden move and did not respond favorably. He acknowledged that emergency relief might be appropriate in these extreme circumstances, but he insisted that any motion asking him to enjoin state officers must be made in writing, served on opposing counsel, and made the subject of argument. Vines, for his part, said he would prepare such a motion and a brief outlining the basis of his argument. With that, the matter of emergency relief was put to one side.

Over the weekend, Levin pursued the idea of asking for preliminary relief and, to underscore his commitment, held a news conference to announce his intention to file a motion forthwith. See PH, 8-26-75. The others finally agreed to file a joint motion asking for an immediate order closing the doghouse. The delay allowed Lamar and Newman to develop a response. In answer to the plaintiffs' joint motion, the defense insisted that the punishment cells were really not so bad as Boone and Sarver would have the court believe. Only six of the ten cells were "normally" used, and those six were equipped with ordinary washbasins and commodes—all in "working order." Each cell, according to the defense, was "scrubbed down with disinfectant on the average of once a week," and prisoners kept in the cells were checked by guards "four to six times a day." While it was true that there were no lights in the cells, it was not true, as some witnesses had suggested, that the cells were "almost totally dark." In any event, it was argued, electric lights could not be installed in the cells for fear that inmates would "short them out" in an attempt to cause a "power breakdown." Prisoners might even electrocute themselves. In sum, according to Lamar and Newman, the plaintiffs' witnesses had stretched the truth in aid of their own "biased" judgment that isolation should not be employed as punishment. Judge Johnson did not respond to this early attempt by the plaintiffs to obtain interim relief. He dealt with the issues raised only later, after the defense rested, as explained in the text.

10. RL, 8-2-82. Lamar does not recall clearly who, beyond himself, Baxley, Sullivan, and Long, may have been attendance. He does recall that Long played no significant role in the meeting. Vickers does not recall being consulted about the decision to concede a constitutional violation. JV, 7-26-82.

11. RL, 8-2-82. It is true that at least one reporter, Peggy Roberson, understood Sullivan's comments of a month earlier to mean that the defendants might "plead guilty" in the prison litigation. BN, 7-8-75. There is no evidence, however, that the defense made the decision to concede constitutional error that early. Others, who did not attend the meeting at Long's home, have expressed to me different explanations of the defense tactic. For example, MM, 8-19-81 (guessing that the defense conceded because state authorities were "getting kicked around in the press"); RK, 4-20-83 (guessing that Lamar anticipated that further defense witnesses would be "demolished" on cross-examination).

12. I rely on Bronstein's recollections for most of the description in the text, but I amend his account slightly to conform to what appears in the court reporter's transcript. AB, 8-18-81; RS, 5-29-82.

13. AB, 8-18-81; RS, 5-29-82; GT, 3-8-82; MM, 8-19-81; RK, 4-20-83.

14. The joint decree made exceptions for escapees and parole violators who might be captured and returned to the prison system. The defendants made no immediate objection to the order placing a temporary "cap" on the system's population but, in a related motion, 10-1-75, Larry Newman explained that state statutes required that prisoners due to be released at expiration of sentence must be discharged from a state penal institution. Newman asked, then, that the joint decree forbidding the acceptance of new prisoners be relaxed to permit prison

authorities to accept prisoners from county jails only long enough to process them for release. Taking the view that the administration of prisoners' release could be accomplished without a physical transfer to Mt. Meigs, Judge Johnson denied the motion summarily. Order, 10-9-75. The only objection the defendants raised to the new standards for isolation cells came in the form of a request to suspend exercise for segregated prisoners on weekends, when a shortage of staff made supervision difficult. Judge Johnson also rejected that request. Order, 10-8-75.

15. AJ, 8-22, 25-75; MA, 8-29-75 (including Lamar); WP, 9-4-75. See WJ, 8-28-75; NY, 8-30-75.

16. MM, 8-19-81.

17. See TN, 10-7-75; FT, 12-18-75; BN, 12-18-75; JE, 12-2-75; Locke, EL, 11-21-75; Pearson, OD, 12-10-75.

18. HT, 10-28-75; VT, 12-26-75; AJ, 12-26-75; ST, 12-26-75 "Victimless" crimes, AJ, 12-26-75; Turner, ST, 12-26-75; Simpson, HT, 10-28-75; Heflin, FT, 11-11-75. For Wallace's proposals, § 954–58, 1975 Leg. Sess. See MR, 10-29-75. Curiously, George McMillan and Maston Mims chose this same time to propose a bill establishing a mandatory minimum sentence for offenders using weapons to commit crimes. §689, 1975 Leg. Sess.

19. On Locke's position, AC, 10-26-75; CT, 10-26-75; DS, 12-5-75. On Wallace's position, BN, 10-19, 28-75; MR, 10-29-75. See MA, 11-2-75 (reporting that Wallace did not expend "great effort" on the "crime package" because his lieutenants were preoccupied with the state budget); OD, 11-27-75 (reporting Rep. G. J. Higginbotham's prediction that a special session would be called to deal with prison crowding); MA, 11-2-75 (reporting Wallace's plan to call a special session to reconsider his "crime package"). See PH, 1-11-76 (reporting the ACLU's demand for a special session to deal with prison problems). For Hill's statement, FT, 11-20-75; CT, 11-20-75. On other Wallace statements, TN, 1-21-76; MA, 11-13-75. The Department of Mental Health, whose projects were also included in the bond issue, hoped to spend part of the $7 million allotted to it for a new facility for the "criminally insane." BN, 11-11-75. See MA, 1-9-76 (reporting the ACLU's opposition).

20. On the damage actions, AJ, 11-20-75. Johnson, TN, 11-5-75.

21. Hale, BN, 10-16-75. "Happy," MA, 11-4-75; "neglecting," BN, 10-16-75; "talked," PH, 10-16-75. On the prison name change, MA, 9-10-75. "Waiting," MA, 12-29-75.

22. On some minor matters, Johnson referred as well to the equal protection clause of the Fourteenth Amendment.

23. Conrad to AB, 1-21-76 (NPP); Bronstein, Press release, 1-13-76; Suitts, BN, 1-14-76; HR, 2-14-76; CP, 1-22-76; MI, 1-22-76; ON, 1-22-76; Folsom, SA, 1-22-76; Johnson, MI, 2-19-76.

24. ON, 1-22-76; ET, 1-16-76; EC, 2-1-76. See AJ, 1-24-76 (collecting editorials from around the state). For national press accounts, *Time,* 1-26-76; WJ, 2-6, 4-15-76. On the Prison Project's strategy, MM, 8-19-81.

25. Lamar, BN, 1-14-76; WP, 1-15-76; Locke, NT, 1-23-76. I collect Wal-

lace's statements from several sources. Some accounts differ slightly from others, but the discrepancies are without substantive significance. BN, 1-14, 30-76; MA, 1-14, 15-76; DE, 1-15-76; AC, 1-15-76; PH, 1-30-76 (reporting on Wallace's statement in Massachusetts). Wallace's critics found the "thugs and judges" comment a source of amusement. Perhaps, they said privately, the involvement of judges in state government was comparatively new. But thugs had been exercising authority in Alabama since 1962—when Wallace had first been elected. SS, 5-17-85. Wallace later apologized for the "barbed wire enema" statement. FT, 4-18-77. On the governor's strategy, BN, 1-15-76; MA, 1-16-76.

26. For national press accounts, SP, 1-14, 23-76; WJ, 4-15-76; NY, 2-1-76. The same theme was featured in a subsequent segment of the CBS television program, "60 Minutes," broadcast on 4-17-77. Johnson, AJ, 1-31-76. See NY, 1-18-76 (carrying Tom Wicker's lament that Wallace was "back in the gutter"). But see NY, 1-26-76 (carrying a more perceptive account by Ray Jenkins of the AJ); MG, 8-13-76 (carrying a story prepared by *Guardian* reporters sent to Alabama to investigate).

27. For example, BN, 1-25-76 (piecing together evidence taken in court). "Solutions," PH, 1-15, 19-76; AJ, 1-15, 16-76; BN, 1-18-76; Greer & Hill, FT, 1-14-76.

Chapter 5

1. Cost Analysis for Implementation of Federal Court Order: Alabama Prison System (1976). The plaintiffs were not displeased with the study. They considered Fowler to be an essential ally, and they respected Toohey's professionalism. At the same time, Bronstein saw in the "cost" issue an opportunity to channel Alabama toward enlightened penal policies that the Prison Project had hoped the litigation would produce. If state authorities could not be persuaded to change the Alabama penal system for any other reason, then perhaps they could be convinced to change it to avoid the great expense of operating large, maximum security prisons under the conditions prescribed in the order. Bronstein first commissioned the American Bar Association's Correctional Economics Center to do an independent study that would focus on the savings associated with the policies he wanted Alabama to pursue. That project stumbled, however, and much time was lost before Bronstein concluded that the ABA group would never finish. Still bent on having a study, Bronstein then persuaded the Edna McConnell Clark Foundation to finance an investigation by Nagel's American Foundation in Philadelphia. That group produced a valuable report that built on the earlier University of Alabama study and placed emphasis where Bronstein wanted it. Yet the new report was not circulated until March 1977—too late to influence greatly the state's initial course. Bronstein's first project is described in Axilbund to AB, 10-26-76 (NPP); AB to Axilbund, 11-1-76 (NPP); Wayson to AB, 12-20-76 (NPP); AB to Stanley, 12-28-76 (NPP). His second project is described in Nagel to AB, 12-20-76 (NPP); AB to Nagel, 12-22-76 (NPP). The American Foundation report was circulated to interested parties and sub-

mitted to the court under the title, The Alabama Prison System: An Analysis and Estimate of the Cost and Economic Considerations Resulting from the Orders of the United States District Court (1977). See Press release, 3-18-77 of the United States District Court (1977). See Press release, 3-18-77 (NPP).

2. FJ, 4-19-83; RN, 5-11-82.

3. 376 U.S. 254 (1964).

4. RN, 5-11-82.

5. RN, 5-11-82; RN to Beto, 1-15-76 (HRC).

6. Beto, 6-28-82. See also RN, 5-11-82.

7. Humphrey to MM, 1-26-76 (NPP); "buckshot," PH, 3-1-76; "henhouse," Murton to RN, 2-18-76 (HRC). For Beto's reaction, Beto, 6-28-82. See Memo, 2-13-76 (HRC).

8. Beto, 6-28-82.

9. RN to Beto, 3-15-77 (Beto); Ussery to Beto, 3-10-77 (HRC); FJ to RN, 3-18-76 (HRC).

10. RN, 5-24-82 (recalling that he urged Johnson to make the members of the parole board parties to the prison cases); RN to Ussery, 3-22-76 (HRC); RN to Thagard & Friend, 3-25-76 (HRC); RN to JL, 4-2-76 (HRC); JL to RN, 4-14-76 (HRC). On more public efforts to influence the board, MA, 3-20-76; FT, 3-20-76; HT, 3-27-76. On Nachman's continuing efforts, RN to JV, 5-19-77 (HRC); RN to JL, 6-9-77 (HRC); RN to Sellers, 6-24-77 (HRC). The Alabama parole board similarly rejected the path followed in Georgia, where parole authorities issued a blanket decree reducing most inmates' sentences by a full year. Order of Commutation, 10-27-75; BN, 10-28-75. Locke asked Alabama authorities to consider doing the same for 500 local prisoners, MA, 11-14-75, and John Hale added that twice that number could safely be released early. HT, 10-30-75. The Alabama board's executive director, L. B. Stephens, insisted, however, that the board had no such authority, BN, 10-28-75, and Bill Baxley quickly registered his opposition. BN, 11-2-75. Governor Wallace said flatly that what had happened in Georgia simply would not "happen here." MR, 10-31-75. That sentiment drew wide support. For example, BN, 11-2, 6-75; HT, 11-1-75.

11. Staton to RN, 1-14-76 (HRC); Staton, Nachman & Locke, MA, 2-1-76.

12. Beto, MA, 2-5-76; MR, 2-5-76; "collision course," AJ, 2-3-76.

13. RN, 5-11-82; telephone conversation, RN, 5-5-82.

14. RN to JL, et al., 10-29-76 (HRC); Radney to RN, 11-5-76 (GT).

15. FJ, 4-19-83; FJ to RN, 2-6-76 (HRC); FJ to RN, 6-4-76 (HRC):

> I realize that the members of the Board of Corrections cannot personally operate the facilities under their control. However, these facilities are under their control, and they are charged with the responsibility ... of supervising and ensuring the elimination of the horrendous conditions detailed in the ... report.

16. RN to JL, 6-16-76 (HRC); RN to JL, 9-29-76 (HRC); RN to FJ, 5-10-76 (HRC).

17. "Hotseat, insinuations," MA, 2-15-76. See PH, 2-5-76; BN, 2-6-76; MR, 2-6-76; OD, 2-11-76; TN, 2-14-76. On the "dove hunt" issue, MA, 2-6-76. "Whipping boy," AJ, 2-11-76; "publicity," AS, 2-8-76.

18. "Explosion, slouched," MA, 2-22-76. On the meeting, Beto, 6-28-82; RN, 5-11-82.

19. Harding, MA, 7-29-76; McMillan, AJ, 8-5-76. On the task force bills, MR, 3-3-76.

20. "Cold day," BN, 4-8-76. See *Corrections Digest,* 5-5-76.

21. See AJ, 6-23-76; HT, 3-21-76; MA, 3-25, 4-1-76; PH, 4-1, 9, 30-76; BN, 4-9, 5-26, 6-16, 30, 7-29, 8-2-76; MR, 4-1-76. "Splendid," RN to GM, 5-6-76 (HRC); FJ, 4-19-83. On the Legislative Prison Task Force, RN, 5-11-82; Act No. 84, Reg. Sess. 1976 (creating the Board of Corrections Management and Performance Evaluation Committee); Sen. Res. No. 108, Reg. Sess. 1976 (asking Johnson to appoint the task force to monitor compliance with the order); RN to FJ, 8-5-76 (HRC); Order, 8-17-76:

> The legislature of Alabama has . . . clearly recognized that statutory powers and authority conferred upon the executive and administrative officials to operate the corrections system . . . have not been carried out in accordance with legislative purpose and policy; and that the acts and omissions of these state officials have contravened not only the mandates of the Constitution . . . but the statutory policy of the legislature of Alabama as well. . . .
>
> The Court is of the opinion that the supervisory powers which inhere in the Legislative Task Force by virtue of its permanent status will be of considerable assistance to the Court in the implementation of its orders. This Court commends the legislature of Alabama for its laudable willingness to cooperate with the Court in this common purpose and endeavor.

22. Locke, MA, 7-31-76; McMillan, MA, 8-18-76; Vickers, AJ, 8-19-76.

23. See MA, 8-18, 19, 31, 9-28-76; AJ, 8-19-76; PH, 7-30-76.

24. On Staton, FJ to File, 6-1-76 (HRC); Staton to FJ, 6-1-76 (HRC); Vickers, MR, 5-28-76. On Robinson, FJ to File, 6-2-76 (HRC); MA, 5-21-76. On other contacts with board members, FJ to RN, 7-13-76 (HRC) (explaining that Johnson had spoken to C. E. Carmichael); JV to FJ, 8-18-76 (HRC) (acknowledging a meeting).

25. On new facilities, CT, 3-14-76; MA, 3-18, 4-1-76; BN, 5-2, 20-76; HT, 5-20, 11-21-76. Beasley, FT, 7-31-76; Wallace, MA, 4-4-76.

26. Beto to JL, 3-5-76 (HRC); "get-tough," HT, 3-27-76. On Locke's plan, HT, 3-27, 31-76; MA, 3-27-76; PH, 3-29-76; AS, 3-31-76.

27. On sheriffs, MA, 5-4-76; AJ, 7-12-76. On expenses, FT, 10-15, 11-10-76. On prosecutors, BN, 4-2, 6-13-76. On Judge Thetford, AJ, 7-23-76. On worsening jail conditions, BN, 1-28-76; CT, 2-22-76; FT, 7-22-76. Some local authorities took legal action. Judge Johnson permitted the Wilcox County Commission to intervene in the prison cases but, when the commission attempted to name various state financial officers as additional defendants in an effort to coerce payment for the upkeep of backlogged prisoners, Johnson refused to entertain what he viewed as a dispute between state authorities over state law issues. Order, 7-2-76.

28. On the conflict between Thetford and Russell, *McKinney v. Locke,*

Case No. 4374-76, Circuit Court for Montgomery County, Order, 12-30-76; MA, 12-22, 30, 31-76; TN, 12-31-76. Petition for Instructions, 1-3-77. On Johnson's order in Houston County, BN, 9-18-76. For the resolution, Order, 1-4-77. On Lauderdale County, Order, 11-24-76.

29. On the search for a north Alabama site and local opposition, MR, 4-22-76; MA, 10-7, 10, 11-11, 12-16-76; HT, 11-7-76, 7-31-77; HN, 11-12, 22-76, 5-10, 18-77; DD, 11-19, 21, 22-76; PH, 12-12-76; AC, 12-29-76. Beasley, HT, 12-15-76, 7-27-77; Wallace, HN, 11-23, 12-23-76; HT, 12-23-76; MA, 2-9-77; AJ, 7-27-77; AS, 8-30-77. On the politics of site selection, TN, 7-29-77; AJ, 7-31-77. For editorial commentary, HN, 11-15, 12-24-76; HT, 11-18-76, 7-31-77; AJ, 12-3-76; MA, 12-17-76; BN, 5-16-77; TN, 8-1-77.

30. On the Elmore County site, MA, 7-27-77; OD, 7-28-77. On the south Alabama sites, MA, 8-3, 4-77; AS, 8-7-77; HT, 8-7-77; UH, 8-11, 18, 9-15-77; AO, 8-24-77; PH, 9-1-77.

31. On the HRC meeting, RN to HRC, 3-5-76 (HRC); AJ, 3-19, 20-76; BN, 3-20-76; PH, 3-20-76; MA, 3-20-76. On the Nachman and Beto speeches, BN, 5-6-76; MA, 5-14, 18-76; DD, 5-20-76; AS, 5-20-76. Locke, MA, 5-28-76.

32. Nachman, MA, 9-15, 10-22-76; AJ, 10-22-76; Beto to FJ, 10-13-76 (HRC). Quotations, MA, 10-23, 28-76; BN, 11-2-76. On the general pressure to dismiss Locke, PH, 9-27, 10-25-76. For the defense of Locke and Wallace by Vickers and McCorquodale, AJ, 5-27, 11-11-76; CT, 9-28-76; MA, 11-11-76; AO, 11-12-76. On the general allegation that Wallace acted irresponsibly, MA, 5-29, 7-27, 11-21-76. See also MA, 1-9-77 (containing year-end interviews with Beto and Locke).

33. FT, 3-25-76; AJ, 3-26-76.

34. OD, 5-6-76; HN, 5-6-76. I rely for pieces of this explanation of Wallace's maneuver on editorials and analytical articles in Alabama newspapers. For example, BN, 5-9-76 (Ralph Holmes); EC, 5-9-76; AS, 5-9-76 (Mike Sherman); ST, 5-11-76 (Paul Davis); AO, 5-17-76.

35. BN, 5-6-76; JE, 5-7-76. See HN, 5-22-76; FT, 5-25-76; BN, 5-25, 7-21-76; PH, 5-25-76; CT, 7-21-76. Beasley used his regular column, "Issues in State Government," carried by a number of Alabama newspapers, as a vehicle for pursuing his point of view. For example, BT, 5-19-76; CR, 8-26-76. I rely for parts of this analysis of Beasley's behavior on contemporaneous editorials and articles. For example, ST, 5-11-76 (Paul Davis); *Alabama Home Record,* Summer 1976, No. 6 (Civil Liberties Union of Alabama newsletter).

36. Acts of Alabama, Act No. 182, p. 176 (1976); Beto to JL, 7-30-76 (HRC); McMillan, MA, 11-7-76; PH, 11-11-76; Graddick, MR, 7-31-76; Wallace, Veto message, 7-20-76.

37. Beto to JL, 7-30-76 (HRC); Baxley (by Evans) to JL, 9-8-76 (HRC).

38. Admin. Reg. No. 420, 9-20-76; Locke, MA, 9-21-76; Robinson, AO, 9-20-76. On the release of jail prisoners, BN, 9-16-76; AC, 9-26, 11-7-76. On the diminution in the prison population, PH, 9-24-76; BN, 10-7-76; MA, 11-7-76; HT, 11-8-76. Order, 11-9-76. See BN, 10-29-76; NY, 12-5-76; AJ, 11-10-76; PH, 11-11-76.

39. McMillan, BN, 9-21-76; prosecutors, PH, 11-10-76; MR, 12-3-76. On mistaken discharges, AJ, 11-24-76; MA, 12-5-76. Beasley, MR, 11-19-76; CT, 11-19-76; others, AO, 11-10-76; PH, 11-11-76; FT, 11-18-76; MR, 11-18-76; Locke, ST, 11-8-76; Locke & Vickers, HT, 9-30-76; FT, 11-9-76; BN, 11-9-76; MA, 11-9-76; Nachman, MA, 12-2-76. On amendments, HN, 10-27-76; MA, 11-7-76; MR, 12-2-76.

40. BN, 11-25-76; MA, 11-25-76. The attorney general had previously revealed his plans to Locke. Baxley to JL, 11-25-76 (GT) (explaining that Baxley and his staff had made a "careful study" and "found" a provision of the state constitution on which to rely). For editorials on the "good time" episode, BN, 9-20, 11-5, 27-76; FT, 11-14-76; DE, 12-3-76; AO, 11-26-76; MA, 11-26, 30-76; AJ, 11-30-76; PH, 11-30-76.

41. BN, 11-25-76. See AJ, 11-25-76; AO, 11-29-76. Judge Clarence Allgood in the Northern District dismissed one suit on the theory that only state law issues were at stake and the proper interpretation of the "good time" statute was "within the sound discretion of the Attorney General of Alabama...." *Torris v. Alabama Bd. of Corrections,* Civ. Action No. 77-A-0068-S, Order, 2-23-77. In the Southern District, Judge Hand acknowledged that prisoners might have federal claims, but he chose to delay federal adjudication of those claims until the courts of Alabama had been asked to decide whether Baxley's interpretation of state law was correct. *Dickerson v. Locke,* Civ. Action No. 76-628-H, Order, 12-20-76. Judge Johnson, too, abstained. He agreed that an authoritative decision on the retroactivity question under state law should be obtained before a federal judge treated the federal questions that would be presented if Baxley's view were sustained. If the state courts held that the "good time" statute was retroactive after all, the judicial decision would supersede Baxley's second opinion, and the board would presumably satisfy complaining prisoners by giving them the benefit of the law. If, on the other hand, the state courts decided that the "good time" statute could not be applied retrospectively, there would be time enough for a federal court to determine whether the different treatment of prisoners exhibiting good behavior before and after the effective date of the new statute constituted a violation of the Fourteenth Amendment. Unlike Hand, however, Johnson did not dismiss the lawsuit filed in the Middle District but, instead, invoked an innovative provision of Alabama law permitting a federal court to put specific questions of state law to the Alabama Supreme Court. By certifying the retroactivity issue to the state's highest court, Johnson saved the prisoners concerned the expense, effort and, most important, the time that would otherwise have been spent litigating the issue initially in the lower state courts. With the help of Edward Still and William M. Dawson, lawyers provided by the ACLU, a group of prisoners was able to obtain a prompt decision from the Alabama Supreme Court. Readers should know that I wrote the brief on behalf of the prisoners and made the (unsuccessful) argument before the Alabama Supreme Court. That court sided with the attorney general. *Baker v. Baxley,* 348 So.2d 468 (Ala. 1977). Back in federal court, Baxley insisted that the disparate treatment of the prisoners deprived of retroactive "good time" could be held

unconstitutional only if the plaintiffs proved that the change in state policy was made deliberately to penalize prisoners denied early release. In an attached affidavit, Baxley now insisted that the first opinion on the retroactivity issue had been "based upon a misapprehension of law" and that the second opinion represented his "good faith" interpretation of the Alabama Constitution. *Baker v. Baxley,* Civ. Action No. 76-413-N, Affidavit of William J. Baxley, 7-25-77. The plaintiffs were unable to prove otherwise. Even if they had demonstrated that Baxley had simply bent to political pressure and altered his position in order to prevent the release of more inmates, it was not clear that Judge Johnson would have found that motivation constitutionally invalid. The litigation over the use of the new "good time" law ended in summary judgment for the defense.

42. "Grab back," MA, 1-18-76. On Judge Johnson's new policy, FT, 4-11-76. Johnson recalls that Judge Rives respected this policy in other cases in which the two sat together. FJ, 4-19-83.

43. On Baxley's indecision, AJ, 1-14-76; MA, 1-18-76; "negotiate," PH, 2-5-76. See AJ, 1-30-76; MA, 1-31-76. Baxley originally filed a motion for a new trial, 1-25-76, but later shifted to a (more appropriate) request for rehearing, 2-25-76. See BN, 2-25-76; MA, 2-25-76. See Schlotterback to JL, 3-31-76 (NPP). The statement from the AUM faculty, 3-31-76, was also signed by Dr. Ronald H. Rogers, Arthur W. Hyland, and Norman R. Cox, MA, 4-2-76.

44. FJ, 4-19-83. In addition to granting Baxley's request for permission to find an alternative to the Center for Correctional Psychology and denying his request to alter the space requirement for individual cells, Johnson reduced the number of "mental health professionals" the prison system must employ, altered the conditions that must obtain in punitive segregation, and eliminated the requirement that prisoners be given shampoo. He refused to lift requirements that prisoners with health or religious reasons be given special diets and that all inmates be granted visiting privileges. Order, 3-5-76; BN, 3-6-76. For press criticism, DD, 4-14-76; BN, 4-9-76.

45. Beto, 6-28-82.

46. On Beto's speech, MR, 5-20, 21-76; AJ, 5-24-76. On Judge Johnson's perception, FJ, 4-19-83.

47. Lawson purported to represent only the state of Alabama in *Pugh,* only Governor Wallace in *James,* and the state again in *Newman.* Baxley purported to represent the members of the Board of Corrections, Commissioner Locke, and several wardens in all three cases. In addition, Baxley filed on his own behalf in *Newman,* having never moved to dismiss the original complaint against him personally. Lawson's attempt to limit his representation to Wallace and the state was understandable. He had been summoned by the governor when the attorney general, who would usually speak for the state and its officers, refused to act. Baxley's papers were more puzzling. The state was plainly a named party in both *Pugh* and *Newman,* yet Baxley omitted reference to it in his notices. The confusion was not resolved when, weeks later, Scears Barnes and Tom Radney entered their appearances on behalf of Locke and the board members—"in connection with the Attorney General's Office for the State of Alabama." Barnes to

Wadsworth, 10-14-76 (NPP). Nor were the questions laid to rest by Larry New-man's letter to the clerk insisting that Baxley represented all the defendants and that the clerk should serve documents on all parties-defendant by addressing them to Newman. Newman to Wadsworth, 6-25-76 (NPP).

The Eleventh Amendment states that the "Judicial power of the United States shall not be construed to extend to any suit in law or equity, commenced or prosecuted against one of the United States by Citizens of another state, or by Citizens or Subjects of any Foreign State." Lawson's argument that that amendment barred the suits in *Pugh* and *James* would become significant in the Supreme Court. Lawson also contended that the Three-Judge Court Act, 28 U.S.C. §2281, barred Johnson's order to the extent it displaced state policies. See *Kennedy v. Mendoza-Martinez,* 372 U.S. 144, 154 (1963) (reading the statute to "prevent a single federal judge from being able to paralyze totally the opera-tion of an entire regulatory scheme" by the "issuance of a broad injunctive order"). This argument was not without force—at the time it was made. Finally, Lawson argued that the Seventh Amendment, guaranteeing the right to trial by jury in common law cases, entitled the defendants to a jury trial—this on the theory that the named plaintiff in *Pugh* would rely on Johnson's legal determi-nations in pursuit of compensatory damages from the defendants. See *Curtis v. Loether,* 415 U.S. 189 (1974).

48. Judge Johnson instructed the clerk to file the January 13 order in the *Newman* drawer. Order, 1-31-76. That action was not noted in the press, and neither Johnson nor DeMent recalls the purpose of the order. FJ, 4-19-83; ID, 7-20-82. Nachman suggests that Johnson may have wished to associate his new order with *Newman* in order to ensure some basis for the appointment of the HRC if the appellate court overturned important aspects of the order with respect to *Pugh* and *James* alone. The 1972 order in *Newman* had, of course, already been sustained on appeal. RN, 5-11-82. The consequence was confusing, inasmuch as it was questionable whether an order that had once been approved by the Fifth Circuit was subject to yet another appeal. The parties nonetheless treated the three cases as though they had been consolidated in the district court, and both Baxley and Lawson purported to appeal in *Newman* as well as in *Pugh* and *James.* Lawson later obtained an order consolidating the cases for appeal, but even then the appealability of the *Newman* order was not examined. The circuit court clerk was concerned that the litigants in the *Newman* case be rep-resented on appeal and to that end wrote to Phelps, inviting him to submit a brief. When Phelps failed to reply, the clerk informed other counsel that no sub-mission from the original *Newman* plaintiffs was expected. Wadsworth (by Stiebing) to Counsel, 2-23-77 (NPP). On the Justice Department's involvement on appeal, SW, 3-29-83; Landsberg to ID, 5-19-76 (JD); Days to McCree, 5-18-76 (JD).

Bronstein obtained permission to appear for the National Prison Project on the strength of the project's appointment by Judge Johnson "with full rights of a party." AB to Wadsworth, 5-6-76 (NPP); Wadsworth (by Ganucheau) to AB, 6-23-76 (NPP). Finally, in yet a further illustration of the confusion attending the appeal, the court of appeals noticed that a fourth case, styled *McCray v. Sullivan,* was scheduled to be heard at roughly the same time as *Pugh, James,* and *Newman.* Apparently on the assumption that this *McCray* case was the same *McCray* case that had figured in *Pugh* and *James* below, the circuit appointed Segall to make the argument for the plaintiffs. Wadsworth (by Ganucheau) to RS, 6-29-76 (NPP). In fact, this was an entirely different matter, albeit involving the same named plaintiff who had attacked prison conditions before Judge Hand. Segall prepared the case and made the argument nontheless, but his work had nothing to do with the appeal in the *McCray* conditions suit. RS, 4-11-82. That appeal was decided with the *Pugh* and *James* cases. *McCray v. Sullivan,* 559 F.2d 292 (5th Cir. 1977). In the end, counsel saw the danger of confusing the circuit court with their own disorder regarding who represented whom and resolved the difficulty by filing joint briefs on each side.

49. 547 F.2d 1206 (5th Cir. 1977).

50. 433 U.S. 119 (1977).

51. Another new decision, *Costello v. Wainwright,* 430 U.S. 325 (1977), diffused the "three-judge court" issue. See also *Morales v. Turman,* 430 U.S. 322 (1977). See Joint Reply Brief; Joint Supplemental Brief of Appellees and Amicus Curiae; Joint Supplemental Brief of Appellants. See also AS, 3-24-77 (quoting lawyers on the likely impact of the *Costello* decision).

52. AB, 4-21-82. Memories regarding the argument are dim, disclosing nothing of substantive moment. The transcript is unavailable.

53. Judge Coleman declined to be interviewed with respect to the *Pugh* and *James* cases directly. The account in the text is extrapolated from a more abstract discussion of prison suits generally. Coleman, 9-20-83. See MA, 9-20-77 (expressing a similar reaction to Coleman's opinion, apparently without benefit of an interview). Quotations, *Newman v. Alabama,* 559 F.2d 283 (5th Cir. 1977).

54. Motion to Stay Mandate, 11-11-77.

55. AB, 4-21-82; RK, 4-22-83; SW, 3-29-83; Barnett to Landsberg, 11-10-77 (JD). Compare PH, 9-17-77 ("Court upholds decree"), with DS, 9-18-77 ("Johnson overstepped authority"), and EL, 9-18-77 ("Appeals Court modifies Johnson's prison order"). On the plaintiffs' ultimate appraisal, RK, 4-22-83; AB, 4-21-82.

56. AB, 4-21-82. On Burger's recommendation, B. Woodward & S. Armstrong, The Brethren 160 (1979).

57. *Alabama v. Pugh,* 438 U.S. 781 (1978). In the same term, the Supreme Court approved a small piece of Judge Henley's work in the Arkansas prison case, now denominated *Hutto v. Finney,* 437 U.S. 678 (1978). In an opinion by Justice Stevens, the Court sustained an order prohibiting punitive isolation for more than thirty days and held that state officials could be ordered to pay fees consistent with the Eleventh Amendment, even if the money came from the state treasury. Only Justice Rehnquist objected to Stevens' treatment of the thirty-day rule; several justices dissented from his decision regarding attorney fees. For Johnson's action, Order, 9-6-78.

58. FJ, 4-19-83. On the appointments, NY, 12-14-76, 8-18, 26, 27, 28, 9-9, 10-11, 12-77; BN, 8-17-77; PH, 8-17-77. Nachman, RN to HRC, 4-15-77 (HRC); Johnson, FJ to Counsel, 11-2-77 (NPP). For the transfer to Judge Pittman, Order, 11-3-77. Pittman formally returned jurisdiction to Johnson, Order, 3-21-78.

Chapter 6

1. "Together," Second Biennial Report of the Inspectors of Convicts (1888); "trained experts," H. Hart, Social Progress in Alabama: A Second Study of the Social Institutions and Agencies of the State of Alabama 36 (1922).

2. On the plan, BN, 12-5-74. See MA, 12-5-74. Swafford, MA, 5-9-75. See MA, 5-11-75.

3. Readers should know that I was personally involved in the "classification" phase of the Alabama prison cases. I was recruited by Toohey, and compensated by the Alabama Law Institute, to assist Fowler with legal issues that might arise in connection with his work in the prison system. In my capacity as part-time legal advisor to the Prison Classification Project, I participated in many of the episodes on which I report in this chapter. While I acknowledge this involvement in the interest of candor, I do not suggest that my presence was influential in any important sense. In truth, I merely had a good seat from which to observe others.

4. FJ, 4-19-83.

5. On DeMent's recommendation of Fowler, ID, 7-20-82. Fowler and Brodsky corresponded with Swafford and Dr. Erwin Stasek, who had worked with Swafford. For example, Swafford to SB, 1-27-76 (PCP); Stasek to RF, 2-2-76 (PCP). Fowler explained to Stasek that he had not been "completely" surprised by the order's mention of the center. RF to Stasek, 2-18-76 (PCP). On contacts with the Bureau of Prisons, SB to RF, 1-29-76 (PCP). On cooperation with Toohey, Toohey to RF, et al., 2-27-76 (PCP); RF notes, 2-4-76 (PCP).

6. Stasek warned Fowler that he would face resistance. Stasek to RF, 2-2-76 (PCP). On perceptions, KW, 7-21-82; SB, 5-18-19, 27, 31-82; RF, 6-23-82.

7. Motion for Rehearing, 2-23-76. "Comparably qualified," Order, 3-5-76. On the plaintiffs' efforts, GT, 3-8-82; RK, 4-22-83; RS, 5-29-82; MM, 4-23-82. Conrad, Affidavit of Alvin Bronstein, 4-19-76. "Panel of experts," Order, 5-20-76.

8. Plan for Classification of Inmates, 4-15-76; Clements to RF, et al., 5-26-76 (PCP); Objections to Defendants Plan for Classification of Inmates, 6-8-76; Order, 6-9-76.

9. RF to JL, 6-3-76 (PCP); RN to JL, 6-7-76 (PCP); SB notes, 6-12-76 (PCP).

10. RF to RN, 6-15-76 (PCP); JL to RN, 6-15-76 (PCP).

11. SB notes, 6-12-76 (PCP).

12. RN to RF, 6-17-76 (PCP). Fowler did ask the AUM group to prepare a

draft of a new classification plan but, on receiving their work, he reported to Judge Johnson that it was "editorial in nature" and thus unacceptable. RF to FJ, 6-24-76 (PCP).

13. RF notes, 6-20-76 (PCP); RF to FJ, 6-23-76 (PCP).

14. RF notes, 6-25-76 (PCP). For the modified plan itself, RF to FJ, 6-25-76 (PCP). For Fowler's later report to Nachman, RF to RN, 6-30-76 (PCP).

15. Order, 6-28-76. See AJ, 6-29-76; BN, 6-30-76.

16. RF to Thigpen, 6-29, 30-76 (PCP); Thigpen to RF, 7-2-76 (PCP). Over the next year and a half, the University of Alabama advanced the PCP a great deal of money. While the Board of Corrections did reimburse the university for verified expenditures, payments were obtained in some instances only through additional litigation and explicit court orders. For example, Order, 4-1-77.

17. "Cramped," RF to Moore, 7-19-76 (PCP).

18. RF memoranda, 7-4, 15-76 (PCP); RF, 6-23-82. See RF to Staff, 6-30-76 (PCP) (outlining plans); RF memo, 7-5-76 (PCP) (covering administrative matters); RF memo, 7-13-76 (PCP) (outlining initial procedures). See Fowler, Classification as a Means of Rehabilitating a Correctional System: The Alabama Experience (PCP); Clements, A Report on the Alabama Prison System (PCP); Brodsky, Psychology at the Interface of Law and Corrections: The Alabama Correctional Psychology Experience (PCP).

19. RF, 6-23-82; SB, 5-18-76; SB memo, 7-21-76 (PCP) (quoting Fowler as saying that his "main goal" was to "reduce the population by a quarter"); RF memo, 7-13-76 (PCP) (arguing that prisoners at less secure institutions should be classified early in hopes that some might be appropriate for work release); see Clements memo, 7-23-76 (PCP) (complaining that permanent personnel seemed to dislike prisoners).

20. KW, 7-21-82; RF, 6-23-82.

21. "Hell, Doc," KW, 7-21-82. See RF memoranda, 7-7, 21-76 (PCP). I rely here on my interviews with Fowler, Brodsky, and Warren and on my own inferences drawn from their comments and behavior. I hasten to make clear that no one, least of all Warren, has confirmed, or could confirm, that Warren actually thought through the tactics I ascribe to him or, indeed, knowingly engaged in them. I believe, however, that my appraisal is consistent with, and rests comfortably on, the hard data available.

22. The procedure for eliciting and meeting objections from Warren and Nagle was described precisely in the classification project's published rules. In actuality, none of the participants adhered to specific forms and timetables, however, and the rendition in the text captures the truth of the story better than the rules themselves. The rules went through several drafts in the summer of 1976 and were presented on occasion to Judge Johnson. The final version can be found in Center for Correctional Psychology, Prison Classification Project Summary and Materials, Report No. 32 (January 1977). On their explanation for delays in reviewing files sent to them, Nagle & KW to LB, 8-6-76 (PCP).

23. SB notes, 7-29-76 (PCP). Accounts of similar cases appear elsewhere in

the files. On one occasion in 1975, a "snitch" assigned to Holman by Nagle was brutally murdered within a day of his arrival. See *Gullatte v. Potts,* 654 F.2d 1007 (5th Cir. 1981).

24. The policies followed by Warren's staff and Fowler's attitude toward them were discussed in Fowler's progress report to Judge Johnson, 8-13-76. See also Beto to RF, 7-2-76 (PCP).

25. RF, 6-23-82. RN to RF, 7-22-76 (PCP); RN to JL, 8-4-76 (PCP); RF to Champion, 7-23-76 (PCP); RF to Nagle, 7-23-76 (PCP). An attachment to Nachman's letter of August 4 borrowed language from the procedural rules then being used by the PCP. I drafted some of that language, and I was present in Nachman's office when he dictated the August 4 letter to Locke. I did not attend the anterior conference with Judge Johnson in which the judge approved the language.

26. JL to Beto, 7-12-76 (HRC); Beto to RN, 7-15-76 (HRC) (describing a telephone call from Locke). Beto recalls that he himself was doubtful that classification should be in the hands of inexperienced academics. Beto, 6-28-82. JL to RN, 7-29-76 (PCP); RN to FJ, 8-2-76 (HRC).

28. "Final authority," Evans & Maxwell to Board Members, 8-6-76 (GT).

29. Evans & Maxwell to Board Members, 8-6-76 (GT); RK to RF, 8-6-76 (PCP). See RN to File, 8-5-76 (HRC). In the longer run, Johnson's attempt to substitute informal arrangements for additional orders was turned against him. In the wake of the conference in chambers, Lawson moved to reopen the record on appeal to add some of Nachman's most truculent letters purporting to speak for the judge, many of which concerned classification, in hopes those letters would persuade the appellate courts that both the HRC and the PCP were unduly intrusive—*because* they worked with and for Judge Johnson informally. Johnson denied Lawson's motion on the formal ground that the Nachman letters were not evidentiary exhibits, but Lawson remained free to put his motion and Johnson's disposition of it in the record. Judge Coleman's opinion, which, of course, concluded that the HRC must be disbanded, included statements indicating that the court had examined the letters. A year later, in response to a request from Bronstein, Judge Johnson refused to give the National Prison Project access to internal documents touching the PCP. The judge explained that he did not consider those materials part of the record. AB to FJ, 8-4-77 (NPP); FJ to AB, 8-8-77 (NPP).

30. On Staton's call, Perry to FJ, 8-6-76 (HRC); Staton & JV to FJ, 8-12-76 (HRC). On Warren and Staton, KW, 7-21-82.

31. The informal style of the proposal advanced by the board members indicates that it was their work alone. For evidence of the meeting with Johnson, JV to FJ, 8-18-76 (HRC). On Fowler's concerns, RF to SB, 9-1-76 (PCP). For the critiques of the Staton-Vickers letter, SB to RF, 8-30-76 (PCP); RF to RK, 8-30-76 (PCP). For Toohey's new estimate, Toohey to RF & SB, 8-18-76 (PCP).

32. Order, 8-18-76. Nachman recalls that Johnson added the requirement

that prisoners be assigned the minimum custody grade consistent with security in light of the permanent staff's undue emphasis on security concerns. RN, 5-11-82.

33. On work at other institutions, RF to SB, 8-30-76 (PCP). On the demand for more staff, RF to JL, 8-19-76 (PCP). For reports to Judge Johnson, RF to FJ, 9-1-76 (PCP); RF to FJ, 9-21-76 (PCP). On Warren's plan, KW, 7-21-82. For the plan itself, Motion, 9-13-76: Alabama Board of Corrections, Special Classification Project (with attachments). Fowler and Brodsky were sufficiently impressed with Warren's plan to renew pleas for a cooperative effort. RF to JL, 9-17-76 (PCP). Yet state authorities were no longer prepared to acquiesce in such an arrangement. RF, 6-23-82; KW, 7-21-82.

34. *APA Monitor,* September/October 1976. Quotations, RF to Moore, 7-19-76 (PCP). RF to JL, 8-31-76 (PCP); RF to FJ, 8-31-76 (PCP). See FT, 9-26-76; MA, 9-29-76; TN, 9-29-76.

35. SB notes, 8-24-76 (PCP). Order, 9-24-76. See BN, 9-24-76; MA, 9-24-76.

36. For an example of petulance on Warren's part, KW to RF, 10-11-76 (PCP). Staton, Vickers and Robinson, MA, 10-7-76. See SB notes, 9-28-76 (PCP) (commenting that "there is little or no sense that we are in charge"). RF to RN, 10-14-76 (PCP).

37. RN to JL & Board Members, 10-18-76 (PCP); RN to JL & Board Members, 10-29-76 (PCP); RN to RF, 11-3-76 (PCP).

38. RF to ID, 11-1-76 (PCP). Press reports, MA, 12-31-76; TN, 12-31-76; HT, 12-31-76. Quotation, KW & Nagle to Staff, 11-22-76 (PCP). See also JL to Wardens, 9-23-76 (PCP); JL to All Concerned, 12-10-76 (PCP). For Barnes' report, Interim Classification Compliance Report and Motion to Extend Time, 12-27-76. The chill between state authorities and the PCP was such that Warren and Nagle told the permanent staff to "route" any contacts with PCP members "through" their supervisors. Nagle to Prof. Svc. Personnel, 11-23-76 (PCP); KW & Nagle to Social Svc. Personnel, 12-10-76 (RS). At least one member of Nagle's staff was subjected to disciplinary proceedings for allegedly violating the "no contact" rule. RS to MM, 12-30-76 (RS) (explaining that the staff member, Isabell Moore, was found "not guilty" after an administrative hearing). See also Ellis to PCP Staff, 12-21-76 (PCP) (describing a telephone call at home from a member of Nagle's staff afraid to call from the office).

39. RF to JV, 9-20-76 (PCP); Motions, 10-21, 11-18-76.

40. Quotations, RF notes, 12-12, 15-76 (PCP). Order, 12-14-76.

41. Motion, 12-21-76; see RN to FJ, 1-19-77 (GT) (explaining that the use of custody grade changes as punishment remained an issue). Fowler sent a series of memoranda to Johnson, explaining his reasons for refusing to bend to the blanket policies. RF to FJ, 12-23-76 (GT); RF to FJ, 1-13-77 (PCP). On the reference to Gwaltney, Order, 1-11-77; Gwaltney to Counsel, 1-13-77.

42. I attended the initial hearing, 3-18-77. See also SB notes (PCP). For Gwaltney's decision, Report, 3-29-77; Order, 3-31-77; see BN, 4-2, 5-6-77; HT, 4-19-77; MA, 4-19-77. On Baxley, Objections to the Court-Ordered Modifica-

tion of Alabama Work Release Program Procedure, 5-4-77 (outlining the offenses of the prisoners concerned). Orders, 5-5, 6-77 (amending Gwaltney's ruling to the extent it might have suggested that prisoners erroneously placed in the community could not be retrieved). For press reports, AJ, 5-6-77; PH, 5-7-77. On the return of inmates, BN, 5-7-77. At the time, George McMillan charged that Locke had not misunderstood Johnson, but had placed questionable prisoners on work release deliberately to embarrass the judge. BN, 6-14-77. On the parties' positions, RF, 6-23-82.

43. Newman, BN, 5-25-77; Barnes to Newman, 3-11-77 (Barnes). MR, 5-21-77; OD, 5-25-77; PH, 5-25-77; BN, 5-27-77. Report of the Magistrate, 6-9-77; Order, 6-10-77; see AJ, 6-13-77.

44. Order, 4-21-77. "Blink," RN to Radney, 4-25-77 (HRC); "confidence," JV to RN, 3-31-77 (HRC). See AJ, 4-22-77; MA, 4-22-77.

45. RF to ID, 3-7, 10-77 (PCP). On DeMent's request for a monitoring plan, RF to RN, 10-14-76 (PCP); see SB to RF & Fisher, 11-29-76 (PCP). For the plan itself, RF to FJ, 12-14-76 (PCP); RF to RN, 12-17-76 (PCP). "Emergency," RN to RF, 12-21-76 (PCP). On the plan to employ Boyles, RN to JL & Board Members (undated) (HRC); RN to Boyles, 4-20-77 (HRC); see RF to Boyles, 4-13-77 (PCP) (offering to cooperate). On the recruitment of Fowler's graduate students, Fisher to SB (handwritten and undated) (PCP).

46. On Locke's attitude, JL to RN, 10-22-76 (PCP); Radney to RN, 1-14-77 (PCP); MA, 10-26-76; BN, 10-26-76. Locke agreed to meet with Nachman and DeMent early in January to discuss the monitoring issue. RN to JL, 1-20-77 (HRC). Fowler was invited, but declined to attend. RF to RN, 1-21-77 (PCP); SB to RF & Jones, 2-7-77 (PCP); RF to Staff, 2-8-77 (PCP). Fowler explained to Nachman that he had a previous engagement and thus maintained a formal willingness to cooperate, but a handwritten note in the margin of an internal memo indicates that Fowler thought it unwise to attend the meeting. He distrusted Nachman's objectives and feared the outcome of any cooperative effort. Indeed, Fowler declined even to permit state authorities to see the plan he and his staff had drafted. Barnes to Counsel, 2-28-77 (PCP); ID to Barnes, 4-4-77 (PCP). For Nachman's formal proposal, Motion, 6-20-77.

47. For the clerk's letter, Wadsworth (by Ganucheau) to Counsel, 7-14-77 (NPP). The players skirmished over the form of Nachman's proposal. Inasmuch as it was put forward as a suggestion from the HRC, Barnes complained that it was in the form of a motion, as though it came from a party to the litigation. Response, 6-23-77; Motion to Strike, 6-6-77. Larry Newman insisted in the same vein that if Nachman purported to take the role of a party he was subject to formal interrogation. Newman to RN, 7-14-77 (NPP). In the end, Judge Johnson resolved the difficulty be accepting the monitoring plan as a report from his own agents—Nachman and the HRC.

48. Transcript, 7-19-77; RF to FJ, 7-18-76 (PCP). I have been unable to verify whether Judge Johnson received Fowler's letter prior to his conference with counsel on July 19.

49. Lawson to Wadsworth, 7-25-77 (NPP); AB to Wadsworth, 7-22-77

(NPP). When I first noticed that Fowler's letter to Johnson was written in the eight-day period between the clerk's letter to counsel and Bronstein's response, and when I calculated the time required for posting, I, too, suspected that one of the lawyers on the prisoners' side of the litigation must have prompted Fowler to make such an explicit and timely statement to the court. Yet Bronstein, Segall, and Knowles deny asking Fowler to write the letter; Fowler does not recall being asked. Then, too, there are earlier, very similar letters in the record. One, RF to FJ, 2-24-77, includes this statement.

> In response to the Court's [Johnson's] request, the University of Alabama Center for Correctional Psychology has completed the classification of all inmates in the Alabama State Prison System who entered the system before September 23, 1976. We have dismissed all but two employees who are compiling the data from the classification process.

While it seems unlikely that the timing of Fowler's letter of July 18 was merely coincidental, there is no reason to believe that it misrepresented events. The PCP had completed its work, save for the disagreements resolved in the proceedings before Gwaltney, six months before the letter from the circuit court clerk.

50. *Newman v. Alabama,* 559 F.2d 283, 290 (5th Cir. 1977). Motion, 10-24-77; Lawson to Wadsworth, 10-25-77 (NPP).

51. Clements, A Selective Summary of Current Deficiencies in the Alabama Prison System: Classification and Mental Health (1978) (unpublished) (PCP).

52. SS to Counsel, 1-3-77 (NPP).

Chapter 7

1. Petition to Modify Cell Use, 10-10-77.

2. RK, 5-6-83. In light of Judge Johnson's order of 11-3-77, transferring jurisdiction of the *Pugh* and *James* cases to Judge Pittman while Johnson was considering an appointment to be director of the FBI, it would seem that these matters should have come before Pittman for action. Pittman's order returning the prison cases to Johnson was not filed until 3-21-78. I have been unable to resolve the discrepancy. Inasmuch as the transfer was largely a matter of form, however, these niceties have little significance.

3. Compliance Report, 3-15-78.

4. See Motion to Reopen Discovery, 3-20-78; RK to Beasley, et al., 5-4-78 (NPP); F. Rundle, Report of Inspection of Medical and Psychiatric Problems and Services, Kilby and Fountain Correctional Centers, Department of Corrections, State of Alabama (1978) (NPP); American Foundation, Staffing for Alabama's Prison System, 11-30-78 (NPP). "Impressed," Nagel to RK, 6-14-78 (NPP); Barnes, Response to Request for Admissions, 5-25-78. Barnes later amended this statement to add information regarding the new prisons the board intended to construct, but the essential concession that the prison system could

not be brought into compliance in the near future remained intact. Amended Response, 6-6-78.

5. On Racette's charges, HT, 5-4-78. The Foshee brothers had been convicted on "check-kiting" charges in 1976, but their convictions had been reversed on appeal. In the summer of 1978, when the events described in the text occurred, it was uncertain whether they would be brought to trial again. Both brothers were later tried and convicted again in Judge Johnson's court. MA, 11-10-78. Still, Wheeler's status within the prison system was unclear, apparently because Wilkinson, who had served as his defense attorney, also chaired the Board of Corrections and, in that capacity, forced the board to discuss his client's case in open session. AS, 1-3-79. Staton and Vickers were quite prepared to sack Foshee immediately but, with Wilkinson recusing himself and Hamner abstaining, it was difficult to obtain an authoritative vote. TN, 12-14-78 (reporting indecision when Carroll was absent). Circumstances became even more complicated when Foshee accused Staton of using his position to further the interests of a company in which Staton held stock, and the Alabama State Ethics Commission initiated an investigation. DD, 12-15-78. The matter hung on for some time while Staton and Vickers asked Baxley for an attorney general's opinion on whether Foshee could retain his position pending a second appeal. MA, 12-13-78. Ultimately, Foshee offered his resignation. FT, 1-4-79.

On Holmes' allegations, MA, 5-25-78. On Bennett's background and ties to the Wallace family and Vickers, AJ, 12-3-78; JH, 7-28-82. On his transfer, PH, 6-1-78. A bit later, a nurse and a medical assistant who had been dismissed at Tutwiler Prison charged that both Locke and Bennett had neglected inmate patients at that institution. AJ, 9-1-78; MA, 9-1-78.

6. For Johnson's request, Order, 7-11-78. On the efforts by Bronstein and Myers to obtain advice from others, MM to FJ, 3-10-78 (NPP); AB to Ohlin, 3-10-78 (NPP); Conrad to MM, 3-14-78 (NPP); Breed to MM, 3-14, 15-78 (NPP); Nathan to MM, 8-15-78 (NPP). On the plaintiffs' recommendations, MM to FJ, 6-8, 8-28-78 (NPP). The federal government endorsed the NPP's recommendation that Vincent Nathan serve as "master." Days (by Whinston) to FJ, 9-1-78 (NPP). On Barnes' recommendations, Barnes to FJ, 8-31-78 (NPP). Johnson's apparent decision to delay any appointment prompted periodic letters from Myers describing the continued availability of the Prison Project's nominees. For example, MM to FJ, 9-1, 10-27-78 (NPP). In June, Barnes took the position that the appointment of an outsider was "premature." Barnes to FJ, 6-30-78 (NPP). On the fire marshal's report, AJ, 8-14-78; PH, 8-15-78. Noting similar concerns about the new Staton facility, the prisoners' lawyers asked Judge Johnson for an order preventing Locke from moving prisoners into that institution until the fire marshal could inspect and approve it. RS to FJ, 6-30-78 (NPP). On the state examiners' report, PH, 7-12-78; BN, 7-25-78; RK to Nagel, 7-14-78 (NPP) (stating that the judge had ordered state authorities to give him a "listing of their 20,000 acres of land" but that the "full implications" of Johnson's interest in the agricultural fields were not yet known).

7. Commissioner Locke provided the information regarding crowding at

Kilby and the population of sentenced prisoners in the jails in a deposition taken in connection with the litigation concerning the Jefferson County Jail. Locke deposition, *Thomas v. Gloor,* Civ. Action No. 77-P-66-S (N.D. Ala., 3-9-78). Accord Minutes of Social Svc. Staff Meeting, 1-17-78 (NPP). See WJ, 1-20-78 (taking stock of the Alabama cases in the wake of the appeal). On the Shelby County Jail, BN, 9-7-77. On the action in Birmingham, PH, 5-2-78. On the grand jury reports, HT, 9-1-78. On the sheriffs' association proposal, ML, 7-14-78.

8. See generally *Wyatt v. Walker,* Civ. Action No. 76-P-0775-W (N.D. Ala.) (the Tuscaloosa case); *Thomas v. Gloor,* Civ. Action No. 77-P-66-S (N.D. Ala.) (the Birmingham case); *Bibb v. Montgomery County,* Civ. Action No. 76-380-N (M.D. Ala.) (the Montgomery case); *McCray v. Purvis,* Civ. Action No. 5620-69-H (S.D. Ala.) (the Mobile case). See also *Nicholson v. Choctaw County,* 498 F. Supp. 295 (S.D. Ala. 1980) (an order by Judge Pittman regarding unconstitutional conditions in the Choctaw County Jail); *Parrish v. Lauderdale County Commission,* Civ. Action No. 79-G-0301-NW (N.D. Ala., 6-25-82) (an order by Judge J. Foy Guin regarding the Lauderdale County Jail); PH, 12-3-82. Locke used his authority to transfer prisoners from one jail to another in response to the order in Tuscaloosa. JL to Walker, 12-9-77 (NPP). In some instances, Dr. Warren sent classification teams to local jails to identify prisoners who could be shipped to low-security facilities in the state system. KW to JL, 12-12-77 (NPP) (explaining what had been done in Tuscaloosa). On Pointer's initial order in Birmingham, PH, 8-29-78. For the order requiring payments to prisoners, Order, 4-16-80. On the public outcry, PH, 10-23, 29-81. On Varner's release orders in Montgomery, MA, 9-29-79. Varner continued to issue similar orders periodically, whenever the population in the Montgomery County Jail rose above the limit. For example, Order, 3-25-82.

9. The history of the Houston County litigation is reported in *Adams v. Mathis,* 458 F. Supp. 302 (M.D. Ala. 1978), aff'd, 614 F.2d 42 (5th Cir. 1980). See AJ, 3-2-78. Locke's motion for clarification was filed on 3-20-78.

10. For the new decree, Order, 3-31-78. A bit later, Judge Hand, who had joined Johnson in the original order establishing the "cap" on the prison system's population, issued an order similar to Johnson's March 31 decree in his own case, *McCray v. Purvis.* Order, 5-4-78. The quotations in the text are taken from a typed version of Johnson's statement appearing in Bronstein's files and dated 4-4-78. See also PH, 4-5-78.

11. Knowles' contacts with other lawyers handling jail cases are reflected in his correspondence. For example, RK to Chappell, 6-10-78 (NPP); RK to Galanos, 7-10-78 (NPP); RK to Turner, 10-3-78 (NPP). For Knowles' request, Motion for Further Relief, 4-17-78. See Drake to Pointer, 4-20-78 (NPP) (explaining the theory of the new motion to Judge Pointer).

12. RK, 6-21-83.

13. Lawyers for state authorities insisted that Johnson should defer to the judges in other districts regarding particular jails and should, at all events, post-

pone any further action until after the parties finished preparations for a new hearing on the extent to which the prison system now met the standards fixed by the January 13 order. Response, 5-1-78.

14. On the new Staton facility, MA, 6-12, 26-78. On the plaintiffs' desire to prevent the construction of new prisons, RS, 5-29-82; RK; 4-22-83.

15. Knowles does not now recall some of the matters reported in the text. I rely on what he does remember and what appears in his notes of the meeting contained in the NPP files. Other notes, dated 5-4-78, suggest that Barry Teague, who had recently succeeded Ira DeMent as U.S. attorney in Montgomery, may have spoken previously with Judge Johnson about ordering the release of some jail prisoners. The notes report that "Johnson . . . felt strongly about not letting people out." Inasmuch as Knowles cannot recall the occasion for the notes, and the date they carry would put his apparent conversation with Teague prior to the meeting discussed in the text, I hesitate to suggest that Judge Johnson was actually consulted about the parties' plan and rejected it so early. For Knowles' account of the lawyers' agreement, RK to Galanos, et al., 5-15-78 (NPP).

16. On Johnson's failure to rule on the plaintiffs' motion, RS, 5-29-82. On Locke's explanation for his resignation, MR, 7-13-78; AS, 7-13-78. On rumors that Locke was forced to leave, MA, 7-16-78. On Locke's personal resistance to the release of prisoners, LB, 6-28-82. On Vickers' role in Bennett's selection, JH, 7-28-82. On the appointment of Bennett and Cooper, BN, 7-14-78. On Bennett's immediate personnel changes, PH, 7-22-78. Locke was given the title of associate commissioner and was assigned to ensure sanitary conditions at the state's institutions. A year later, Commissioner Britton asked him to resign. RB to JL, 7-9-79 (Barnes). Cooper was convicted of violating Alabama's ethics law. Because of his prior position, arrangements were made for him to serve his three-year sentence in a federal facility in Florida. PH, 11-14-81.

17. On Bennett's initial statements, BN, 7-14-78. On the new bond issue, MA, 7-14-78; AS, 7-14-78; PH, 7-15-78; FT, 8-21-78. On the political opposition, BN, 7-16-78. The local ACLU affiliate opposed the bond issue on the ground that the revenues would be spent on new prisons. For editorials supporting the bond issue, AJ, 11-1-78; BN, 11-1-78; PH, 11-2-78. The quotations in the text are taken from Knowles' notes on a conversation with Barnes, dated 7-27-78, and Taylor's notes on a subsequent discussion with Barnes, dated 8-23-78 (NPP).

18. RK, 4-22-83; Conversation with Knowles, 10-31-80.

19. Memories are dim regarding the precise timing of the meeting with Judge Johnson and the persons in attendance. Knowles recalls that only he and Barnes were there; Segall remembers that he, too, was present. RK, 4-22-83; RS, 5-29-82.

20. "Homework," RK, 5-6-83. On the Washington meeting, Agenda memo, 8-5-78 (NPP). The quotation from Johnson appears in Knowles' handwritten notes on the conference, included in the NPP files. On the prisoners' lawyers' expectations, RS, 5-29-82; MM, 4-23-82. "Show and tell," LB, 7-28-82.

21. There is no official transcript of the hearing, but Myers' handwritten notes appear in the NPP files. Locke, PH, 9-19-78; Gordon, MA, 9-19-78; Clements, BN, 9-21-78; inmates, MA, 9-20-78.

22. "Still critical," DD, 9-22-78; "trying," BN, 9-20-78; Bennett, TT, 9-21-78.

23. See Order, 10-19-77 (substituting Teague for DeMent as amicus in *Pugh* and *James*); Drake to Gordon, 2-24-78 (GT) (announcing Knowles' departure from the Tuscaloosa firm); JC to Vines, 7-11-78 (US) (announcing Carroll's entry); Notice of Withdrawal, 8-18-80 (requesting formal withdrawal for Myers). Taylor did not file a formal motion for three more years. Motion for Withdrawal, 9-1-81.

24. Newman to Gordon, 3-24-78 (NPP) (announcing Newman's transfer); Order, 9-13-78 (approving Lawson's withdrawal). See AJ, 7-8-77 (announcing Hamner's appointment); BN, 6-27-78 (announcing Wilkinson's elevation to the chair).

25. BN, 7-30-78 (complaining that the prisons were not being discussed by gubernatorial candidates); AS, 9-27-78 (describing Graddick's primary victory); HT, 12-10-78 (carrying an early interview with Graddick in which he insisted he was not "blood thirsty"); TN, 1-14-82 (reporting that Graddick opposed lethal injection as a means of carrying out the death penalty on the ground that a painful death would constitute a more effective deterrent to crime). "Eyes," PH, 2-6-85 (noting that Graddick later denied making the statement "in the context in which it has been used").

26. Post-trial Brief, 10-11-78; Defendants' Reply, 10-26-78; Bennett, MA, 11-29-78.

27. On Bennett's difficulties with the board, BN, 12-14, 21-78; MA, 12-17, 20-78; AJ, 12-14-78. On Britton, Beto, 6-28-82; RB, 7-13-82.

28. Order, 12-18-78. Decisions were initially postponed when the board flirted with the idea of shifting responsibility for construction plans to a "blue ribbon panel" of citizens, chaired by Robert Davis of the Alabama Law Enforcement Planning Agency, and including Roland Nachman, Ira DeMent, and Laurie Mandell. The notion that such an ad hoc group would or could accept responsibility for the plan Johnson had ordered was unrealistic at best. Staton and Vickers recognized as much and, accordingly, short-circuited the scheme by denying Davis' request for time in which to work. In the end, the panel was proposed, undercut, and discarded before some potential members had agreed to serve. On the division within the board and the "blue ribbon panel," BN, 12-18-78, 1-10-79; PH, 1-5, 6, 10-79; HT, 1-4-79; MR, 1-4-79. DeMent declined to serve on the panel because of what he called his "obvious conflict of interest." ID to Davis, 1-9-79 (US) (referring to a letter to Davis from Nachman insisting that such a committee would require too much time to do a responsible job). Reports on board members' positions on specific projects are in conflict. John Hale recalls that Hamner was "instrumental in going to Union Springs" and that he and the others openly offered to trade their votes on other projects in order

to further their own favored sites. Hale admits, however, that he could "never understand that Union Springs situation." JH, 7-28-82. For the board's ultimate plan, Board of Corrections Plan for Utilization of Present Revenue Resources, 1-17-79. The members' votes were reported in an amendment to the plan, dated 1-24-79. Knowles and Myers filed a lengthy response, which attacked the construction projects proposed at Union Springs, Wadley, and Heflin. Their position was supported by an affidavit from Fred D. Moyer, who had reviewed the prison system in connection with the study done by the University of Alabama three years earlier. Moyer found the new plan to offer no serious promise of facilities that would meet the standards fixed by Johnson's orders. Response of Plaintiffs and Amici, 2-5-79.

29. "Ball game," MA, 12-19-78.

30. My account differs in minor respects from those of others. Howell Raines reported at the time that Judge Johnson "sent word" to James that he was available to discuss the prison cases and the mental health case, *Wyatt,* with the governor-elect. Raines failed, moreover, to identify the "intermediary" who arranged the conference with Johnson and the "new intermediary" who presented the "receiver" idea to the judge and drafted James' petition. NY, 2-12-79. Writing more recently, Professor Yarbrough reports that Johnson did not meet with James until after the latter's inauguration in mid-January. T. Yarbrough, Judge Frank Johnson and Human Rights in Alabama 223 (1981). Raines mentioned no sources; Yarbrough cites an interview with the judge. I have been able to put the dates of the initial meetings much earlier and to reveal the roles played by McMillan and Nachman. FJ, 4-19-83; GM, 3-21-83; RN, 5-28-82, 3-15, 23-83. See also Letter from James, 5-13-83 (stating that the "first concern" was "the operational aspect of the prison system" and that "the only way [the governor] knew to break the log jam was to gain operational control").

31. RN, 3-15-83; Petition of Governor of Alabama for Appointment as Temporary Receiver, 2-2-79.

32. Memorandum, 2-2-79. See *Newman v. Alabama,* 466 F. Supp. 628 (M.D. Ala. 1979).

33. For the common view that Johnson would never have appointed anyone but the governor to take charge of the prison system, RN, 3-23-83; RS, 5-29-82; cf. Johnson, In Defense of Judicial Activism, 28 Emory L.J. 901, 911-12 (1979) (maintaining that the appointment of James increased state responsibility for the prison system).

34. FJ to Days, et al., 2-5-79 (JD); Order, 2-5-79. On the governor's action, LB, 3-9-83. Bennett was shrewd enough to recognize that the demise of the board, within which he had been losing support, did not mean safety for his own position. Accordingly, he attempted to impress James with his own vision. He advocated that all three rural construction projects be abandoned, that Fountain and Draper be closed within a few years, and that all new construction be located in the north near Birmingham. L. Bennett, A Presentation, 2-79 (Bennett); RB, 7-13-82.

35. RS, 5-29-82; SW, 3-29-83. On the allegations concerning Britton's performance in Arkansas, SW to File, 3-19, 20-79 (JD); SW to Goff, 3-21-79 (JD); PH, 3-23-79.

36. Order, 6-14-79.

37. On Johnson's nomination, NY, 2-14, 3-31-79. On his heart condition, PH, 10-17-81 (reporting surgery to clear a blocked artery). See *Hutto v. Finney,* 437 U.S. 678, 681 n.2 (1978) (noting that Judge Henley retained the Arkansas prison case after taking a circuit judgeship). RB, 7-13-82; RN, 5-12-82. On the last drive, BN, 7-10-79.

Chapter 8

1. On Varner's appointment and the allegations concerning black jurors, J. Goulden, The Benchwarmers 329–30 (1974). On his experience in Macon County, BN, 11-14-81. On his concern about damages actions from jail prisoners and ascription of blame to the legislature, RV, 8-21-82. On some lawyers' concern that Varner might undercut Johnson's accomplishments, SW, 3-29-83.

2. GT, 3-8-82; RN, 3-15-83; AB, 3-30-83.

3. RB, 7-13-82; Britton deposition, 5-1-79. The legislation establishing the Department of Corrections appears as Ala. Code §14-1-15, et seq. On the continuing search for a Jefferson County site, BN, 6-10-79. James initially attempted to persuade the authorities in St. Clair County that a new prison would not discourage residential development. They resisted his arguments, however, and promptly convinced the owner of the site penal authorities had identified, the Kimberly-Clark Corporation, to renege on its earlier decision to sell. When James threatened to take the site anyway by condemnation, local officials countered with their own eminent domain action, contending that they wished to have the land for a public park. Judge Varner concluded that St. Clair authorities were frustrating James' performance of his duties as receiver and enjoined further activities on their part. Kimberly-Clark then sold the parcel to the Department of Corrections under protest. PH, 9-11, 18, 19, 25, 10-25, 11-13-79, 1-10, 26-80; BN, 9-24-79; MA, 9-12, 17, 26, 28, 30-79, 1-25-80; SA, 9-30-79; James to McClendon, et al., 11-9-79 (telegram) (GT); Motion of Receiver, 11-19-79; Order, 11-19-79; Response of St. Clair County Commissioners, 12-3-79; Orders, 1-8, 17, 2-8-80; Memorandum and Permanent Injunction, 3-4-80.

4. RK, 6-21-83. On James' budget for the prison system, PH, 1-18-80; MA, 1-18-80. On violence within the institutions, Reports of MacArthur Davis, 4-1, 6-18-79 (GT) (reporting a stabbing death and an apparent suicide at Holman); Report of Edward Wright, 7-10-80 (GT) (reporting an apparent homicide at the Henry County Jail); Totty to Wright, 7-13-80 (GT) (reporting threats against a prisoner's life). On guard violence, Report of MacArthur Davis, 8-11-80 (GT) (describing the shooting in the agricultural fields); King to Evans (undated) (GT) (reporting on Hopper's shooting of the escapee). See PH, 4-15-80 (further describing the Hopper incident); MA, 6-2, 12-5-80 (describing a

series of allegations of beatings of prisoners by guards). On the stopgap proposals for additional space, Compliance Report, 11-19-79; MA, 12-4-79.

5. "Crucial," RK to GT, et al., 1-14-80 (GT); "reasonable," Response to Receiver's Compliance Report, 6-19-80. On the meeting, MM notes (NPP).

6. Taylor's aside was noted at the bottom of a letter from Knowles scheduling several meetings to discuss preparations for the hearing. Memo, 9-25-80 (NPP).

7. Beto to RB, 10-1-80 (HRC).

8. Nachman's posture is described in Knowles' undated, handwritten notes on conversations with Carroll (NPP). See also RN, 3-15-83; JC, 5-31-83; RK, 6-21-83; SW, 3-29-83.

9. JC, 5-31-83; RK, 6-21-83.

10. Objections of Temporary Receiver to Deposition and Motion for Protective Order, 8-13-80; RK to Barnes, et al., 9-30-80 (NPP); RK to Conrad, 10-1-80 (NPP). Nachman also asked Judge Varner for a protective order for Britton, but that effort was only half-hearted.

11. RK, 6-21-83; JC, 5-31-83; SW, 3-29-83; RS, 5-29-82; RN, 3-15-83.

12. Order, 10-9-80; James to Teague, et al., 10-9-80 (attached); MA, 10-10-80. See also AJ, 12-14-80. On the relation between the new deadlines and projected construction, SW, 3-29-83. The consent decree provided for the appointment of Kenneth Schoen, a Minnesota corrections specialist whom Bronstein had consulted regarding classification and now an officer of the Edna McConnell Clark Foundation, to "monitor" compliance with its terms. Schoen, however, spent little time in Alabama and presented no serious threat to Britton's authority. For a rare report from Schoen, Schoen to Barnes, 2-26-82 (NPP). Schoen's appointment was of some psychological concern. State officials charged (at least privately) that the Clark Foundation had provided the Southern Poverty Law Center with financial backing and that Schoen, accordingly, had a conflict of interest. For example, Hopper to Barnes, 4-30-82 (Barnes). In truth, it was not John Carroll's organization, but Bronstein's National Prison Project that depended on the Clark Foundation for funding. AB, 8-17-81. The October 9 order also committed James to satisfy the Justice Department with a new contract for medical services with the Brookwood company. SW to RN, 12-10-80 (US).

13. On Graddick's criticism of parole authorities, BN, 7-19-81. On the poor progress at new prison sites, Quarterly Report of Receiver, 5-2-81. On Britton's report and statements, PH, 12-11-80; MA, 12-10-80, 1-30-81. For the letter to Barnes and Nachman, JC to Barnes, et al., 1-16-81 (NPP). Officials in St. Clair County retained Bill Baxley, now in private practice, to sue state authorities on the questionable ground that their construction plans had proceeded without an environmental impact statement, required by federal law. See Shults to James, 12-10-79 (US); PH, 1-29-81.

14. RK, 6-21-83; JC, 5-31-83. See RK to RN, 3-10-82 (NPP); Drake to RV, 3-24-81 (NPP).

15. 433 U.S. 267 (1977).

16. Motion to Require the Provision of Sufficient Funds, 3-9-81; Brief in Support of Motion, 3-9-81.

17. Conversation with RK, 5-20-81; RK, 6-21-83; JC, 5-31-83; MA, 5-20-81; Inmate List, 6-29-81. Two local newspapers, the *Montgomery Advertiser* and the *Birmingham News,* filed actions to obtain access to the lists of inmates provided to Varner. Knowles and Bronstein, who were employed by an arm of the American Civil Liberties Union, were ambivalent regarding the apparent conflict between the newspapers' first amendment claim and their sense that the interests of their inmate-clients would not be served by the publication of the lists. In the end, they took no public position but agreed privately that the interests of their clients in this instance were paramount. For example, RK to AB, 10-27-81 (NPP); AB to RK, 11-2-81 (NPP). At least one inmate attempted to intervene in hopes of having his name added to the list. Motion on Behalf of Ray Anthony Ragland, 7-17-81. Later, Lawson filed an additional document in which he insisted that his comments regarding the release of prisoners had been made in the context of his opposition to what he called "judicial funding," that he had not intended to speak for those who might be affected by the release of prisoners, and that he certainly had not meant to endorse the release of convicts as sound policy. Response of "New" Defendants, 7-21-81.

18. On the deadlines in Mobile and Birmingham, PH, 5-1, 29-81. On Britton's statements, PH, 5-19, 29-81; MA, 6-3-81. On Graddick's charges and Britton's denial, PH, 6-10-81; TN, 6-12-81. On street interviews, TN, 6-7-81. On the petition, PH, 6-17-81. For an editorial, TN, 7-12-81. Graddick, BN, 7-12-81; PH, 7-13-81; McMillan, GM to RV, 7-13-81 (NPP); BN, 7-16-81; TN, 7-14-81.

19. On Baxley's candidacy, PH, 10-2-81. On the "modular" housing proposal, Temporary Housing Plan, 6-11-81; PH, 6-13, 17, 23, 26, 7-3-81; TN, 6-10, 13-81.

20. 452 U.S. 337 (1981). See Motion for Emergency Relief, 6-15-81; TN, 6-16-81 (reporting Drake's motion). I rely on contemporaneous conversations with Knowles for the interstices reported in the text here and below. Knowles received some support from an unexpected source. Two legislators, Donald Harrison and Jack Venable, joined a number of Elmore County residents in an attempt to intervene in the prison cases to argue against the use of modular units to house more prisoners near their homes. Motion to Intervene, 9-16-81. A bit later, the same would-be litigants asked for permission to participate as amici curiae. Nachman filed an objection on James' behalf, and Judge Varner refused the intervention. Varner did permit Harrison, an attorney, to participate as an additional amicus curiae, but Harrison did not become heavily involved. Motion of Temporary Receiver, 9-28-81; Order, 10-15-81.

21. Orders, 6-15, 16-81. On Graddick's reaction to *Chapman,* PH, 6-18-81. For Carroll's argument, TN, 6-16-81. On the report that 400 inmates might be released, TN, 7-14-81.

22. On the Texas case, *Ruiz v. Estelle,* 503 F. Supp. 1265 (S.D. Tex. 1980),

650 F.2d 555 (5th Cir. 1981). On the statute in Michigan, *Oakland County Prosecuting Attorney v. Michigan Dept. of Corrections,* 305 N.W.2d 515 (Mich. 1981). On the Fifth Circuit's action, *Hamilton v. Morial,* 644 F.2d 351 (5th Cir. 1981). On the riot in Georgia, PH, 6-16-81.

23. Order, 7-15-81; NY, 7-16-81; PH, 7-14-81; TN, 7-15-81.

24. BN, 7-19-81; PH, 7-16-81.

25. Britton, PH, 7-4, 17, 31-81; TN, 7-6-81; Meese, *Philadelphia Inquirer,* 5-14, 20-81; Smith, 29 Crim. L. Reptr. 2235 (6-10-81); Bronstein, AB, 3-30-81. Reynolds later confirmed his efforts to conclude the case in Texas. NY, 12-19-81.

26. BN, 7-16-81; TN, 7-16-81; PH, 7-18-81.

27. Motion to Intervene, 7-16-81; Intervenor's Answer, 7-16-81; TN, 7-16-81.

28. Motion for Joinder of Fob James, 7-16-81.

29. Graddick, TN, 7-16, 17, 18-81.

30. James, BN, 7-16-81; TN, 7-17-81; PH, 7-18-81; Knowles, TN, 7-17-81; editorial, TN, 7-17-81. See TN, 7-19-81 (carrying commentary by Kendal Weaver contrasting James favorably with Wallace in his response to federal court orders). On the riot in Texas, BN, 11-22-81.

31. On the meeting with Hines, TN, 7-18-81. On the release of prisoners' names, PH, 7-18-81. On paring the number of prisoners to be released, Orders, 7-22, 23-81; PH, 7-17-81; TN, 7-19, 21-81; MA, 7-21-81. On the parole cases, TN, 10-28-81.

32. Motion of Temporary Receiver, 7-17-81; Plaintiffs' Response, 7-20-81; Order, 7-20-81.

33. Motion to Stay, 7-22-81 (district court); Notice of Appeal, 7-22-81 (district court); Motion to Stay, 7-22-81 (circuit court). SW, 3-29-83 (reporting Reynolds' position); Response of Temporary Receiver, 7-22-81; Additional Response of Temporary Receiver, 7-23-81; Response of the Plaintiffs, 7-22-81; Order, 7-23-81 (circuit court) (denying a stay). See PH, 7-23-81 (reporting on Varner's actions).

34. Application for Stay, 7-23-81 (Supreme Court); Objection of Fob James, 7-23-81; Memorandum of Respondents-Plaintiffs, 7-23-81; AB, 8-18-81; Order, 7-23-81 (Powell, J.) (granting the stay).

35. PH, 7-24-81 (reporting the statement from Graddick's office). For the editorial, PH, 7-25-81. Order, 7-25-81 (Powell, J.) (vacating the stay). Graddick filed yet another application for a stay with Chief Justice Warren Burger who, following practice, referred the request to the full Court. Nothing came of that action, however, inasmuch as the Court postponed decision until September and then issued a terse denial. Justice Powell attached another opinion to the Court's order, now acknowledging that Graddick was a party but standing firm in his earlier judgment that the attorney general was not entitled to a stay. In any event, according to Powell, the matter was now moot. *Graddick v. Newman,* 453 U.S. 928 (1981).

36. Nachman, RN, 3-23-83; prisoners, BN, 7-26-81. See also TN, 7-26-81; PH, 7-27-81; NY, 7-26-81.

37. On Varner's attitude, RV, 8-21-82; JC, 5-31-83; RN, 3-15-83. On plans to place two prisoners to a cell in new facilities, TN, 6-24-81; PH, 7-9, 11-81.

38. On Graddick's views, TN, 7-25, 27-81; PH, 7-27-81. On new offenses charged against freed inmates, PH, 7-28-81; TN, 7-31-81; BN, 11-29-81. On James' soul-searching and reaction to the news article, JS, 5-31-83. On the recidivism rate for the prisoners released in July, BN, 6-11-82.

39. On the governor's actions, Hopper deposition, 9-28-81. On the lease revenues, PH, 10-2-81. "Trailer park," Prehearing Memorandum, 11-12-81. On the Holman riot, PH, 9-2-81; TN, 9-2-81. For the governor's motion, Request of Receiver for Postponement of Consideration of Further Release of Inmates, 8-28-81. See TN, 9-4-81; PH, 9-4-81. For Varner's reaction, Order, 9-8-81; PH, 9-10-81.

40. On James' personal contacts with Reagan, TN, 7-27-81; PH, 7-28-81. There is no evidence that James and Reagan actually discussed the Alabama prison cases. On the meetings with Justice Department officials in which the prison cases were discussed, JS, 5-31-83; SW, 3-29-83; JC, 5-31-83.

41. Memorandum of the United States, 9-23-81. I rely for much of what appears in the text on personal conversations with Whinston, Knowles, and Carroll on the day of the hearing for which Whinston's memorandum was written, 11-12-81.

42. Conversation with RK, 9-28-81.

43. Graddick deposition, 10-28, 11-19-81. On the plaintiffs' view, RK, 6-21-83. On Nachman's, RN, 3-23-83.

44. I went to Montgomery for the hearing, discussed their preparation with the attorneys, and waited outside in the hall with reporters when Judge Varner closed the proceeding. The quotations in the text are taken from the transcript prepared by the court reporter. Hearing Transcript, 11-12-81. If Varner had not himself ordered the proceeding to be recorded, Whinston would have requested it on instructions from his superiors. The *Montgomery Advertiser* objected to the closed hearing and filed suit to force Judge Varner to open similar proceedings in the future. PH, 11-13-81; TN, 11-13-81. Nachman recalls that Varner may have preferred to be in his office instead of the court room not to avoid publicity, but to nurse a sore neck. RN, 3-23-83.

45. On the plaintiffs' thinking during and immediately following the hearing, Conversation with RK & JC, 11-12-81. Nachman made his arguments both in the hearing and in a later letter to Varner. RN to RV, 12-8-81 (NPP). See also RK to RV, 11-16-81 (NPP) (continuing the argument over when new prisons would be open and the capacity they would offer); RN to RV, 11-17-81 (NPP) (insisting that more prisoners might be housed in new facilities a bit sooner). See also CG et al., to RV, 12-9-81 (NPP).

46. RV, 8-4-82.

47. Order, 12-14-81.

48. For press reaction, PH, 12-15, 19-81; BN, 12-15-81. For a critical editorial, TN, 12-20-81. "Good possibility," TN, 12-15-81; Graddick, TN, 12-15-81; PH, 12-16-81.

49. Hopper, TN, 12-13-81; BN, 12-13-81; PH, 12-11-81; Varner, PH, 12-16-81.

50. Notice of Appeal, 12-16-81; Motion for Stay, 12-16-81; Joinder of Governor James in Request for Stay, 12-18-81; Motion for Reconsideration and Stay, 12-17-81. On Graddick's blanket objection, PH, 12-17-81. On James' position generally, PH, 12-18-81. Hopper's office discovered during this period that a few prisoners on the list provided to Judge Varner did not fit the criteria that Varner had asked the commissioner to apply. TN, 12-16-81 (reporting Carroll's comment that any such errors were entirely ascribable to the commissioner's staff).

51. Transcript of Hearing, 12-18-81; Opinion and Order, 12-22-81. Judge Varner did amend his order in another respect; he substituted the names of additional prisoners to replace those removed from the original list for various reasons. For the most important documents, Emergency Motion for Stay, 12-16-81; Brief in Support of Emergency Motion, 12-17-81; Memorandum in Opposition to Motion for Stay, 12-20-81; Memorandum of Respondents-Plaintiffs and Respondents-Amici Curiae, 12-20-81.

52. Graddick, PH, 12-22-81; see TN, 12-22-81. On the argument schedule, Order, 12-23-81; TN, 12-23-81.

53. Notice of Appeal, 12-28-81; Joinder in Appeal, 12-28-81; RN, 3-23-83. See Brief of Governor Fob James, 12-30-81 (also signed by Samford).

54. 441 U.S. 520 (1979).

55. 449 U.S. 1312 (1981).

56. Inasmuch as the order below was, in theory, an instruction to the receiver and to the defendants from the district judge and not, in the ordinary fashion, a judgment won by the plaintiffs, Knowles and Carroll styled their brief on appeal as a certificate of interested parties, 1-28-82.

57. Brief for the United States as Amicus Curiae (draft), 1-26-82; SW to Reynolds (undated) (JD). See also SW, 3-29-83.

58. I rely here and in what follows on contemporaneous conversations with the lawyers involved in the appeal and my own observations at the time. My attempt to obtain a transcript of the appellate arguments was unsuccessful. Letter from Thomas H. Reese, Circuit Executive, 6-18-82; see Interim Rules of the United States Court of Appeals for the Eleventh Circuit, Rule 24(g). News accounts of the proceeding were superficial. For example, PH, 2-8-82; TN, 2-9-82. Accordingly, I rely on my own notes.

59. I interviewed Judge Varner between the oral argument and the circuit court's decision and came away with the impression that, at that time at least, the plaintiffs' expectations regarding his willingness to invoke the contempt power were very close to the mark. RV, 8-4-82.

60. *Newman v. Alabama,* 683 F.2d 1312 (11th Cir. 1982).

Chapter 9

1. Varner, PH, 12-22-82. On crowding, TN, 6-27-82. On Jefferson County, PH, 3-20-82. On the protests in the Tennessee Valley, PH, 4-13, 7-23, 24, 26, 27, 29, 8-4, 6, 10, 9-1, 3, 10, 11-16-82; TN, 8-31-82. Another site in Colbert County was also investigated in this period. PH, 3-29, 5-5-82. On more fines in Tuscaloosa and Mobile, TN, 11-29-82; PH, 10-30-82. Pointer later forgave some of the fines he imposed in Birmingham on the theory that they had served their instrumental purpose. PH, 11-30, 12-1-82.

2. Graddick, BN, 3-21-82. On Baxley and McCorquodale, BN, 8-29-82. On Wallace, BN, 8-29, 11-7-82; PH, 10-27-82. On the promise to abort the Limestone County project, PH, 1-25-83. On McMillan, BN, 8-29-82; PH, 6-7, 8-25, 27, 9-20, 21-82. Emory Folmar, the Mayor of Montgomery and the likely Republican nominee for governor, was if anything less interested than the Democrats in prison reform. Folmar openly opposed the Limestone County project, but warned local citizens that he might not be able to stop it if Governor James was able to begin construction before he, Folmar, assumed office. PH, 9-17-82.

3. On the significance of the *Jaffree* case for James' thinking, JS, 5-31-83. The specifics of the litigation are explained in the Supreme Court's opinion, *Wallace v. Jaffree,* 472 U.S. 38 (1985). On James' visit to the Supreme Court, PH, 9-16-82.

4. James, TN, 11-30, 12-1-82.

5. On the "jurisdiction" issue, RN, 3-23-82. "Ball game," PH, 12-1-82.

6. On the discussions with Reynolds, SW, 3-29-83; JS, 5-31-83; PH, 7-27, 28, 30, 8-18, 19, 20, 21-82; TN, 8-19, 11-30-82. On James' multiple objectives, RN, 3-23-83; JS, 5-31-83.

7. James to RV, 7-23-82 (NPP); RK to RV, 7-28-82 (NPP); RK to RV, 8-6-82 (NPP).

8. Varner, RV, 8-4-82. Application for Order to Fob James, Joseph Hopper, and Charles Graddick to Show Cause Why They, and Each of Them, Should not be Fined and/or Imprisoned for Contempt, 8-23-82; PH, 8-24-82; TN, 8-24-82; Motion of Charles Graddick for Modification, 9-8-82; CG to RV, 9-7-82 (NPP). Barnes filed a similar motion on Hopper's behalf, Motion to Dismiss and Alternatively Petition to Modify, 9-7-82.

9. I attended the conference mentioned in the text, 8-23-82, and spoke at that time with most of the players, including Hopper. On the order for another plan, Thrower to Barnes, 8-25-82 (NPP). For the plan itself, James & Hopper to RV, 9-7-82 (NPP).

10. RN, 3-23-83. For the plaintiffs' thinking, I rely on contemporaneous conversations with Knowles and Carroll, 8-23-82. See also JC, 5-31-83; RK, 6-21-83; SW, 3-29-83; RN, 3-23-83. I also rely here on conversations with Knowles and Carroll on 11-1-82, the day of the conference described below.

11. JC, 5-31-83; James deposition, 10-22-82. I rely for my description of Nachman's thinking on Carroll's understanding and my own inferences from

the circumstances. Nachman himself declines to discuss Governor James' performance under formal interrogation.

12. RN, 3-23-83; JC, 5-31-83; RK, 6-21-83; Conversation with RK, 11-1-82. I attended the conference described in the text by special permission of Judge Varner and rely here in part on my own notes and impressions.

13. I rely here on several conversations with Knowles during the period described and on my formal interview with him, 6-21-83.

14. Here, I rely on my own notes and impressions of the pretrial hearing, 12-1-82. That hearing was held in open court. When I arrived expecting to be admitted again to Judge Varner's chambers, I found him in an outer office about to leave for the court room. The Eleventh Circuit had just sent him a special order, obtained at the instance of the *Montgomery Advertiser,* instructing him to make this proceeding open to the public. See *Newman v. Graddick,* 696 F.2d 796 (11th Cir. 1983). I was not present during any bargaining sessions and, indeed, understood that the parties wished to conceal their discussions from public view. I am confident, however, that my account accurately reflects the negotiations that took place and the positions of the parties.

15. RN, 3-23-83; JS, 5-31-83.

16. Conversation with Mitchell W. Dale, 1-3-83; SW, 3-29-83; SW to Peabody (undated) (JD); Peabody to Reynolds, 12-30-82 (JD); Wilkinson to Reynolds, 1-12-83 (JD).

17. I attended the hearing and rely for the impressions voiced in the text on my own notes and contemporaneous conversations with the individuals involved. Quotations are taken from the official transcript of the proceedings.

18. On James' desire to testify, Conversation with George Beto, 1-3-83. On the confusion over the governor's resignation, RN, 3-23-83; RK, 6-30-83. Judge Varner formally accepted James' resignation a week later. Order, 1-11-83. Other defense witnesses were similarly loose with numbers. Greg Utley, an official with the Alabama Public Health Service, testified that the prisons complied with relevant state environmental requirements "on the average." Under cross-examination, however, he conceded that his "average" figure obscured the point that several institutions, taken individually, scored well below acceptable standards. Many facilities that now passed muster, moreover, did so on the strength of a very recent round of inspections conducted in anticipation of this hearing.

19. RN, 3-23-83; JS, 5-31-83; RK, 6-10-83.

20. JS, 5-31-83; RK, 6-10-83.

21. I attended the meeting described in the text and rely for my description of the negotiations on my own observations and contemporaneous conversations with the participants.

22. RK, 6-10-83. I was excluded from a subsequent session with Nachman at which the prisoners' lawyers put their proposal forward. Thomas Lawson attended that late afternoon meeting. The plaintiffs understood that he represented Governor Wallace, but Lawson was evasive on that issue.

23. I rely for my account of Whinston's thinking on contemporaneous con-

versations with him and Dale. On the drafting sessions with James and Hopper, RN, 3-23-83; JS, 5-31-83.

24. I rely here on contemporaneous conversations with Knowles and Carroll.

25. Lawson & Wallis to RV (undated) (NPP). The tone of this letter aborted a planned meeting between Wallace's advisors and Judge Varner on 1-11-83.

26. In a telephone conversation with Knowles on 1-10-83, Varner confessed his hopes that the threat of contempt might yet move Graddick to relent. For Varner's judgment, Opinion, 1-18-83. On the appeal, Notice of Appeal, 1-28-83. Smyly also prepared an alternative settlement agreement, which Graddick was prepared to endorse. Inasmuch as it would have diluted the October 9 order, the plaintiffs declined to consider it. See Smyly to (RK), 1-11-83; MA, 1-13-83.

27. Memorandum of the United States, 1-14-83; Order, 1-18-83. For press reports, TN, 1-13, 14-83. For the editorial, PH, 1-15-83.

28. On Beto and Conrad, RK to Conrad, 1-24-83 (NPP); RN to RV, 1-27-83 (NPP); Motion, 1-28-83; Order, 2-8-83. On the riots in Virginia and New York, TN, 1-10-83. On the disturbance in Florida, PH, 1-23-83. On the hangings in Alabama, PH, 1-24-83.

29. FS, 7-30-86.

30. Graddick, TN, 2-2-83; Smith, MA, 1-13-83; TN, 2-11-83.

31. PH, 2-24-83. Wallis promptly announced that he could find no way to rescind the Limestone County contract. PH, 2-4-83.

32. Request to Implementation Committee, 1-19-83; RK to McAlpine, 1-21-83 (RK); RN to FS, 2-16-83 (RK); Conversation with RK, 2-16-83.

33. The committee held its initial meeting in stages. In the morning, the committee met privately in Nachman's law offices to map strategy; in the afternoon, the group met publicly with Smith in his office. I did not attend the committee's morning meeting and rely here on a later conversation with Knowles and on interviews with Knowles and Nachman, 4-20-83 and 3-23-83, respectively. I did attend the afternoon session in the commissioner's office. See also BN, 2-17-83; PH, 2-18-83.

34. FS, 7-30-86. I attended the Implementation Committee's meeting with the board and rely here on my own notes. I rely on Knowles for the report that Graddick had telephoned Lambert prior to the meeting. For confirmation of the meeting, RN to Lambert, 3-3-83 (RK); Beto to RN, 3-1-83 (RK).

35. I attended the meeting, 3-15-83, at which the commissioner announced the SIR program. For his own description, FS to RN, et al., 4-7-83 (RK). Smith also agreed to make changes in the department's medical care contract, to negotiate for additional space for mentally handicapped inmates, to refurbish certain living areas, and to identify realistic staff levels. FS to RN, et al., 3-7-83 (RK). On the committee's reactions, RN to FS, 3-15-83 (RK); RN to JC, et al., 4-4-83 (RK); RN to Conrad & Beto, 4-4-83 (RK).

36. Conrad to FS, 3-18-83 (RK); Conrad to Beto, et al., 3-18-83 (RK). For

the initial news reports, TN, 3-15, 16-83; BN, 3-27-83. On the sheriffs, PH, 5-16-83; TN, 5-16-83. On the Burgess affair, PH, 5-4, 5-83. For an illustrative report on citizen reaction, BN, 3-20-83. On Smith's explanations, PH, 3-16, 31-83; BN, 3-27-83. There is reason to doubt that Graddick himself was aware of the plan prior to its announcement. Conversation with Smyly, 3-15-83 (indicating not). Yet Smith insists that the attorney general's advisors were informed and actually approved the scheme as long as only "property offenders" were involved. FS, 7-30-86. Wallace was hospitalized during this period, but Smith understood that the governor approved the SIR plan. FS, 7-30-86. For favorable editorials, TN, 3-16-83; PH, 3-17-83.

37. AJ, 5-13-83; PH, 5-12, 13-83. On the opening at St. Clair, PH, 5-26, 30-83. On meeting the July 1 deadline, PH, 6-30-83. Smith's relative success with innovative ideas won him some measure of national attention. See *Esquire*, 12-85.

38. FS to RN, et al., 5-10, 6-15-83 (RK). On the committee's reaction, PH, 5-21-83. On the recommendation regarding staff levels, PH, 5-26-83. Nachman, RN to FS, 6-1-83 (RK).

39. On Wallace's health, PH, 4-20, 5-30-83. On his legislative proposals, PH, 4-27-83. On new taxes and the legislative response, PH, 4-16, 20-83. For the committee's initial report, Beto, et al., to RV, 5-20-83 (RK).

40. JC to RN, et al., 7-11-83 (RK); Conrad to JC, 7-13-83 (RK); RK, 6-21-83.

41. On Smith's address, PH, 6-21-83; Telephone memo, 6-20-83 (RK). On the meetings in July, AJ, 7-21-83; BN, 7-21-83. For Smith's report, Final Compliance Report, 7-20-83. For press criticism, BN, 7-24-83. For the committee's second report, Beto, et al., to RV, 7-21-83 (RK). I rely in some measure for what is in the text on contemporaneous conversations with Knowles. For evidence of deteriorating relations, see RK to FS, 9-8-83 (RK) (complaining that the commissioner had failed to send the committee promised reports); Wilson to RK, 9-19-83 (RK) (expressing surprise and disappointment at Knowles' tone); RK to Wilson, 9-26-83 (RK) (regretting any sharpness). Smith was hostile to the Implementation Committee from the outset. FS, 7-30-86.

42. See *State of Alabama ex rel. Charles A. Graddick v. Freddie V. Smith*, Civ. Action No. CV-83-1262-PH; PH, 8-16-83; AJ, 9-11-83. For criticism of Graddick, TN, 8-17-83. For background on Graddick's actions, CG to FS, 8-12-83 (RK); Smith deposition, 9-23-83.

43. Motion for Emergency Relief, 9-29-83. For the committee's communication to the court, Beto, et al., to RV, 10-14-83 (RK). The hearing was held on 10-26-83. For Varner's judgment, Opinion and Order, 11-4-83.

44. Smith essentially requested permission to continue the SIR program in a motion for declaratory relief, filed with his response on 10-1-83.

45. See Conrad, et al., to RV, 11-3-83 (RK); RN to FS, 10-27-83 (RK); RN to CG, 10-27-83 (RK); RN to Lambert, et al., 10-27-83 (RK). On the legislature's actions, MA, 11-11-83; PH, 11-23-83; TN, 11-16, 18-83.

46. Notice of Appeal, 11-4-83; Petition to Modify, 11-21-83; see Wilson to

RN, et al., 12-15-83 (RK). On Graddick's attempt to obtain financial assistance from Smith's department, MA, 5-25-84. On Varner's new order holding Smith in contempt, PH, 12-8, 23-83; TN, 12-23-83.

47. On the committee's request for a new plan, RK to FS (undated) (RK). On Smith's initial proposals and the comments by Nachman and Graddick, MA, 1-13-84; PH, 1-12, 13-84. On Smith's plan to overpopulate the Jefferson County prison, MA, 2-18-84. For Carroll's opposition, JC to RN, et al., 2-16-84 (RK). For Smith's predictions, Smith deposition, 3-12-84.

48. For the committee's views, RN to RV, 3-12-84 (RK). Knowles, Memoranda, 2-20, 4-13 & 8-23-84 (RK). Conrad to Beto, et al., 4-17-84 (RK). I rely on a contemporaneous conversation with Knowles for my report on Nachman's successful argument within the committee.

49. *Newman v. Graddick,* 740 F.2d 1513 (11th Cir. 1984).

50. On Smith's ultimatum, TN, 10-26-84. RK to Conrad, et al., 10-15-84 (RK); JC to RN, et al., 10-8-84 (RK); Conversation with JC, 10-9-84. Carroll's consultant was Pat McManus, a well-regarded penologist from Minnesota.

51. On new negotiations, RN to Conrad, et al., 11-14-84 (RK); RK to File, 11-26-84 (RK). Bruce Ritchie, a reporter with the *Montgomery Advertiser,* attended and recorded the negotiating sessions on 11-26-84. I rely here in part on his recording.

52. Quotations, PH, 11-28-84; BN, 11-28-84. For other contemporaneous press reports, NY, 11-23, 28-84; PH, 11-27-84; MA, 11-28-84. For the *Post Herald* comment, PH, 11-29-84.

53. On Graddick's threat to appeal, TN, 11-28, 29-84. For the order itself, Order, 11-27-84.

54. FS, 7-30-86.

55. NY, 4-16-85; PH, 4-16, 17, 19-85; BN, 4-21-85.

56. Conversation with RK, 5-8-85. JC to Wilson, 5-28-85 (RK); Wilson to JC, 6-10-85 (RK); RN to JC & Wilson, 6-11-85 (RK). For the committee's initial contact with the principals, RK to Wilson, 9-11, 10-2-85 (RK). For Smith's statements, MA, 11-13-85.

57. On the charges against the guards and Smith's actions, MA, 10-9, 10, 12-4, 16-85, 1-16, 17-86. In the end, state authorities settled the inmates' civil actions arising from these events by making cash payments to each prisoner. On the individual prisoner complaints received by Knowles, RK to Conrad, 1-21-86 (RK); Conrad to RK, 5-31-86 (RK). On Smith's objection to paying Knowles' fees, Bright to RK, 9-11-86 (RK); FS, 7-30-86. On the agreement to channel such complaints to Smith's grievance process, RK to Wilson, 2-20-86 (RK); RK to Hildreth, 4-18-86 (RK); FS, 7-30-86. Crowding in particular continued to plague the prison system during the initial three-year life span allowed the Implementation Committee, and at the end of that period the committee asked for and received an order of renewal from Judge Varner. Conversation with RK, 1-15-88. Order, 12-30-87. See AJ, 12-29-87; TN, 12-31-87. Thereafter, a new (Republican) governor, Guy Hunt, appointed a relative moderate, Morris Thigpen, to succeed Smith as commissioner. MA, 2-4-87. Despite Thigpen's efforts, and the

efforts of a special task force chaired by Chief Justice C. C. "Bo" Torbert of the Alabama Supreme Court, the prison system remained out of compliance with various provisions of the court's orders in July 1988, when the committee sought yet another extension. By then, the motivating factor driving the committee members to remain in place was only their abiding, yet occasionally faltering, belief that the Alabama prison system seemed *always* to need outside review of some sort, however feeble. Conversation with RK, 7-19-88.

58. FS, 7-30-86.

59. On the jail renovation crews, AJ, 12-22-85.

60. For Smith's concessions that the system was not in compliance with the court's orders, Smith deposition, 1-7-87. See also AJ, 1-14-87; PH, 1-16-87; MA, 1-15-87.

61. FS, 7-30-86. On the new prisons, MA, 10-11, 15-85.

62. On the commissioner's consistent warnings that the state courts would sentence more prisoners to occupy additional bed space, MA, 10-11-85. Smith pressed the construction of more prisons in the south until his departure at the end of Governor Wallace's term and thus left the incomplete projects for his successor, Morris Thigpen. AJ, 12-16-86; BN, 12-16-86; MA, 12-16-86. Thigpen, in turn, faced both the momentum of projects well under way and spirited criticism of the plans from outsiders, including the members of the Implementation Committee who were convinced that more building would not answer Alabama's crowding problems. AJ, 2-5-87; BN, 2-5-87. Fred Smith attempted to retain a role in the department by appointing himself to a civil service position as associate commissioner just before surrendering the commissioner's position to Thigpen. He later pleaded guilty to a criminal charge of submitting improper expense vouchers during his tenure as commissioner and was dismissed from state government employment. In March 1988, Smith was killed when his speeding car left an interstate highway near Montgomery. The medical examiner reported that he was legally intoxicated at the time of the crash. TN, 3-31-88; MA, 4-8-88.

Select Bibliography

Penology and Prisons

F. Allen, The Decline of the Rehabilitative Ideal (1981).

American Friends Service Committee, Struggle for Justice (1971).

Correctional Institutions (R. Carter, D. Glaser & L. Wilkins, eds. 1977).

D. Cressey, The Prison: Studies in Institutional Organization and Change (1961).

F. Cullen & K. Gilbert, Reaffirming Rehabilitation (1982).

L. DeWolf, Crime and Justice in America (1975).

D. Fogel, We Are the Living Proof: The Justice Model for Corrections (2d ed. 1979).

J. Gillin, Criminology and Penology (3d ed. 1971).

G. Hawkins, The Prison: Policy and Practice (1976).

J. Jacobs, New Perspectives on Prisons and Imprisonment (1983).

J. Jacobs, Stateville: The Penitentiary in Mass Society (1977).

D. Jones, The Health Risks of Imprisonment (1976).

D. Lipton, R. Martinson & J. Wilks, The Effectiveness of Correctional Treatment (1975).

K. Menninger, The Crime of Punishment (1966).

J. Mitford, Kind and Usual Punishment (1973).

N. Morris, The Future of Imprisonment (1974).

N. Morris & G. Hawkins, The Honest Politician's Guide to Crime Control (1970).

J. Moynahan & E. Stewart, The American Jail (1980).

T. Murton, The Dilemma of Prison Reform (1976).

L. Orland, Prisons: Houses of Darkness (1975).

H. Packer, The Limits of the Criminal Sanction (1968).

Prisoners in America (Ohlin, ed. 1973).

R. Quinney, Class, State & Crime: On the Theory and Practice of Criminal Justice (1977).

R. Roberg & V. Webb, Critical Issues in Corrections: Problems, Trends and Prospects (1981).

M. Sherman & G. Hawkins, Imprisonment in America (1981).
R. Singer, Just Deserts: Sentencing Based on Equality and Desert (1979).
R. Somer, The End of Imprisonment (1976).
G. Sykes, Crime and Society (2d ed. 1967).
G. Sykes, The Society of Captives (1958).
Twentieth Century Task Force on Criminal Sentencing, Fair and Certain Punishment (1976).
A. von Hirsch, Doing Justice (1976).
N. Walker, The Aims of a Penal System (1966).
N. Walker, Sentencing in a Rational Society (1971).
L. Wilkins, Evaluation of Penal Measures (1969).
Gardner, The Renaissance of Retribution—An Examination of Doing Justice, 1976 Wis. L. Rev. 781.
Morris, Impediments to Penal Reform, 33 U. Chi. L. Rev. 627 (1966).
Nagel, On Behalf of a Moratorium on Prison Construction, 23 Crime & Delinq. 154 (1977).
Takagi, Revising Liberal Conceptions of Penal Reform: A Bibliographic Overview, 5 Crime & Social Justice 60 (1976).

Penal History

G. De Beaumont & A. de Tocqueville, On the Penitentiary System in the United States and its Application in France (reprted. 1964).
M. Foucault, Discipline & Punish: The Birth of the Prison (1979).
E. Goffman, Asylums (1961).
J. Heath, Eighteenth Century Penal Theory (1963).
J. Howard, The State of the Prisons in England and Wales (Bicentennial ed. 1977).
M. Ignatieff, A Just Measure of Pain: The Penitentiary in the Industrial Revolution, 1750–1850 (1978).
G. Killinger & P. Cromwell, Penology: The Evolution of Corrections in America (1973).
O. Lewis, The Development of American Prisons and Prison Customs, 1776–1845 (reprted. 1967).
W. Lewis, From Newgate to Dannemora: The Rise of the Penitentiary in New York, 1796–1848 (1965).
B. McKelvey, American Prisons: A History of Good Intentions (1977).
D. Melossi & M. Pavarini, The Prison and the Factory: Origins of the Penitentiary System (1981).
G. Rusche & O. Kircheimer, Punishment and Social Structure (1978).
G. Playfair, The Punitive Obsession (1971).
D. Rothman, Conscience and Convenience: The Asylum and its Alternatives in Progressive America (1980).
D. Rothman, The Discovery of the Asylum (1971).
J. Sellin, Slavery and the Penal System (1976).

N. Teeters, The Cradle of the Penitentiary: The Walnut Street Jail at Philadelphia, 1773–1835 (1955).

N. Teeters & J. Shearer, The Prison at Philadelphia, Cherry Hill: The Separate System of Penal Discipline, 1829–1913 (1957).

F. Wines, Punishment and Reformation: An Historical Sketch of the Rise of the Penitentiary System (reprted. 1972).

Hirsch, From Pillory to Penitentiary: The Rise of Criminal Incarceration in Early Massachusetts, 80 Mich. L. Rev. 1179 (1982).

Alabama Penal History

T. Abernethy, The Formative Period in Alabama, 1815–1828 (1965).

E. Clark, The Abolition of the Convict Lease System in Alabama, 1913–1928 (M.A. Thesis, University of Alabama, 1949).

R. Cobb, History of the Penitentiary (1882).

A. Going, Bourbon Democracy in Alabama: 1874–1890, 170–90 (1951).

H. Hart, Social Progress in Alabama: A Second Study of the Social Institutions and Agencies of the State of Alabama (1922).

F. Lee, A View of Alabama Prisons (1960).

R. March, Alabama Bound: Forty-five Years Inside a Prison System (1978).

A. Moore, History of Alabama and Her People 978–83 (1927).

M. Moos, State Penal Administration in Alabama (1942).

H. Patterson & E. Conrad, Scottsboro Boy 97–131 (1950).

B. Reeves, Alabama Prison System, 1820–1955 (1956).

A. Tullos, The Alabama Prison System: Recent History, Conditions, and Recommendations (1973) (unpublished manuscript).

Annual Report of the Secretary, Transactions of the Third Nat. Prison Reform Congress 273–76 (1874).

Cunningham, The Convict System of Alabama in its Relation to Health and Disease, in Proc. of the Nat. Prison Assoc. 108–41 (1889).

Dawson, Address, Proc. of the Nat. Prison Assoc. 82–85 (1888).

Ford, The Bar's Responsibility for Prison Reform, 34 Ala. Lawyer 356 (1973).

Hill, Experience in Mining Coal with Convicts, in Proc. of the Nat. Prison Assoc. 388–98 (1897).

Lee, The Lease System of Alabama, in Proc. of the Nat. Prison Assoc. 104–18 (1890).

McCullough, Alabama Prisons Today, 19 Ala. Lawyer 380 (1958).

Oates, The County Jail, in Forty-First Annual Session of the Nat. Conf. of Charities and Correction (1914).

Quadrennial Reports of the Inspectors of Convicts, 1888–1934.

Scott, Annual Address, in Proc. of the Nat. Prison Assoc. 27–28 (1901).

Statement of the Cost of Each Species of Manufacture Carried on in the Penitentiary (1844).

Tutwiler, Prison Schools in Alabama, in Proc. of the Nat. Prison Assoc. 215–20 (1889).

Judge Johnson

J. Bass, Unlikely Heroes 78–82 (1981).

W. Douglas, The Court Years 128–32 (1980).

L. Friedman, Southern Justice 192 (1965).

D. Garrow, Protest at Selma (1978).

W. Greenhaw, R. Crow & C. Prigmore, The New G-Man: Frank Johnson of the FBI (unpublished manuscript).

R. Kennedy, Judge Frank Johnson, Jr., A Biography (1978).

V. Navasky, Kennedy Justice 23 (1971).

R. Norrell, Reaping the Whirlwind: The Civil Rights Movement in Tuskegee (1985).

B. Taper, Gomillion v. Lightfoot (1962).

T. Yarbrough, Judge Frank Johnson and Human Rights in Alabama (1981).

Brill, The Real Governor of Alabama, *New York,* April 26, 1976.

Johnson, The Alabama Punting Syndrome, The Judges' Journal, Spring, 1979, at 4.

Johnson, Commencement Remarks, Yale (1980).

Johnson, The Constitution and the Federal District Judge, 54 Tex. L. Rev. 903 (1976).

Johnson, Responsibility for Integrity in Government, 35 Ala. Lawyer 12 (1974).

Johnson, The Role of the Federal Courts in Institutional Litigation, 32 Ala. L. Rev. 271 (1981).

Johnson, In Defense of Judicial Activism, 28 Emory L.J. 901 (1979).

Johnson, Supremacy of the Law, 30 Ala. Lawyer 287 (1969).

Maxwell, Tough Judge, *Wall Street Journal,* April 15, 1976.

Bill Moyers' Journal, Judge: The Law & Frank Johnson (1980).

The Real Governor, *Time,* January 26, 1976.

Reform Litigation

B. Ackerman, Reconstructing American Law (1984).

R. Carp & C. Rowland, Policymaking and Politics in the Federal District Courts (1983).

O. Fiss, The Civil Rights Injunction (1978).

N. Glazer, Courts and Social Policy (1978).

M. Harris & D. Spiller, After Decision: Implementation of Judicial Decrees in Correctional Settings (1977).

D. Horowitz, The Courts and Social Policy (1977).

I. Jenkins, Social Order and the Limits of Law (1980).

National Association of Attorneys General, Implementation of Remedies in Prison Conditions Suits (1980).

M. Perry, The Constitution, The Courts & Human Rights: An Inquiry into the Legitimacy of Constitutional Policy-Making by the Judiciary (1982).

M. Rebell & A. Block, Educational Policy-Making and the Courts: An Empirical Study of Judicial Activism (1982).

M. Shapiro, Courts: A Comparative and Political Analysis (1981).

Bell, Serving Two Masters: Integration Ideals and Client Interests in School Desegregation Litigation, 85 Yale L.J. 470 (1976).

Brakel, Special Masters in Institutional Litigation, 1979 A.B.F. Res. J. 543.

Brodsky, Prison Class Action Suits: The Aftermaths, in Abnormal Offenders, Delinquency & the Criminal Justice System (J. Gunn & D. Farrington eds. 1982).

Brodsky & Miller, Coercing Changes in Prisons and Mental Hospitals: The Social Scientist and the Class Action Suit, in Prevention Through Political Action and Social Change (J. Joffe & G. Albee eds. 1981).

Burt, Pennhurst: A Parable, in In The Interest of Children (R. Mnookin ed. 1985).

Chayes, The Role of the Judge in Public Law Litigation, 89 Harv. L. Rev. 1281 (1976).

Chayes, The Supreme Court, 1981 Term—Foreword: Public Law Litigation and the Burger Court, 96 Harv. L. Rev. 4 (1982).

Clune, A Political Model of Implementation and Implications of the Model for Public Policy, Research, and the Changing Roles of Law and Lawyers, 69 Iowa L. Rev. 47 (1983).

Clune & Lindquist, What "Implementation" Isn't: Toward a General Framework for Implementation Research, 1981 Wis. L. Rev. 1044.

Dan-Cohen, Bureaucratic Organizations and the Theory of Adjudication, 85 Colum. L. Rev. 1 (1985).

Diver, The Judge as Political Powerbroker: Superintending Structural Change in Public Institutions, 65 Va. L. Rev. 43 (1979).

Drake, Enforcing the Right to Treatment: *Wyatt v. Stickney,* 10 Amer. Crim. L. Rev. 587 (1972).

Eisenberg & Yeazell, The Ordinary and the Extraordinary in Institutional Litigation, 93 Harv. L. Rev. 465 (1980).

Engel & Rothman, The Paradox of Prison Reform: Rehabilitation, Prisoners' Rights, and Violence, 7 Harv. J. of Law & Pub. Policy 413 (1984).

Fiss, The Supreme Court, 1978 Term—Foreword: The Forms of Justice, 93 Harv. L. Rev. 1 (1979).

Fletcher, The Discretionary Constitution: Institutional Remedies and Judicial Legitimacy, 91 Yale L.J. 635 (1982).

Frug, The Judicial Power of the Purse, 126 U. Pa. L. Rev. 715 (1978).

Galanter, Palen & Thomas, The Crusading Judge: Judicial Activism in Trial Courts, 52 So. Calif. L. Rev. 699 (1979).

Glazer, Should Judges Administer Social Services? 50 Pub. Int. 64 (1978).

Goldfarb & Singer, Redressing Prisoners' Grievances, 39 Geo. Wash. L. Rev. 175 (1970).

Hirschkop & Millemann, The Unconstitutionality of Prison Life, 55 Va. L. Rev. 795 (1969).

Kirp, Legalism and Politics in School Desegregation, 1981 Wis. L. Rev. 294.

Mishkin, Federal Courts as State Reformers, 35 Wash. & Lee L. Rev. 949 (1978).

Nagel, Controlling the Structural Injunction, 7 Harv. J. of Law & Pub. Policy 395 (1984).

Nagel, Separation of Powers and the Scope of Federal Equitable Remedies, 30 Stan. L. Rev. 661 (1978).

Nathan, The Use of Masters in Institutional Reform Litigation, 10 Toledo L. Rev. 419 (1979).

Neisser, Is There a Doctor in the Joint? The Search for Constitutional Standards for Prison Health Care, 63 Va. L. Rev. 921 (1977).

Owens, Classifying Black Inmates: The Alabama Prison Classification Project, in Blacks & Criminal Justice (C. Owens & J. Bell eds. 1977).

Robbins & Buser, Punitive Conditions of Prison Confinement: An Analysis of *Pugh v. Locke* and Federal Court Supervision of State Penal Administration Under the Eighth Amendment, 29 Stan. L. Rev. 893 (1977).

Rudenstine, Judicially Ordered Social Reform: Neofederalism and Neonationalism, 59 So. Calif. L. Rev. 449 (1986).

Schuster & Widmer, Judicial Intervention in Corrections: A Case Study, 42 Fed. Prob. 10 (Sept. 1978).

Symposium: Judicially Managed Institutional Reform, 32 Ala. L. Rev. 267 (1981).

Turner, Establishing the Rule of Law in Prisons: A Manual for Prisoners' Rights Litigation, 23 Stan. L. Rev. 473 (1971).

Yarbrough, The Alabama Prison Litigation, 9 Justice System Journal 276 (1984).

Comment, Equitable Remedies: An Analysis of Judicial Utilization of Neoreceiverships to Implement Large Scale Institutional Change, 1976 Wis. L. Rev. 1161.

Note, Beyond the Ken of the Courts: A Critique of Judicial Refusal to Review the Complaints of Convicts, 72 Yale L. J. 506 (1963).

Note, Complex Enforcement: Unconstitutional Prison Conditions, 94 Harv. L. Rev. 626 (1981).

Note, The Courts, HEW, and Southern School Desegregation, 77 Yale L. J. 321 (1967).

Note, Decency and Fairness: An Emerging Judicial Role in Prison Reform, 57 Va. L. Rev. 841 (1971).

Note, Implementation Problems in Institutional Reform Litigation, 91 Harv. L. Rev. 428 (1977).

Note, Institutional Reform Litigation: Representation in the Remedial Process, 91 Yale L. J. 1474 (1982).

Note, Judicial Intervention and Organization Theory: Changing Bureaucratic Behavior and Policy, 89 Yale L. J. 513 (1980).

Note, Mastering Intervention in Prisons, 88 Yale L. J. 1062 (1979).

Note, Monitors: A New Equitable Remedy?, 70 Yale L. J. 103 (1960).

Note, The Role of the Eighth Amendment in Prison Reform, 38 U. Chi. L. Rev. 647 (1971).

Note, The *Wyatt* Case: Implementation of a Judicial Decree Ordering Institutional Change, 84 Yale L. J. 1338 (1975).

Special Project, The Remedial Process in Institutional Reform Litigation, 78 Colum. L. Rev. 784 (1978).

Index

315